RESEARCH IN
SOCIAL MOVEMENTS,
CONFLICTS
AND CHANGE

Volume 12 • 1990

RESEARCH IN SOCIAL MOVEMENTS, CONFLICTS AND CHANGE

A Research Annual

Editor: LOUIS KRIESBERG
Department of Sociology
Syracuse University

VOLUME 12 • 1990

 JAI PRESS INC.

Greenwich, Connecticut   *London, England*

CONTENTS

LIST OF CONTRIBUTORS

Marjorie L. DeVault

Department of Sociology
Syracuse University

William E. Feinberg

Department of Sociology
University of Cincinnati

Roberto M. Fernandez

Department of Sociology
University of Arizona
Tucson

Norris R. Johnson

Department of Sociology
University of Cincinnati

David Kowalewski

Division of Social Sciences
Alfred University

Doug McAdam

Department of Sociology
University of Arizona

Bronislaw Misztal

Department of Sociology and
    Anthropology
Indiana University-Purdue University
Fort Wayne

Chris R. Mitchell

Center for Conflict Analysis
    and Resolution
George Mason University

Terrell A. Northrup

Program on the Analysis and
    Resolution of Conflicts
Syracuse University

Benjamin S. Orlove   Division of Environmental Studies
                                        University of California
                                        Davis

Gail A. Quets   Department of Sociology
                                        Columbia University

Carlo E. Ruzza   Department of Sociology
                                        Harvard University

John L.P. Thompson   School of Public Health
                                        Columbia University

Erich Weede   Forschungsinstitut für Soziologie
                                        Universität Köln
                                        West Germany

INTRODUCTION

Social movements, conflicts, and change are not only phenomena to be explained. The persons engaged in bringing about social change, in waging a struggle or trying to resolve one, or in mobilizing support for a social movement organization offer their own interpretations of their actions. Their accounts and justifications often are regarded by social analysts as more than another aspect of the phenomena to be explained. These accounts often provide or significantly influence the way analysts themselves frame their explanations.

Many, if not most, of the major new ideas in the understanding of social movements, conflicts, and change have come from outside the academy. This can be illustrated by the diffusion of ideas arising from the women's movement, the European peace movement, and the conflict resolution movement. For example, the American women's movement and associated feminist thinking has profoundly affected academic interpretations of all aspects of social and intellectual life.

Practice also affects academic theorizing because the practice itself is theoretical and academics distill general ideas from practice. In trying to bring about social change, generate or sustain social movement organizations, and wage social conflicts, activists apply specific ideas derived from more general ideas. They may even write and talk about what they have done in order to teach their followers and co-workers. Academic-based analysts then examine what activists do in trying to resolve conflicts, wage struggle, or bring about particular social changes. They sometimes study different efforts and compare the results, intended and unintended.

The influence between activists and academically-based analysts can also flow from the academy to the field. The research findings and interpretations by social analysts may influence the activists about what they are doing and what they might do. Academic analyses may help activists to understand the structural constraints within which they are acting.

Finally, empirical studies and theoretical elaborations may be the source of new ideas about social movements, conflicts and change, independent of the thought and actions of partisans in the field. Research and theory construction have dynamics of their own, as new findings and elaborations build on old ones and challenge them. These developments may remain unknown to the activists or if known may seem irrelevant to their efforts.

Many of these points can be illustrated by the transforming social changes in the Soviet Union, in Eastern Europe, and in many other parts of the world which erupted at the end of the 1980s. The ideas emerging from the new social movements, especially the peace and environmental movements, influenced students, intellectuals, and broad sectors of the population. These movements were transnational in scope. They raised awareness of environmental degradation and of the risks of increased military arms. They also gave credence to alternatives: to reliance on popular forces, on nonviolence, on conversation, and on local autonomy.

The dramatic events and underlying forces for change will impact on the research agenda of analysts of social conflicts, movements, and change. We will see increased research about nonviolent means of conflict. Interest in the role of collective behavior in bringing about social change may also be rekindled. There is some recognition that once government officials began to give room for expressions of dissent, in response to pressures from below as well as from above, social movement organizations were pushed aside by action in the streets.

On the other hand, ideas that were developed in academic institutions and other research settings influenced peace movement activists and political leaders. For example, this was the case for ideas about nonprovocative defense, civilian-based defense, and other alternative security policies.

In reviewing the contributions to this volume, I will note how they illustrate some aspect of the relationship between theory and practice. Each has her or his own set of concerns pertaining to the contribution.

The chapter by Doug McAdam and Robert M. Fernandez demonstrates the cumulative and evolving nature of research and theory about social movement organizations. They view recruitment in relational terms, as an emergent property of groups. They compare recruitment to the 1964 Mississippi Freedom Project at two university campus sites: Berkeley, California and Madison, Wisconsin. The long history of civil rights activism on the Berkeley campus relative to Wisconsin affected the recruitment process in complex ways. For example, in Berkeley, groups of similar activists were likely to participate in the Project even after controlling for individual-level factors. Such findings may not provide short-term policy guides for activists, but they suggest long-run consequences that would be encouraging for activists taking a long-term perspective.

Norris R. Johnson and William E. Feinberg use a computer simulation model to examine the relations among conditions of ambiguity, information seeking, suggestibility, and consensus in crowd behavior. The computer simulations indicate, for example, that increasing suggestibility contributes directly to achieving consensus more quickly and to a more extreme consensus. The computer simulations allow for analyzing indirect effects as well as direct ones, yielding some results not predicted by theory. Extrapolating their results, the authors find support for theories that postulate the effect of suggestibility on crowd processes and outcomes, matters of possible renewed interest after the 1989 events in Eastern Europe.

Bronislaw Misztal analyzes three alternative, non-conventional social movements in Poland, the Independent Education Movement, the Freedom & Peace Movement, and the Orange Alternative Movement. He argues that these movements, although for the few, mark a new chapter of social life. He accords importance to the social context of social movements, comparing the state socialist and capitalist systems. The alternative movements in Poland therefore cannot be explained in terms of the new social movements theories developed in capitalist societies. His discussion broadens our conceptions of the nature and role of social movements and provides insights about the movements from below which contributed to the social transformation of Poland.

David Kowalewski provides an historical-sociological analysis of the U.S. sanctuary movement to assist Central American refugees and to oppose U.S. foreign policy there. He explains the emergence and effects of the movement in terms of the conjunction of long standing traditions and of new developments, including the new theological approaches, the transnational and ecumenical character of the movement, and the U.S. government's unresponsive and repressive policy. Such an historical perspective might seem to have little value to social movement organization activists since they are unable to alter those historical conditions. Yet activists choose justifications, seek supporters, and select activities to undetake. Which choices will be relatively effective depends on how they fit the circumstances. Analyses such as this one about the sanctuary movement can be read as providing information about what does and does not fit well.

Carlo E. Ruzza examines conceptions of strategy in two kinds of Italian peace movement organizations: one seeking to influence the government and one seeking to change the lifestyles of individuals. On the basis of a content analysis of meetings and of interviews with leaders in each kind of organization, for example, he finds that the cadres' conception of instrumentality differs between the two organizations. Furthermore, he argues that rationality should be redefined in relation to collective identities; he points out that for many religious people activism is worthwhile simply if they can bear witness. This analysis builds on the resource mobilization and new social movements theories, adding specifications and elaborations.

Benjamin S. Orlove examines violent uprisings in Peru which did not transform that society. He compares two theoretical approaches in explaining the uprisings: the mode of production perspective, exemplified by Jean Piel and Eric Hobsbawm, and the political economy framework, exemplified by Eric Wolf. His detailed analysis relates to several general issues, including the relative weight of external forces and of local conditions, the relevance of objective interests and of subjective perceptions, and the relations of the rebellions to an export economy. He concludes that the political economy approach gives a fuller and in some aspects a more accurate interpretation than the mode of production framework. The general issues he examines have relevance for understanding the nonviolent revolutions now transforming many societies. They also bear on the struggles in many Third World countries, which continue to be waged while the global context changes.

Marjorie L. DeVault draws on the feminist perspective and experience from the women's movement to illuminate a fundamental question in the analysis of conflicts. Some theorists have argued that certain unequal conditions or relations constitute structural violence or objective conflict, whether or not persons in the situation so perceive them. However one defines social conflicts, the relationship between objective conditions and subjective awareness of a social conflict is critical. DeVault examines the ways in which inequalities in the performance of housework tasks provide women with the bases for consciously recognized social conflicts. She suggests reasons for the difficulty women have in framing complaints about housework and in sustaining conflict over the division of labor.

C. R. Mitchell draws from the conflict resolution literature in his analysis of the 1972 settlement of the conflict between the Sudanese government and the South Sudanese Liberation Movement. His chapter is intended to examine whether the peacemaking efforts and agreement in that case might serve as an example for emulation in the settlement of other wars. He discusses possible lessons about (1) the time when leaders of warring parties come to consider the option of seeking a settlement rather than continuing the war, (2) the intervention by intermediaries which proves successful, and (3) the structure of acceptable agreements over issues of regional autonomy or secession.

John L. P. Thompson and Gail A. Quets analyze the conflict in Northern Ireland, comparing it to the Holocaust, to help account for the emergency of genocidal conflict. They regard genocide as one end of a continuum, not as one side of a dichotomous variable. Moreover, they regard genocide as multidimensional. They emphasize the importance of the normative climate in the movement toward genocide, in addition to the organizational resources of bureaucracies and states and the destructive capability of advanced technology. Recognizing elements which contribute to movement along the continuum ending in genocide might suggest possible ways of interrupting such movement.

Terrell A. Northrup draws on feminist thought to enrich our understanding of the concept of security. Peace researchers and peace activists have been extending the term security so that it embraces more than military-based threat as defense. The "new thinking" in the Soviet Union has incorporated much of this reconceptualization. Northrup suggests a fundamental basis for different conceptions of security. Using semantic differential scales, she found that male and female undergraduate students differed in the concepts they associated with war, peace, and security; the concepts of masculinity and femininity were also found to be associated with somewhat different sets of concepts.

Erich Weede compares two theoretical approaches to explaining income redistribution and income inequality in industrial democracies. According to the democratic class struggle line of reasoning, the lower classes can improve their relative income by collective action through unions and political parties. According to the public choice line of reasoning, the privileged classes, with better information and resources, can use the democratic system to their own advantage. He assesses these and other arguments by examining income inequality in contemporary industrial democracies. Among his findings, is the conclusion that there is little *robust* support for the democratic class struggle line of reasoning.

Policy implications can be inferred from all these papers, and issues of practice help frame the research. The actions of partisans in the field are not wholly separate from the efforts of the analysts to explain, interpret, or influence what the activists are striving to accomplish.

I am indebted to colleagues at Syracuse University and in other institutions for reviewing papers submitted for publication in this volume. They include: Michael Barkun, J. David Edelstein, James M. Fendrich, Jeffrey M. Haydu, Stephen P. Koff, William Mangin, Allan Mazur, John Nagle, Pamela Oliver, Richard Ratcliff, Mark Rupert, David A. Snow, Howard Tamashiro, Charles Tilly, A. Dale Tussing, Miles Wolpin, and Mayer N. Zald.

Louis Kriesberg
Series Editor

MICROSTRUCTURAL BASES OF RECRUITMENT TO SOCIAL MOVEMENTS

Doug McAdam and Roberto M. Fernandez

Among the topics that have most concerned researchers in the field of social movements is that of differential recruitment (Jenkins 1983, p. 528; Zurcher and Snow 1981, p. 449). What accounts for individual variation in movement participation? Why does one individual get involved while another remains inactive? Traditionally, these questions have been answered by reference to various "personalogical" (Zukier 1982) accounts of movement recruitment. The basic assumption underlying such accounts is simply that it is some characteristic of the individual activist that compels them to participate. Among the individual attributes most frequently seen as productive of activism is a strong attitudinal affinity with the goals of the movement or a well-articulated set of grievances consistent with the movement's ideology. Some authors attribute the individual's ideological leanings to the effects of early childhood socialization (Lewis and Kraut

Research in Social Movements, Conflict and Change,
Volume 12, pages 1-33.
Copyright © 1990 by JAI Press Inc.
All rights of reproduction in any form reserved.
ISBN: 1-55938-065-9

1972; Thomas 1971). Others describe them as a byproduct of more immediate social-psychological dynamics. For example, relative deprivation theorists see the motivation to activism growing out of the perception that "... one's membership group is in a disadvantaged position, relative to some other group" (Gurney and Tierney 1982, p. 34). Regardless of these differences, all grievance- or attitudinally-based models of activism locate the motive to participate within the individual actor. This assumption has informed any number of otherwise different accounts of participation in political or religious movements (Braungart 1971; Fendrich and Krauss 1978; Flacks 1967; Glock 1984; Geschwender 1968; Searles and Williams 1962).

However, the emergence and increasing influence over the last decade of resource mobiization and political process perspectives in the study of social movements has led to growing dissatisfaction with the individual motivational accounts of recruitment. The following statement by Snow et al. (1980, p. 789) cuts to the heart of these objections: "However reasonable the underlying assumption that some people are more (psychologically) susceptible than others to movement participation, that view deflects attention from the fact that recruitment cannot occur without prior contact with a recruitment agent." It matters little if one is ideologically disposed toward participation if he or she lacks the structural or network contact that would "pull" them into protest activity (see Snow et al. 1983). Consistent with this argument, a number of recent studies have demonstrated the decisive role of structural, rather than attitudinal factors, in encouraging activism (Bibby and Brinkerhoff 1974; Bolton 1972; McAdam 1986; Orum 1972; Rosenthal et al. 1985; Snow et al. 1980; Von Eschen et al. 1971). A similar argument has been made for recruitment to religious movements (Harrison 1974; Heirich 1977; Stark and Bainbridge 1980).

As impressive as this body of evidence is, the structural or network accounts of movement recruitment suffer from both conceptual and empirical shortcomings. Conceptually, the problems stem from a lack of precision in the way the central concepts and ideas underlying the structural/network model have been defined. The imprecision centers on the particular identity of the networks, relationships or communities and the manner in which these network/structural factors facilitate recruitment (Wallis and Bruce 1982, p. 105).

At least two different agents have been identified in the literature as midwives to the recruitment process. The first of these agents, formal organizations, can facilitate recruitment in two ways. First, individuals can be drawn into a movement by virtue of their involvement in organizations that serve as the associational network out of which a new movement emerges (Rosenthal et al. 1985; Curtis and Zurcher 1973). Second, established organizations can also serve as the primary source of movement participants through what Oberschall (1973, p. 125) has termed "bloc recruitment." In this pattern, movements do not so much emerge out of established organizations as they represent a merger of such groups. For example, Hicks (1961) has described how the Populist party was created through a coalition of established farmers' organizations. Both of these patterns highlight the organizational basis of much movement recruitment, and support Oberschall's general conclusion: "mobilization does not occur through recruitment of large numbers of isolated and solitary individuals. It occurs as a result of recruiting blocs of people who are already highly organized and participants" (1973, p. 125).

The second agent that has been identified as important in the recruitment process is the individual activist. Here, the emphasis is on the necessity for prior *personal* contact with a *single* activist who introduces the recruit to the movement. Empirical support for the importance of a prior relationship with a single activist can be found in Gerlach and Hine (1970), Snow et al. (1980), and White (1970).

If the full explanatory power of the structural/network perspective is to be realized, the central concepts and ideas underlying it will have to be refined and further specified. How are structural positions best conceptualized? Which structural positions are especially productive of activism? Are informal friendship networks as effective as formal organizational affiliations? Within such networks, are "weak ties" as good a basis for recruitment as "strong ties?"

Apart from these conceptual questions, the network accounts of recruitment have tended to share at least two major empirical shortcomings which we hope to address here. First, they have tended to infer the importance of structural or network factors from data drawn exclusively from activists. Very few of these studies ever compare matched groups of activists and non-activists on the structural or network dimensions thought to facilitate recruitment. Thus, for example, Snow et al. (1980, p. 787) cite a number of studies in support of their claim that "...recruitment...is strongly influenced by structural proximity, availability, and affective interaction with movement members." But in all of the studies they cite, no attempt was made to compare the structural positions of activists and non-activists prior to entrance into the movement. It is at least possible, then, that non-activists would exhibit structural links to the movement similar to those of activists.

Second, the structural or network studies of recruitment have generally based their conclusions exclusively on structural or network data. Having demonstrated a high level of contact between potential recruits and movement members, structural theorists have generally been content to attribute causal significance to this contact. They may well be right in doing so. On the other hand, it is possible that both the contact and the individual's subsequent activism are the result of individual background factors that have not been controlled.

In this study, we address both the empirical and conceptual problems evident in past research on recruitment to social movements as we seek to extend the microstructural analysis of movement recruitment. Toward these ends, we develop a model of recruitment to the 1964 Mississippi Freedom Summer Project (McAdam 1988; Rothschild, 1982) at two sites: the University of California at Berkeley and the University of Wisconsin at Madison. We address the empirical limitations of past research on network/ structural factors in recruitment in two ways. First, our data allow us to model the recruitment process for groups of activists and non-activists *prior* to their participation (or non-participation) in the social movement. Second, our data also allow us to control for a number of individual-level variables while studying the importance of network variables as predictors of movement participation. By examining data for two recruitment sites, we are also able to examine the extent to which micro level recruitment processes are contextually specific.

Regarding the conceptual problems discussed above, we hope to contribute to this literature by bringing some of the conceptual and methodological rigor of formal network analysis (Burt 1980) to bear on the topic of recruitment. First, we will address both the organizational and interpersonal bases of recruitment by including organization-based and interpersonal network measures in our models predicting recruitment to the Freedom Summer project. Second, we go beyond past research on network or structural factors in recruitment by conceptualizing social structure in a more precise and complete manner. While researchers have called for increasing attention to the "...social fabric of ...preexisting social relations" (Zald and McCarthy 1979, p. 238-9), few have examined the fine texture of the social fabric, i.e., the microstructure of preexisting social relations among potential recruits. The approach we develop in this paper focuses on the fine structure of social relations among potential recruits to the Freedom Summer campaign.

Our approach is to adopt the perspective of each individual in defining the social context of recruitment: from every individual's perspective, all the other individuals in their immediate social environment constitute the social context. Rather than, as has been typical in past research, extracting each individual from their social context and examining only certain aspects of the individual's structural position (e.g., comparing if activists exhibit more social contacts then non-activists; Oliver 1984), we examine the actual *patterns* of relationships among all potential recruits that form the social context in which each individual is embedded. Moreover, we conceive of this social context in multidimensional terms. We locate potential recruits in a web of "multiplex" relations (see Burt 1980) by examining multiple relations among all potential recruits simultaneously.

Our strategy is to conceptualize the social context of recruitment in relational terms. Moving to the relational level corresponds to making the fundamental unit of analysis the dyad or pair of individuals (see Lazarsfeld and Menzel 1961, p. 431). In shifting to the dyad as the unit of analysis, we move away from the methodological individualism that has characterized traditional studies of recruitment to social movements (Fireman and Gamson 1979). As such, we treat relations as an emergent property of groups, not reducible to individuals (Lazarsfeld and Menzel 1961). Whereas traditional studies take individuals as social atoms and treat social structure as external to individuals, we embed each individual in the web of social relations that constrain or facilitate their behavior (see Granovetter 1985).

In the context of this study, we conceptualize the social process underlying recruitment to social movements as reflecting joint decision proceses among potential Freedom Summer recruits. Stated another way, we hypothesize that interpersonal influences among the applicants to the Freedom Summer program are likely to follow an "I'll go if you'll go" pattern. In-depth follow-up interviews with Freedom Summer volunteers revealed that many of these individuals described their decision to attend Freedom Summer as determined jointly with friends (McAdam 1988). To the degree that the decision to participate in Freedom Summer reflects such interpersonal influences among potential recruits, then individualistic conceptualizations of the recruitment process will fail to capture the effects of social structural position on recruitment. By examining the results of the model for two different recruitment sites (Berekeley and Wisconsin), we study the role that structural context plays in the recruitment process. By virtue of its more faithful representation of social structure, the model we develop in this paper has the potential of more fully uncovering the social bases of recruitment than traditional individual-level studies of recruitment to social movements.

THE MISSISSIPPI FREEDOM SUMMER PROJECT

This paper will apply the perspective on recruitment we developed above to a single, highly visible case of high risk/cost activism (see McAdam 1986): the 1964 Mississippi Freedom Summer project. In this section, we briefly describe the Freedom Summer project in general, and examine the historical record of civil rights activism at the two recruitment sites we study (Berkeley and Wisconsin). This will set the stage for our analysis of the role that recruitment context plays in predicting participation in the Freedom Summer project.

The Misssissippi Freedom Summer campaign brought hundreds of primarily white, northern college students to Mississippi for the summer of 1964 to help staff freedom schools, register black voters and dramatize the continued denial of civil rights to blacks throughout the South. The Freedom Summer campaign was both costly and risky. Volunteers were asked to commit an average of two months of their summer to a project that was to prove physically and emotionally harrowing for nearly everyone. Moreover, they were expected to be financially independent in this effort; they were not only asked to give up their chance of summer employment elsewhere, but to support themselves as well (for a detailed description of Freedom Summer, see McAdam 1988).

Prior to their participation in the campaign, all prospective volunteers were required to fill out detailed applications providing information on, among other topics, their organizational affiliations, college activities, and reasons for volunteering. On the basis of these applications (and, on occasion, interviews), the prospective volunteer was either accepted or rejected. However, acceptance did not necessarily mean participation in the campaign. In advance of the summer, many of the accepted applicants informed campaign staffers that they would not be taking part in the project after all. Completed applications for all three groups—rejects, participants and withdrawals[1]—were copied and coded from the originals which are located in the archives of the Martin Luther King, Jr. Center for the Study of Non-Violence in Atlanta and the New Mississippi Foundation in Jackson, Mississippi. These applications provide a unique source of archival data for assessing the relative importance of various factors in recruitment to high risk/cost activism.

It is important to note that these data were collected during a relatively late phase of the Freedom Summer mobilization. This is important because network factors are usually seen as crucial in the initial phases of the mobilization process (see Snow et al. 1980) drawing individuals into the movement and socializing them to share the goals and ideologies of the movement. Because our data are for individuals who have already applied to participate in the Freedom Summer project, the measures we derive below are only relevant to the applicants to Freedom Summer. Therefore, our data are not appropriate to study the early phase of the Freedom Summer mobilization, i.e., in getting individuals to apply to Freedom Summer.

While our data cannot address the factors that attracted individuals to apply to the Freedom Summer project in the first place, they are ideally suited for studying the network or other factors that maintain commitment to the Freedom Summer Campaign among the set of applicants to the project. Unlike much prior research which studies activists *after* the onset of the campaign in question, our study provides data on individuals before their participation or non-participation in the movement. Therefore, for this late stage of the process, we are able to identify the factors that distinguish between participants and withdrawals.

The Activist Context: University of California at Berkeley

When one thinks of 1960s activism and especially student demonstrations, it is hard not to think of the University of California at Berkeley. One mistake people make, however, is to assume that this era of conflict was inaugurated by the Free Speech Movement that erupted in the fall of 1964 (for descriptions of the Free Speech Movement, see Draper 1965; Heirich 1968; Lipset and Wolin 1965). In fact, the Berkeley campus had already been witness to nearly five years of sporadic activism by the time the Free Speech movement got under way.

For all intents and purposes the foundation of the activist community at Berkeley was laid in 1957 with the founding of SLATE, the leftist student political party that would play a dominant role in campus politics throughout the 1960s. The driving force behind the founding of SLATE was an undergraduate sociology major named Mike Miller. The fact that Miller remained in 1964 a central figure in civil rights organizing at Berkeley attests to the strength and continuity of the activist subculture on campus. SLATE grew in size and strength in the period 1957-1960, helping to mobilize leftist political sentiment at Berkeley. But campus (and Bay area) activism took a quantum leap forward the spring of 1960 through a series of demonstrations at the San Francisco City Hall protesting the House Un-American Activities Committee (HUAC) hearings that were being held inside. Hundreds of Berkeley students took part in the demonstrations, with scores being arrested and others injured in what proved to be a harbinger of many later confrontations between police and students.

Campus activism did not subside in the wake of the anti-HUAC demonstrations. Instead, the spread of the black student sit-in movement in the South only galvanized and refocused the energies of Berkeley's activist community. In 1961, following a speech on campus, Student Non-Violent Coordinating Committee (SNCC) chairman, John Lewis, challenged the Berkeley activists to initiate civil rights activity of their own. In response,

Mike Miller—now a graduate student—and others formed a university chapter of the Friends of SNCC. Later, another group of students established a campus chapter of the Congress of Racial Equality (CORE). Later still, active chapters of these same two organizations were organized in the city of Berkeley. By early 1963, then, the Berkeley community had emerged as a veritable hotbed of civil rights activity. To coordinate this activity, an Ad Hoc Committee Against Discrimination was created in the fall of 1963. It was this group that was to spearhead an escalating campaign of civil rights protest in the months leading up to Freedom Summer. Moreover, virtually all of the Berkeley volunteers to the summer project were active in this campaign.

The beginning of the campaign, and the ostensible reason for founding the Ad Hoc Committee was a series of demonstrations directed against a chain of drive-in restaurants that purportedly practiced discrimination in the hiring and promotion of black employees. "At Christmas students picketed Berkeley merchants who refused to sign a non-discriminatory hiring agreement or to report the number of minority employees on their payroll each month" (Heirich 1968).

In 1964 the Ad Hoc Committee supported a "shop-in" campaign initiated by the San Francisco Chapter of CORE. The campaign brought pressure on a leading grocery chain to cease discriminatory hiring practices. This campaign was so effective that the chain signed a non-discrimination agreement with CORE on March 2, 1964. Buoyed by this victory, some 100 civil rights activists, including many from Berkeley, ignored a restraining order, and that same night initiated picketing against the Sheraton-Palace Hotel in San Francisco. "In the next few weeks literally thousands of students took part. More than nine hundred persons were arrested in the various Sheraton-Palace demonstrations, including about two-hundred students enrolled at the Berkeley campus" (Heirich 1968, p. 45). Of those Berkeley Freedom Summer applicants for whom data are available, nine of thirteen participants and one of four no-shows were arrested in those demonstrations. Before the spring semester ended, major campaigns involving many Berkeley students were also launched against several automobile dealers and the Bank of America (Meier and Rudwick 1973). All were charged with practicing discrimination in the hiring and promotion of blacks. As in the Sheraton-Palace demonstrations, these latter two campaigns were marked by mass arrests.[2]

Thus, on the eve of Freedom Summer, the activist subculture at Berkeley was a community with a long and intense history of civil rights activism. Virtually all the Berkeley applicants were embedded in this community and a party to its history. As such, they stand in a very different relationship to the summer project than those who applied from Wisconsin.

The Activist Context: University of Wisconsin at Madison

The University of Wisconsin offers a marked contrast to Berkeley with regard to the level of leftist activism on campus immediately prior to Freedom Summer. While the university had had its share of socialist and communist organizing during the thirties, leftist political activism was all but nonexistent on campus during the period leading up to Freedom Summer. Although the Midwest is generally regarded (incorrectly) as the birthplace of a resurgent Students for a Democratic Society (SDS), Wisconsin was without a chapter of the organization until the spring of 1964. Even then, the chapter remained among the smallest and least active of the 29 campus groups affiliated with the organization (Sale 1973, p. 122).

More relevant for our purposes is the absence of major civil rights organizing on campus prior to the summer. The university did not have a CORE chapter. Nor did Madison, the city in which the University is situated. There was no Friends of SNCC chapter in town either. The only civil rights group operating in the area was a small campus chapter of the Friends of SNCC. But even it had confined its activities to fund-raising and sponsorship of an occasional speaker. As one of the Wisconsin volunteers told the second author in a recent interview:[3]

> There was little happening [on campus]. You know you'd read about Birmingham or wherever and you felt really out of it...It felt very distant and you wanted to be where the action is [sic].

In contrast to Berkeley, then, one gets the impression that the activist community at Wisconsin was small, untried, and not particularly well-organized. It is even questionable whether we can speak of an activist community at this time in Wisconsin at all. Certainly the network of activists that constituted the community was much less well-developed than at Berkeley. The contrast between the size, strength, and history of these two communities may hold the key to understanding the very different dynamics of Freedom Summer recruitment at Berkeley and Wisconsin.

DATA AND METHODS

In past work (McAdam 1986), we have shown that network processes are strong predictors of participation for all the Freedom Summer applicants.

However, the network processes examined in that work were studied without reference to the local recruitment context. Subsequent analyses showed that the proportion of applicants that participated in Freedom Summer differed widely across recruitment context. This led us to consider the possibility that the Freedom Summer recruitment processes, especially micro level network processes, might be highly contextually specific.

Our goal in this paper is to examine the microstructural bases of recruitment to the Freedom Summer project within two university contexts. The university or college corresponds to the original recruiting context and aims of the movement (McAdam 1988). We limit our attention to the populations of 40 applicants from Berkeley and the 23 applicants from Wisconsin. Unlike our past work, the bounded nature of the groups and the small number of individuals in each group has the advantage of allowing us to examine the role of little-studied small group network processes in social movements (Fine and Stoecker 1985). A comparison of the data for the two universities allows us to assess the degree to which these micro level network processes are contextually specific.[4]

As we described above, we develop a model of the effects of network relations and social comparisons at the dyad level of analysis on joint decisions to participate in the Freedom Summer campaign.[5] The dependent variable (participation) is measured at the dyadic level by forming all possible (unordered) pairs of individuals and coding pairs sharing participation (both members of the pair participating in the Freedom Summer project) as a one, and a zero otherwise. If we consider all possible unordered dyads among the 40 applicants to Freedom Summer from Berkeley, we generate 780 unique relations $[((40*40)-40)/2=780]$, and the 23 applicants from Wisconsin generate 253 relations $[((23*23)-23)/2=253]$. Of the original 40 individuals applying from Berkeley, 31 attended Freedom Summer. When we convert these data to dyads, there are 465 dyads where both members participated in the Freedom Summer campaign $[((31*31)-31)/2=465]$. At Wisconsin, 10 of 23 individuals participated in the Freedom Summer project, yielding 45 dyads $[((10*10)-10)/2=45]$ where both members participated in Freedom Summer.

As we discussed above, we are interested in studying "I'll go if you'll go" decision processes among the Freedom Summer applicants. Our hypothesis is that individual decisions to attend are likely to be interdependent if the individuals are linked by various social relations. In our model, we examine dyads for evidence of joint decisionmaking. Such evidence would appear as effects of independent variables, such as network relations and social comparisons between dyad members, on the probability of both members of the dyad participating in Freedom Summer.

Note, however, that we are not studying *agreement* between the members of the dyads in whether or not they went to Freedom Summer. Such agreement would be shown by having dyads where both members did not participate, as well as dyads where both members participated, coded as one. Following many other studies of the effects of social integration (e.g., Festinger et al. 1950; Ekland-Olson 1982; Newcomb 1959), we see network and social comparison processes as increasing conformity with the group norm, which in this case, is to participate in the Freedom Summer campaign (recall the subjects had all applied to participate). Therefore, although it might have been possible for individuals to have been socially influenced by eventual non-participants to *not* attend Freedom Summer, our hypothesis is that social ties, even to people who did not eventually participate, will lead individuals to be more likely to participate in the summer project.

In preliminary analyses, we tested this hypothesis by coding the dependent variable as a trichotomy (agree to go, agree not to go, and disagree) and, using multinomial logistic regression, we examined whether the process by which subjects agree to participate is the same as agreeing *not* to participate. If individuals are being socially influenced to not attend by having ties to eventual non-participants, then we would observe that social ties between members of the dyad would increase the probability of non-participation. However, the results for both Berkeley and Wisconsin showed that the effects of the independent variables were in opposite directions for joint attendance and joint non-attendance (both compared to one member of the dyad attending, and the other not attending). This is inconsistent with the idea that network and social comparison processes would produce agreement between dyad members on participation (either both attending, or both not attending Freedom Summer). Being tied makes joint non-attendance *less* likely, and joint attendance *more* likely. This same pattern emerged for all the regressors described below.[6] For these reasons, we are interested in studying joint participation, rather than agreement about participation in Freedom Summer.

Among the independent variables, we include two measures at the relational level of analysis (for all unordered dyads of applicants) of the strength of interpersonal ties that existed among applicants prior to the Freedom Summer project. This information was coded from a question on the application which asked the subject to list at least ten persons they wished to be kept informed of their summer activities. Reflecting the well-articulated public relations goals of the project, this information was gathered in an effort to mobilize a well-heeled northern white liberal constituency who might put pressure on reluctant public officials to modify their stance on civil rights issues. Most of the applicants seemed to be very aware of this goal: the most common categories of names supplied by the applicants were parents, parents' friends, professors, ministers, and any other noteworthy *adults* they had contact with. Quite often, however, the applicant would include another applicant or well-known activist in their list of names.

Following the "strength of weak ties" argument (Granovetter 1973; Liu and Duff 1972), we distinguish "strong" and "weak" ties. Persons listed directly on the subject's application were coded as strong ties, where a one indicates the existence of a tie, and zero indicates the absence of a tie. Because we do not have information on the intensity of the tie, we measured indirect ties as a proxy for indirect "bridging" ties. We coded persons not listed on the subject's application to whom they were indirectly linked by way of intervening strong ties. A few of these weak ties were mediated by people who, while mutually chosen by applicants, were not themselves applicants to Freedom Summer. These interpersonal choices were coded for all dyads for each university separately. It should be noted that applicants were not directly asked about each of the other applicants in their university context.[7]

For the purposes of the analyses presented here, both of these relations were symmetrized, i.e., if person i chose person j, but person j did not reciprocate the relation, we imposed a j-i relation. Symmetrizing the data simplifies the analyses because half the dyads in each case become redundant and can be excluded from the analyses. Also, as we will show below, the strong and weak ties matrices are quite sparse, and symmetrizing allows us to increase the density of independent variables. Finally, the dependent variable is by definition symmetric (i.e., if person i shares participation at Freedom Summer with person j, then person j must share participation with person i). Therefore, the direction of the relation is of no substantive importance. For these reasons, and because of the content of the relation (see above), we think it is reasonable to impute mutual social relations on the basis of only one person's choice and to examine only the presence or absence, and not the direction of the relation.

Regarding the interpersonal relation variables, we will examine which *type* of relation is more effective in recruiting activists. Granovetter (1973) and others (e.g., Liu and Duff 1972) have argued that by virtue of their ability to bridge large social distances, "weak" ties are more important to social diffusion processes than "strong" ties. To the degree that the recruitment process is governed by social diffusion or communication processes (see Rogers and Kincaid 1981), then we would expect weak ties to be a more important determinant of activism than strong ties. However, as McAdam (1986) has argued, weak ties may not suffice for recruitment to incidents of high risk/cost activism. Because of the dangers involved in high risk/cost activism, strong interpersonal ties may be necessary for recruiting activists to such episodes. Since Freedom Summer was certainly an incident of high risk/cost activism, we would expect strong interpersonal ties to be a more important determinant of activism than weak ties. Note that because dyads linked by strong ties are indicative of small friendship groups, the hypothesis that strong ties are more important than weak ties in recruitment corresponds to Zald and McCarthy's (1979, p. 240) speculation that small friendship groups provide the fundamental building blocks of aggregation of individuals into social movements.

In addition to these interpersonal measures of network position, we also include a relational measure of shared organization ties (see Fernandez and McAdam 1987a, 1987b). This is similar to the approach taken by Rosenthal et al. (1985) in their analysis of the nineteenth century women's movement. This measure is based on subjects' reports of their organizational affiliations on the applications. The vast majority of these are campus organizations (e.g., the Friends of SNCC) and ties among recruits on the basis of shared organizations are exclusively through campus and local organizations. Because these organizations tend to be small, sharing membership in these organizations implies face-to-face encounters that are likely to be crucial in micromobilization processes (Gamson et al. 1982:1-12). We used Breiger's (1974) method of analyzing overlapping memberships to construct measures showing the number of organizations shared for all 780 dyads at Berkeley and 253 dyads at Wisconsin.

Regarding ties between recruits on the basis of shared organizations, we are interested in two questions. First, we examine if shared organization ties facilitate recruitment, independent of other effects. Second, we examine if organizational ties are more important than interpersonal ties in predicting activism. Note that unlike past research which discusses the *number* of social movement organizations (Curtis and Zurcher 1973; McCarthy and Zald 1977, p. 1218) that recruits are involved in, our approach examines the effects of the *pattern* of overlapping membership on recruitment.

In addition to these measures of structural position, we also incorporate individual background data into our model. Because our model has been conceptualized at the relational level of analysis, the individual level data must be matched for each member of the dyad. A number of strategies have been proposed for mapping individual-level data onto dyads (cf. Laumann et al. 1974; Lincoln 1984). We incorporated the individual level data in two ways. First, in order to control for individual level effects, we computed the dyad level average on each of a number of individual level characteristics:

parental income, years of education, gender (1=male), past level of civil rights involvement, and in-state versus out-of-state residence.

Parental income, gender and years of education are likely to reflect individual constraints on participation. Students with low parental income are less likely to be able to go without a summer job (recall that Freedom Summer volunteers were not paid). Because of parental and peer sex-role expectations, we expect females to be less likely to participate in the Freedom Summer project than males. Also, followiong Orum (1972) who found that class standing was positively related to activism, we expect subjects who are more advanced in their educational careers to be more likely to attend Freedom Summer. This is because integration into the local activist community is likely to increase with class standing. We see past civil rights involvement as reflecting the individual's attitudinal affinity with the goals of the civil rights movement and/or previous integration into activist networks. Finally, we distinguish in-state versus out-of-state residence and hypothesize that applicants who are from out-of-state are likely to be freer of parental constraints than applicants attending college in their state of home residence.[8]

We also included individual-level data in our model in another way. Because of our focus on the group bases of recruitment in this paper, we conceptualize the effects of individual's background on participation as being mediated in part by interpersonal comparisons on the basis of background characteristics. Following the large body of research on interpersonal attraction which documents the tendency for individuals with similar attitudes and backgrounds to interact (e.g., Newcomb 1961), we see similarity on background characteristics as an important relational variable indicating interpersonal affinity. Therefore, in this conception, it is not the absolute levels of the background variables that lead pairs of recruits to jointly participate in Freedom Summer, but the relation between the characteristics of the pair, i.e., similarity. Such similarity of background characteristics among pairs of individuals has been termed "homophily" (Lazarsfeld and Merton 1964); heterophily is the opposite concept and refers to dissimilarity in background characteristics (see Rogers and Bhowmik 1971). We therefore compute homophily-heterophily measures (computed as the absolute value of differences in the pair; for a similar approach, see Tuma and Hallinan 1979) for the background variables discussed above. For each of these variables, heterophily is indicated by a positive effect because larger numbers indicate differences, and homophily is shown by a negative effect as smaller numbers indicate similarity.[9]

Past research has related the idea of homophily-heterophily to the concept of tie strength (e.g., Rogers and Bhowmik 1971). By virtue of their interpersonal affinity, homophilous dyads are more likely to be found among strongly tied dyads, and because of the large social distance between heterophilous dyads, weak ties are more likely to be found among heterophilous dyads. As Liu and Duff (1972, p. 366) put it:

> ...homophilous communication has structural limitations to diffusion, so that information tends to re-circulate among those who already possess the same information. Heterophilous communication, seemingly facilitated by weak ties...allows new ideas to enter the network of homophilous relationships...

Therefore, for the same reasons that we expect strongly tied dyads to be more likely to participate in Freedom Summer, we posit that homophily is likely to be an important factor determining dyads' activism, especially in incidents of high risk/cost activism such as Freedom Summer. Parallel to the discussion above regarding weak ties, if the recruitment process is largely governed by social diffusion processes, then we will find heterophily predicting joint decisions to attend Freedom Summer.

We hypothesize that for both Berkeley and Wisconsin, the relational (homophily and heterophily) and structural (strong, weak, and organizational membership ties) variables will affect the likelihood of dyads participating in Freedom Summer, independent of the effects of the individual background variables (pair-level averages). By comparing the models for Berkeley and Wisconsin, we will address the question of the role that recruitment context plays in determining participation in the Freedom Summer campaign. In particular, we seek to examine if the recruitment context modifies the interpersonal comparison (relational) and network processes that we hypothesize determine participation in Freedom Summer.

ANALYSIS

We begin our analyses of the microstructural processes governing recruitment to the Freedom Summer project by presenting descriptive information for the dependent variable (shared participation), and each of the three sets of independent variables (network, relational, and averages) for both Berkeley and Wisconsin. We then specify a multivariate model predicting participation at the dyad level of analysis. Our strategy is to first investigate the total effects of the network (strong, weak, and organizational ties), relational, and dyad-level average variables on participation, and then to examine the partial effects of these variables.

Table 1 presents means and standard deviations for the variables used in these analyses for both Berkeley and Wisconsin. The means

Table 1   Means and Standard Deviations for Dyad-Level
Variables for Applicants from Berkeley and Wisconsin

	Berkeley [N=780]		Wisconsin [N=253]	
	Mean	St. Dev.	Mean	St. Dev.
Dependent Variable:				
Activism	.596	.491	.178	.383
Network Variables:				
Strong Ties	.018	.133	.032	.176
Weak Ties	.104	.352	.075	.264
Organizational Ties	.145	.352	.095	.332
Relational Variables:				
Income (in 1000s)	4.802	4.694	3.096	2.232
Education	1.432	1.1055	1.874	1.330
Gender (male=1)	.481	.500	.443	.497
Past Activism	7.858	6.211	6.901	6.280
In-state	.513	.500	.474	.499
Dyad-level Averages:				
Income (in 1000s)	10.191	3.273	7.963	1.826
Education	15.575	.882	15.00	1.099
Gender (1=male)	.625	.338	.696	.319
Past Activism	7.6225	4.883	6.000	4.463
In-state	.500	.349	.652	.330

for zero-one dichotomous variables can be interpreted as the proportion of dyads in the category coded one. The number of dyads sharing relations (dyads coded as ones) as a proportion of all possible dyads indicates the density of a network. The means for the dependent variables indicate that 60 percent of the dyads at Berkeley and 18 percent of the dyads at Wisconsin attended Freedom Summer. This difference in density on the dependent variable for the two recruitment sites reflects the fact that over three-quarters (77.5 percent) of individuals applying from Berkeley eventually participated in Freedom Summer while less than half (43.4 percent) of the individuals from Wisconsin attended Freedom Summer. Therefore, whatever the processes by which recruits maintain commitment to the Freedom Summer project, the outcomes are certainly different for the two sites.

If we consider the independent variables, only 2 percent of the dyads at Berkeley have strong ties linking the individuals compared to 3 percent of the dyads from Wisconsin. Although the percentage of strong ties is slightly lower for Berkeley, the absolute number of relations is much higher at Berkeley (780 vs. 253). The pattern for the weak ties is reversed, however. Over 10 percent of the Berkeley dyads are linked by weak ties compared to over 7 percent of the Wisconsin dyads. This indicates that, controlling for differences in the size of the networks at the two sites, the degree of social integration indicated by strong and weak ties among the applicants at the two sites are roughly comparable.

Considering the organizational ties variable, the average number of shared memberships in organizations is .145 at Berkeley and .095 at Wisconsin. Because the variable is not dichotomous (recall the coding reflects the number of organizations dyads share), in a strict sense, the mean cannot be interpreted as the density of the shared organization network. However, because very few of the relations are non-dichotomous (dyads that are tied by shared membership in multiple organizations), the percentage of dyads tied by shared membership in at least one organization are very similar to the proportions indicated by the means. For Wisconsin, the percentage is 8.3 percent, while the comparable percentage at Berkeley is over 50 percent higher at 14.5 percent.

The relatively low densities for the network variables indicate that, at least at this stage in the recruitment process, the applicants to Freedom Summer from Berkeley and Wisconsin are not very closely integrated. As we discussed above, the spareseness of these networks is probably due in part to the suboptimal measurement of these variables. Moreover, the small differences in the densities for the interpersonal networks are not likely to explain the large difference observed in the outcome variable. This leads us to believe that structural position in these networks alone is unlikely to explain recruitment to Freedom Summer. Of course, the relative importance of these network factors is an empirical question that we will address in the multivariate analyses.

Turning to the means for the relational variables, we find that dyads exhibit a high degree of homophily on education at both Berkeley and Wisconsin, i.e., disagreement on this variable is quite low.[10] For both schools, the average difference in years of education is less than two years. This is not surprising when we consider that all the people applying to the Freedom Summer program at these two schools were enrolled students. As measures of agreement on this individual variable, the high degree of homophily exhibited here indicates that there is little potential for the recruitment process to operate through heterophily on education. As we described above, we see heterophily as reflecting social diffusion processes by bridging the larger social distances that are likely to exist among dissimilar dyads.

On the other hand, the degree of homophily is lower for the other variables considered. We find that dyads at both Berkeley and Wisconsin exhibit a high degree of heterophily on family income. For Freedom Summer, dyads differ by almost $5,000 on average, while at Wisconsin the average differences are just over $3,000. For both schools, the averages for state of residence indicate that about half the pairs of Freedom Summer applicants are heterophilous meaning that half the dyads have one individual that resides in the same state as the university (either California or Wisconsin) while the other is from out of state. A similar pattern is found for gender: for both schools, a little less than half the pairs are made of individuals of different genders. The average level of disagreement on the level of past civil rights activism are also quite high. At Berkeley, an average of almost eight points separate individuals on the past activism scale, while at Wisconsin the average difference is almost seven points. These high levels of disagreement indicate that there is considerable variation in past civil rights activism. Unlike the education measures where there is little variation, the high degree of variation in past civil rights activism allows the possibility that the recruitment process may operate through heterophily on this variable.

Finally, Table 1 shows the means for the dyad-level averages of the independent variables. The means show that at Wisconsin the dyads average 15 years of education, while at Berkeley the average is slightly over 15 and a half years. The only across-school differences that are substantively worth noting are those for parental income and past activism. At Berkeley, dyads' average family incomes are over $2,000 more than dyads applying from Wisconsin. Regarding past activism, applicants from Berkeley show an average activism score that is over a point and a half greater than the average activism score for applicants from Wisconsin. Since these two variables are likely to increase the probability of participation in social movements, these variables are likely to explain the high rate of participation at Berkeley.

We turn next to the results of models predicting participation. Because the dependent variables is dichotomous (shared participation in Freedom Summer versus not), we use techniques of logistic regression analysis (see Aldrich and Nelson 1984). Table 2 presents the results of logistic regressions predicting participation for dyads at both Berkeley and Wisconsin with only the network variables as predictors.[11] When we consider the effects of the interpersonal networks, we find that they are weak predictors of joint-participation in Freedom Summer. For both schools, the Delta P coefficients show that the effect of strong ties on the probability of joint participation are positive but quite small in magnitude. At Berkeley, the effect of weak ties is also small, but contrary to our hypotheses the effect is negative. However, the results for Wisconsin show that weakly tied dyads are more likely to participate

Table 2. Logistic Regression Analyses Predicting Participation in the
Freedom Summer Project for Berkeley and Wisconsin
(Elasticities for Dummy Variables in Parentheses)

	Berkeley			Wisconsin		
	Coeff.	Delta P.[a]	Elasticity[b]	Coeff.	Delta P[a]	Elasticity[b]
Strong Ties	.297	.069	[.002]	.544	.094	[.014]
Weak Ties	−.350	−.086	−.015	.731	.132	.045
Organizational Ties	.653	.143	.145	1.200	.240	.094
Constant	.330			−1.787		
Mean of the Depend. Var.	.596			.178		
-2Log-Likelihood	1046.62			223.04		
Pseudo-[c] R-square	.005			.058		

[a]Change in probability resulting from a unit change in the independent variable when the effect is evaluated at the mean (Petersen, 1985:131).
[b]Percent change in the probability resulting from a percent change in the independent variable when the equation is evaluated at the means of the independent and dependent variables.
[c]Calculated as (Lc−Lm)/Lc where Lc and Lm are the log-likelihood statistics for equations with just the constant and the substantive model respectively.

in Freedom Summer, although the magnitude of this effect is still quite small.

Table 2 does show larger effects of organizational network ties for both schools: dyads sharing memberships in campus organizations are more likely to attend Freedom Summer than dyads not sharing such memberships. This is consistent with the notion that shared organization ties imply face-to-face encounters among applicants, that lead to increased conformity with the group norm, which is to attend Freedom Summer. A comparison of the Delta P coefficients for the organization ties variable shows that shared organizations is a stronger predictor of participation at Wisconsin than Berkeley. The pseudo R-square measure (Aldrich and Nelson 1984) shows that the model explains less variation at Berkeley (.005) than at Wisconsin (.058). This is despite the fact that there is less dyadic variation to explain at Wisconsin (compare the means of the dependent variables). Interestingly, for Wisconsin, the constant is negative indicating that structurally isolated dyads (dyads lacking strong, weak, and organizational relations) are less likely to participate in Freedom Summer than dyads sharing such ties. However, disconnected dyads at Berkeley are still likely to participate in the Freedom Summer project. This is probably due to the relatively high rate of participation at Berkeley.

Table 3. Logistic Regression Analyses Predicting Participation
in the Freedom Summer Project with Relational
and Dyad-Level Average Variables
(Elasticities for Dummy Variables in Parentheses)

	Berkeley			Wisconsin		
	Coeff.	Delta P.^{a}	Elasticity^b	Coeff.	Delta P^a	Elasticity^b
Relational:						
Income (in 1000s)	.009	.002	.017	−.286	−.038	−.728
Education	.024	.006	.014	−.028	−.004	−.044
Gender (male=1)	.037	.009	[.007]	−5.417	−.177	[−1.972]
Past Activism	−.046	−.011	−.148	.006	.0009	.036
In-state	.051	.012	[.011]	.192	.030	[.075]
Dyad Averages:						
Income (in 1000s)	−.081	−.020	−.334	−.213	−.029	−1.397
Education	.213	.051	1.338	−1.268	−.120	−15.632
Gender (male=1)	−.345	−.085	−.226	9.167	.822	12.780
Past Activism	.169	.040	.520	.282	.045	1.390
In-state	−.483	−.120	−.098	−2.131	−.153	−1.143
Constant	−2.269			1.406		
Meanof the Depend. Var.	.596			.178		
−2Log− Likelihood	971.832			116.136		
Pseudo^c R-square	.076			.510		

^{a}Change in probability resulting from a unit change in the independent variable when the effect is evaluated at the mean (Petersen,1985:131).
^{b}Percent change in the probability resulting from a percent change in the independent variable when the equation is evaluated at the means of the independent and dependent variables.
^{c}Calculated as (Lc−Lm)/Lc where Lc and Lm are the log-likelihood statistics for equations with just the constant and the substantive model respectively.

Table 3 presents the effects of the relational and dyad-level averages on participation. For both schools, the most important effects are among the dyad-level averages. As we described above, controlling for homophily, the averages measure individual-level tendencies toward participation. Consistent with our expectations, for both Berkeley and Wisconsin, dyads that have been highly active in civil rights are more likely to participate than dyads that have not been active in the past. The Delta P coefficients reveal that the change in probability due to unit change in average civil rights activism are comparable for the two schools (Berkeley = .040; Wisconsin = .045), although in percentage terms, the increment is much larger at Wisconsin (1.390 vs. .520). In contrast, the effects of years of education are in opposite directions for the two schools: at Berkeley more highly educated dyads are more likely to participate in Freedom Summer, while at Wisconsin the opposite is true. Preliminary analyses showed that this pattern surfaces at the individual level. The magnitudes of the Delta P coefficients show that the decrease in probability of participation associated with a year's increase in education at Wisconsin is more than double the magnitude of the increase in the probability of participation due to a year's increase in education at Berkeley (−.120 vs. .051). Moreover, as the elasticities show, the education effects are the strongest effects in each of their respective equations: at Wisconsin, the decrease in the probability of participation associated with a percent increase in education is over 15 percent: for Berkeley, the corresponding increase is over 1 percent.

The effects of average gender are quite different for the two schools. At Berkeley, males are moderately less likely to participate in Freedom Summer than females, while at Wisconsin the effect of gender is very strong, and in the opposite direction. In fact, none of the women who applied from Wisconsin participated in the program. For both sites, the effect of average parental income is negative indicating that dyads from less affluent families are more likely to participate in Freedom Summer than dyads from more affluent backgrounds. This runs counter to our hypothesis that affluence would be positively related to participation because more affluent dyads would be better able to take a summer off without paid employment (recall that participation in Freedom Summer was unpaid). We have no explanation for why this pattern should surface at both schools. We might speculate that the counterintuitive results are due to the indirect nature of the areal measure of parental income (see above). Consistent with our hypothesis about the greater parental constraints that in-state applicants face, dyads whose home residence is out-of-state are more likely to participate in the Freedom Summer campaign. Here too, there is a language difference in the effect of this variable across site. The tendency for out-of-state applicants to participate is very strong at Wisconsin, but only slight at Berkeley.

Turning to the relational variables, we find the effects of the homophily-heterophily measures are much weaker than the dyad-level averages. For Berkeley, the only effect worth discussing is that of past activism. There is a slight tendency for dyads that are homphilous with respect to past activism to participate in Freedom Summer. There is no evidence of a similar process at work at Wisconsin: the corresponding effect at Wisconsin is nil, and in the opposite direction. However, at Wisconsin, two effects emerge among the relational measures. First, there is a strong tendency for dyads that are similar with respect to their parental income to participate in Freedom Summer. Second, there is also a strong effect of gender homophily on the chances of participation. As we mentioned above, all the Wisconsin participants were male. When read in concert with the effect of average gender, the results show that males are likely to participate, and to do so in single-sex (male) dyads.

Finally, a comparison of the pseudo-R-squares for Tables 2 and 3 show that the set of relational and dyad-level average variables explain much more of the variation in participation than the set of network variables.[12] Similar to the results in Table 2, the pseudo-R-square measures show that the model in Table 3 is much better at explaining variation in participation at Wisconsin than at Berkeley.

Table 4 presents the final model predicting Freedom Summer participation with the network, relational, and dyad-level averages. For Berkeley, the network variables have only small effects once the relational and dyad-level average variables are controlled. This implies that the effect of interorganizational ties we noted in Table 2 is explained by the relational and dyad-level average variables. Given the lack of network effects, it is not surprising that the effects of the other variables are virtually identical to those presented in Table 3 for Berkeley. Among the relational variables, only past civil rights activism remains as a fairly weak predictor of participation. This effect is negative indicating that dyads that are homphilous with respect to this variable are more likely to attend Freedom Summer than dyads that are heterophilous with regard to their past activism. As we discussed earlier, homophily is consistent with a recruitment pattern that mobilizes tightly-knit groups of similarly active individuals. Among the dyad-level averages, the same pattern of effects emerges as in Table 3. Consistent with our expectations, there is a tendency for more highly educated dyads to participate in Freedom Summer. Also, dyads composed of experienced civil rights activists are more likely to attend Freedom Summer than dyads with less experience in civil rights protest. Also consistent with our hypothesis, out-of-state students are slightly more likely to participate in the summer project than in-state students. Finally, contrary to our hypothesis, males are less likely to participate in the summer project than females, and more affluent dyads are less likely to participate in the Freedom Summer campaign.

If we consider the model for Wisconsin, we find that, although it is modest by comparison to the other effects in the model, the effect of organizational ties on joint-participation is stronger after the relational and dyad-level

Table 4. Logistic Regression Analyses Predicting Participation
in the Freedom Summer Project with Network, Relational
and Dyad-Level Average Variables
(Elasticities for Dummy Variables in Parentheses)

	Berkeley			Wisconsin		
	Coeff.	*Delta P.[a]*	*Elasticity[b]*	*Coeff.*	*Delta P[a]*	*Elasticity[b]*
Network:						
Strong Ties	.070	.017	(.0005)	−.885	−.096	[−.023)
Weak Ties	−.264	−.065	−.011	.033	.005	.002
Organizational Ties	.457	.104	.027	1.916	.417	.150
Relational:						
Income (in 1000s)	.009	.002	.018	−.243	−.033	−.619
Education	.026	.006	.015	−.037	−.005	−.057
Gender (male=1)	.042	.010	(.008)	−5.873	−.178	(−2.137)
Past Activism	−.043	−.010	−.137	.055	.008	.312
In-state	.049	.012	(.010)	.341	.050	(.133)
Dyad Averages:						
Income (in 1000s)	−.085	−.021	−.349	−.243	−.033	−1.538
Education	.223	.052	1.405	−1.358	−.125	−16.751
Gender (male=1)	−.340	−.084	−.223	8.762	.821	12.215
Past Activism	.163	.039	.512	.184	.028	.906
In-state	−.468	−.116	−.095	−1.969	−.149	−1.056
Constant	−2.440			3.555		
Mean of the Depend. Var.	.596			.178		
-2Log- Likelihood	969.816			109.917		
Pseudo[c] R-square	.078			.536		

[a]Change in probability resulting from a unit change in the independent variable when the effect is evaluated at the mean (Petersen, 1985:131).
[b]Percent change in the probability resulting from a percent change in the independent variable when the equation is evaluated at the means of the independent and dependent variables.
[c]Calculated as Lc-Lm)/Lc where Lc and Lm are the log-likelihood statistics for equations with just the constant and the substantive model respectively.

average variables are controlled. This effect is positive showing that dyads that are linked by joint membership in local organizations are more likely to participate in Freedom Summer than dyads that are not linked by such ties. This is consistent with the results of other quite different models of the Freedom Summer recruitment for Wisconsin (Fernandez and McAdam, 1987a, 1987b). However, similar to the results in Table 3, the strong and weak ties variables are only very weakly related to participation at Freedom Summer. Analyses not reported here have shown that these variables are not related to participation even after the organizational ties variable is removed from the model. Therefore, these results show no evidence of recruitment being affected by either social diffusion (weak ties) or small friendship group (strong ties) processes after the other variables in the model are controlled.

The final model for Wisconsin shows a number of other changes compared with the models presented in Table 3. Among the relational variables, the addition of the network variables to the model changes two of the effects for Wisconsin (compare Tables 3 and 4). First, the effect of homophily with respect to family income becomes somewhat weaker when the network variables are controlled. Especially in light of the counterintuitive negative effect of average parental income (see below), it is unclear why this is the case. Second, the effect of heterophily on past civil rights activism is substantially stronger after the network variables are included in the equation. In marked contrast with Berkeley where a pattern of homophily on past civil rights activism is associated with participation, the pattern at Wisconsin is one of heterophily with respect to past civil rights activism. As we discussed above, this pattern shows that dyads that are composed of individuals with widely varying histories of civil rights activism are more likely to participate than dyads composed of individuals with similar histories of civil rights activism. This is consistent with a "leader-follower" recruitment pattern where a relatively inexperienced applicant is drawn into participation by a veteran civil rights activist.

The addition of the network variables leaves the effects of a number of dyad-level average variables unchanged. Contrary to our expectations, less affluent dyads are more likely to participate in Freedom Summer, and more highly educated dyads are less likely to participate in the Freedom Summer program than less educated dyads. Consistent with our expectations, male applicants are more likely to participate than female applicants, and applicants from out-of-state are more likely to participate in Freedom Summer than in-state applicants.

Among the dyad-level averages, only one change is worth noting, i.e., the effect of past activism is weaker after the network variables are controlled. Consistent with our hypothesis, the effect remains positive showing that applicants with more activist experience are more likely to participate in Freedom Summer. This implies that structural position in the interorganizational network explains part of the tendency for experienced civil rights activists to participate in Freedom Summer. This is probably because past civil rights activism serves to affect participation in the Freedom Summer campaign *through* location in the interorganizational network (recall that many of the organizations are campus-based activist organizations; also see Fernandez and McAdam 1987a, 1987b). That is, past civil rights activism is likely to *cause* position in the local interorganizational network, which in turn serves to increase the chances of participation in the Freedom Summer campaign. Because position in the network is a more proximate cause of participation than past civil rights activism, network position tempers the effect of past civil rights activism (for a detailed discussion of this point, see Fernandez and McAdam 1987b).

DISCUSSION

In this paper, we have explored the role of structural factors in recruitment to social movements. Using data for applicants to the Freedom Summer project from two universities, we developed a model of recruitment that incorporates structural factors as predictors of participation in the summer project. We hypothesized that interpersonal influences among the applicants will follow an 'I'll go if you go" pattern. Unique among studies of social networks and social movements, we developed dyad-level models to examine the influence of networks, interpersonal comparison, and individual-level factors on joint participation in the Freedom Summer campaign for two contexts: the University of California at Berkeley and the University of Wisconsin at Madison.

The results of this model have several important implications regarding the microstructural bases of social movements. First, the results lend support to the notion that structural availability is a determinant of participation in social movements, but that the effects of structural and other variables on participation are highly contingent on the recruitment context. While the strongest effects for both schools are the individual-level determinants of participation (measured by the dyad-level averages), some effects of the network and relational variables remain after the individual-level variables are controlled. For one of the two recruitment sites (i.e., Wisconsin) structural position in the organizational ties network appears as a predictor of participation independent of the other variables. However, we could find no evidence of this process operating at the University of California at Berkeley. In contrast with Wisconsin, where the effect of organizational ties is strengtehened by the addition of controls, the gross effect of the organizational ties variable is explained by the addition of the relational and dyad-level averages so that the net effect of structural location in the organizational network was negligible for Berkeley.

On the other hand, the final model for Berkeley did show an effect of homophily with respect to past civil rights activism: dyads that are similar in their histories of civil rights protest were more likely to participate in the Freedom Summer program than dissimilar dyads, independent of the individual-level propensity for past activists to participate. However, there is no evidence of a comparable process at work at Wisconsin. In fact, the opposite appears to have been the case: dyads that are heterophilous with respect to past civil rights activism are more likely to participate in Freedom Summer than dyads with similar histories of activism. Therefore, it appears that the recruitment context not only affects the rate of participation in Freedom Summer, it also modifies the process by which structural and other factors affect joint decisions to participate in Freedom Summer.

Second, these analyses are also suggetive of the complex interplay between structural and individual-level background factors in producing participation. In addition to having an independent effect on the probability of participating in Freedom Summer, structural position in the Wisconsin organizational ties network also tempers the individual-level effect of past civil rights activism. The fact that this pattern does not surface at Berkeley indicates that the recruitment context not only affects the kinds of social influences that serve to maintain commitment to the movement, but the context also affects the manner in which these social influences combine with individual-level factors to predict participation.

Finally, because the context apparently plays a crucial role in the mobilization of potential recruits, we need to address which facets of the overall structural context of recruitment have these far-reaching consequences. With only two contexts, any description of the role of recruitment context must be seen as highly speculative. Nevertheless, we may offer some tentative hypotheses.

We think that they key difference between the Berkeley and Wisconsin recruitment contexts is the history of civil rights activism at the two campuses. Our discussion of the history of civil rights activism on the two campuses showed that Berkeley had had a long history of civil rights activism prior to the Freedom Summer recruitment. Moreover, many of the Berkeley applicants were members of the well-developed activist community on campus. It is likely that this feature explains why Berkeley proved to be such fertile ground for recruitment to Freedom Summer. At Berkeley, the activist community served to reinforce commitment to the project on an almost daily basis. The fact that groups of similar activists were likely to participate in the Freedom Summer project at Berkeley, even after individual-level factors were controlled, is consistent with this interpretation.

In contrast, Wisconsin lacked a similarly intense activist community with a tradition of civil rights protest. Consequently, the Freedom Summer recruitment was less successful there. While the Freedom Summer applicants from Wisconsin were the pioneers of civil rights protest on campus, they did not engage in these early efforts as solitary individuals: commitment to the Freedom Summer campaign was apparently also maintained by integration in a campus and community-based organizational network.

Seen in this light, these results are consistent with a conception of recruitment contexts as the residue of protest culture that is left by incidents of past activism. However, this residue is not neutral in its effects; it forms the basis of subsequent mobilizations by affecting the actions of potential recruits. The effects of the context can be felt at both the individual level, perhaps by raising the social costs of movement non-participation and the benefits of participation, and the group level by affecting the number and form of interactions among potential recruits. For these reasons, the context is likely to exert an important influence on all the processes involved in the Freedom Summer recruitment, including those related to the structural variables.

If our description of the recruitment context as a residue of past activism is correct, then time becomes an important variable for understanding the nature of recruitment to social movements. This is not surprising, for the time-dependent nature of social movements has long been recognized. Therefore, it is possible that the residue of the protest culture might have operated quite differently at an earlier point in the Freedom Summer recruitment. For example, network factors may have played an important role at an earlier phase in the Freedom Summer recruitment at Berkeley. As a result of the extraordinary level of civil rights activity on the Berkeley campus, the already well-developed organizational network might have served an important communication function, thereby encouraging people to apply. This is consistent with the results of a classic diffusion of innovation study (Coleman et al. 1966) which shows that these effects are important during the early phases of the diffusion process in distinguishing adoptors from non-adoptors, but that network effects dissipate toward the end of the process. In terms of the Freedom Summer recruitment, network factors might have been important in the early phases for informing individuals who are predisposed to participate in the program, but the more stubborn hold-outs identifed during the later phases of the process are not likely to be drawn into participation by social network contacts. If this is the case, then by studying this late phase of the Freedom Summer recruitment we will have missed the most important effect of these networks during the formative phase of the recruitment process. Unfortunately, we do not have available any data that would allow us to test this intriguing hypothesis.

While we cannot test hypotheses about the earlier phase of the recruitment process, we will be able to bring more data to bear on the questions that motivated this paper. It is important to realize, however, that our conjectures in these matters are supported by the qualitative information we have on the history of activism at these two universities. As more cases become available, we will be able to develop a full contextual model of participation in Freedom Summer. Such a model should allow us a better specification of the complex interrelationships between structural factors and recruitment contexts in their effects on participation in social movements.

ACKNOWLEDGMENTS

An earlier version of this paper was presented at the 1986 meetings of the American Sociological Association. The second author gratefully acknowledges the support of the Rockefeller Foundation in undertaking this research. The first author gratefully acknowledges the support of a Guggenheim Fellowship, and a grant from the National Science Foundation. We would like to thank Ken Dauber, Paul DiMaggio, Roger Gould, Mark Granovetter, Charles Kadushin, Yong-Hak Kim, David Knoke, Jim Lincoln, John McCarthy, Jim Shockey, Michael Sobel, and Harrison White for their helpful advice and criticisms at various stages of the project.

NOTES

1. Very few of the applicants to Freedom Summer were rejected. Of the original 1,068 applicants to Freedom Summer, only 55 were rejected. Seven hundred and twenty participated in the program, and 239 withdrew. The participation status of an additional 54 applicants could not be determined, and these cases have therefore been coded as missing. All of the applicants we analyze in this paper were either participants or withdrawals.

2. See acounts on the front pages of the *Daily Californian*, March 1, 1964; March 6, 1964; March 14, 1964; April 20, 1964.

3. The following account is taken from the transcript of a three hour in-depth interview conducted with a former Freedom Summer volunteer. The interview is one of 80 that were conducted as part of a follow-up study of all applicants to the summer project. The results of this research are reported in McAdam (1988).

4. Note that our data constitute the population of applicants from Berkeley and Wisconsin. Therefore, we eschew statistical significance tests and interpret the model we present here as descriptive of historical events at Berkeley and Wisconsin. Because the network ties linking members of dyads are collective properties of the settings, we think that the units that one would need to vary in order to generalize to other settings are the recruitment contexts

themselves. From this perspective, this paper is a detailed analysis of two case studies and runs all the risks that case studies normally run in terms of representativeness of the findings. We are in the process of obtaining the data that are required to determine the networks for respondents from other colleges and universities. We will address the representativeness of these findings in subsequent work by examining other recruitment contexts as the data become available.

5.   In other work (McAdam 1986; Fernandez and McAdam 1987a, 1987b), we have studied the recruitment process for Freedom Summer applicants at the individual level of analysis. However, there are very different processes being modelled in those papers. The most important contrast between this and our previous work is the fact that joint decisionmaking does not play a role in our previous models of recruitment. Consequently, social comparison processes (see below) are not examined in our previous studies. Because of differences in both the processes being modelled and the contextually specific nature of data being studied here, the results presented below are not directly comparable to those reported in our past work.

6.   Note that we could not estimate full multinomial logit models for the trichotomy. Proctor (1969, 1979) has shown that the number of degrees of freedom for models with a dependent variable that is derived from a nodal variable (such as individual participation in Freedom Summer) and is studied at the relational level of analysis is simply the number of individuals. With only 23 individuals at Wisconsin, the final multinomial logit model used more degrees of freedom than were available, making estimation impossible. This is because the multinomial logit model for the trichotomy fits twice as many parameters and therefore uses twice the number of degrees of freedom as the binomial logit model. Our strategy was to estimate various combinations of the sets of independent variables (network, relational, and individual; see below) taking care not to use all the degrees of freedom. With only a very few exceptions, the pattern of effects for joint participation and joint non-participation were in opposite directions. Because of the small number of degrees of freedom, and the fact that the results of the multinomial analyses do not offer any evidence that joint non-participation is more likely among dyads that are tied, we have chosen to present the binomial logit analyses predicting joint attendance vs. joint non-attendance and disagreement combined.

7.   This feature of the measurement of the interpersonal data may introduce undesireable biases (Holland and Leinhardt 1973; Lindzey and Byrne 1968). In particular, we believe that our data underestimate the actual numbers of the interpersonal ties among the applicants. However, we think the data we have available are well-suited for measuring particularly salient interpersonal ties. Especially for an instance of high risk/cost activism such as Freedom Summer (McAdam 1986), it is reasonable to assume that very salient ties are likely to be most important in individuals' decisions to participate. When we also consider the other unique strengths of these data, we think the benefits of using these data outweigh the risks that derive from the suboptimal measurement of the interpersonal networks.

8.   With the exceptions of parental income and past civil rights activity, the individual-level coding of these variables is straightforward. Both participants and withdrawals were asked to list on their applications any previous civil rights activities they were involved in. We assigned a numeric value to each activity reflecting its intensity relative to other forms of civil rights activism. The idea here is to distinguish between what Oliver (1984) has called token and active contributions to collective action. For example, participation in the Freedom Rides is assigned a score of "7," while contributing money to a civil rights organization is designated a "1." We then assign each subject the sum of the points for the activities reported on their applications.

Unfortunately, applicants were not asked about their parents' income so that we had to resort to a crude, indirect measure of parental income. Students provided the names and addresses of their parents on their applications. Using these addresses, we coded the median family income for the appropriate Census tract or for the city or county if the address was outside of a Standard Metropolitan Statistical Area, for every applicant. Only one applicant is not covered by this procedure: one student listed an overseas embassy as the parents' address (the father was a U.S. ambassador at the time). We coded this student's father's income from the State Department's 1964 Foreign Service List.

9.   Our focus on homophily-heterophily bears an important similarity to the approach of recent research that focuses on group heterogeneity of resources as a determinant of collective action (see Oliver et al. 1985, p. 28-30). However, our approach is different from that of Oliver et al. (1985) in that they conceive of group heterogeneity at a high level of aggregation (in their example, the neighborhood) and see such heterogeneity as potentially forming the bases of a critical mass in a threshold model of collective behavior. In contrast, our model of the process sees group heterogeneity operating at the most micro level (the smallest possible group, the dyad), and does not explicitly seek to identify collective action thresholds.

10.   Note that the homophily/heterophily variables are measuring the amount of individual-level heterogeneity in the group, and partitioning it on a dyad-by-dyad basis. We are testing the hypothesis that, in addition to individual-level processes measured by the dyad-level averages, similarity or differences on background characteristics will affect the probability of the dyad participating in Freedom Summer by means of interpersonal comparison processes discussed above. As such, we are studying the covariation of this heterogeneity in background characteristics with the joint-decision to participate in the summer project.

11.   For each school, we present the raw logistic regression coefficient and two transformations of the raw effects, denoted as "Delta P" and "Elasticity" in the tables. Delta P shows the change in the probability of participation (rather than the log-odds) resulting from a unit increase in the independent variable (Petersen 1985). Because of the non-linear nature of the logistic regression model, Delta P will differ depending on where the effect is evaluated. For the results presented here, the effects are evaluated at the mean. The elasticity expresses the change in the probability in percentage form; it is the percent change in the probability of participation resulting from a percent change in the independent variable. For qualitative variables such as strong ties, a percent increase is meaningless; for this reason, the elasticities for dummy variables are placed in parentheses.

12.   This comparison may be misleading because the models presented in Table 3 use more degrees of freedom than the models in Table 2. Correcting for this difference between the models in Tables 2 and 3 by calculating the improvement of fit per degree of freedom still shows that the set of relational and dyad-level average variables explain more variation in participation per degree of freedom than the network variables.

REFERENCES

Aldrich, J. H. and F. D. Nelson. 1984. *Linear Probability, Logit, and Probit Models.* Beverly Hills, CA: Sage.
Aveni, A. F. 1978. "Organizational Linkages and Resource Mobilization: The Significance of Linkage Strength and Breadth." *The Sociological Quarterly*, 19:185-202.
Bibby, R. W. and M. B. Brinkerhoff. 1974. "When Proselytizing Fails: An Organizational Analysis." *Sociological Analysis* 35:189-200.
Bolton, C. D. 1972. "Alienation and Action: A Study of Peace Group Members." *American Journal of Sociology* 78:537-61.

Braungart, R. G. 1971. 'Family Status, Socialization, and Student Politics: A Multivariate Analysis." *American Journal of Sociology* 77:108-29.

Breiger, R. L. 1974. 'The Duality of Persons and Groups." *Social Forces* 53:181-89.

Burt, R. S. 1980. "Models of Network Structure." *Annual Review of Sociology* 6:79-141.

Coleman, J. S., E. Katz and H. Menzel. 1966. *Medical Innovation: A Diffusion Study.* Indianapolis: Bobbs-Merrill.

Curtis, R. L. and L. A. Zurcher, Jr. 1973. "Stable Resources of Protest Movement: The Multi-Organizational Field." *Social Forces* 52:53-60.

Draper, H. 1965. *Berkeley: The New Student Revolt.*New York: Grove Press.

Ekland-Olson, S. 1982. "Deviance, Social Control and Networks." *Research in Law, Deviance and Social Control* 4:271-99.

Fernandez, R. M. and D. McAdam. 1987a. "Multiorganizational Fields and Recruitment Contexts: Network and Contextual Factors in Recruitment to Freedom Summer." Unpublished manuscript, Department of Sociology, University of Arizona.

_____ 1987b. "Multiorganizational Fields and Recruitment to Social Movements." in Bert Klandermans (ed.), *Organizing for Social Change: Social Movement Organizations Across Cultures.* Greenwich, CT: JAI Press.

Fendrich, J. and E. S. Krauss. "Student Activism and Adult Left-wing Politics: A Causal Model of Political Socialization for Black, White and Japanese Students of the 1960s Generation." Pp. 231-55 in Lewis Kriesberg (ed.), *Research in Social Movements, Conflict and Change* Vol. 1:231-55.

Festinger, L. S. Schachter, and K. Back. 1950. *Social Pressures in Informal Groups.* New York: Harper and Row.

Fine, G. A. and R. Stoecker. 1985. "Can the Circle be Unbroken? Small Groups and Social Movements." *Advances in Group Processes* 2:1-28.

Fireman, B. and W. A. Gamson. 1979. "Utilitarian Logic in the Resource Mobilization Perspective. Pp. 8-44 in Mayer N. Zald and John D. McCarthy (eds.), *The Dynamics of Social Movements: Resource Mobilization, Social Control, and Tactics.* Cambridge, MA: Winthrop.

Flacks, R. 1967. "The Liberated Generations: An Exploration of the Roots of Student Protest." *Journal of Social Issues* 23:52-75.

Gamson, W. A., B. Fireman and S. Rytina. 1982. *Encounters with Unjust Authority.* Homewood, Illinois: Dorsey Press.

Gerlach, L. P. and V. H. Hine. 1970. *People, Power, Change: Movements of Social Transformation.* Indianapolis, Indiana: Bobbs-Merrill.

Geschwender, J. 1968. "Explorations in the Theory of Social Movements and Revolution." *Social Forces* 47:127-35.

Glock, C. Y. 1964. "The Role of Deprivation in the Origin and Evolution of Religious Groups." R. Lee and M. Marty (eds.), *Religion and Social Conflict.* New York: Oxford University Press.

Granovetter, M. S. 1973. "The Strength of Weak Ties." *American Journal of Sociology* 78:1360-80.

_____ 1985. "Economic Action and Social Structure: The Problem of Embeddedness." *American Journal of Sociology* 91:481-510.

Gurney, J. N. and K. J. Tierney. 1982. "Relative Deprivation and Social Movements: A Critical Look at Twenty Years of Theory and Research." *Sociological Quarterly* 23:33-47.

Harrison, M. L. 1974. "Sources of Recruitment to Catholic Pentecostalism." *Journal for the Scientific Study of Religion* 13:49-64.

Heirich, M. 1968. *The Beginning: Berkeley, 1964.* New York: Columbia University Press.

_____ 1977. "Change of Heart: A Test of Some Widely Held Theories of Religious Conversion." *American Journal of Sociology* 83:653-80.

Hicks, J. D. 1961. *The Populist Revolt.* Lincoln, Nebraska: University of Nebraska Press.

Holland, P. W. and S. Leinhardt. 1973. "The Structural Implications of Measurement Error in Sociometry." *Journal of Mathematical Sociology* 3:385-111.

Jenkins, C. 1983. "Resource Mobilization Theory and the Study of Social Movements." *Annual Review of Sociology* 9:527-53.

Laumann, E. O., L. Verbrugge and F. U. Pappi. 1974. "A Causal Modelling Approach to the Study of a Community Elite's Influence Structure." *American Sociological Review* 39:162-74.

Lazarsfeld, P. F. and H. Menzel. 1961. "On the Relation between Individual and Collective Properties." Pp. 422-40 in Amitai Etzioni (ed.), *Complex Organizations: A Sociological Reader.* New York: Holt, Rinehart and Winston.

Lazarsfeld, P. F. and R. K. Merton. 1964. "Friendship as Social Process: A Substantive and Methodological Analysis." Pp. 18-66 in Monroe Berger, Theodore Abel, and Charles H. Page (eds.), *Freedom and Control in Modern Society.* Princeton, NJ: Van-Nostrand.

Lewis, S. H. and R. E. Kraut, 1972. "Correlates of Student Political Activism and Ideology." *Journal of Social Issues* 28:131-49.

Lincoln, J. R. 1984. "Analyzing Relations in Dyads: Problems, Methods and an Application to Interorganizational Research." *Sociological Methods and Research* 13:45-76.

Lindzey, G. and D. Byrne. 1968. "Measurement of Social Choice and Interpersonal Attractiveness." Pp. 452-525 in G. Lindzey and E. Aronson (eds.), *The Handbook of Social Psychology.* Vol. II. Reading, MA: Addison-Wesley.

Lipset, S. M. and S. Wolin. 1965. *The Berkeley Student Revolt.* New York: Doubleday Anchor.

Liu, W. T. and R. W. Duff. 1972. "The Strength in Weak Ties." *Public Opinion Quarterly* 36:361-66.

McAdam, D. 1986. "Recruitment to High-risk Activism: The Case of Freedom Summer." *American Journal of Sociology* 92:64-90.

_____ 1988. *Freedom Summer.* New York: Oxford University Press.

McCarthy, J. D. and M. N. Zaid. 1977. "Resource Mobilization and Social Movements: A Partial Theory." *American Journal of Sociology* 82:1212-1241.

Meier, A. and E. Rudwick. 1973. *CORE, A Study in the Civil Rights Movement, 1942-1968.* New York: Oxford University Press.

Newcomb, T. M. 1959. "The Study of Consensus." Pp. 277-92 in R. K. Merton, L. Broom and L. S. Cottrell (eds.), *Sociology Today: Problems and Prospects.* Volume II. New York: Harper and Row.

_____ 1961. *The Acquaintance Process.* New York: Holt, Rinehart and Winston.

Oberschall, A. 1973. *Social Conflict and Social Movements.* Englewood Cliffs, New Jersey: Prentice-Hall.

Oliver, P. 1984. "'If You Don't Do It, Nobody Else Will': Active and Token Contributors to Local Collective Action." *American Sociological Review* 49:601-10.

Oliver, P., G. Marwell and R. Teixeira. 1985. "A Theory of the Critical Mass. I. Interdependence, Group Heterogeneity, and the Production of Collective Action. *American Journal of Sociology* 91:522-56.

Orum, A. 1972. *Black Students in Protest: A Study of the Origins of the Black Student Movement.* Washington, D.C.: American Sociological Association.

Petersen, T. 1985. "A Comment on Presenting Results from Logit and Probit Models." *American Sociological Review* 50:130-1.

Proctor, C. H. 1969. "Analyzing Pair Data and Point Data on Social Relationships, Attitudes and Background Characteristics of Costa Rican Bureau Employees." *Proceedings of the Social Statistics Section, American Statistical Association.*

_____ 1979. "Graph Sampling Compared to Conventional Sampling." Pp. 301-318 in Paul W. Holland and Samuel Leinhardt (eds.), *Perspectives on Social Network Analysis.* New York: Academic.

Rogers, E. M. and D. L. Kincaid. 1981. *Communication Networks: Toward a New Paradigm for Research.* New York: Free Press.

Rogers, E. M. and D.K. Bhowmik. 1971. "Homophily-heterophily: Relational Concepts for Communication Research." *Public Opinion Quarterly* 34:523-28.

Rosenthal, N., M. Fingrutd, M. Ethier, R. Karant, and D. McDonald. 1985. "Social Movements and Network Analysis: A Case Study of Nineteenth-century Women's Reform in New York State." *American Journal of Sociology* 90:1022-54.

Rothschild, M. A. 1982. *A Case of Black and White: Northern Volunteers and the Southern Freedom Summers, 1964-1965.* Westport, CT: Greenwood.

Sale, K. 1973. *SDS.* New York: Random House.

Searles, R. and J. A. Williams, Jr. 1962. "Negro College Students' Participation in Sit-ins." *Social Forces* 40:215-20.

Snow, D. A., L. A. Zurcher, Jr. and S. Ekland-Olson. 1980. "Social Networks and Social Movements: A Microstructural Approach to Differential Recruitment." *American Sociological Review* 45:787-801.

_____ 1983. "Further Thoughts on Social Networks and Social Movements." *Sociology* 17:112-20.

Stark, R. and W. S. Bainbridge. 1980. "Networks of Faith: Interpersonal Bonds and Recruitment to Cults and Sects." *American Journal of Sociology* 85:1376-95.

Thomas, L. E. 1971. "Family Correlates of Student Political Activism." *Developmental Psychology* 4:206-14.

Tuma, N. B. and M. T. Hallinan. 1979. "The Effects of Sex, Race, and Achievement on Schoolchildren's Friendships." *Social Forces* 57:1265-85.

Von Eschen, D., J. Kirk and M. Pinard. 1971. "The Organizational Substructure of Disorderly Politics." *Social Forces* 49:529-44.

Wallace, R. and S. Bruce. 1982. "Network and Clockwork." *Sociology* 16:102-7.

White, J. W. 1970. *The Sokagakkai and the Mass Society.* Stanford, California: Stanford University Press.

Zald, M. N. and J. D. McCarthy (eds.). 1979. *The Dynamics of Social Movements: Resource Mobilization, Social Control, and Tactics.* Cambridge, MA: Winthrop.

Zukier, H. 1982. "Situational Determinants of Behavior." *Social Research* 49:1073-91.

Zurcher, L. A. and D. A. Snow. 1981. "Collective Behavior: Social Movements." Pp. 447-82 in M. Rosenberg and R. Turner (eds.), *Social Psychology: Sociological Perspectives.* New York: Basic.

AMBIGUITY AND CROWDS:

RESULTS FROM A COMPUTER

SIMULATION MODEL

Norris R. Johnson and William E. Feinberg

Interactionist perspectives in social psychology at least since Sherif's work have assumed that conditions of ambiguity produce information-seeking behavior and heighten susceptibility to social influence. Sherif and Sherif (1969, p. 70) have summarized the relationship by concluding that "the more unstructured the stimulus situation, the greater the effectiveness of social influences."

This assumption has been central in a number of theories of collective behavior, which often characterize the phenomenon as reflecting a response to situations of structural ambiguity.[1] When characterized in that way, collective behavior is defined as the process through which members of a collectivity seek information to define an ambiguous situation, generate agreements concerning the appropriate action in the situation, and develop a group response to the situation (see, e.g., Turner and Killian 1987, passim).

Research in Social Movements, Conflict and Change,
Volume 12, pages 35-66.
Copyright © 1990 by JAI Press Inc.
All rights of reproduction in any form reserved.
ISBN: 1-55938-065-9

Directly studying ambiguity and the resulting reliance on others for direction within actual episodes of collective behavior presents difficulties rarely overcome. Discussions are usually based on descriptive accounts of collective behavior episodes or on experimental work with individuals or small groups, which is only indirectly related to collective behavior. Heirich's (1971) account of the initiation of student protest at Berkeley in 1964, which details the information exchange and social influences which ultimately led to crowd action, is probably the best descriptive evidence of the process in an actual crowd episode.

An example of laboratory work with individuals was reported by Ball-Rokeach (1973), who experimentally created "pervasive ambiguity," arising when there is insufficient information to construct a definition of a situation, and produced both the predicted information-seeking activity and the reliance on others for definitions of the situation. Ball-Rokeach viewed the work as within the collective behavior framework implied above and as supporting Shibutani's (1966) view of rumor as a collective definition of an ambiguous situation. The classic small group studies are, of course, those of Sherif discussed below, but another excellent experimental study—more closely related to collective behavior—is work by Gamson, Fireman, and Rytina (1982), whose laboratory simulation demonstrated the interactive, group-formation process through which an aggregate mobilizes to resist unjust authority.

The work reported here represents another method of simulating the collective behavior process. We have developed—and reported elsewhere (Johnson and Feinberg 1989)—a computer simulation model of behavior in crowds which permits us to experimentally vary indicators of ambiguity and to test hypotheses concerning ambiguity's effect. This research focuses on the impact of differing levels of ambiguity on outcomes of the interaction process in crowd formation. Specifically, we are concerned with how variation in ambiguity affects the consensus for action reached by a relatively spontaneous, protesting crowd, as indicated by the time required to reach consensus, and the point of consensus on a scale of action-choices (see below) that ranges from least to most "radical."[2]

THEORETICAL BACKGROUND

The theoretical and computer simulation model grows most directly from Turner and Killian's (1987) use of the idea of ambiguity and the consequent *suggestibility* to account for the emergence of norms guiding collective behavior; however, the model is also compatible with other collective behavior theories. Our synthetic model and its computer simulation translation, as well as another hypothesis test based on the model, are reported elsewhere (Feinberg and Johnson 1988; Johnson and Feinberg 1989) and are not repeated here; only an outline of the theoretical model and necessary details of the simulation model are included.

Ambiguity and Social Order

The focus on ambiguity, suggestibility, and group norms began with Sherif's research (Sherif 1966 [1936]) using the auto-kinetic effect. That research began with assumptions about individual responses to a lack of perceptual clarity, and moved to hypotheses concerning the emergence of social norms. Individuals were shown to reply more readily on the judgment of others when objective information on which to base their own responses was less available; thus, ambiguity facilitated the development of group norms. That relationship between ambiguity and suggestibility is also central to sociology's explanatory framework: social organization provides structural and normative guides for human social action. Absent those guides, individuals must search for cues in the immediate situation, which includes co-present others. In the absence of other information, cues from others are more readily accepted.

Interactionist theories of collective behavior flow directly from the above. The problem in the study of collective behavior is to account for coordinated activities in the absence of functioning norms and role relations (Turner and Killian 1987, p. 4). Turner and Killian's emerging norm approach to collective behavior argues that members of unorganized groupings collectively define the situation and the approporiate response to it; they then enforce that definition as a norm. Weller and Quarantelli (1973) elaborated this approach by arguing that either norms or social structure (or both) emerged from the interaction.[3]

The Nature of Suggestibility

These approaches and our model assume that ambiguity heightens susceptibility to the influence of others; thus, ambiguity is directly related to suggestibility. Suggestibility is viewed as a *social* rather than an individual variable. As Turner and Killian wrote:

> When the interaction of men in an ambiguous situation is regarded as collective problem solving, suggestibility... refers to the heightened responsiveness of the individual to cues provided by others when situational anchorages are inadequate (1972, p. 32).

Within that social framework, suggestibility is a property of the social situation, i.e. the lack of clarity; thus, it varies with ambiguity rather than across individuals. The increased suggestibility resulting from ambiguous situations is also not a generalized response but represents a tendency to respond to suggestions that are consistent with the emerging conception of appropriate action which has begun to assume a normative character (Turner and Killian 1987, p. 78). Normative influences in unclear or ambiguous situations, then, rather than psychological dispositions, produce suggestibility; the degree of ambiguity, rather than psychic states of individuals, influences the amount of suggestibility.[4]

Physical Movement in Milling

A second impact of ambiguity—in addition to heightened susceptibility to influence—is increased information-seeking activity. When the response to ambiguous situations of collectivities (rather than individuals) is of interest, an additional consequence of the information-seeking response to ambiguity emerges: physical movement of members of the collectivity. That is, if we postulate information-seeking within a collectivity distributed within a defined space, then a logical consequence is that such activity involves physical movement within the space to seek information from others. Those "others" are also seeking information. Collective behavior theories (e.g., Turner and Killian 1987) propose that out of their mutual search emerges a consensual definition of the situation, in the manner suggested by Sherif's work, and of the action appropriate for the situation. But the interactive process to which Turner and Killian refer, the milling process, includes both physical movement and communication. This physical movement, both of individuals and of small groups, can have a number of effects. One important effect is the formation of relatively homogeneous small groups, which provides a microstructure for the crowd. We suggest that physical movement and the emerging structure have consequence for the relation of ambiguity and consensus formation not evident in research on individual responses to ambiguity or in small groups research focusing on the symbolic communication alone.

Ball-Rokeach (1973) does refer to both verbal and "action" aspects of information seeking, including in the latter looking for cues in the physical surroundings; however, physical movement would have been minimal within the space in which her experiment was conducted and therefore was not discussed. She does report that experimental subjects were more likely to stand alongside, and to interact with, persons perceived to be like themselves. This implies at least some purposive movement of those subjected to the ambiguous situation.

Our framework suggests that the restructuring activity of collective behavior creates definitions both of the situation and of the behavior appropriate for the situation (i.e., norms) and a rudimentary social structure as well; the latter is a consequence of individuals forming into relatively homogeneous small groups, with these small groups constituting the larger collectivity. We view both the physical movement—as information-seeking activity—and the susceptibility to influence (suggestibility) as varying with ambiguity,[5] and thus use them as indicators of ambiguity in our computer model described below. This focus on small group structure, a rudimentary structure that changes as movement occurs, should lead to impacts of ambiguity not apparent in individual and small group research.

THEORETICAL EXPECTATIONS

Sherif's work and inferences from other work led to the hypothesized set of relations modeled in Figure 1. Ambiguity—particularly the probability of shifting action-choice (labeled PSHFT in the computer model)—is expected to have a positive effect on extremity of consensus and a negative effect on time to consensus (number of cycles). Previous literature is less clear about the level of information seeking, the other aspect of ambiguity, which is indicated by the probability of physical movement (designated as PMOVE in the model). Our initial discussions of relationships involving PMOVE are necessarily more speculative than for other relationships in the model and our ultimate interpretation of the effects of PMOVE is a post hoc one.

The work probably most crucial to the hypothesized relationships in the figure is that of Sherif and Harvey (1952), which showed that situations of high ambiguity result in more rapid convergence and more extreme judgments. Shibutani's (1966) discussion of rumor grew from a similar framework, and he used similar reasoning to hypothesize that the form of a rumor varied with ambiguity (suggestibility): rumors were likely to be extreme, i.e., less consistent with cultural norms, when suggestibility was high. Although our experiments with a less complex computer simulaton model (Johnson and Feinberg 1977) a decade ago did not find the hypothesized relation of suggestibility with extremity of choice, the simplicity of that earlier model leads us to regard that lack of confirmation as a weak test of the hypothesis.

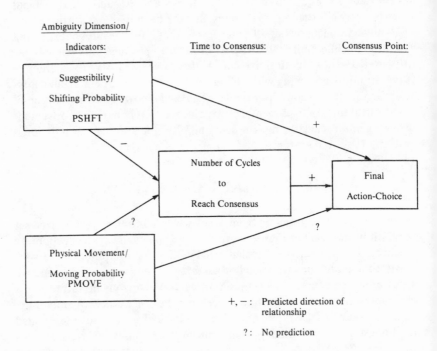

Figure 1.   Predictions of Relationships among Ambiguity Indicators,
Time to Consensus, and Consensus Point

Both the work of Sherif and Harvey and the defining criteria for ambiguity and suggestibility themselves lead to predictions of a negative relationship of suggestibility with time required to reach consensus. Ambiguity leads to dependence on others for cues, i.e., to suggestibility. When ambiguity is high, other bases on which to make judgments are less available; therefore, reliance on the judgments of others is greater. The evidence from the work by Sherif and Harvey is compatible with that set of assumptions; they showed that the rapidity of convergence on a common standard varied with the ambiguity of the situation, with greater ambiguity leading to a more rapid convergence.

The overall effect of the other dimension of ambiguity, physical movement (indicated by the probability PMOVE), is unclear. A greater likelihood of physical movement (as information seeking) can, on the one hand, lead to more rapid consensus as persons locate others with action choices similar to their own and compatible with the suggested action. On the other hand, increased movement also might allow those with action choices imcompatible with the action suggested to find more readily compatible partners and anchor their contrary positions, thus inhibiting the achievement of consensus. Depending on the relative strength of these two opposing strains, three different hypotheses are possible—positive effect, negative effect, or cancelling of effects. Without research evidence to guide a prediction, we designate the link with a "?".

The theoretical discussions suggest a direct negative relationship of suggestibility and time to consensus, with lesser time to consensus required under conditions of greater suggestibility, and a direct positive relation of suggestibility and consensus reached, with more extreme consensus points expected when suggestibility is high. Our previous research (Johnson and Feinberg 1977) revealed a possible total negative relationship between suggestibility and consensus, with consensus achieved at less extreme positions under conditions of high suggestibility, apparently contradictory to the predictions. Examination of this current model helps to resolve the apparent contradictions.

Evidence from recent research with the present computer model (Johnson and Feinberg 1989), in which ambiguity was not varied, showed that crowds achieve a more extreme consensus as the time required for reaching consensus increases. Thus, the positive sign accompanies the arrow from "Number of Cycles to Reach Consensus" to "Final Action Choice." If the direct relation of time to consensus with consensus position reached is indeed positive (as those earlier results show) and the direct relation of suggestibility with time to consensus is negative (as hypothesized), then the fact that the overall relation of suggestibility and consensus is slightly negative or zero (as in our 1977 results) is not incompatible with the theoretical expectation that the direct relation of ambiguity (suggestibility) and consensus is positive. For those results to occur, given the observed relations of suggestibility with consensus position and with time to consensus, the direct relation between time to consensus and consensus point must be positive and strong. Thus, the prediction of a positive relation between time to consensus and the extremity of the consensus position reached can be derived deductively as well as inferred from the results of our recent study cited above (Johnson and Feinberg 1989).

The prediction of a sign for the direct effect of physical movement on final action-choice is even more problematic than the prediction for the effect of movement on time to consensus, as we have even less to guide us in the case of the movement-final action-choice relationship. Yet we would not be surprised if we found the sign from physical movement to final action-choice to be the opposite of the sign to time to consensus. We arrived at that conclusion from first assuming that physical movement as an aspect of ambiguity has the same weak *total* relationship with final action-choice as does suggestibility, and then using the same deduction used above for the direct relationship between suggestibility and final action-choice (consensus). Thus, we "predict" that the sign of the effect of movement on action-choice will be negative if the effect of movement on time to consensus is positive, will be positive if the other sign is negative, and will be zero if the other relationship is insignificant.[6]

CROWD SIMULATION

The theoretical and computer-simulation model has been synthesized from theoretical and empirical work focusing on interaction within crowds and on structural constraints on that interaction. Within this framework, a crowd is considered as a decision-making group with many of the characteristics of other such groups; thus, we assume that the same set of social concepts used for analyzing other social forms is appropriate for the study of collective behavior. Specifically, we assume that those present within the ambiguous situation attempt collectively to restructure the situation, to form themselves into interacting groups through which they arrive at a consensus for appropriate behavior.

Crowd Heterogeneity

The model assumes that gatherings that develop into acting crowds involve individuals with varying motives and initial intentions. Assuming that type of heterogeneity, we assign to each individual an integer value from 1 to 10 representing a point on an "action-choice" scale ranging from least to most "radical" action. The initial individual action-choices are not seen as simply reflecting attitudes or emotional states of individuals, but as expectations of occupants of positions within social networks, or roles. For instance, the position of young, unemployed male is likely to encourage or permit behavior different from that of the position of older, employed female. A particular individual's choice and consequent scale value assigned is thought to be situationally determined and is regarded as combining in an unexplicated way both individual motivational states and a number of external social constraints.[7]

The model focuses on the overall distribution of action-choices in the crowd, which can vary to represent crowds of different types. Classical crowd theory would suggest a homogeneous grouping located at the extreme high end of the action-choice scale. Within our model, the classical assumptions could be represented by a skewed distribution with a high mean and small variance of action choice. Contemporary crowd theory, however, (e.g., see Turner and Killian 1987), postulates much greater crowd heterogeneity. Thus, we vary this aggregate property in the *initial* distribution to represent various possibilities, such as skewed left distribution to reflect classical theory, a "normal" distribution to reflect the kind of heterogeneity implied by Turner and Killian (1987) and by McPhail and Miller's (1973) discussion of the assembling process, and a skewed right distribution as a theoretical contrast to the classical model. The aggregate distribution also provides the continuing status of the crowd as it seeks to reduce ambiguity as well as establishing an initial condition. The distribution changes as a consequence of the processes in the model, frequently producing a final consensus of action choices (see below).

Small Groups Processes

The model assumes that persons assemble in crowds within small groups, providing an initial rudimentary structure for the crowd (based on work by Aveni [1977], McPhail [1985], and others). The process then involves intragroup as well as intergroup interaction and social influence. Suggestions by many and research by Meyer and Seidler (1978) led us to assume a moderate relationship between initial physical location and initial action-choice. Those most "radical" may be nearer the center of the space, with those less radical typically located farther from the center, although other factors, such as time of arrival, also affect physical location.

Intragroup interaction has two consequences, each of which contributes to small group homogeneity. Group members can be influenced by another member of their group to change their action-choice to one closer to that of the source of influence, of, if they are sufficiently deviant from the group, can move physically away from the group. Thus, group interaction and physical movement contribute both to the emergence of a consensus (emergent norm) and to small group formation (emergent structure). A reaction to the influence cue reflects both the content (action-choice) of the cue relative to the recipient's own choice and social influences (i.e., the number of others in the group holding his/her own position and the number holding the position represented by the influence cue).

Groups which in this manner develop sufficient internal homogeneity might then direct some influence cue (verbal or nonverbal) toward the other groups, which may or may not receive the cue (with a probability that depends partly on their physical distance from the influence source). Influence is assumed to be produced by either verbal or nonverbal (behavioral) cues, such as a raised, clenched fist or an upraised middle finger. Crowd members may react to the influence cue by changing their action-choices toward the position of the influence source or physically moving, in much the same way as in response to the intragroup source. If as a result consensus for crowd action is reached, the process ends; if consensus is not reached, the process begins anew with intragroup interaction. In the manner just described, over a series of cues advocating particular actions—what Turner and Killian (1987, p. 85) refer to as a succession of potential keynoters—the crowd is structured by individuals coalescing into small groups, and consensus for crowd action is reached. Our theoretical model—and our simulation—end with the achievment of this consensus, or with the failure to reach consensus (which is defined as occurring after some prescribed number of sequences).

Our conception of consensus does not assume that a homogeneity of motives or of actions has emerged, simply that the requisite agreement on the course of action to be supported has developed. As Turner and Killian write, "even when a norm defining an appropriate line of action has emerged, individuals may comply externally without agreeing internally" and "... may participate in different ways and yet contribute to the common objective" (1987, p. 90). The primary criterion for crowd action is a large reduction of variability—rather than total agreement—in action choice sufficient to produce among participants a sense of consensus.

THE COMPUTER SIMULATION MODEL

The translation of the above theoretical model into a computer simulation model begins with the physical space in which the modeled crowd assembles. The space is organized into 14 concentric circles about a central core; the 14 circles are subdivided into eight sectors radiating from the center. The 113 circle-sector combinations (14 x 8 = 112, plus the central core) constitute locations that can be occupied by up to six participants, for a maximum

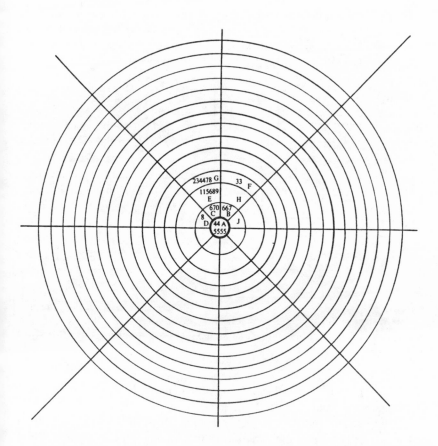

Figure 2. Abstracted Physical Space Used in the Model

capacity of 678 people (see Figure 2; the numbers and letters are used in a later discussion).[8]

This brief discussion of the computer simulation model follows the sequence shown in Figure 3. Many of the details and rules of the model are omitted; these are available in Johnson and Feinberg (1989).

The first step in the model is to assemble an initial number of individuals ("size" parameter) in the physical space; the proportional distribution ("initial distribution" parameter) of these individuals on the 10-point scale of action-choices is entered separately and combined with the initial number to produce a frequency distribution, by action-choice, of the crowd.

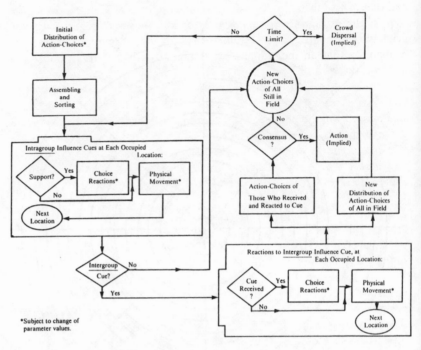

Figure 3.   Schematic of Computer Model

The crowd is then subjected to assembling and spatial sorting rules ("assembling" and "sorting" parameters), beginning with the random selection of an action-choice on the 10-point scale, followed by a random selection of how many individuals (to a maximum of three) with that choice will be placed together at the same location. The location is determined by first finding their distance from the central core, and then the sector within the particular concentric circle.

Once assembling and spatial sorting are completed, the milling process begins. It consists of a series of *recurring* events involving influence attempts and reactions both within and among the small groups that provide the microstructure of the crowd. We assume the events occur in this sequence: *intra*group influence cues and reactions occur at each of the locations occupied, followed by an *inter*group influence cue emanating from a single group and reacted to by other groups and individuals in the total physical space.

We also assume that all members of a small group know perfectly the action-choices of all in the group and assess support for their own choice, and that of all others, in the same way. That mutual assessment is the first step in the intragroup influence process and is based on a metric for evaluating support which assumes that greater support increases the probability that an individual will attempt to influence the group: each action-choice c in the group receives three points for each individual having that exact choice c, two points for each individual having either choice $c+1$ or $c-1$, and one point for either $c+2$ or $c-2$. An attempt to influence the small group will then be made if the group has at least three members and if the highest scoring choice receives at least seven points.[9] Intragroup influence attempts would be made in locations A, B, and G in Figure 2 by individuals with action-choices 5, 6, and 4, respectively. Each of those choices receives a score of at least seven points according to the coding scheme.

An influence attempt is followed by reactions by the members of the group. Individuals whose action-choices are different from that of the influence source either maintain their choice or shift *toward* that of the source. The amount of shift is determined by a binomial process; the absolute difference in positions between individual and influence source yields the number of trials (and thus maximum shift) in the process. The probability of success in the binomial trials can vary among individuals according to whether the individual who might shift has an action-choice supporting that of the influence source, and, if not, what support the individual enjoys; the model assumes that the individual probabilities are functions of an underlying shifting probability (PSHFT, a parameter) that varies with suggestibility, a dimension of structural ambiguity (as discussed above and in Johnson and Feinberg 1977; 1989).

The second dimension of ambiguity is physical movement, indicated by the value of the probability of moving (PMOVE), a parameter. Following an influence attempt within a small group, the members of the group are now subject to the risk of physical movement in response to the choice of others in the group. The risk of *staying* at the same location is based on the complement of the moving probability (i.e., 1-PMOVE); the risk reflects factors discussed earlier and varies according to an individual's support and the distance between the choice of the individual and of the influence source (if there was one in the group). The values of the moving probability (PMOVE) reflect directly the degree of ambiguity. Variation in these two parameters—PSHFT and PMOVE—is one of the bases for the hypotheses tested here.

The direction of the potential move depends on the relation of the individual's choice to that of the influence source. The distance of a move can be only one unit, i.e., from one concentric band to the next within the same sector, or from one sector to an adjacent one in the same band. If an individual is a supporter of the influence source, then the directions for a move are equiprobable. If more "radical" than the influence source (7 or 8 at G in Figure 2, for example), then there is a directional bias favoring a move toward the central core; less radical potential movers are subject to a directional bias away from the central core. In each case, the direction is found using a random number. If there is no room at the potential mover's new location (such as at E), the move does not occur; density can thereby interfere with movement.

After all the events subsumed by "Intragroup Influence Cues" have had a chance to occur at all the occupied locations in the field, the milling process continues with the possibility of an "Intergroup Influence Cue." The attempt to influence all in the field arises from the small group closest to the center of the space[10] that also has sufficient consensus about a proper course of action.

The same metric used to assess the level of support for intragroup influence attempts is employed here to assess whether a small group of at least four members will provide the intergroup influence attempt. The criterion score is raised here to at least 12 points for one action-choice, held by at least two individuals. An intergroup influence cue would come from location A in Figure 2, the central core in the abstract space we have assumed. Action-choice 5 is assessed a score of 16 here.

If the cue is received—modeled as a probabilistic process in which the likelihood of receiving the cue declines with increasing distance from its source—by members of a small group, they react in much the same way as to intragroup attempts. Action-choice reaction is a binomial process; the number of trials is determined by the distance between the choices of the individual and the source, and the single-trial probability is a function of the shifting probability, PSHFT. This probability function varies according to the distance between the individual's choice and that of source and the number of one's supporters, just as described above for reactions to intragroup influence cues.

Members of all groups are then subject to the risk of physical moves; each individual's risk is a function of the moving probability, PMOVE, and depends on whether the cue was received, scale distance of the action-choice from the source, and number of supporters.

Those individuals still in the field who received and reacted to the cue are now assessed to see whether the influence attempt has brought about a consensus for defining the situation and agreeing on a course of action. Those who did not receive the cue are not considered in assessing consensus.

The first criterion for consensus is that at least 50 percent of those in the field must have received the cue. Second, the modal choice among the recipients of the cue must be the same as the choice (reflected in the cue) of the influence source; there cannot be more than one modal choice among these reactors. Finally, either at least 75 percent of these recipients and reactors share the modal action-choice or at least 95 percent have choices at mode-1, or mode+1 (with at least 50 percent at the mode). The criteria reflect a need to reduce variability of choices in the crowd in order for consensus to emerge, as well as having a means for recognition of the course of action by a sufficient number of people.

If a consensus does emerge, action by the crowd is implied: the model ceases operation with fulfillment of the consensus criteria. If a consensus has not emerged, or if there was no intergroup influence cue, the model considers whether the milling process will continue with new intragroup and intergroup influence attempts or whether a time limit (a parameter) has been reached. The model measures time in cycles, with a cycle spanning the intragroup influence events and the events that compose the intergroup influence attempt, if it occurs. If the time limit, set at 50 cycles in the experiments reported below, is reached without consensus being achieved, the crowd remaining in the field is assumed to disperse.

RESULTS

Parameters

For this experiment we ran the model 25 times under each of 81 conditions defined by combinations of the four parameters that were varied. The crucial parameters for these tests were the measures of underlying suggestibility (PSHFT) and the underlying probability of changing physical locations (PMOVE), both construed as indicators of ambiguity. Values for the former were set at .05, .15, or .25. PMOVE took values of .10, .30, or .50.

The "size" parameter took values of 100, 300, or 500. The proportional "initial distribution" had conditions "skewed right," "normal," and "skewed left"; these have an increasing mean value on the 10-point scale of action-choice.[11] All runs used assembling by groups, in which one, two, or three individuals of the same action-choice were randomly and equiprobably selected for initial physical location.

The gathering of individuals was initially located in space (the "sorting" process) according to a binomial probability process described in Johnson and Feinberg (1989); each of the runs used what we call "moderate" sorting, in which the probabilities have a relatively narrow variation and thus produce considerable spatial overlap of the action-choices.

Initial Results

Although not part of the predictions, we first examine the variation in the numbers of simulated crowds achieving consensus and how that variation might be affected by our indicators of ambiguity. Generally, we expect that greater ambiguity will lead to greater dependence on others and thus a greater probability of reaching a consensual position. There is little overall variation in the frequency of reaching consensus when the maximum number of cycles is set at 50; most crowds reach consensus. Most departures from the maximum 25 successes are found in various conditions that include a skewed right initial distribution. If we consider the successes and failures in reaching consensus only in the skewed right runs, and ignore the size variable, both ambiguity indicators (PSHFT and PMOVE) are significant (at .05) positive predictors of the proportion successful p and of arcsin p (see Snedecor and Cochran 1967, pp. 327-29). The overall R^2 is equal to .684 when predicting p and equal to .744 predicting arcsin p[12].

Those runs using the skewed right distribution when initial crowd size is 300 seem to have the most "variation" in successes among the three size conditions within that initial condition. When we consider only that limited condition, there is no significant prediction of the proportion successful p or of arcsin p by either ambiguity indicator. But the partial slopes in both these equations are quite close to those found when successes were aggregated across size categories (above),[13] suggesting that the lack of statistical significance is due to the lower number of cases in the latter situation rather than a change in the effects of PSHFT and PMOVE.

These findings are supported by alternative analyses using logit, probit, and log-linear techniques. The logit and probit procedures yielded significant results (at .001) for the aggregate skewed-right outcomes and for the effects of both PSHFT and PMOVE, but significance was absent when only the outcomes with size equal to 300 were considered. A log-linear analysis emulating multiple regression (Goodman 1972) and predicting the dichotomous outcome of success or failure to achieve consensus provides results similar to these other statistical techniques. Thus, the alternative statistical analyses all support the description of both the shifting probability (PSHFT) and the moving probability (PMOVE)—the indicators of the respective ambiguity dimensions of suggestibility and physical movement—affecting the chance of a crowd reaching consensus, at least within the context of the skewed-right distribution.

Table 1. Number of Simulated Crowds Reaching Consensus (Maximum = 25),[a] by Initial Distribution, Initial Crowd Size, and Probabilities of Shifting Action-Choices (PSHFT) and Changing Locations (PMOVE)

Initial Distribution:		Skewed Right			Normal			Skewed Left		
PMOVE:		.10	.30	.50	.10	.30	.50	.10	.30	.50
Size	PSHFT									
100	.05	19	23	22	25	25	25	25	25	25
	.15	22	23	25	25	25	25	25	25	25
	.25	25	24	25	25	25	25	25	25	25
300	.05	20	21	21	25	25	25	25	25	25
	.15	15	20	21	25	24	25	25	25	25
	.25	21	24	23	25	25	25	25	25	25
500	.05	24	25	23	25	25	25	24	25	25
	.15	24	25	25	25	25	25	25	25	25
	.25	24	24	25	25	25	25	25	25	25

[a]For those runs reaching consensus within the time limit of 50 cycles.

We sought to assess the effect of the 50-cycle time limit on the number of crowds successfully reaching consensus, recognizing that the results could be influenced by the somewhat arbitrary cycle limit. A 35-cycle limit produced results for numbers of successful crowds that were not much different from the results in Table 1. Further reduction of the time limit to 25 cycles *did* produce considerably more variation in the numbers of successful crowds. The analysis of those results still showed both ambiguity indicators to be significant predictors of a crowd achieving consensus, although PMOVE had somewhat more influence here than it did with 50 cycles.[14] These overall results, then, confirm the expectations that greater ambiguity leads to a greater tendency to reach a consensus.

Test of the Model

The predictions drawn from our theoretical argument and from earlier simulation results were displayed above in Figure 1. The suggestibility dimension of ambiguity—indicated by the probability of shifting action-choice (PSHFT)—is expected to have a positive effect on extremity of consensus and a negative effect on time to consensus (number of cycles).

The other variable dimension of ambiguity—physical movement, indicated by the probability of movement PMOVE—did not allow singularly convincing predictions of effects on time or consensus point, but these effects are subject to investigation. Finally, the time necessary for consensus is predicted to have a positive effect on the action-choice that is the final point of consensus.

Thus, the model we suggest is subject to three hypothesis tests of effects predicted on the basis of several sources (those indicated by positive or negative signs in Figure 1). In addition, the effect of the moving probability (PMOVE) on both the consensus position and the time needed to reach it (indicated by the question marks in Figure 1) can be assessed.

Both initial distribution and crowd size are regarded as contextual variables here, since the two probabilities that are indicators of ambiguity are the focus. That decision is also justified because the correlation[15] between initial distribution[16] and final consensus for the 1,966 successful simulated crowds is .90, thereby overwhelming the opportunity for either of the ambiguity indicators to affect that outcome of interest. The initial distribution variable also affects the time to consensus ($r = -.275$). Crowd size is not significantly correlated with time to consensus or the final consensus, however (but see note 7).

Thus, we looked for the effects of the two ambiguity indicators on final consensus value and time to consensus within nine contextual conditions (three initial distributions by three initial crowd sizes). The variation in number of cycles and in final consensus (when achieved) to be accounted for varies considerably among the nine contextual conditions; the disaggregation should simplify the search for effects and the tests of the influence of ambiguity by obviating potential problems arising from heteroscedasticity.

Table 2 reports the mean time to consensus, along with the unbiased standard deviations for each of the nine PSHFT-PMOVE combinations within each of the nine size-initial distribution contexts. These means appear to vary in a complex pattern, both within and between contexts. We used regression analysis to search for simple descriptions of this complex pattern and as tests of our predictions.

Table 3 reports the partial slopes (b) and standardized slopes (B) when predicting the number of cycles (time) with the ambiguity indicators PSHFT and PMOVE. Each of the contexts in which size is equal to 500 (any distribution) produces parsimonious models requiring only PSHFT as a predictor of time (b varies between -3.79 and -4.41, and R^2 is considerable, varying between .580 and .753). For the other six contexts, both the shifting probability (PSHFT) and the moving probability (PMOVE) are significant

Table 2. Mean ($\hat{\sigma}$) Number of Cycles Needed to Reach Consensus[a], by Initial Distribution, Initial Crowd Size, and Probabilities of Shifting Action-Choices (PSHFT) and Changing Locations (PMOVE)

	Initial Distribution:	Skewed Right			Normal			Skewed Left		
	PMOVE:	.10	.30	.50	.10	.30	.50	.10	.30	.50
Size	PSHFT									
100	.05	31.6	26.4	24.5	21.0	18.6	18.2	18.6	15.4	14.1
		(5.51)	(8.23)	(6.67)	(7.37)	(3.77)	(5.18)	(6.56)	(4.35)	(2.99)
	.15	16.4	14.6	12.8	9.8	8.7	8.1	7.4	6.5	7.5
		(6.67)	(8.33)	(6.56)	(4.16)	(2.04)	(2.61)	(2.40)	(1.83)	(2.35)
	.25	15.4	8.5	7.3	10.3	5.2	6.1	5.0	4.6	4.6
		(6.93)	(3.24)	(3.18)	(8.46)	(1.72)	(3.30)	(2.56)	(1.38)	(1.19)
300	.05	29.7	23.5	23.1	23.4	19.6	19.9	19.5	16.2	16.4
		(5.47)	(3.59)	(5.81)	(6.80)	(5.29)	(7.47)	(4.91)	(3.72)	(3.27)
	.15	14.2	9.9	15.2	8.9	8.2	7.6	7.8	6.6	5.8
		(7.28)	(1.86)	(11.32)	(2.72)	(2.79)	(2.10)	(2.87)	(1.26)	(1.47)
	.25	10.9	8.5	7.8	6.6	5.3	4.6	4.8	4.8	4.0
		(6.51)	(6.45)	(6.66)	(4.09)	(1.63)	(1.50)	(1.13)	(1.30)	(1.71)
500	.05	27.8	22.4	23.3	19.9	19.6	18.4	18.8	20.0	17.9
		(3.67)	(2.40)	(6.36)	(4.18)	(5.16)	(4.35)	(4.93)	(5.51)	(4.37)
	.15	10.6	8.6	8.5	7.7	6.2	6.2	7.6	6.7	7.0
		(5.66)	(1.38)	(1.26)	(1.90)	(0.83)	(1.56)	(5.21)	(2.51)	(5.56)
	.25	6.2	5.3	8.8	4.1	3.6	3.8	3.9	3.7	3.7
		(2.42)	(1.20)	(11.58)	(1.33)	(0.86)	(0.97)	(1.20)	(0.90)	(0.85)

[a]For those runs reaching consensus within the time limit of 50 cycles.

negative predictors of time, with PSHFT clearly the more important predictor: b for PSHFT varies between -2.82 and -4.21, while that for PMOVE varies between $-.40$ and -1.58 (PSHFT's partial slope is at least twice as large—and usually at least four times as large—as that of PMOVE).[17] Thus, the theoretical prediction of a direct negative effect of the shifting probability on time to consensus is confirmed. The analysis also points to a negative effect of the moving probability on time to consensus, with magnitude depending on context.

Table 3.   Regression Analyses Predicting Number of Cycles Needed to Reach Consensus[a], by Probabilities of Shifting Action-Choices (PSHFT) and Changing Locations (PMOVE), within Initial Distribution and Initial Crowd Size Contexts

Initial Distribution:		Skewed Right		Normal		Skewed Left	
		b	B	b	B	b	B
Size							
100	PSHFT	−4.205***	−.694	−3.023***	−.676	−2.823***	−.779
	PMOVE	−1.581***	−.261	−0.733**	−.164	−0.400***	−.110
		$R^2 = .541$***		$R^2 = .484$***		$R^2 =.619$***	
300	PSHFT	−4.052***	−.691	−3.867***	−.783	−3.213***	−.834
	PMOVE	−0.777*	−.128	−0.570**	−.115	−0.487**	−.126
		$R^2 = .495$***		$R^2 = .627$***		$R^2 =.712$***	
500	PSHFT	−4.414***	−.761	−3.863***	−.866	−3.786***	−.815
	PMOVE	−0.334***	−.058	−0.273***	−.061	−0.143***	−.031
		$R^2 = .583$***		$R^2 = .753$***		$R^2 =.664$***	

[a]For those runs reaching consensus within the time limit of 50 cycles.
*** $p < .001$;   ** $p < .01$;   * $p < .05$.

Table 4 shows the mean consensus (and unbiased standard deviation) for each of the nine PSHFT-PMOVE combinations within each of the nine contexts. As we have already indicated, the initial distribution variable is highly correlated with the consensus reached, so these mean values are shown without any attempt to characterize their variation among the several conditions. We again chose to characterize the variation within the specific contexts using regression analyses.

The results of the regression analyses, in which various combinations of PSHFT, PMOVE, and number of cycles to reach consensus were used to predict the final consensus, are given in Table 5. These results provide tests of the prediction of a direct positive effect for PSHFT and of the prediction[18] of a direct positive effect of number of cycles on final consensus; the results also provide a description of the effect of PMOVE, which was left unpredicted.

Table 4. Mean ($\hat{\sigma}$) Consensus Achieved[a], by Initial Distribution,
Initial Crowd Size, and
Probabilities of Shifting Action-Choices (PSHFT)
and Changing Locations (PMOVE)

Initial Distribution:		Skewed Right			Normal			Skewed Left		
PMOVE:		.10	.30	.50	.10	.30	.50	.10	.30	.50
Size	PSHFT									
100	.05	3.74	4.04	4.32	6.04	6.16	6.04	8.12	8.12	8.24
		(1.05)	(1.11)	(0.95)	(0.79)	(0.99)	(0.79)	(0.67)	(0.67)	(0.44)
	.15	4.00	4.52	4.48	6.04	6.00	5.96	8.20	8.04	8.24
		(1.11)	(1.16)	(1.12)	(0.93)	(1.00)	(0.79)	(0.71)	(0.73)	(0.72)
	.25	4.32	3.71	3.96	6.20	6.28	6.52	8.36	8.56	8.24
		(1.35)	(1.04)	(1.17)	(1.00)	(1.02)	(0.82)	(0.70)	(0.77)	(0.66)
300	.05	4.15	3.95	4.19	6.16	6.48	6.28	8.40	8.20	8.44
		(0.88)	(1.02)	(1.08)	(0.85)	(0.71)	(1.02)	(0.50)	(0.65)	(0.58)
	.15	4.27	3.95	4.81	6.48	6.38	6.40	8.48	8.48	8.24
		(1.10)	(0.83)	(1.47)	0.77)	(0.88)	(0.82)	(0.59)	(0.51)	(0.52)
	.25	4.48	4.58	4.52	6.44	6.68	6.36	8.52	8.60	8.36
		(1.03)	(1.10)	(1.16)	(0.92)	(0.80)	(0.70)	(0.59)	(0.65)	(0.57)
500	.05	3.50	3.56	3.74	6.08	6.08	6.16	8.17	8.32	8.20
		(0.88)	(0.65)	(0.96)	(0.49)	(0.57)	(0.55)	(0.38)	(0.48)	(0.41)
	.15	3.33	3.32	3.32	6.04	6.00	6.00	8.28	8.28	8.16
		(0.76)	(0.48)	(0.56)	(0.68)	(0.41)	(0.50)	(0.61)	(0.54)	(0.47)
	.25	3.58	3.29	3.84	6.00	5.96	5.92	8.32	8.24	8.12
		(0.72)	(0.55)	(1.46)	(0.65)	(0.54)	(0.40)	(0.56)	(0.44)	(0.53)

[a]For those runs reaching consensus within the time limit of 50 cycles.

We considered statistical predictions of consensus from suggestibility (PSHFT), physical movement (PMOVE), and time (number of cycles) that ignore any possible interaction effects. In the three contexts involving the skewed right initial distribution, each of these exogenous variables is significantly and positively related to the consensus value: cycles has the largest standardized slope (B), while PMOVE has the smallest standardized effect. In the other six contexts, PMOVE has no significant effect, and PSHFT and cycles remain significantly positive in their effects. PSHFT and

Table 5.   Regression Analyses Predicting Final Consensus[a],
by Probabilities of Shifting Action-Choices (PSHFT),
Changing Locations (PMOVE), and Number of Cycles,
within Initial Distribution and Initial Crowd Size Contexts;
Main Effects and Best-Fit Models

Initial Distribution:		Skewed Right		Normal		Skewed Left	
		b	*B*	*b*	*B*	*b*	*B*
Size							
100	PSHFT	0.279***	.398	0.224***	.404	0.164***	.393
	PMOVE	0.161***	.231	0.059	.106	0.019	.044
	Cycles	0.070**	.604	0.053***	.428	0.038**	.330
		$R^2 = .173$***		$R^2 = .109$***		$R^2 = .060$**	
	Best model:	I1; $R^2 = .275$***		M1; $R^2 = .098$***		M1; $R^2 = .058$**	
300	PSHFT	0.513***	.779	0.373***	.736	0.319***	.904
	PMOVE	0.131**	.192	0.045	.088	0.013	.036
	Cycles	0.100***	.892	0.084***	.822	0.088***	.959
		$R^2 = .435$***		$R^2 = .260$***		$R^2 = .283$***	
	Best model:	M2; $R^2 = .435$***		I2; $R^2 = .315$***		I2; $R^2 = .502$***	
500	PSHFT	0.389***	.757	0.194***	.593	0.266***	.884
	PMOVE	0.070**	.136	0.013	.040	−0.014	−.047
	Cycles	0.089***	1.010	0.060***	.815	0.071***	1.090
		$R^2 = .432$***		$R^2 = .117$***		$R^2 = .405$***	
	Best model:	I2; $R^2 = .445$***		I2; $R^2 = .315$***		I2; $R^2 = .549$***	

[a]Within the time limit of 50 cycles.
*** $p < .001$;   ** $p < .01$;   * $p < .05$.
Model M1: Effects of PSHFT, Cycles;
    M2: Effects of PSHFT, PMOVE, Cycles;
    I1: Effects of PSHFT, PMOVE, Cycles, PSHFT*Cycles, PMOVE*Cycles;
    I2: Effects of PSHFT, Cycles, and PSHFT*Cycles.

cycles have approximately equal standardized slopes in the four contexts combining sizes 100 and 300 with normal and skewed left distributions; number of cycles has a considerably greater standardized effect than PSHFT in the normal and skewed left conditions when size equals 500. (We also note the two (*B*) values in the table that are problematically greater than 1.)

Finally, all but one of the R^2 values is significant at the .001 level, with the exception significant at the .01 level.[19] R^2 is generally lower when size equals 100 than for the other two size contexts, and the skewed right distribution—the context in which PMOVE has a significant effect on consensus value—yields typically higher R^2 values than the other two distributions.

Overall, these results confirm the predicted positive effects of both suggestibility (PSHFT) and time to consensus (number of cycles) on final consensus point in all the contexts. On the other hand, PMOVE appeared to have a positive effect on final consensus in only three of the contexts, all involving the skewed right distribution, and no significant effect in the others.

We should also note that some of the signs for PMOVE in the equations of Table 5 do correspond in opposition to the signs in Table 3, as "predicted" above: the significant positive Bs for PMOVE in Table 5 (skewed right, 100 and 300) occur in conjunction with significant negative effects in Table 3; and two insignificant effects (normal and skewed left, 500) appear for PMOVE in both equations. In none of the other five contexts do the signs agree with the conjecture, but in each context the disagreement with the "prediction" is weak; that is, the disagreement is between a significant effect and an insignificant one rather than between two significant effects on the same sign, and the weak disagreements also result in the assumed weak *total* relationship between movement and final action-choice (consensus).

One way of summarizing the results is to determine the proportion of the variation in consensus explained by the ambiguity indicators taken together, and to ask whether that amount of explanation is statistically significant. This determination requires controlling for the effect of the time needed for consensus, given the hypothetical model (depicted in Figure 1) that governed this investigation. The appropriate measure of statistical explanation is the squared multiple-partial correlation coefficient, discussed in detail, along with its test of statistical significance, by Namboodiri, Carter, and Blalock (1975, pp. 189-93).

The squared multiple-partial correlations for predicting consensus value—controlled for time to consensus—by both ambiguity indicators together are shown in Table 6. The values, for each of the nine size-initial distribution contexts, are all statistically significant at the .01 level (or less). The amount of statistical explanation does vary considerably among the contexts; however, these correlations tend to confirm the importance and explanatory power of both ambiguity indicators in the skewed right contexts, compared to the other contexts.

We must note two aspects of this part of our analysis, however, First, the effect of the physical-movement indicator—PMOVE—of ambiguity is included in the multiple-partial calculation even in those contexts in which PMOVE did not have a significant direct effect on consensus. The inclusion,

Table 6.   Proportion of Variation in Consensus[a],
Controlled for Time to Consensus,
Explained by Both Ambiguity Indicators Together (PSHFT and PMOVE),
within Initial Distribution and Initial Crowd Size Contexts:
Squared Multiple-Partial Correlations

Initial Distribution: Size:	Skewed Right	Normal	Skewed Left
100	.106***	.100***	.060**
300	.367***	.217***	.253***
500	.307***	.097***	.310***

[a]For those runs reaching consensus within the time limit of 50 cycles.
*** $p < .001$;   ** $p < .01$;   * $p < .05$.

we believe, is appropriate to assessing the total effect of ambiguity.[20] Second, the calculation of the coefficients considers only the separate effects of the ambiguity indicators and time; any interaction effects are clearly not amenable to separation and control of the time aspect alone while simultaneously including the ambiguity components.[21] Yet, it does seem clear, despite our cautions, that ambiguity affects both the time required to reach consensus and the action-choice consensus achieved.

Summary of Results

In all nine of the conditions suggestibility (indicated by PSHFT) has a direct negative effect on the time to consensus and a direct positive effect on final action-choice consensus;[22] these agree with our predictions indicated in Figure 1. The time to consensus (number of cycles), as predicted, exerts a direct positive effect on the final action-choice in all nine conditions of joint variation of initial distribution and crowd size.[23]

On the other hand, the physical movement indicator of ambiguity— PMOVE—typically had no direct effect on the consensual action-choice (except in the skewed right conditions) but did have a direct negative effect on time (particularly with size less than 500), similar to (but smaller than) the effect of PSHFT, the other indicator of ambiguity. These were effects we left unpredicted but sought to understand, although we attempted a deductive conjecture about the relation between the signs of the effects of movement on time and on consensual action-choice. We believe that deduction was appropriate—although perhaps too strong in its expectations of significant opposite signs—and was borne out by the results.

A synthesis of the patterns typical of the nine conditions suggests an overall model in which both ambiguity indicators (PSHFT and PMOVE) have direct negative effects on the number of cycles, with the final consensus a result of the direct positive effects of PSHFT and the number of cycles. Thus, the indicator PMOVE typically has no direct effect on final action-choice, except in the skewed right conditions that are most unfavorable to the achievement of consensus. Overall, then, ambiguity has a significant effect on final consensus, even after controlling for time needed to reach consensus.

CONCLUSION

The results of the computer simulation show the predicted direct and joint effects of suggestibility. These effects, and those considered unpredictable from previous theory and research, provide general support for the model of the relationship of ambiguity and consensus. Increasing suggestibility led to achieving consensus more quickly and to achieving a relatively more extreme consensus. Moving had a similar but lesser effect on the time to consensus, but typically had no direct effect on the final consensus achieved.

The data from the simulations clarified some effects not obvious in either individual or small-group studies of ambiguity and suggestibility. Two important differences between this model and that implied by research on small groups are noted. First, the model assumed that—in order to reflect the collective behavior process—structural ambiguity must be considered as influencing both suggestibility and physical movement within the space in which a potential crowd had gathered. Additionally, the time required to reach consensus was postulated as having a mediating effect on the relationships between ambiguity indices and the extremity of the consensus.

Interpreted within this model, the results show that the effect of ambiguity on the consensus reached is indeed more complex than revealed in studies of individuals or small groups. Although the *direct* effect of suggestibility on consensus is positive and is negative on time to consensus as predicted from previous work, the *overall* effect is not so unambiguous. Suggestibility, on the one hand, reduces time to consensus and leads *indirectly* to a less extreme consensus, since the effect of time to consensus on the extremity of the consensus reached is positive and strong, i.e., a longer period of time is required to reach an extreme consensus. On the other hand, higher suggestibility leads *directly* to more extreme consensus. Thus, the overall effect of suggestibility on consensus is mediated by time to consensus, producing a weak total relationship.

This examination thus provides a resolution of the unexpected finding in our previous research (Johnson and Feinberg 1977) of the negative relation of ambiguity to the extremity of the consensus reached. Although the direct effect of suggestibility on consensus is positive as predicted by the theories, the overall effect, including the indirect effects as well (because of the mediating effect of time to consensus), is negative or zero.

The consequences of physical movement—conceived as information-seeking behavior and considered as a separate indicator of ambiguity—are much more dependent on context than is true for suggestibility. Physical movement has a significant negative effect on time to consensus when the crowd is small enough[24] and presumably there is room for movement to occur; the effect is considerably smaller than that of suggestibility. Only with skewed right distributions did physical movement have a significant positive effect on consensual action-choice. While this contextual variation of the effects of movement appears confusing—particularly in contrast to the more unequivocal effects of suggestibility—we want to emphasize that the overall pattern of relationship of movement with time and consensus is similar to that of suggestibility, the other aspect of ambiguity. That similarity of pattern and weak *total* relationship between ambiguity and consensus allowed the speculation—somewhat supported by the results—about the paired effects of movement on time and on consensus. Hindsight suggests that the contextual variation affecting the impact of physical movement interferes with the speculated pairing of effects.

This research provides theoretical clarification of linkages of ambiguity with outcomes of interaction. In doing so, it shows the importance of distinguishing between individual suggestibility as a product of the absence of perceptual clarity—the response of subjects in Sherif's autokinetic experiments or in Ball-Rokeach's study—and the simultaneous responses of multiple, mutually influencing individuals within a crowd, also acting in the absence of the normative clarity usually provided by the social order. The manner in which the time required for consensus mediates the ambiguity-consensus relation seems important, and although the effect of movement was weak, it did contribute to the greater complexity of the relationships.

Much of the research on which this model of consensus formation in crowds was based came from studies of laboratory groups rather than from actual crowds. Although computer simulation models of crowds may seem even more removed from the reality of a protesting, perhaps violent, crowd, the simulation model by its capability of considering the joint effects of multiple variables is more "realistic" than are the small group experiments, at least in one sense. The results produced here clearly do not conflict with that presumed "reality." The overall results of the simulation outcomes are generally compatible with the predictions based on theoretical expectations, and they are intuitively sound. They also clarify relationships that are not easily studied in the real world, a potentially important contribution of simulation models. In this particular case, an unexpected result from a previous computer simulation study—showing that ambiguity and the extremity of the consensus reached were related in an unexpected way—led to predictions that clarified relationships confirmed in the experiments with this second, more complex, computer model.

If we extrapolate from these results to actual crowds we find support for those crowd theories that postulate the effect of suggestibility on crowd processes and outcomes. The amount of movement within the physical space in which crowds are located (considered as an index of information-seeking behavior) also has an impact; however, the impact of movement is less than that of suggestibility. The effect of information-seeking is possibly limited as well by situational conditions, particularly by crowd size and the resultant crowding that limits movement. To the extent that suggestibility and information-seeking are crucial indicators of ambiguity, and that they are is suggested by collective behavior theory, these results make more tenable those theories which depend on notions of situational ambiguity.

The fact that the results and the conclusions in another study using the present model (Feinberg and Johnson 1989) also corresponded with theoretical expectations—along with the results and conclusions reported here—produce greater confidence in both the theoretical crowd model and its computer simulation translation.

Moreover, the interaction between the theoretical model and simulation model enhances the synthetic value of the theoretical model. Because the simulation model requires a more detailed and concrete description of behaviors of individuals and groups within a crowd than does the theoretical model, the specification of the theory is enhanced by the synthesis of empirical findings from a variety of sources into the simulation model. Our increased confidence in both models suggests the need to study the behavior of individuals and groups within real crowds to confirm the validity of the synthesis.

ACKNOWLEDGMENTS

The authorship of this paper, and the project which it describes, is the result of an equal, joint effort. We have had a great deal of support, including summer grants for each of us from the Taft Fund at the University of Cincinnati and considerable computer time from the University of Cincinnati Computer Center. Cecil Craig, a mathematician at the University of Cincinnati, provided a solution for a thorny problem we encountered in the design of the simulation model; and P. Neal Ritchey, a colleague in our own department, gave very useful advice about the statistical treatment and presentation of our results. Despite owing so much to so many, the faults of the paper and the project must remain our own.

NOTES

1. Although we refer to structural ambiguity, clearly elements of both culture and social structure are at issue. Our own approach could be referred to, although awkwardly, as "emergent norm and social structure theory." Weller and Quarantelli (1973) imply a similar label. Ball-Rokeach (1973) uses the term "pervasive ambiguity" for a condition in which individuals or collectivities have insufficient information to construct a definition of a social situation. She reports research demonstrating the resultant information-seeking interaction to resolve the fundamental question of meaning. Smelser (1962) similarly refers to "unstructured ambiguity," incomprehensible situations exemplified by disaster.

2. Our computer simulation model focuses specifically on the emergent and extra-institutional groups traditionally considered as collective behavior and traditionally labeled "acting crowds." Thus, our model applies to relatively spontaneous, unplanned gatherings in problematic situations and which have an emergent objective that is, following Lofland, defined as somewhat out of the ordinary (1981, p. 414). Lofland's (1981) discussion of crowd hostilities includes a list of the types of gatherings to which we consider this model applying, although we do not follow his focus on the dominant emotion as a scheme for classifying crowds. We do retain the conventional term "crowd," which has been virtually discarded by recent writers such as McPhail (e.g. McPhail and Wohlstein 1983) in favor of the more neutral label "gatherings."

3. Other collective behavior theorists make similar assumptions relative to social order, ambiguity, and collective behavior. Shibutani's (1966) approach to rumor is in its essentials identical, reflecting a common source and mutual influences. He postulates that rumors emerge from ambiguous situations in response to which persons engage in information-seeking activity. Other very different approaches, including those of Lang and Lang (1961), Smelser (1962), Rose (1962), and Klapp (1972) rely on some conception of unclear, ambiguous situations. Even McPhail (1985) includes within his singular approach a discussion of collective behavior in which multiple individuals faced with a problematic situation generate common instructions for behavior.

4. The general view of increased suggestibility as a result of increased ambiguity is common in collective behavior theories. Lang and Lang (1961, p. 260) see that when persons find themselves in unstructured situations, the same "susceptibility to interpersonal influences that [normally] maintain order is likely to operate as counter-norm contagion which disrupts and modifies the ordinarily valid norms of conduct." The view of ambiguity and suggestibility on

which this paper is based does not rest on assumptions about contagion, but is drawn from sources such as Shibutani (1966, p. 97), cited earlier, who observed that when a situation was highly ambiguous and the demand for information was high, collective definitions were based less on critical deliberations and more on uncritical interchanges.

5.   Movement also varies with other factors that affect either the pressures or opportunities to move, including the salience of the issue, the perceived threat of control forces, physical impediments to movement, or estimates of the probability of finding others like oneself (because of factors such as the amount of available light). As a consequence, both suggestibility and physical movement are functions of ambiguity, but they do not necessarily covary.

6.   Because the "prediction" here is dependent on the empirical outcome rather than on theoretical grounds, we have also labeled this effect with a "?".

7.   Our choice of the term "individual disposition" as the label for this variable in our earlier model (Johnson and Feinberg 1977) had the unfortunate consequence of leading many to interpret our model as emphasizing individual attitudinal states as a major factor in the emergence of crowds and to label our approach as a "convergence model." To avoid that misunderstanding, and to more accurately reflect our concept, we have changed the label to "action-choice." By using this term we hope to make clear that the variable refers to an individual's current choice of an action, a choice influenced by a variety of factors, possibly including—but not dominated by—an attitude state. That the "action-choice" is subject to change—including the possibility of change from one end of the continuum to the other—during the relatively short period of interaction modeled here indicates that it does not represent an enduring attitudinal state. We think of the measure as representing the responses that would be elicited by a continuing poll asking "What action would you be willing to take right now?" Aggregate responses to that hypothetical poll would change constantly during the course of interaction. In fact, crucial to the model is the necessity of constantly assessing the fluctuating distribution of action-choices as that change occurs.

8.   We recognize that the areas of the circle-sector combinations are not equal; these areas generally increase with increasing distance from the center. Because we assume that each location can hold the same number of individuals, maximum density at each location thus generally decreases with increasing distance; ideally, all locations would be identical in area and density. We could not fulfill this ideal in a *simple* abstraction while also preserving the finding of McPhail's (1985) review showing that small groups rarely attain a size larger than six in such gatherings. (The difficulties are discussed in a Technical Note available from the authors.) The abstraction we chose "compromises" by permitting locations in the first four of the concentric circles to be smaller in area than the core, and thus of greater potential density, and those locations in the more distant concentric circles to be larger and potentially less dense. Our choice for the abstract space had the additional benefit of allowing relatively simple solutions for communication and physical movement across the space. Yet we are mindful that the benefits of these compromises exact the cost that the effects of size (and density) in the results of the model's runs might be artifactual. Because of that possibility, we limit our discussion of size to a contextual one.

9.   The model has special rules in the event of action-choices tied on the support metric. These rules, and others, are detailed in Johnson and Feinberg (1989).

10.   Thus, a group located in the core and having sufficient consensus is located at the same distance from the center, the group providing the intergroup influence cue is randomly chosen from these alternative groups.

11.   These three distributions were also used in our earlier model (Johnson and Feinberg 1977). The proportional distributions, by action-choice (including mean and standard deviation), are:

	1	2	3	4	5	6	7	8	9	10	Mean	SD
Skew Rt	.07	.18	.30	.18	.11	.06	.04	.03	.02	.01	3.76	1.91
Normal	.01	.02	.07	.16	.24	.24	.16	.07	.02	.01	5.50	1.62
Skew Lft	.01	.02	.03	.04	.06	.11	.18	.30	.18	.07	7.24	1.91

12. The partial slopes are .019 and .018 for PSHFT and PMOVE, respectively, when predicting the proportion p of successes. When predicting the arcsin p transformation, the corresponding slopes are .049 and .042.

13. The slopes are .020 and .030 (compared with .019 and .018) for PSHFT and PMOVE, respectively, when predicting the proportion p of successes in the skewed-right runs limited to size 300. The respective slopes for the prediction of arcsin p in this limited set of runs is .044 and .050 (compared with .049 and .042).

14. Most of the results to be discussed below using the 50-cycle time limit are not contradicted by analyses (unreported) using the 25-cycle time limit. The lower time limit does yield more complex results, however, partly because the four exogenous parameters—size, initial distribution, PSHFT, and PMOVE—become significantly correlated, rather than independent as with the higher time limit (and the experimental design). The change in relationship among the parameters occurs because the numbers of successes are much more unevenly distributed among the various experimental conditions with the lower time limit. The increased complexity and departure from the original experimental design persuaded us to concentrate on the results with the 50-cycle time limit, as reported in the tables and discussed below.

15. The zero-order correlation matrix considering all the runs together is available for the interested reader.

16. The initial distribution variable was coded 1 for skewed right, 2 for normal, and 3 for skewed left. Initial crowd size was coded in hundreds (for example, code 1 for size 100). PSHFT and PMOVE both used codes 1, 3, and 5, corresponding to .05, .15, and .25 for PSHFT and to .10, .30 and .50 for PMOVE. The actual values for number of cycles and consensus point were used for the outcomes.

17. None of the contexts yielded significantly improved (at .001) R^2 values when the multiplicative interaction term PSHFT*PMOVE was included in the prediction equation. We used the restrictive .001 level for interaction terms in order to balance two somewhat competing goals of this research: testing some predicted relationships, and describing some unpredicted ones.

18. The statistical hypothesis resulted from assuming, based on an earlier study, a weak-negative or insignificant total relationship between the shifting probability PSHFT and final consensus. Considering all outcomes together (not context-specific), the correlation between PSHFT and consensus is .013. The simple correlations within the size-distribution contexts indicate that PSHFT and final consensus are typically unrelated; while the only two significant (out of nine) correlations are positive, each is less than .20.

19. We also considered some possible interaction effects among the three predictors, PSHFT, PMOVE, and number of cycles, using only first-order interaction terms such as PSHFT*cycles. As shown in Table 5, inclusion of first-order interactions significantly improved (at .001) upon the R^2 of the main-effects prediction equation in six of the nine contexts. Only

one (skewed right of size 100) of those six equations included interaction terms involving PMOVE: the other five do not include PMOVE in any form. One of the main effect equations— for skewed right crowds of size 500—includes PMOVE among the significant predictors, but an equation including PSHFT*Cycles, but not PMOVE, yields a significantly greater R^2. An analysis of signs in the interaction supports the outcomes of the main-effects equations.

20. The results of Table 5 indicate clearly that suggestibility (PSHFT) generally would dominate physical movement (PMOVE) in their relative contributions to the overall effect of ambiguity on the consensus reached, however.

21. The restriction may lead to our underestimating here the variation explained by ambiguity.

22. The positive effect of PSHFT on final consensus value is inferred from the sign of the regression coefficient for PSHFT in the main-effects models in those six situations where the best-fit model includes interaction terms. In five of these six conditions the sign of the coefficient for the term PSHFT*Cycles also agrees with that for PSHFT.

23. Inferences similar to those indicated in the preceding note about the effect of PSHFT were made for the time variable (cycles).

24. "Small enough" specifically means under 500 in the runs of the model. But for reasons discussed in note 8, we should be cautious about viewing size too literally in these runs. It is reasonable, however, to interpret the results to mean that there is some size above which movement is inhibited, thereby blocking out any possible effect of variation in PMOVE. An anonymous reviewer made this and other useful suggestions about interpreting the contextual variation of the effects of PMOVE.

REFERENCES

Aveni, A. 1977. "The Not-so-lonely Crowd: Friendship Groups in Collective Behavior." *Sociometry* 40: 96-9.

Ball-Rokeach, S. J. 1973. "From Pervasive Ambiguity to a Definition of the Situation." *Sociometry* 36: 378-89.

Feinberg, W. E. and N. R. Johnson. 1988. "'Outside Agitators' and Crowds: Results from a Computer Simulation Model." *Social Forces* 67: 398-423.

Gamson, W. A., B. Fireman, and S. Rytina. 1982. *Encounters with Unjust Authority.* Homewood, IL: Dorsey.

Goodman, L. A. 1972. "A Modified Multiple Regression Approach to the Analysis of Dichotomous Variables." *American Sociological Review* 37: 28-46.

Heirich, M. 1971. *The Spiral of Conflict: Berkeley, 1964.* New York: Columbia University.

Johnson, N. R. and W. E. Feinberg. 1977. "A Computer Simulation of the Emergence of Consensus in Crowds." *American Sociological Review* 42: 505-21.

_____ 1989. "Crowd Structure and Process: Theoretical Framework and Computer Simulation Model." In *Advances in Group Processes: Theory and Research,* Vol. VI, edited by Edward Lawler and Barry Markovsky.

Klapp, O. E. 1972. *Currents of Unrest: An Introduction to Collective Behavior.* New York: Holt, Rinehart, and Winston.

Lang, K. and G. E. Lang. 1961. *Collective Dynamics.* New York: Thomas Y. Crowell.

Lofland, J. 1981. "Collective Behavior: The Elementary Forms." Pp. 411-46 in *Social Psychology: Sociological Perspectives,* edited by Morris Rosenberg and Ralph Turner. New York: Basic Books.

McPhail, C. 1985. "The Social Organization of Demonstrations." Paper presented at the annual meeting of the American Sociological Association, Washington.

McPhail, C. and D. L. Miller. 1973. "The Assembling Process: A Theoretical and Empirical Examination." *American Sociological Review* 38: 721-735.

McPhail, C. and R. Wohlstein. 1983. "Individual and Collective Behaviors Within Gatherings, Demonstrations, and Riots." Pp. 579-600 in *Annual Review of Sociology* Vol. 9.

Meyer, K. and J. Seidler. 1978. "The Structure of Gatherings." *Sociology and Social Research* 63: 131-53.

Namboodiri, N. K., L. F. Carter, and H. M. Blalock, Jr. 1975. *Applied Multivariate Analysis and Experimental Designs.* New York: McGraw-Hill.

Rose, J. D. 1982. *Outbreaks: The Sociology of Collective Behavior.* New York: Free Press.

Sherif, M. 1966 [1936]. *The Psychology of Social Norms.* New York: Harper and Row.

Sherif, M. and O. J. Harvey. 1952. "A Study of Ego-Functioning: Elimination of Stable Anchorages in Individual and Group Situations." *Sociometry* 15: 272-305.

Sherif, M. and C. Sherif. 1969. *Social Psychology.* New York: Harper and Row.

Shibutani, T. 1966. *Improvised News: A Sociological Study of Rumor.* Indianapolis: Bobbs-Merrill.

Snedecor, G. W., and W. G. Cochran. 1967. *Statistical Methods* (sixth edition). Ames, IA: Iowa State University.

Smelser, N. 1962. *Theory of Collective Behavior.* New York: Free Press.

Turner, R. H. and L. A. Killian. 1972. *Collective Behavior* (2nd edition). Englewood Cliffs, NJ: Prentice-Hall.

———— 1987. *Collective Behavior* (3rd edition). Englewood Cliffs, NJ: Prentice-Hall.

Weller, J. M. and E. L. Quarantelli. 1973. "Neglected Characteristics of Collective Behavior." *American Journal of Sociology* 79: 665-85.

ALTERNATIVE SOCIAL MOVEMENTS IN CONTEMPORARY POLAND

Bronislaw Misztal

Two major theoretical dilemmas dominate the discourse in contemporary analyses of social movements. First, the problem of utmost importance is whether social movements are a manifestation of agency or structure. This dilemma takes several forms: do people act in social movements primarily and only as the bearers of social structure (Althusser 1970)? Or are they rational agents who select their options based on choices they have made themselves (Anderson 1980)? Do people participate in social movements primarily in order to secure resources or benefits generated through political activity (Oberschall 1978; McCarthy and Zald 1973)? Or are they prompted by the desire to achieve non-tangible goods, moral values and the sense of solidarity (Gamson 1979; Jenkins 1983)? Are social movements the factors of change in the contemporary world (Misztal 1988)? Or are they the collective action of actors at the highest level, marking a transition from one societal type to another and being the manifestation of the end of workers' movements (Touraine 1981)?

Research in Social Movements, Conflict and Change,
Volume 12, pages 67-88.
Copyright © 1990 by JAI Press Inc.
All rights of reproduction in any form reserved.
ISBN: 1-55938-065-9

This heuristic dilemma does not find clear theoretical solution in the light of social movements research in the West: it is possible to demonstrate that social movements are born because the resources become available either due to some regular historical processes or because of historical aberrations (Parsa 1988), but it also possible to see that at the conception of social movements lies structural dynamics, which initiates transition from one type of rule (frequently authoritarian) to another (Oxhorn 1988; O'Donnell and Schmitter 1986).

Secondly, in response to the agency-versus-structure dilemma, social scientists (Eder 1982; Cohen 1982; Offe 1983, 1985; Kitschelt 1985) have invented a new category, that of "new" social movements suggesting that these are agents of structural change in capitalist welfare states or in socialist states, respectively. Such new movements are seen as being a response to the increased control and mediation of society by formal state apparatuses, and as possessing an "axial principle" or a drive to societal self-management. Therefore, "new" movements reflect the allegedly new social situation, whereby "social conflicts move from the traditional economic/industrial system to cultural grounds" (Melucci 1984, pp. 826). The new systemic contradictions of the 1980s are reflected in movements that become "a network of small groups submerged in everyday life" (Melucci 1984, pp. 831) where the traditional distinctions between the State and civil society do not suffice.

The observers of the Western scene hope that movements will eventually re-create social classes and accordingly mobilize their societies (McNall 1986), whereas the observers of Eastern European scene bear contradictory expectations (Bakuniak and Nowak 1987), hoping for the movements to cut across traditional class barriers and to assume the role of representative of the entity of societal components vis-a-vis the party-state.

Neither the former (agency vs structure) nor the latter (the "old" vs "new" movements) approach seem adequate to the developments in contemporary Poland, where the spectrum of social movements is especially rich. In this paper I contend that neither the agency vs structure nor the "old" vs "new" movements approach possess the explanatory abilities to grasp the complexity of social movements emerging in Eastern Europe, and in Poland more specifically I also argue that since World War II Poland was the stage on which social movements of the modern era of state socialism rehearsed and celebrated their premieres.

In 1945 and 1948 nationalistic tendencies led to the first German and Jewish exoduses, respectively, that were to be completed two decades later, after an unprecedented wave of commotion which has not yet fully been explained. While ethnic migration has been strictly controlled by the

Communist governments and did not really take off until after the Helsinki agreements, thousands of Germans and Jews were forced to leave. Although the whole process was devised "by a joint decision of the victorious allies" (Davies 1982, pp. 565) ethnic antagonisms were aroused for the first time in the after-war history. The Jewish migration was shamefully forced again in 1968, while the German migration was revived in the early 1970s.

In 1956 two different movements came into the open: workers' claimed more self-government, and intellectuals claimed more openness and cultural freedoms. Interestingly, apart from the time coincidence, the two movements were not historically correlated. Both were a sociological novelty and with only some delay they were followed by movements in other Eastern European countries: Hungary and Czechoslovakia. In Hungary, the popular demands resulted in an aborted workers' revolution. In Czechoslovakia, on the other hand, the intellectual call for freedoms led to the aborted Prague Spring.

In 1968 students took to the streets of Warsaw some two months ahead of their French or Italian counterparts and nineteen years ahead of their colleagues in Communist China. While it is true that students in Poland failed to bring the authoritarian regime to its knees, they have, nevertheless managed to socialize the entire generation to the conditions of social struggle. Even more importantly, to paraphrase Foucault (1988, pp. 162), the events in Poland in March 1968 demonstrated that penal justice was beginning to function entirely in the name of social protection and no longer in the name of law. Therefore, the student movement of 1968 was also the rehearsal for one of the last stages of the authoritarian regime, the one that revealed its nature, and the one which acquainted the then young population with the principles of collective action. One more argument can be made about the 1968 student movement. It revealed the fundamental weakness of collective action in state socialist society—the inability to make viable social and political coalitions. Students failed because they were alone. A similar situation occurred at least three times in the future, culminating in 1981 when the absence of coalition between the Solidarity and the moderate Party rank-and-file resulted in the dramatic breakdown of democracy.

In 1970 the principal pre-Solidarity rehearsal took place in the Northern regions of Poland. It came unrecognized for its significance, although this particular wave of protests resulted in political succession. Its quality of a social movement was smokescreened by the immediate character of economic demands and by the fact that the military forces were able to crush the struggle, while the political skills of the new power elite effectively diluted the contents of the protest into a set of gradually satisfied economic vindications. Again, I argue that one can see the events in Poland of 1970-

1971 as an important rehearsal before yet another historical era—the one of "glasnost" or "perestroika." The early 1970s in Poland were clearly marked by increased political mobilization towards restructuring of the state and economy. Not only did it fail, but it also led to yet another social movement rehearsal.

In 1976 the goal unachieved twenty years earlier was made attainable by the mobilization of leading intellectuals and workers so as to create the first cross-class coalition. It resulted in the independent education movement that is analyzed in this paper.

In 1980 a peculiar mixture of the sacred and the secular brought tabernacles to the industrial plants and made religiously devout workers mix their demands for religious freedoms with the demands of agnostic intellectuals for cultural liberties. The result was a situation whereby workers became more politically astute, while intellectuals became more dependent on the Church.

Historically speaking, therefore, I claim that precipitating factors have worked faster and more clearly in Poland than in other countries of the bloc. It took forty years of Communism to reveal that the system is unable to overcome ethnic cleavages between the Hungarians and Rumanians, between the Russians and the Lithuanians or Estonians. But in Poland the system did not manage to mask the existing ethnic tensions. It took almost as much time to reveal that workers have a certain subjectivity which cannot be ignored, but in Poland it was already visible in the mid-1950s. The students are an extremely powerful political force, yet with the exception of Poland one could think that the "real socialism" has managed to subdue the vigor of the youth. I would hesitate to seek those factors at work within the national character of the Poles, since any historical generalization based on such a premise would inevitably be biased. Instead, I propose that for a mixture of historical reasons the political system of communism in Poland was least effective and contained cracks from the onset. Poland was probably the only country of the bloc where the system has been implemented by the Russians rather than by the local folks. For the four decades of its existence it contained the nucleus of independence from the state—private farming. Poland was originally a peasant society, and it was the peasant class from where the recruitment to the "new" classes (new working class, new intelligentsia) was possible. Unlike other countries of the bloc, Poland also had a tradition of vivid "cultural class" and the unbreakable links with the Western culture. The combined effect of class structure (peasant domination), cultural tradition (independence and ability to penetrate the Western cultures), and the historical presence of the solid edifice of the Catholic Church amounted in the peculiar sacralization of the quotidien. While other countries of the bloc have managed to educate the new cadres of secular apparatchiks, in Poland, on the contrary, even the Party-State became vulnerable to the faith and ethics of Catholicism. To say that Poland contributed to cracks within the entire bloc would probably be an unqualified statement, yet certainly due to the particular fabric of which the Polish socio-political and cultural systems were made, the transition from authoritarianism was the play which first rehearsed in Poland.

If one accepts such a premise, the developments surrounding social movements in Poland should be monitored more closely, since they bear historical and sociological significance and since they may outline the direction of similar changes elsewhere in the bloc. I also argue that the alternative (i.e., neither "old" nor "new") character of those movements in Poland is, in many respects, unprecedented and that those movements exhibit traces of cultural currents which characterize the turn of historical eras, while possessing, at the same time, features of organizations found elsewhere in the Western hemisphere. I also argue that the non-conventional character of those recent movements results from the essence of the political fabric of state socialism: from an attempt to control the vastest spheres of social life, combined with unpreciseness of operational rules of control, imperfectness of such control and from spontaneity of social life.

THE INDEPENDENT EDUCATION AND PUBLISHING MOVEMENT

The thesis that Poland is a rehearsal stage for many unconventional social movements could probably be best illustrated by an independent education movement.

Historically speaking, Poland has a long (perhaps a century long) tradition of "flying universities," which originated in 1883 on Polish territories annexed then by Russia (Buczynska-Garewicz 1985, p. 28), and continued in the 1940s under the Nazi occupation. What makes those two cases distinguishably different from the most recent one, however, is that Polish education had been non-existent both in 1880s and in 1940s when the occupant states imposed their own control of curricula and instruction, eradicated Polish language and supervised the process of simultaneous de-politicization and de-polonization. Therefore, the underground, independent education emerged as a way of retaining national character, tradition, and history when statehood was absent.

In recent history, however, the reason for the emerging independent education movement was different. The state did exist and "supplied" society with its own system of education which has been inadequate to the cultural and political needs of extensive social structure, where large numbers of educated people were politically mute, while those politically determined were historically and sociologically illiterate. Hence the independent education, which by necessity had to take the semi-legal form, emerged as a complementary effort to parallel the official organization of instruction and eventually to override the debilitating effect the official system had had on society.

Ever since the Communist takeover in 1944, education has been a domain of the state monopoly, with a centrally administered school structure and politically controlled curricula. Although centralized, the educational system supervised by the state intentionally provided differential instruction to various categories of recipients. The high school system provided selected students with fairly general and liberal arts oriented education, since most if its alumni were supposed to enter colleges of various kinds. The high school system was heavily controlled in its offerings in such subjects as history or literature, and the ideological indoctrination was probably the most scrupulous here. The interpretation of history was washed out from any politically sensitive contents (like the history of Polish-Russian and Polish-Soviet relations, or the role of the Jewish community in Poland).

Alternative to high schools was the system of vocational training where the humanities were almost absent from the curriculum. Subsequently, this sytem was less controlled. Vocational education was supposed to provide the national economy with skilled workers. Similarly, higher education (college and university) was divided between liberal arts and technical divisions, with the latter being subjected to considerably more liberal indoctrination than the former. Such differentiated educational system reflected the authorities' attitude of producing the brainwashed intelligentsia on the one hand, and the technically skilled but politically or socially illiterate masses of workers, on the other. One can describe the system of education in Poland as similar to the beehive, where some individuals are fed with specially prepared food, while others are bred to be workers.

The structural differentiation of the official educational system bore considerable significance for an alternative education movement. While the white-collar segments of the Polish population remained relatively conformist and did not rebel, workers, on the other hand, have had a history of protests ever since 1956.

Independent education movement dates since approximately 1976, i.e., the period of heavy persecution of workers, that followed the wave of price riots in June, 1976. While the educated layers of Polish society remained depoliticized and inactive, a group of intellectuals have—in response to political hardships suffered by the workers—created the Committee for Workers' Defense (KOR). Almost simultaneously, although independently, the underground publishing house NOWA, and a number of underground periodicals were created, thus ploughing the ground for the future crop. At this time a very narrow group of historically aware but politically handicapped intellectuals decided to offer basic instruction in civil liberties, law, economics and history so as to arm the workers into a more efficient means of defense against the totalitarianism of the system. The first leaflets and courses dealt with an effective defense during police interrogation, instructed how to deal with the police acting without a search warrant, and explained the legal difference between being a suspect and a convicted "criminal" (political acts deemed illegitimate were branded as crimes). One can say that the scope of terror and its random character have largely contributed to the spread of underground education, since the need for social self-defense became apparent to wide layers victimized by the state.

In fact, the Committee for Workers' Defense (KOR) has been a vanguard, cultural group, that was able to adequately recognize the historical demand for knowledge and has played the role of a catalyst for change. The group eventually transformed itself into a Committee of Societal Defense (KOS), broadening its scope of action and targeting at society at large. In 1978 sixty-one intellectuals, writers, artists and students established the Association for Academic Studies (TKN). The new organization pronounced that needs for scholarly, objective knowledge are not adequately satisfied by the existing official institutions. With this step a narrow initiative of social defense has been transformed into a social movement seeking change of a considerable fragment of social reality. What followed was a range of discussion groups, courses and seminars, run by the leading intellectuals, who met in individual apartments or at facilities provided by the church. While the TKN provided some tutelage as far as organization of instruction was concerned, the learning collectives were independent and did not follow any centralized program or attempt to achieve a coordinated goal. With such horizontal growth of the movement the scope of instruction widened as well, covering basic subjects in history, sociology or philosophy that would be sought in vain in the official university curriculae. Originally the "workers only" audiences grew as well, and included high school and university students, and peasants. Numberwise, an estimated total participation in the activities of "flying universities" and the Association for Academic Studies (TKN) was approximately 500 students in two principal "basins"—Warsaw and Cracow.

In 1979 the political harrassment had led to an almost complete halt of informal gatherings and discussion groups. The law enforcement agencies were successful in their attempt to intimidate and prohibit intellectuals from any organized and independent efforts. They were, however, unable to stop the free thinking, nor were they able to restrain the activity of the infrastructural network which gained its peak output of book production.

To put it in economic terms, independent education in Poland was possible grace to almost simultaneous mobilization of "supply" and "demand," with the latter slightly lagging behind the former. Therefore, the movement was sparked by a group possessing a relatively narrow social base, but anticipating adequately the historical momentum, whereby the repression of societal needs for truth and objectivity were coupled with the rising crisis of moral values and with an era of frustrated economic (consumeristic) expectations. This stage was not marked by any significant and objective demand for academic or libertarian instruction, since such needs were latent at that time. What was characteristic at that time, however, was developing and making operational of the human and material resources infrastructure, notwithstanding the limited social bases for such an effort. What is clear, however, is the attempt—on the part of the core group of organizers—to force change if not necessarily on the state institutions, then at least on the minds of individuals who make up the fabric of society.

Independent education as a social movement in Poland went through four stages of resource mobilization. In the first stage, the rank-and-file members of society have become mobilized with respect to their needs for unrestrained and uncontrolled access to knowledge. In the second stage, the group of potential instructors, who at the same time could be university teachers, historians, activists, practitioners etc. have become mobilized so as to offer a resource instruction for prospective audiences. The third stage consisted of production of a wide network of free (i.e., uncontrolled) publications, thus mobilizing authors, editors, printers etc., so the educational material would be available. In most cases this would involve not that much printing of textbooks in traditional, scholarly sense, but preparing publications to cover the gaps in the official propaganda in such areas as novels, historiography, literary essays, critiques, etc. Finally, in the fourth stage, the distributing network became mobilized, for there could not be education without libraries, distributors and organizers. In Poland those four networks had emerged in a parallel way, but not necessarily as a result of the same organizational and mobilizational effort.

Subsequently to the emergence of Solidarity, which forced the authorities to some immediate, though short-lived concessions, the independent education became semi-legalized. Under the auspices of various level Solidarity bodies, the evening universities, seminars and courses were organized. The curriculum of such instruction was quite an extemporaneously political one, and was limited to history, economics and current affairs. The instruction was complemented by a rapid expansion of publishing activities, with over 2,000 news-letters, journals and bulletins being distributed systematically. At this stage, also, the independent education movement attempted some change in the official educational institutions, and the authorites were pressed for an update of compulsory curricula of instruction in history, the Polish language and literature, and the social sciences.

Although its agenda is relatively loose, one can, I believe, list the most recurring issues of the independent education movement in Poland.

Civil Rights and Self-Defence

A considerable part of the independent instruction dealt with the "know-how" of the use of civil rights when citizens are being confronted with oppression by the state. Knowledge of penal and civil codes and also information about operational procedures of the state militia (police) and its political branch (S.B.) were an important part of the underground teaching. One can say that this item on the movement's agenda was of significant importance for awakening the legal consciousness and legal literacy of Polish society.

History of Poland

Since teaching history in schools of all levels was considered to be an extremely sensitive political issue, this knowledge has been traditionally heavily controlled by the state. The textbooks used for school teaching had conspicuous blank spots, as they skipped periods of less glamorous past or remained mute about the historical events which would shed new light on the politics of Poland.

History, Structure and Determinants of Poland's Relations with Her Neighbors

Poland has three neighboring countries: Germany, Czechoslovakia and Russia (now the U.S.S.R.). Her relations with its neighbors have never been smooth; with the events of meddling into Russian politics in the early ages, to the Soviet extermination of the Polish intellectuals and army officers in the most recent past; with Poland participating in the annexation of the Czech territory to the most recent events of territorial controversies between the two countries; from the several centuries-long history of Polish-German wars, through the German extermination of the Polish population during the World War II, to the forced migration of Germans out of territories annexed by Poland after the war. The official historical interpretations said little or nothing about those less popular events, and the independent education movements contributed to the increased awareness of the Poles of their politics regarding neighboring countries.

Ethnic Minorities

For several decades Poland has been portrayed as an ethnically monolythic society, and the issues of Jewish exodus, forced resettlement of Ukrainians, Bielorussians and Germans were non-existent in the official literature. Similarly, until most recent times, the history of Poland was silent about the role Jews played in the cultural and political development of the country. Several systematic courses and the ad hoc speeches have increased the knowledge of this aspect of Polish history.

Polish Presence Abroad

For centuries the most non-conformist men of arts and letters exited the country to settle in more friendly cultures, where they would become visible and appreciated members of the cultural community. In Poland, however, there has been a traditional silence around those, who left and lived abroad. The underground education movement spread the knowledge of writings of Czeslaw Milosz, the Literature Nobel Prize Winner, as well as worked towards inclusion in the Polish national heritage of all those, who, although living apart and away from the country remained culturally Polish.

In early 1989, when this paper was completed, the movement still remains unconcerted, without clear organizational structures or the governing bodies. Subsequently it is pluralized and consists of enterprizes of various character.

One can, I claim, consider independent education to be a social movement in Poland, since it satisfied all major definitions of movements, or conditions for an endeavor to be a movement rather than an initiative or an institution. The existence of Solidarity has somehow outshone the independent education, but to a major degree the workers' movement would not have been possible without the preceding, continuous and systematic mobilization of those who teach and those who are being taught.

THE "FREEDOM & PEACE" MOVEMENT

Historically speaking, the appearance of the—originally anti-militaristic—group known as Freedom & Peace (WiP) was sparked by the events which followed the martial law in Poland and the wide use of the military forces to extinguish the wave of political and social commotion, and to dash the hopes of the people for a better and more human life. The very use of the Army for such a disgraceful goal sat oddly with the traditional values of Polish society, where for centuries the Army has enjoyed a virtually universal respect, and where the officer's rank used to have—in the 1918-1939 period—prestige equal only to that of a university professor. Public opinion polls conducted in the period directly preceding the military truncation of Solidarity showed that the Army ranked behind the Church and the Union as the most trusted public institution. Also, despite the fact that it apparently remained the armored fist of the Communist State, the Army itself was never the subject of direct or indirect attacks on the part of various opposition groupings, which otherwise had singled out the Communist Party, the political police, and the local administration for having compromised the idea of socialism in Poland.

The appearance of the Freedom & Peace movement in April, 1985 marks a departure from this traditional attitude, that can only be attributed to a classical cognitive dissonance experienced by at least some segments of society.

In search for the causes of such a dissonance, one can point to the fact that during martial law the conscripts risked being used in the "pavement politics," or against the street riots, pretty much in the same way the army was used against repressed societies in countries like South Africa, Argentina, Chile and Israel. Indeed, many conscripts and also ranks of instantly drafted army reserve were used as auxiliary forces at the trouble spots. While certainly not everybody drafted would be exposed to such actions, and not everybody exposed would experience a conflict of values, the cases existed when people refused to serve and/or to carry out orders. The situation was further complicated by the requirement of the oath of allegiance, which not only included the recognition of the Army being an instrument of the "People's Power" (i.e. the Communist rule), but also the allegiance to "fraternal armies" (i.e., armed forces of other Communist States, the Red Army most notably).

The Freedom & Peace movement was officially proclaimed in April, 1985 in Cracow, after a court trial of a member of the Independent Student Union (NZS) in the city of Wroclaw. The student objected to the wording of the oath and not to the service per se. The student was sentenced anyway, despite the hunger strike of several core members of the group. Later the same year there were reports of at least a dozen harrassments, detentions, trials and sentences given to those who objected the oath, and to those who defended them. The official line was that objection to the oath was equal to the refusal to serve, and thus is subversive to the very interests of Poland. Separately from politically determined refusals to take an oath, there were several cases of religiously motivated refusals, which mostly included Jehovah's Witnesses, who certainly do not make a political opposition group.

While the movement's genesis is clear, its current profile is certainly at least complex. Various observers attribute to the movement several wishful characteristics, varying from that of the anarchism to that of complete libertarianism, or to a simple model of a peace movement. In fact, the programmatic document as well as the latter activity indicates that the Police Freedom and Peace movement creates a peculiar mixture of humanitarian, libertarian, environmental, philosophical and political agendas. What follows, is a more systematic look at those agendas and the way they compare with the general attitudes prevailing in Polish society and/or with the agendas of other movements.

Human Rights

Of the several human rights, Freedom & Peace concentrates on the ones of prisoners. In this respect the movement creates an absolutely unique group in Polish society, since there is no other group systematically proclaiming equal rights to those deprived of freedom. Unlike the majority of Polish society, the movement is opposed to capital punishment. Interestingly, during the debate on capital punishment it was only the government and the Freedom & Peace movement who proposed to abolish the death penalty, while the overwhelming majority of the society supported the punitive measures. If there is an organization with an agenda similar to Freedom & Peace, it is certainly the Amnesty International.

National Liberation

The movement stands for the rights of the ethnic minorities in Poland, and for the rights of Poles who constitute a minority in other countries. Polish society, until now, did not have a particular agenda of equal opportunity for ethnic minorities, and the Belorussians, Tatars, Germans or Jews were deprived of political representation.

World Peace

The movement's stance is two-fold. Firstly, it stands for tolerance in Poland, and proposes to allow alternative civilian service to those for whom the military service would be in confict with moral, political, or religious beliefs. Secondly, the movement stands for disarmament and global demilitarization. Unlike the Western Peace movements, the Freedom & Peace, however, seeks the master key to disarmament in abolishing state violence against citizens at home, i.e., in Poland.

The Environmental Issue

The movement concentrates on banning nuclear energy and technology. The issue is pretty timely in Poland, since the country has entered a period of considerable energy deficit and the construction of nuclear power plants is under way. It also becomes apparent that for economic reasons (need of hard currency) the East Bloc countries now accept dumping toxic waste on their territories—an issue which creates immediate environmental problems.

Hunger and Poverty

As in the case of the issue of world peace, the movement's perspective is first of all domestic. It stands for demilitarization of Eastern Europe as a means for successfully dealing with poverty. It also points out that Poland itself is facing a problem of poverty and malnutrition and is sliding towards a dependent economic model. Hence, the hunger problem has some extemporaneous and domestic meaning and is not dealt with as an abstract issue.

Philosophical Sense of Existence

Unlike any other, non-religious movement in Eastern Europe, Freedom & Peace is concerned with the lacking sense of existence, decline of personal relations and other forms of anomie. In a country where moral, philosophical and psychological problems are piling up, the movement's stance can be only compared to the one taken by the base communities in Latin America. In both cases the reconstruction of ethos seems to be the most fundamental societal task.

Tolerance

The movement stands for tolerance and understanding and for the appreciation of alternative approaches to solving world's problems.

However, leaving apart all those particular issues, which make the multi-faceted profile of the Freedom & Peace in Poland, there is one aspect of its program which certainly creates a common frame for all the movement's claims and approaches. This is clearly a political stance, which dominates its program. Whatever the issue, whatever the problem, the movement adopts the domestic perspective whereby the state, the state-socialist state, mediates all issues and hence is ultimately responsible for them. "Real socialism" as it is called by the movement, is seen as the system with no restraints, no checks and controls, no democratic balances. Social, economic, and technological forces are allowed to develop freely and are only limited by organizational, infrastructural or technical shortcomings. It is best seen when Freedom & Peace speaks for the victims of the Chernobyl disaster. The immediate problems of the radioactive fall-out seem secondary, what gains prominence, instead, are the systemic conditions which lack participation, control and security. Totalitarianism is the main object of the movement's attack, and its various guises consist the principal source of the movement's worries.

THE "ORANGE ALTERNATIVE" MOVEMENT

The "Orange Alternative" became nationally visible in the second half of the 1980s. However, a group which called itself "The New Culture Movement" (NCM) attempted to stipulate new directions for artistic and political contesting actions in 1981. At a time of dashed hopes and conflict of values the movement sought to deepen aesthetic sensitivity, to build constructive ethics and to establish broadly humanistic social relations. In October, 1981, it organized a march which proclaimed freedom of imagination and condemned "symmetry" as a too predictable order of society. However, the demonstration did not correspond to the general climate of social life: vindications, strikes, negotiation of populist demands, hunger marches called for a new order, while the NCM proposed no order at all. The street art which was promoted by the NCM was certainly distant from mainstream political life in Poland of the early 1980s. Poles were busy re-creating the fabric of civil society, digging trenches for the long forthcoming confrontation with the Party-State.

Parallel to the conspicuous militancy of the student associations, was the NCM's apparent concern with problems of peace. Despite the different political agendas held during the days preceding martial law, several thousand people came to the meeting which turned out to be the first large-scale happening.

The first issue of the *Orange Alternative* (the publication which gave the official name to the movement), appeared in Fall, 1981. The journal received considerable circulation and attention among youth circles in Wroclaw for its thorough graphics. The movement proclaimed its own Manifesto which contained three principal statements. Firstly, it proposed that imagination is the key to individual freedoms. Secondly, it suggested that politics and politicians have, albeit unwillingly, contributed to the survival or re-birth of free imagination and of sur-realism. This survival came about even despite the temporarily successful ideology of rationalism. Thirdly, it stated that the entire world can be seen as an object of art and that surrealism makes it possible to treat the world as a play.

It is significant that at a time when workers, peasants, and students, indeed practically everybody, turned themselves towards some form of overtly religious behavior, the "Alternative" proclaimed individual, artistic and intellectual freedoms. Interestingly, at the same time Adam Michnik, an individual identified in the West with leading oppositionist forces, praised the ten commandment and the Bible (*Kontakt* 7/8 1988, pp. 53) as the sole utopia worth believing and the only real spiritual force capable of fueling the revolutionary masses. The Alternative, instead, was critical of the left, the right and the sacred, pointing to the political bigotry which dominated the Polish social scene. The movement's social criticism, however, went unnoticed since martial law was imposed soon thereafter and most of the "alternative" discourse lost its immediate relevance.

Paradoxically, however, the long period of military rule bolstered the agenda of the Orange Alternative. Everyday life and the praxis of survival under the conditions created by the generals had become so schizophrenic that a rank-and-file member of society could hardly make any sense of it. During the years of state socialism common people had at least been able to believe in some ideals: such notions as the "industrial transformation of the economy," "increased supply of consumer goods," etc., created some guidelines for individual consciousness. The political failure of Solidarity and the economic-managerial failure of the generals left society with nothing to put its faith in. Therefore, when Martial Law was eased, the "Alternative" worked out its own techniques of organizing collective episodes so as to correspond to the subliminal expectations of the younger segment of the Polish population. The youth and adolescents were among those most affected by the hopelessness of the post-martial law era.

The events organized by the Orange Alternative are called "carnivals" and their principal aim is to do away with "grey reality." The carnivals attempt to overcome the boredom of street life, making it more joyful and colorful. Hence the Alternative draws young people to the streets, offers them some theatrical-like performances, partly improvised, partly developed from a well-prepared scenario. Originally it assumes a dualism of roles: some people perform, while some others watch. But the main purpose of the movement is to cheer up and mobilize the young masses: colorful clothing (orange, red. etc.), paper decorations (the "Aurora" cruiser), posters, masks, gremlin hats, and banners with quasi-serious slogans ("We are For!", "Love the People's Police!", "Long Life to the Undercover Agents!" etc.). Common games, chants and dances are constant elements of the street performances and the performers peacefully allow the police to detain them. On the St. Nicholas Day (December 6) 1987 the streets were full of the "orange happeners," who strolled around with their hands full of candy which they gave out freely to passersby. The St. Nicholas celebration was organized under the auspices of "friendship with (economic) reform" making this serious political issue a target of laughter. In 1987 the Orange Alternative organized 15 different events: "The Parade of the Casseroles" (April), "Gremlins in Peoples' Poland" (June), 'Away With the Heat Weather" (August), "The Anti-War Manifesto" (September), "Who is Afraid of the Toilet Paper," "The Day of Militiaman," "Direct Action," "The Day of the Army-Manouvers," "Rockmelon in the Mayonnaise," "Toilet Paper-Part Two" (October), "Eve of the Revolution," "Referendum-a Support Meeting" (November), "St. Nicholas," "The Evening of Three Kings," and "The Orange-Blue Toast" (December).

During 1988 there has been approximately a dozen street events including one major happening in Warsaw, where the Orange Alternative came out on the day traditionally celebrated as the anniversary of the creation of the secret police. Scores of young people gathered around the statue of Felix Dzherzhynski, the founding father of the Soviet secret police, laying wreaths and chanting their love of policemen. The protest scenario had undergone surrealistic reversion; it was simply awkward to arrest demonstrators who were declaring their friendship with the police forces.

The Orange Alternative highlights the paradoxes of social life better than any serious social criticism ever could. It points to the fact that the clergy, the party apparatachiks and the military all belong to the same category, and that the bureaucracy wields totalitarian control over average citizens.

The Orange Alternative is not a fixed social organization nor is it a regular movement which, like Solidarity would have a negative program (i.e., the agenda of issues to which the movement is opposed). Instead, the Alternative is completely unpredictable, floating and flexible. It responds to the pettiness of back official and oppositional forces, it mocks the grandioze and meaningless decorativeness of Polish life, it tries to help people to rid themselves of ambivalence and ambiguity. Its major accomplishment is its de-mythologization of the political order, its doing away with fear, and its normalization of street protests. The Alternative ran contrary to the original goals of the military government which wanted to inculcate fear and obedience and to mythologize the sources of its political power. It runs as well against the original goals of Solidarity, which attempted to normalize the underground political coalition between the banned trade union and Catholic organizations. It also runs contrary to the grand formulas of Soviet perestroika, which have captured the minds of the Westerners and of some East Europeans. To put it in a nutshell, the Orange Alternative is a cabaret movement. But, as Marcin Wolski, a prominent satyrist, says, life in Poland has long outdone the cabaret. The Orange Alternative, therefore, has only kept up with the pace of life.

Although bringing any order into the agenda of the surrealistic movement is a fairly difficult task, below follows listing of the main issues on the movement's agenda.

Nonsensical Aspects of the Quotidien

As indicated earlier in this paper, life in Poland is a coalescence of several not only surrealistic but paranoiacal regulations which came into effect at various times and which now create a patchwork of nonsense. Coupons for various merchandise, spontaneous waiting lines controlled by the social, i.e., informal committees are just a few examples. The nonsensical aspects of social life provide an extremely plausible theme for the happenings.

Comical Aspects of the Quotidien

Everyday life contains several celebrations (like the Women's Day on the 8th of March) which are completely meaningless, yet continue to be celebrated by the state. The movement most frequently selects those aspects to weave around them a new, and surrealistic meaning of the happening.

Embarassing Aspects of Polish History

Such facts like the role played by Dzerzshynski, a Polish nobleman, in the creation of the first security police in the U.S.S.R., or the role the Polish army played in quashing the Czechoslovak uprising in 1968 are used by the movement to satyrically criticize political decisions and acts.

CONCLUSION

The three movements described here certainly differ from the picture of social movements in Eastern Europe that most of the readers might have after following the reports on Solidarity in Poland, ethnic unrest in the Soviet Union, or political and ethnic turmoil in contemporary Yugoslavia. The Independent Education Movement, the Freedom & Peace Movement, and, finally, the Orange Alternative Movement mark a qualitatively new chapter in social movements' development.

The very issue of social structural belongingness of their members is debatable for it is—at this stage—theoretically and analytically impossible to distinguish any particular structural criteria for their emerging. Similarly, it would be impossible to ascribe to those movements the capacity of making rational choices, not for the lack of rationality in the movements' agendas, but for the reason of incompatibility of value structures. The rationality of the Orange Alternative is not the rationality of society at large. Choices made by the Freedom & Peace movement, especially where it deals with military issues certainly run against reason of the State and the immediate political interests of Poland in her geopolitical environment. But, again, the system of values to which Freedom & Peace movement has adopted the system of values that might be characteristic of the twenty first century—where neither wars nor immediate politico-military threats exist, it is possible to consider dismantling some of the central state's functions.

The alternative social movements in contemporary Poland are also non-conventional in yet another way. While it is easy to point to resources or benefits which are being generated through the activity of such a giant movement like Solidarity, and it is equally possible to identify the non-tangible goods to be achieved by movements like the Independent Students' Movement, the benefits derived through the activities of Orange Alternative are more difficult to identify.

Hence those alternative movements cannot be seen as a manifestation of neither agency nor structure. Nor do they fit the "new" movements theory. Eyerman is unequivocal in his criticism of the explanatory abilities of the "old" vs "new" theories, pointing out that "on the basis of their criteria of universality and centrality drawn from their respective theories of historical development" different authors come to contradicting conclusions "regarding the potentialities of the various new social movements" (1984, p. 81). For the state socialist society, the theory, as I indicated elsewhere (Misztal 1984), does even not exist. Therefore, in order to free oneself from the "tyranny of theory" (Goldfarb 1987), I propose that social movements in Poland do really rehearse before making it to other societies. And they do so prompted by the precipitating factors which I have already explained in the introductory remarks.

I contend in this paper that the alternative, non-conventional social movements, as they appear in contemporary Poland, mark a new chapter of social life. They by-pass the traditional areas of class politics, they ignore distinctions between commodified or non-commodified actors, they mobilize otherwise non-mobilizational resources, recruit enthusiasm rather than concern, focus on universal qualities rather than on any immediate gains. Since they are not vindictive, they also escape major truncation attempts by the state. Since they are independent of any particular political constituency they are not (so far) incorporated into the major movement of Solidarity. Their criticism of social life, ability to extract this life's most essential nonsenses, omissions and weaknesses makes them movements for a few. Unlike mass movements, they do not try to recruit large numbers of members, instead they rely on being able to influence audiences and to bring new and alternative values into the everyday life. The social change they effect, if any, cannot be immediately linked to any particular movement's activity and results in increased awareness of large and loose segments of the population.

In order to come up with a simple theoretical remedy that would help the Western reader to understand the non-conventional, or alternative social movements, I propose to accept the following perspective. The way societies develop is through dialectical relationship between the spontaneous (unrestrained) and controlled (restrained) social forces. The former usually appear from below, or within, while the latter usually emerge from above, or without.

The growth of capitalism, the origins of state socialism, and revolutions and major transition periods are usually a dialectical process which involves both types of forces to various degrees involved in the process of change. As I have demonstrated elsewhere (1987), such dialectical dynamics can be seen in the course of the industrialization and urbanization of state socialist societies, being also responsible for emerging social movements. In other terms, the socio-political systems can be organized around the issue of "increased spontaneity" (as capitalism), or "increased control" (as state socialism). At various times, the state may take a stand which is at odds with the central issue of the system. For example, the capitalist state may take a more interventionist stance (the welfare state), or the state-socialist state may take a more spontaneous stance (socialist market economy). Similarly, the social movements which emerge and gain prominence within the given socio-political system can take either a pro-spontaneity, or a pro-control stance. Some social movements, like the labor movement in Sweden

(Fulcher 1987) sway from one to another position. Usually, however, one could figure out the following typology:

The State	Social Movement	
	Pro-Spontaneity	Pro-Control
Pro-Spontaneity	"new" movements in capitalism	"old" movements (labor)
Pro-Control	alternative movements under state socialism	Solidarity and similar movements

When the state supports spontaneous processes (free market, free operation of social forces) regular social movements usually object to some aspect of social reality and propose their own patter of social order. Labor movements, for example, use their "political power to force on the employers reforms proposed by the unions" (Fulcher 1987, p. 246). Similar processes take place in Poland, where before Martial Law, Solidarity collided with the government about the mode of control of the labor situation. After the "round table" in early 1989 the government in Poland tried to introduce more spontaneous measures of social life, and Solidarity, again, stood for some protective, or controlling regulations. The "new" movements in capitalism, as pointed out by Kitchelt (1985) also operate along the spontaneity axis, but theirs is incompatible with the axis along which the state operates. The alternative movements in Poland are the response to the four decades of regulatory attempts on the side of the state. With totalitarian regulations, th semiotics of social life became entirely dependent from the central control. The alternative movements mark a decisive breakthrough here: the Orange Alternative is changing the semiotics of social and urban space, marking it with new meanings, colors and vivacity. The Freedom & Peace movement is changing the semiotics of moral space, giving new meanings to the long-forgotten values. The Independent Education Movement is bringing new meaning to the semiotics of knowledge. It comes without saying that there is a major, qualitative difference between such non-conventional movements and the mass-movements like Solidarity. The difference consists in the sphere of operation, or the space, as I called it above. Solidarity remains within the space of labor, and has as its goal protection of the labor force against unjust exploitation. Therefore, it should be seen as an equivalent of the "old," or labor movements elsewhere. In fact, the "round table" negotiations resemble the process of agrement reached in Sweden between the employees and the employers. "New" social movements in the West do exist within the free, or relatively free space, where the state usually does not intervene into the space occupied by the movements (the green, the environmentalists, the feminist, gay etc.). However, in contemporary Poland the state remains in control of several spheres, and the spontaneity can only be observed within the sphere of the market. The "non-pro-control" movements, therefore, attempt to disassociate such newly discovered spheres from the control of the state. The experience of Freedom & Peace (persecution of several of its members) indicates that the freeing attempts do not come without the struggle of social forces normally involved in the operation of society. Similarly, the alternative movements differ from the "new" movements elsewhere. To put it simply, the "new" movements have "only" to uncover the spheres of issues characteristic of the new stage of societal development; the "alternative" movements have also to free or disassociate such spheres from the overwhelming control of the state apparatus and from the apathy of society members.

One can hypothesize that with the remaining struggle of social forces, where the state apparatus allows some spontaneity only within the sphere of market relations and it does so for the sake of management of the economic conflict, the alternative movements would continue to exist and would invent new, non-conventional measures for returning the forgotten spaces to the social life. One can also hypothesize that if the spheres of spontaneous social development are freed more effectively, the alternate social movements would gradually evolve towards what is known in the West as the "new" movements. Whether alternative movements would spread to other societies and how fast and how adequate this diffusion would be remains yet to be seen.

ACKNOWLEDGMENT

The author wishes to thank Dr. Marek Zelazkiewicz, University of California at Berkely for his helpful ideas on the independent education movement in Poland and also for providing background material on the Orange Alternative movement.

REFERENCES

Althusser, L. 1970. *For Marx*. New York: Vintage Press.
Bakuniak, G., and K. Nowak. 1987. "The Creation of a Collective Identity in a Social Movement." *Theory and Society* 16:401-29.

Buczynska-Garewicz, H. 1985. "The Flying University in Poland, 1978-1980." *Harvard Educational Review* 55:1(February), 20-33.

Cohen, J. 1982. "Between Crisis Management and Social Movements: The Place of Institutional Reform." *Telos* 52:21-40.

Davies, N. 1982. *God's Playground. A History of Poland. Vol. 2. 1795 to the Present.* New York: Columbia University Press.

Eyerman, R. 1984. "Social Movements and Social Theory." *Sociology* 18:1(February), 71-82.

Eder, K. 1982. "A New Social Movement?" *Telos* 52: 5-20.

Foucault, M. 1988. "The Catch-all Staregy?" *International Journal of the Sociology of Law* 16:159-162.

Fulcher, J. 1987. "Labour Movement Theory Versus Corporatism: Social Democracy in Sweden." *Sociology* 21:2(May), 231-52.

Gamson, W. 1975. *The Strategy of Social Protest.* Homewood, IL: Dorsey Press.

Goldfarb, J. 1987. "Tyranny of Theory? Confronting Solidarity." *Sociological Forum* 2:7 (Spring), 422-43.

Jenkins, C. 1983. "Resource Mobilization Theory and the Study of Social Movements." Pp. 527-553 in Ralph Turner and James Short (eds.), *Annual Review of Sociology*: Vol. 9. Palo Alto, CA: Annual Reviews.

Kitschelt, H. 1985. "New Social Movements in West Germany and the U.S." Pp. 273-324 in Maurice Zeitlin (ed.). *Political Power and Social Theory*. Vol. 5. Greenwich, CT: JAI Press Inc.

Melucci, A. 1984. 'An End to Social Movements?" *Social Science Information* 23:4-5, 819-35.

Michnik, A. 1988. Interview. *Kontakt* 7-8, 39-58.

Misztal, B. 1988. "Introduction." in Bronislaw Misztal and Louis Kriesberg (eds.). *Social Movements As A Factor of Change in the Contemporary World. Vol. 10. Research in Social Movements, Conflict and Change.* Greenwich, CT: Press, Inc.

Misztal, B. and B. A. Misztal. 1987. "Uncontrolled Processes in the Socialist City: A Polish Case." *Politics and Society* 15:2, 145-157.

Misztal, B. and B. A. Misztal. 1984. "Urban Social Problems in Poland. The Macro-social Determinants." *Urban Affairs Quarterly* 19:3(March), 315-329.

Misztal, B. and B. A. Misztal. 1984. "The Explanatory Utility of Major Sociological Theories Developed in Poland 1970-1980." *Sociology* 18:2(May), 239-52.

McCarthy, J. and M. N. Zald. 1973. *The Trend of Social Movements.* New York: General Learning.

McNall, S. 1986. "Class Analysis and Social Movements Theory: Towards a Synthesis." *Mid-American Review of Sociology* 11:2, 3-28.

Oberschall, A. 1978. "Theories of Social Conflicts." Pp. 291-315 in *Annual Review of Sociology*. Vol. 4. Palo Alto, CA.: Annual Reviews.

O'Donnell, G. and P. C. Schmitter. 1986. *Transition from Authoritarian Rule.* Baltimore, MD.: The John Hopkins Press.

Offe, C. 1983. "Competitive Party Democracy and the Keynesian Welfare State." *Policy Sciences* 15:2, 225-46.

Parsa, M. 1988. "Theories of Collective Action and the Iranian Revolution." *Sociological Forum* 3:19, 44-71.

Touraine, A. 1981. *The Voice and the Eye. An Analysis of Social Movements.* London: Cambridge University Press.

Wesolowski, W. and B. Mach. 1986. "Unfulfilled Systemic Functions of Social Mobility." *International Sociology*:1.

THE HISTORICAL STRUCTURING OF A DISSIDENT MOVEMENT:

THE SANCTUARY CASE

David Kowalewski

Recently social scientists have employed the framework of historical sociology to illuminate dissident movements (Tilly 1988) and other social phenomena (Abrams 1982; Skocpol 1984; Tarrow n.d.). The method employs a multidisciplinary approach toward significant events and utilizes several tools of historical analysis to apply the insights of the disciplines. Large-scale social phenomena are explained by the historical structuring of institutions resulting from traditional substratums, geographical constants, cycles, and secular trends, which together produce favorable social soil for substantive change (Braudel 1980). By examining the historical conjunctures at which these factors combine, substantial breaks with routine behaviors, and their continuities with the past, can be illuminated (Moore 1978).

This paper utilizes the historical-sociological approach to examine the sanctuary movement to provide refuge to immigrants from Central America,

Research in Social Movements, Conflict and Change,
Volume 12, pages 89-110.
Copyright © 1990 by JAI Press Inc.
All rights of reproduction in any form reserved.
ISBN: 1-55938-065-9

prevent their deportations, and publicly oppose U.S. foreign policy. Sanctuary represents a venerable tradition of political dissent by religious groups. By examining the contemporary manifestation of this old—indeed ancient—mode of religious opposition to the state, one can perhaps see how social movements are molded by the historical conjunctures at which they arise.

OVERVIEW

The study posits the following model for explaining the emergence and behavior of the sanctuary movement. The substratum of political culture embodies the continuing norms held by relevant collectivities involved in the sanctuary conflict. Norms regarding the treatment of refugees articulated in international law, American national tradition, American religious life, and the specific theologies of the major religions constitute the yardstick against which state policy is measured by believers. Yet the content of norms will change as social institutions respond to new challenges. In American churches, the political culture of assisting refugees gained a new dimension, liberation theology, as religious bodies responded to the special problems posed by the secular trend of Third World revolutions, particularly in Central America. Similarly, while the political culture of the U.S. state has contained a norm of some type of counterinsurgency against Third World revolutions which threaten powerful institutional interests, the specific strategy for implementing this doctrine has varied cyclically over time. In the 1980s, the "low-intensity conflict (LIC)" reaction to insurgency became dominant, resulting in the flow of thousands of refugees from Central America to the United States.

The secular trends of enhanced communication and transportation networks, combined with the geographical proximity of Central America to the United States, shaped the flow of U.S. church people to Central America and of refugees to the United States. While religious bodies were beginning to formulate their normative justification for dissent against LIC, thousands of refugees began appearing at their churchsteps. A number of churches initiated protests, using the traditional sanctuary form of organization embedded in their political culture. Yet they substantially broadened the scope of networking with constituents and supporters (transnationalism), added a new organizational composition (ecumenity), and adopted a novel theological emphasis and set of internal activities (liberation theology).

In response, the Reagan administration initiated a similar "LIC" strategy against refugees and sanctuary movement at home. It began deporting the immigrants, particularly those publicly critical of U.S. foreign policy. Thus it was perceived by sanctuary not only as violating the norms of political culture regarding the provision of haven for refugees fleeing state persecution, but indeed as persecuting the refugees itself. It also repressed the activists, thus being perceived as violating America's political culture of free speech and religion.

The administration's strategy actually strengthened the normative justification for dissent and enhanced support for the movement in the United States and abroad. Sanctuary grew and stepped up its tactical militancy. The following sections elaborate the specifics of this historical-sociological model and conclude with generalizations about movement continuity and change.

POLITICAL CULTURES AND NORMATIVE JUSTIFICATIONS FOR DISSENT

Normative tradition and alteration among American believers provide a major clue for solving the mystery of the sanctuary movement. The political cultures of international, national, and religious publics with respect to refugees fleeing state persecution have provided normative justification for sanctuary dissent (Gurr 1970, pp. 193-209). These political cultures form historical ideological substratums with which state policies conform or from which they deviate, thereby affecting the intensity of movement grievances.

Internationally, a large body of law has been developed regarding refugees, including the *Geneva Conventions* of 1949, *Protocols Additional to the Geneva Conventions* of 1977, and other legal instruments (Williams 1986; Nickel 1985). Sanctuary activists claim the U.S. government is violating its own commitment to this international political culture, specifically its ratification of the 1967 *U.N. Protocol Relating to Refugees.* "The policy of this [Reagan] administration," according to *Basta!* (1985:8), the organ of the movement's coordinating body, "violates international law." Sanctuary also criticizes the state for ignoring criteria on treatment of Central American refugees enunciated by the Office of the U.N. High Commissioner for Refugees (UNHCR) (Wilson, 1986).

Nationally, Americans cherish the tradition that the United States was founded, and is still being enriched, by refugees from foreign lands. The tenet of providing refugees from political persecution, especially persecution of believers, is thickly interwoven with other doctrines of American political culture such as freedom of religion, freedom of expression, and separation of church and state. The Puritans, dissident believers fleeing state persecution, left a legacy that protest, especially religiously motivated dissent, was legitimate. The New World was seen as a haven for the politically persecuted. The Statue of Liberty became one of the most powerful symbols of American political culture (Ferris 1986). The state's violation of the American tradition prompted one refugee worker to suggest: "If the U.S. government continues its policy toward Central American refugees, we may as well turn the Statue of Liberty into a Coke bottle" (Proyecto Hospitalidad 1983). Indeed, sanctuary activists regard the state's refugee policy as violating its own law, the 1980 *Refugee Act,* which incorporates this tradition as well as international legal norms. For refugee worker Stacey Merkt, the policy "makes me feel like an alien in my own country" (Interview, U.S. 1986).

American religion also has its refugee political culture. Americans fleeing persecution have historically received sanctuary from churches despite official dispproval. Providing safe haven in churches has deep roots as an effective organizational form of American religious dissent. In colonial times, churches protected escaped political prisoners from British agents. In the nineteenth century, religious groups constructed an underground railroad and provided sanctuary for escaped slaves. During the Vietnam war, sanctuary was offered to conscientious objectors (Brown 1985; Ferber and Lynd 1971, pp. 186-200). Contemporary refugee workers made "conscious connections" with these traditions (McDaniel 1987, pp. 135-147).

Each of the major religious groupings in the United States has its own specific theological tradition regarding assistance to refugees. The more a religious body's belief system is at variance with state policies, the more likely it will assume an oppositional stance (Westhues 1976, p. 311; L. Robinson 1987). The Christian faith was born—quite literally—of a refugee son of refugee parents fleeing state persecution, a point not missed by sanctuary workers (Schultz 1987, p. 7). For Protestants, the Puritan tradition of refugeeism continues to live. Catholic churches in Europe during the Middle Ages were considered sanctuaries for believers and nonbelievers alike (Ferber and Lynd 1971, pp. 189-230). In Latin America, churches have traditionally been regarded as places of safe haven. For Jews, the Exodus story that God is on the side of those fleeing state persecution constitutes a major tenet of their faith. The cities of refuge listed in the Old Testament illustrate the ancient Middle Eastern desert law of providing sanctuary for people fleeing their enemies (Ferber and Lynd 1971, p. 189). The Diaspora made refugee status and state persecution, culminating in the Holocaust, a major historical theme in world Judaism. Jews in the sanctuary movement believe that some of their co-believers live today only because sympathizers responded to their refugee plight (Congregation Beth El 1987). As a movement rabbi put it, the "common element between the death of six million Jews and the oppression of Central Americans is the indifference of the bystanders" (Feinberg 1987, p. 31; Religious Action Center, 1987).

The religious refugee tradition was infused by a new normative current in the minds of many American believers—liberation theology (Blee 1985; Montgomery 1983). Although the notion of sanctuary has a solid theological basis in both Judaism and Christianity, the contemporary movement acquired a new theological emphasis from the normative changes growing out of the Second Vatican Council of the Catholic Church in the 1960s. In response to growing criticism within the Church against institutional ossification and lack of relevance in world Catholicism, especially with respect to the secular trend of Third World insurgencies inspired by nationalistic Marxist, social democratic, and liberal doctrines (Kowalewski 1987b), Pope John XXIII launched the Church on a path of greater concern for the world's poor. The Council advocated a return to Biblical roots and Catholics were urged to work, in solidarity with believers of other faiths and humanitarian nonbelievers, on solving the world's social ills.

The call resonated most deeply in Latin America, where Catholics began to engage in Christian-Marxist dialogues as a means of determining how best to give a "preferential option to the poor." Marxism and Christianity were not seen as necessarily incompatible. The previously perceived contradiction was now regarded as based on peripheral and narrow definitions of both (Roelofs 1988). Increasingly the believer's mission was seen as one of liberating the poor from the structural violence deriving from the capitalist world-economy. The church was to accompany the poor in their exodus from institutional oppression. Conscientizing the masses and broader public, and giving a voice to the voiceless, gave rise to organizational forms (Delegates of the Word and Christian Base Communities [CBCs]), which soon developed political leaders and sociopolitical groupings increasingly in conflict with powerful elites. Believers began to suffer persecution precisely for their religious beliefs, a development which greatly concerned their U.S. counterparts (Tomsho 1987, p. 24).

However, the new theology was fortified by the legitimation rendered by the Latin American Bishops' Conferences in Medellin, Colombia in 1968 and Puebla, Mexico in 1979. Growing numbers of American Catholics, Protestants, and other believers were attracted to the new theology and devoted increasing attention to the Third World (Crittenden 1988, pp. 25-178). Religious groups began to oppose U.S. foreign policy toward those countries. One study of religious stockholder resolutions against U.S. banks in 1972-83, for example, found that 78 percent concerned loans to repressive Third World regimes (Kowalewski and Leonard 1985).

Some U.S. religious groups began to incorporate liberation theology into their belief systems and practices. The flow of Central American refugees was seen as resulting from institutionalized violence and manifested a new historical instance of the Exodus. The obligation of believers was to become conscientized in order to give a preferential option to the poor (Sobrino 1987; Golden and McConnell 1986, pp. 137-144). The social pedagogy advocated by Paolo Freire and used by CBCs was implemented to raise consciousness (*Basta!* 1987h, 1988i). Since the 1960s, a number of religious groups studied in "little courses" (*cursillos*] of liberation theology and established CBCs (Bonpane 1985, pp. 2-3, 19; Austin Religious Community 1986, p. 1). These developments led movement activist Gary MacEoin to assert that, in terms of political struggle for the poor who suffer political persecution, sanctuary "resembles the Latin American CBCs" (1985, p. 28; Crittenden 1988, p. 40). The belief that the United States should be engaged in "liberation not pacification" promoted movement activist Jack Elder to assist the refugees (Interview, U.S. 1985).

LOW-INTENSITY INTERVENTION AND HIGH-INTENSITY IMMIGRATION

In addition to these political cultures, the ideology of the U.S. state provides a final current into the normative justification for sanctuary dissent. Whereas the state's belief in some form of counterinsurgency against uprisings which threaten powerful interests has constituted a norm in the history of U.S. foreign policy (Subcommittee on National Security 1970; Ellsworth 1974; Emerson 1972), the actual strategy of opposing such revolutions has varied cyclically over time. According to the findings of the "mood theory" school of foreign policy, the United States has alternated between extrovert and introvert phases throughout its two-century history (Holmes 1985). If extrovert phases are marked by economic wellbeing and a Congress controlled by the President's party and supportive of aggressive, expansionist foreign involvements with U.S. troops, introvert phases are marked by the opposite features. Whereas consensus marks the extroverted phase, dissensus characterizes the introverted. Economic stagnation imposes financial constraints on foreign adventures. An isolationist public resists the potential costs of large-scale military involvements. News of executive-branch scandals, revealed by the opposition-party majority in houses of Congress and resonating among a disgruntled public, further shackle foreign interventionism (Elder and Holmes 1985, 1986). The introverted mood phase of the late 1960s through the 1980s, often characterized as the

"Vietnam Syndrome," hindered the possibility of large-scale, costly military intervention in Central America (Klare 1982).

These constraints, in conjunction with the secular trend in the scope of revolution which rendered military intervention across the entire Third World increasingly difficult, prompted the Reagan administration to devise an LIC strategy to counteract insurgencies (Kowalewski 1987a). Although the introverted policies of the Carter administration had resulted in U.S. humiliation and contributed to the popularity of Reagan's verbal aggressiveness, the Vietnam Syndrome still limited large-scale actions. The LIC doctrine eschewed the use of U.S. military troops in favor of assisting local militaries in massive sweeps and bombings, civic-action programs, strategic hamleting and model villaging, and psychological operations targeted at civilians. Greater emphasis was placed on political than military efforts. Revolutionary forces would not be immediately targeted, but rather the civilian population, in order to destroy the insurgency's political and social structures (Motley 1985). LIC "aims to separate the enemy from the civilian population" through the use of high-intensity military operations by local armed forces. Conflicts would be deliberately protracted—state guerrilla wars against guerrillas (Barry 1986).

Essential to LIC success is preventing opposition by the U.S. population (Miles 1986, p. 21). To shield especially sensitive foreign-policy programs from an opposition-party Congress and a public wary of interventionism, special attention is devoted to secrecy. High priority is given to operations conducted by the less open executive organs (Central Intelligence Agency [CIA], National Security Council [NSC]). Sympathetic private groups, including networks of rich individuals and foundations (Coors, Americares), transnational corporations (W.R. Grace), religious collectivities (Knights of Malta, Unification Church), and political groups (World Anti-Communist League), are solicited to provide low-keyed support. The strategy is designed to entail a low level of public expenditures, generate few American casualties, and ensure low visibility and consequently minimal public dissent (McConnell 1986).

The administration tried to undermine the religious basis of Central American revolutions—liberation theology—by promoting the ideas embedded in the Santa Fe Document of its 1980 presidential campaign. The theology was described as a political threat, a tool used by Marxist-Leninist forces against capitalism. The institute for Religion and Democracy (IRD) was established in 1981 in Washington, D.C. by private foundations which had supported Reagan's campaign. The IRD pressured U.S. churches to cut off assistance to socially active church groups in Latin America. It launched propaganda attacks against liberation theology in popular magazines. In early 1982, it invited the anti-Sandinista Archbishop of Nicaragua to the United States to receive an award. Its publications claimed that liberation theologians in Nicaragua serve as "agents" for Sandinista security organs (Johnstone 1984; *Envio* 1982; Shaw 1982; Ezcurra 1983; IRD 1983, 1984).

In Latin America, threatened client regimes were encouraged to adopt the Banzer Plan, named after Col. Hugo Banzer of Bolivia and designed to avoid attacking the church as an institution in favor of undermining leftist religious elements through discreditation, infiltration, and harassment (Golden 1985). Since CBCs served as "quarries" for the Nicaraguan revolution, they came under special attack. Efforts were made to prevent transnational religious networking with sympathetic North Americans (Berryman 1984, p. 36). In El Salvador, believers active in human rights work became special targets of repression (Interviews, U.S. 1984). In 1980, four American churchwomen assisting internal refugees were slain by Salvadoran military agents. The latter event galvanized a number of American religious groups and transnationalized the Central American struggle. Similar events in Guatemala had the same effect. Some American believers came to feel a special brand of solidarity with their persecuted and slain co-believers in Central America.

Low-intensity intervention, however, generated high-intensity immigration to the United States from El Salvador and Guatemala. Potential civilian supporters of guerrillas were removed from the zones of insurgent influence and control. In El Salvador, Operation Phoenix was launched to depopulate strategic locales by means of military sweeps and bombings targeted against *las masas,* actions which caused a large-scale exodus of refugees (Interviews, El Salvador 1986). A similar depopulation strategy was implemented in Guatemala. Those civilians who failed to escape the military operations were often killed (Interviews, U.S. 1984).

Although relocation camps were established for those fleeing the operations, they offered less than perfect refuge. Suspected guerrilla supporters were dragged out of the camps for questioning and possible repression (Interviews, El Salvador 1986). The same pattern prevailed at refugee locations in Honduras. In Mexico, refugees had little chance of political asylum and experienced abuse by officials (Crittenden 1988). Guatemalan refugees were intimidated and searched by Guatemalan military units and deported by Mexican authorities (Tomsho 1987, pp. 80-85). Central Americans found little opportunity for employment in the debt-ridden Mexican economy (Interviews, El Salvador 1986; Dilling 1984). Refugees trekked further north, heading for the one institution likely to provide a safer haven—the church. By 1987 some 600,000 Salvadorans and

Guatemalans had entered the United States (*Basta!* 1987a). For many American believers, the flood of refugees resulted directly from "LIC's objective of depopulation" (Golden 1987, p. 8; Bonpane 1985, p. 30; Bell 1987, p. 8; Sobrino 1987, p. 22). "The civilians and their means of subsistence," write refugee workers, "have been the true targets of the army" (*Basta!* 1988a, p. 5). Administration officials with their LIC strategy "are the ones who have caused the current refugeeism" (Elliott 1985, p. 50).

ORGANIZING THE RESISTANCE

In conjunction with these political cultures one must add the geographical fact of Central America's proximity to the United States and the secular trend of enhanced transnational communication and transportation technologies. Together these factors spurred the initiation of sanctuary. The ease with which missionaries were able to communicate the repression of Central America's poor, and to travel to the United States to speak with religious bodies, contributed to the movement's formation. Churches sent delegations to Central America to witness first-hand the plight of the refugees and to communicate the experiences to their congregations (Interviews, U.S. 1986; Wright 1986; McDaniel 1987). This "push" of American believers to Central America coincided with the "pull" of refugees to the United States. In spite of the travel hardships, many refugees, aware of American political cultures, felt that the proximity of the United States made it an attractive magnet promising a safe haven (Interviews, U.S. 1986).

The massive influx of refugees overwhelmed the groups providing relief services. The tragic fates of numerous refugees, who died in drownings and vehicle accidents and who were victimized by unscrupulous "coyotes" promising to bring them across the border, drew more believers into relief work (Subcommittee on Immigration 1985; Tomsho 1987, p. 23). The acceleration of immigration after 1980 led to the realization that, since U.S. policy was in fact creating the refugees, the problem could only be resolved if that policy were reversed (Interviews, U.S. 1986; Bau 1985).

The sanctuary movement initiated its formal and public activities in early 1982. It was inspired by traditional political cultures and liberation theology—an "anti-imperialist Christian mode of thought and action" (West 1984, p. 15; Golden and McConnell 1986, p. 5). Despite Reagan's personal popularity and the electorate's desire to reverse the international humiliations of the Carter era, it was encouraged by an introverted public mood which consistently opposed extensive U.S. involvement in Central America (*Central America Alert* 1983). On March 24, the second anniversary of the assassination of Salvadoran Archbishop Oscar Romero, the first sanctuary was declared. Utilizing the traditional organizational form which had proven effective in the past and with which believers were familiar, Quaker Jim Corbett and others working with the refugees on the Arizona-Sonora border, in cooperation with the Tucson Ecumenical Council, declared the Southside Presbyterian Church a safe haven.

Designed to provide services and frustrate deportations, sanctuaries also gave a "voice to the voiceless" refugees, over 90 percent of whom are poor peasants (*Basta!* 1987f). According to the movement, "sanctuary is a place where refugees can speak the truth" (Golden and McConnell 1986, p. 3). As such, the churches served as fora for critiques of U.S. policy in Central America. The refugees, using simple and tragic stories, have accused the U.S. government of complicity in torture, military sweeps, and the like (*Basta!* 1985; Maschinot 1985).

The conjuncture of political culture substratums, secular trends, cycle, and geography lent unique components to the sanctuary tradition. If historically sanctuaries had sheltered Americans, the new "CBCs" transnationalized the scope of networking by adding a Third World constituency to the tradition. The linkages built up before and during the movement provided an extensive network of transnational solidarity with Central Americans to the movement.

If historically the havens had been almost exclusively denominational in organizational composition, now dozens of ecumenical bodies began to declare sanctuary. When religious groups of different faiths at the local level are suddenly confronted by a common urgent problem demanding an immediate unified response, the possibilities for ecumenism are enhanced. Certainly the flood of refugees called for urgent action. The growing belief that the influx of refugees was not generated by assorted unrelated causes, but rather by a single common enemy, the administration's LIC strategy, proved an additional stimulus to ecumenical dissent (Kowalewski and Greil 1985, p. 273). The call for more ecumenical activities by the Vatican Council and liberation theology provided a further motive for joint religious action. Indeed Corbett, influenced by the connections between the Jewish concept of community and sanctuary, believed himself still a Quaker but perhaps more Jewish than Christian (Davidson 1988, p. 97).

GOVERNMENT REACTION

The public sanctuaries presented a serious challenge to the government's counterinsurgency strategy. The media's attention to the movement threatened to foster mass awareness and opposition (Crittenden 1988, pp. 95, 246). The administration reacted to both refugees and churches in accordance with its low-keyed, secretive LIC strategy. It began extensive deportation of the refugees by the Immigration and Naturalization Service (INS) and non-confrontational, subterranean harassment of movement activists (Barry 1986, p. 61).

The administration asserted that the refugees came for economic not political reasons, represented a burden on the U.S. economy, and faced no persecution when deported home. The deportations provoked the ire of believers working with the refugees (Wipfler 1985, p. 115). Activists cited a Massachusetts Institute of Technology study, which showed that political violence was the main motivation for Salvadoran immigration since 1979 (*Basta!* 1986b; Interviews, U.S. 1986). They pointed to a study by the U.S. government itself, which found that refugees do not substantially burden social services but instead contribute to the economy by creating jobs and providing low-skilled manpower (Select Commission, 1981). Yet, whereas refugees from communist-dominated countries received a high rate of INS acceptance for political asylum (up to 80 percent), the rate for Salvadorans and Guatemalans rarely exceeded 3 percent (Golden and McConnell 1986, pp. 44, 77). According to sanctuary, grants of political asylum would represent a tacit admission that U.S. client states in Central America were in fact repressive. Thus, U.S. military assistance for counterinsurgency could be jeopardized.

In 1980-1986, over 50,000 Salvadorans and Guatemalans were deported back to Central America (Golden and McConnell 1988, pp. 1, 43; Blum 1987, p. 46). Despite assurances by the administration that the deportees faced little danger of persecution, the movement pointed to several studies presenting evidence to the contrary (Subcommittees 1983, pp. 67-77; Political Asylum Project 1983; ACLU Fund 1984). According to testimony by Frank Varelli, a Salvadoran working for the Federal Bureau of Investigation (FBI), the names of Salvadoran deportees were given to the National Guard, a force well known for its repressiveness (Subcommittee on Civil and Constitutional Rights 1987, pp. 20-21; Crittenden 1988, p. 365). Despite allegedly free and democratic elections in El Salvador and Guatemala, human rights abuses, including killings and disappearances, continued (Helsinki Watch 1987, pp. 28-41; Interviews, El Salvardor 1986). The government also armed itself with a legal weapon for deportation in the form of the 1986 *Immigration Reform and Control Act*. By providing legal status only to immigrants arriving before January 1982, it effectively excluded Central Americans, most of whom arrived after 1981.

With respect to sanctuary, any large-scale, open, and confrontational "counterinsurgency"' operations might provoke an isolationist citizenry in no mood to tolerate foreign policy fiascos. High-intensity coercion could damage a Central American policy already in deep trouble. Rather, a minimalist LIC strategy of labeling, intimidation, harassment, and selective arrest was initiated (*Basta!* 1987d, p. 12). In contrast to the Vietnam War era, when some sanctuary sites suffered bloody FBI and police attacks and arrests of conscientious objectors, in the 1980s a low-keyed approach was adopted (Ferber and Lynd 1971, pp. 192-198). INS director Alan Nelson asserted that there were no plans to "bust down church doors" (*Miami Herald* 1983, p. 4). The FBI, CIA, and NSC began surveillance of the movement (*Basta!* 1987d; Davidson 1988, p. 112). An attempt was made to criminalize the movement by attacking refugees as drug smugglers and possible terrorists (*Rio Grande Defense* 1986; Heine 1986; Crittenden 1988). To alienate the broader American religious community from sanctuary, the movement was labeled "politically" rather than "religiously" inspired (Tomsho 1987, p. 163). The IRD accused activists of having a political agenda and using religion to mislead the public (Golden and McConnell 1986, pp. 90-93).

In 1984 the Justice Department and INS embarked on "Operation Sojourner," a program to plant undercover agents in sanctuary groups (Tolan and Bassett 1985). The operation was specifically designed for secrecy; more open options were not considered (Crittenden 1988, pp. 299-304). "Coyotes" infiltrated and taped church services and Bible study groups (King 1985). Activists experienced surveillance and phone-taps (Golden and McConnell 1986, p. 53). Breakins of group offices occurred in nine states (*Basta!* 1987e). According to congressional testimony by the Center for Constitutional Rights, the 1980s witnessed a "growing number of ... FBI visits, Internal Revenue Service audits, customs difficulties, mail tamperings, and breakins, directed against ... people involved in the sanctuary movement."

> Widely known is the use of informants to infiltrate the sanctuary movement.... [T]he government admitted to utilizing three informants. Two ... infiltrated church meetings wearing electronic eavesdropping equipment. The third ... first appeared in San Diego where she became active in the sanctuary movement and attended board meetings of the San Diego Interfaith Task Force.... She later traveled to Tucson ... where she infiltrated the Southside Presbyterian Church... [F]ifteen burglaries have been directed against groups involved in the sanctuary movement (Subcommittee on Civil and Constitutional Rights 1987, pp. 2, 8, 18-19, 21).

The FBI, however, denied that any U.S. government agency was involved in the breakins (Crittenden 1988, p. 351).

In early 1984, three activists charged with illegally transporting refugees, Stacey Merkt, Jack Elder, and Dianne Muhlenkemp, were arrested in Texas. Merkt and Elder were later sentenced. In 1985, numerous arrests and sentences were experienced by sanctuary workers in Arizona.

The government's strategy, however, only accelerated the movement. The new immigration law was criticized as a cynical tool for deportation of embarrassing refugees. Not only were most Salvadorans and Guatemalans excluded from legalization by virtue of date of their arrival into the United States, the traumatized refugees, traditionally fearful of government officials, often refused to register with the INS. Many immigrants, given the hardships and confusion of traveling to the United States, had no proof of their arrival date. The new legal sanctions against employers meant refugees were liable to lose their jobs. To the sanctuary movement, the deportations meant that the refugees were being persecuted by the U.S. government as they had been by their own governments in Central America (Miller 1987).

The repression against sanctuary provoked the ire of activists but was too weak to inhibit the movement. To sanctuary workers, the administration was attacking U.S. churches much as Central American governments attacked theirs. Movement members further identified transnationally with refugee believers persecuted for their faiths. The harassment was also criticized for violating the national political culture of freedom held by the churches (Corbett 1986, p. 6). According to the Sanctuary Coordinating Committee of Milwaukee, "The policy of this]Reagan] administration not only violates international law but our constitutional rights" (*Basta!* 1988h, p. 8). Low-intensity repression provided additional normative justification for dissent.

DEVELOPMENT OF THE MOVEMENT

The political cultures concerning refugees, the transnationalism and ecumenity of the movement, and the unresponsive and repressive policy of the U.S. government all combined to generate national and transnational support for the movement, further stimulating the impulse to dissent (Gurr 1970, pp. 274-316). Whereas the administration maintained that the refugees came for economic reasons and hence would take jobs away from American workers, a 1986 Gallup poll discovered that only 15 percent of the respondents felt immigrants would compete with them for jobs (Pear 1986). In spite of the Central American influx, a national poll found the public still favoring responsible and responsive refugee admissions (Human Rights

Internet 1984, p. 98). At the National Sanctuary Conference immediately after the first indictments in Arizona, the movement received the blessings of the governing bodies of the American Lutheran Church, U.S. Catholic Missionary Association, Rabinnical Assembly, and other religious bodies. Jewish leader Elie Wiesel compared the sanctuary activists to those who assisted Jewish refugees from the Holocaust (Crittenden 1988, pp. 201-202). Some local governmental bodies ordered their employees not to cooperate with the INS in deportations (*Amigos* 1986). The sanctuary sites were supported by a network of 2000 other churches (MacEoin 1985, p. 22). Rev. Jesse Jackson's Operation PUSH opened all its offices to the refugees (Tomsho 1987, p. 166). Some religious groups successfully pressured Western Airlines with stockholder resolutions and threats of boycott to terminate its "death flight" arrangement with the INS to deport Salvardorans (Wolf and Smith 1983). In March 1987 the Supreme Court ruled that refugees do not have to prove "clear probability" of harm if deported, only a "reasonable possibility" (K. Robinson 1987). In April 1988, a Los Angeles federal district court barred deportation of Salvadoran refugees and ordered the INS to end coercive practices designed to force the refugees to leave. It found Salvadorans singled out for special victimization by the INS (*Basta!* 1988f). The wide publicity given to the Iran/ Contragate misdoings, and the specific revelations about Operation Sojourner—scandals characteristic of introverted mood phases—further constrained and delegitimated administration policy and helped legitimate the movement.

Sanctuary also won transnational support. In December 1986 it was presented the Rothko Chapel Award for Commitment to Truth and Freedom. Rev. John Fife, one of the founders of sanctuary, received the prize from ex-president Jimmy Carter and South African Bishop Desmond Tutu. In May 1986, 400 church delegates from 42 countries meeting in France passed a resolution supporting those convicted in the Tucson trial (Davidson 1988, p. 160). Sanctuary had a transnational demonstration effect. In September 1986 sanctuary activists met in Holland with representatives of European churches interested in expanding the sanctuary concept to their own churches for the sake of stopping deportations of Chileans, Kurds, and other Third World refugees (Davidson 1988, p. 160; *Basta!* 1987c). Representatives of the Washington Liaison Office of the UNHCR reported that the United States was failing to fulfill its international legal obligation by systematically deporting Salvadorans regardless of the merits of their asylum claims (*Basta!* 1986a). Amnesty International testified at hearings of the Senate Committee on the Judiciary that the United States was violating its own commitment to international standards on refugees

(Wilson 1986, pp. 13-17). After Stacey Merkt was imprisoned, Amnesty declared her a prisoner of conscience, the first American adopted since 1979 (Amnesty International 1987). In September 1987 on his trip to San Antonio, Pope John Paul II urged Americans to welcome needy Hispanic immigrants. He offered muted support for sanctuary by noting that those Americans who had assisted the refugees had shown compassion despite political problems (Suro 1987).

As a result of the combined factors of normative justification, intensified grievances arising from LIC, and external support, the movement showed continued growth (Crittenden 1988, p. xv). By December 1987 the number of sanctuaries had reached 450, including two states, 28 cities, and 430 distinct religious bodies in 39 states (see Table 1). The movement embraced some 70,000 active participants (Golden and McConnell 1986, pp. 80-95; Davidson 1988, p. 85).

The ecumenical composition of sanctuary is evident in the wide variety of religious groups and the large number of specifically inter-religious sites (14.8 percent). Although the refugees are predominantly Catholic, sanctuaries of this religion represent only 17.4 percent of the total religious havens, with Unitarian, Quaker, and Jewish sites somewhat overrepresented in terms of their proportion of U.S. believers. The multi-faith Chicago Religious Task Force on Central America serves as an information center and clearing house. Several thousand activists of many faiths joined together in a "Sanctuary Celebration" and march in Washington, D.C. in September 1986.

Low-intensity repression sparked increasingly intense manifestations of dissent. Growth accelerated, ecumenity deepened, and tactical militancy escalated. Whereas the number of sanctuaries reached 5.6 per month prior to the Arizona arrests of January 1985, it accelerated to 6.9 in the next two years (author's calculations from *Basta!* 1987b). By trying to coerce a multi-faith movement, the administration gave the churches a common enemy, thereby enhancing ecumenical solidarity (Kowalewski and Greil 1985, p. 277). The movement's tactics became more militant. In 1986, some 76 churches filed a law suit against the U.S. government. In April 1988 an Alliance of Sanctuary Communities was formed, which made tentative plans to take sanctuary to the streets by constructing "refugee camps" across the United States to protest publicly the adminitration's foreign policy (Kaminsky 1988). With respect to the new immigration law, the movement "declare[d its] intention to defy the ... Act ... to the extent necessary to secure life and sustenance to refugees" (*Basta!* 1987a).

In 1987, sanctuary began discussing a further tactical escalation and transnationalization of the movement: the physical accompaniment of

Table 1.   Sanctuary Declarations by December 1987

Collectivities	N	% Sanctuary Declarations	% Religious Groups
States	2	.01	n/a
Cities	28	6.2	n/a
Religion			
Baptist	6	1.3	.4
Brethren	9	2.0	.1
Catholic	73	16.2	17.4
Episcopalian	6	1.3	1.4
Jewish$^{\infty}$	46	10.2	11.0
Lutheran	11	2.4	2.6
Mennonite	13	2.9	3.1
Methodist	14	3.1	3.3
Presbyterian	29	6.4	6.9
Quaker	60	13.3	14.3
Unitarian	68	15.1	16.2
United Church			
of Christ	14	3.1	3.3
Other$^{\infty\infty}$	9	2.0	2.1
Ecumenical$^{\infty\infty\infty}$	62	13.8	14.8
Total	450	99.3$^{\infty\infty\infty\infty}$	99.9$^{\infty\infty\infty\infty}$

Sources: Basta!, "Declared Sanctuaries," December 1987, pp. 45-51, and "New Immigration Law," June 1987, pp. 47-51.
Notes: $^{\infty}$Includes New Jewish Agenda (N = 7).
$^{\infty\infty}$Smaller denominations such as Covenant Church and Church of the Disciples.
$^{\infty\infty\infty}$Ecumenical Councils, Peace Centers, Central American Task Forces, religious houses, University Associations and Campus Ministries.
$^{\infty\infty\infty\infty}$Rounding error.

refugees back to their destroyed villages and towns in El Salvador (*Basta!* 1987g). Responding to an appeal from the Department of Ecclesiastical Base Communities of the Archdiocese of El Salvador, sanctuary workers began traveling to El Salvador to provide transnational protection to those wishing to regain control of their homes from military forces and resume their community lives (*Basta!* 1988b, 1988d, 1988g). The transit from First to Third World embodied both traditional and modern themes of sanctuary's political culture:

> The theology [of accompaniment] ... has both an ancient and modern encarnation. Moses left ... safety ... within the ruling circles of Egypt to accompany his people ....

[It] reach[es] back to Vatican Council II when thousands of priests, nuns, and lay workers left the convent and parish house to live among the poorest in Latin America (McConnell 1988, p. 7).

The trips put movement members in dangerous confrontation with the very military forces which had created the refugees. The *extranjeros* ("internationals") were threatened in the military-controlled media and branded as "foreign agents" serving "the strategy of the FMLN guerrillas" (*Basta!* 1988e, p. 29).

IMPLICATIONS

The historical conjuncture of political cultures and new theological development, an introverted foreign policy mood-phase, secular trends, and geographical constraints helps illuminate the initiation and growth of a highly transnational, ecumenical, and militant religious movement of opposition to government policy. Broad public support for refugees, but lack of support for high-intensity military interventionism, elucidate the historically specific consequences of that policy. The government's LIC strategy resulted in a massive influx of refugees and their protection by a growing number of sanctuary communities. The LIC reaction against the refugees and sanctuary only broadened and deepened the opposition.

The method of historical sociology seems useful in accounting for the rise and development of social movements, in particular their continuity and change. Several continuities are evident. The political culture substratums concerning refugees help account for the churches' active concern for the immigrants as well as the organizational form of dissent. The government's own political culture of counterinsurgency rendered imperative its lack of sympathy with threatening revolutions and its aid to Central American militaries to defeat the uprisings. The resulting flood of refugees, encouraged by geographical proximity, represented an urgent call for religious response.

Yet significant changes flowing from historical alterations can also be observed. The institutional change within the Catholic Church, which tried to become more relevant in the face of ideational challenges, particularly in the Third World, stimulated the development of liberation theology. The new current altered the theological emphasis, internal behaviors, and organizational composition of the sanctuary tradition. The secular trend of transportation and communication made urgent the need to respond to the flood of refugees and accelerated the growth of the movement. It also contributed to the new transnational scope of networking with constituents and supporters and enhanced the movement's domestic and foreign support. The LIC phase of the foreign policy cycle, expressed in the United States by deportations and harassments, heightened tactical militancy.

Like all social movements, sanctuary will gradually disappear from the scene and others will take its place depending on the peculiar historical conjunctions operative at the time. Like all movements, however, sanctuary will leave a normative residue in America's political culture and theological repertoire. The historical legacy may well include a deepened resistance among American believers to government policies. In particular, ecumenical and transnational opposition to U.S. foreign policy may "bring the wars home" to a greater extent than in the past. The traditions left by contemporary sanctuary may imply even more difficulty for the government in legitimating its foreign policy toward the Third World among America's established churches.

REFERENCES

Abrams, P. 1982. *Historical Sociology.* Ithaca, NY: Cornell University Press.

American Civil Liberties Union Fund. 1984. *Evidence of Persons Returned from the U.S. to El Salvador and Subsequently Killed, Imprisoned, or Disappearing.* Washington: D.C.

Amigos de Casa Marianella. 1986. "Council Considers Vote on 'City of Refuge.'" 1 (March): 2.

Amnesty International. 1987. *USA: Church Worker Adopted as Prisoner of Conscience.* London: International Secretariat.

Austin Religious Community for Central America. 1986. *Newsletter* July 12: 1.

Barry, T. 1986. *Low-Intensity Conflict: The New Battlefield in Central America.* Albuquerque, NM: Resource Center.

Basta! 1985. "You Learn How to Torture." April: 13.

———. 1986a. "Sanctuary and GAM Receive Human Rights Awards." December: 19.

———. 1986b. "Responses to the INS." June: 21-23.

———. 1987a. "Declaration of Defiance." March: 34.

———. 1987b. "Declared Sanctuaries: March 1987." March: 45-51.

———. 1987c. "International Sanctuary." June: 41.

———. 1987d. "Para Hacer Nuestro Amor Mas Effectivo." June: 11-16.

———. 1987e. "Sanctuary Breakins." March: 31.

———. 1987f. "Santuario es muy importante." March: 12-15.

———. 1987g. "Santuario y sus refugiados." March: 17-20.

———. 1987h. "Servicio Educacion Popular." September: 15.

———. 1988a. "Accompaniment Rooted in History." Fall: 4-5.

———. 1988b. "Call to Accompaniment." Fall: 18.

———. 1988c. "Evanston Declares Sanctuary." March: 18.

———. 1988d. "Future of the Sanctuary Movement." March: 3-5.

———. 1988e. "Going Home—1988." Fall: 28-29.

———. 1988f. "Orantes-Hernandez Decision." June: 16-17.

———. 1988g. "Refugees in Honduras." Fall: 34.

————. 1988h. "Sanctuary Groups Implicated in FBI Files." March: 8-9.

————. 1988i. "SEP Training Weekends." March: 27.

Bau, I. 1985. *This Ground Is Holy.* Mahwak, NJ: Paulist.

Bell, M. 1987. "Abriendo las Esposas Politicas." *Basta!* June: 8-11.

Bencivenga, J. 1983. "Church Sanctuary: Ancient Tradition in a Modern World." *Christian Science Monitor* August 22: 7.

Berryman, P. 1984. "Basic Christian Communities and the Future of Latin America." *Monthly Review* 36 (July-August): 30-40.

Blee, K. 1985. "The Catholic Church and Central American Politics." Pp. 55-72 in Ken Coleman and George Herring (eds.), *Central American Crisis.* Wilmington, DE: Scholarly Resources.

Blum, C.P. 1987. "Canadian Immigration Policy Changes." *Basta!* June: 45-47.

Bonpane, B. 1985. *Guerrillas of Peace: Liberation Theology and the Central American Revolution.* Boston: South End.

Braudel, F. 1980. *On History.* Chicago: University of Chicago Press.

Brown, R. McA. 1985. "Biblical Concepts of Idolatry." Pp. 55-61 in Gary MacEoin (ed.), *Sanctuary.* San Francisco: Harper and Row.

Central American Alert. 1983. "Opposition Grows to Reagan's War." September: 1.

Congregation Beth El of the Sudbury River Valley. 1987. "Resolution of Sanctuary." *Basta!* June: 34.

Corbett, J. 1986. *Sanctuary Church.* Wallingford, PA: Pendle Hill, Pamphlet No. 270.

Crittenden, A. 1988. *Sanctuary: A Story of American Conscience and Law in Collision.* New York: Weidenfeld and Nicolson.

Davidson, M. 1988. *Convictions of the Heart: Jim Corbett and the Sanctuary Movement.* Tucson, AZ: University of Arizona Press.

Dilling, Y. 1984. *In Search of Refuge.* Scottdale, PA: Herald.

Elder, R. and J. Holmes. 1985. "International Economic Long Cycles and American Foreign Policy Moods." Pp. 239-64 in Paul Johnson and William Thompson (eds.), *Rhythms in Politics and Economics.* New York: Praeger.

————. 1986. "Prosperity, Political Consensus, and U.S. Foreign Policy Moods." Paper presented at the International Studies Association, Los Angeles, March.

Elliott, J. 1985. "The Bible from the Perspective of the Refugee." Pp. 49-54 in Gary MacEoin (ed.), *Sanctuary.* San Francisco: Harper and Row.

Ellsworth, H. 1974. *One Hundred Eighty Landings of U.S. Marines: 1800-1934.* Washington, D.C.: History and Museums Division, U.S. Marines Corps.

Emerson, J.T. 1972. "War Powers Legislation." *West Virginia Law Review* 74: 53-119.

Envio. 1982. "Luchas Ideologicas en las Iglesias Evangelicas en Nicaragua." 15 (September): 1-10.

Ezcurra, A.M. 1983. *Neoconservative Offensive: U.S. Churches and the Ideological Struggle for Latin America.* New York: New York Circus.

Feinberg, Rabbi C. 1987. "Sanctuary: A Jewish Perspective." *Basta!* June: 31-34.

Ferber, M. and S. Lynd. 1971. *Resistance.* Boston: Beacon.

Ferris, E. 1986. *Central American Refugees.* New York: Praeger.

Golden, R. 1985. "Response." Pp. 68-72 in Gary MacEoin (ed.), *Sanctuary.* San Francisco: Harper and Row.

————. 1987. "Communidad: A Base of Liberation." *Basta!* September: 6-10.

Golden, R. and M. McConnell. 1986. *Sanctuary: The New Underground Railroad.* Maryknoll, NY: Orbis.

Gurr, T.R. 1970. *Why Men Rebel.* Princeton, NJ: Princeton University Press.

Heine, J. 1986. "Sanctuary Celebration." *Amigos de Casa Marianella* 1 (November): 6.

Helsinki Watch Committees and Lawyers Commitee for Human Rights. 1987. *Critique: A Review of the Department of State's Country Reports on Human Rights Practices for 1986.* New York and Washington, D.C.

Holmes, J. 1985. *Mood/Interest Theory of American Foreign Policy.* Lexington, KY: University Press of Kentucky.

Human Rights Internet. 1984. "Poll Finds U.S. Public Favors Responsive, Responsible Refugee Admissions." *Reporter* 10 (September-December): 98.

Institute for Religion and Democracy. 1983. *Briefing Paper* 1 (March).

————. 1984. *List of Publications.* Washington, D.C.

Interviews, El Salvador. 1986. Author's conservations with refugees; Salvadoran human rights workers; and North American human rights workers, journalists, and volunteers in refugee camps.

Interviews, U.S. 1984-86. Author's conversations with refugees; representatives of Salvadoran Catholic Church; sanctuary activists; legal aid and social service workers; journalists; and religious groups active on Central American issues.

Johnstone, D. 1984. "New Inquisition on Liberation Theology." *In These Times* November 21-December 4: 9.

Kaminsky, L. 1988. "Sanctuary Movement." *Basta!* June: 25-26.

King, W. 1985. "Activists to Persist in Assisting People Fleeing Latin Lands." *New York Times* January 16: 10.

Klare, M. 1982. *Beyond the Vietnam Syndrome: U.S. Foreign Policy in the 1980s.* Washington, D.C.: Institute for Policy Studies.

Kowalewski, D. 1987a. "Core Intervention and Periphery Revolution." Paper presented at the Southwest Social Science Association, Dallas, March.

————. 1987b. "Periphery Revolutions in World-System Perspective." Paper presented at the International Studies Association, Washington, D.C., April.

Kowalewski, D. and A. Greil. 1985. "Ecumenism—Soviet Dissident Style." *Sociological Analysis* 46 (Fall): 275-286.

Kowalewski, D. and R. Leonard. 1985. "Established Banks and Established Churches: A Study of Stockholder Resolutions." *Review of Religious Research* 27 (September): 63-76.

McConnell, M. 1986. "Bringing the War Home." *Basta!* June: 9-11.

————. 1988. "Theological Reflections on Accompaniment." *Basta!* Fall: 7-9.

McDaniel, J. 1987. *Sanctuary: A Journey.* Ithaca, NY: Firebrand.

MacEoin, G. 1985. *Sanctuary.* San Francisco: Harper and Row.

Maschinot, B. 1985. "Salvadoran Muzzled." *In These Times* February 20-26: 4.

Miami, Herald. 1983. "Church Aid to Refugees Discussed." July 3:4.

Miles, S. 1986. "The Real War: Low-Intensity Conflict in Central America." *Report on the Americas* 20 (April-May): 17-46.

Miller, S. 1987. "The Immigration Control Act." *Basta!* December: 3-5.

Montgomery, T.S. 1983. "Liberation and Revolution." Pp. 83-93 in Martin Diskin (ed.), *Trouble in Our Backyard.* New York: Pantheon.

Moore, B. 1978. *Injustice: The Social Bases of Obedience and Revolt.* White Plains, NY: M.E. Sharpe.

Motley, Col. J. 1985. "A Perspective on Low-Intensity Conflict." *Military Review* January 1: 3-11.

Nickel, J. 1985. "Ethical Issues." Pp. 95-108 in Gary MacEoin (ed.), *Sanctuary.* San Francisco: Harper and Row.

Pear, R. 1986. "U.S. Has Split Feelings on Immigration." *Cape Cod Times* July 3: 1, 18.

Political Asylum Project. 1983. *Salvadorans in the U.S.* Washington, D.C.: American Civil Liberties Union.

Proyecto Hospitalidad. 1983. *Sanctuary.* Audio-visual cassette, San Antonio.

Religious Action Center. 1987. *Providing Sanctuary: The Jewish Role.* Washington, D.C.

Rio Grande Defense Committee Newsletter. 1986. "War on Drugs—War on Aliens." October: 3.

Robinson, K.1987. "Simpson-Rodino." *In These Times* May 6-12:9.

Robinson, L. 1987. "When Will Revolutionary Movements Use Religion?" Pp. 53-63 in Thomas Robbins and Roland Robertson (eds.), *Church-State Relations.* New Brunswick, NJ: Transaction.

Roelofs, H. 1988. "Liberation Theology: The Recovery of Biblical Radicalism." *American Political Science Review* 82 (June): 549-66.

Schultz, G. 1987. "Carta." *Basta!* June: 6-8.

Select Commission on Immigration. 1981. *U.S. Immigration Policy and the National Interest.* Washington, D.C.

Shaw, T. 1982. "Mimeographs Roar in Propaganda War." *Washington Post* March 7: 4.

Skocpol, T. 1984. *Vision and Method in Historical Sociology.* London: Cambridge University Press.

Sobrino, J. 1987. "Analysis Teologico del Movimiento Santuario." *Basta!* June: 19-24.

Subcommittee on Civil and Constitutional Rights. 1987. *Oversight Hearing on Breakins at Sanctuary Churches and Organizations Opposed to Administration Policy in Central America.* Washington, D.C.: Committee on the Judiciary, U.S. House of Representatives.

Subcommittee on Immigration and Refugee Policy. 1985. *Hearings on Extended Voluntary Departure Issues.* Washington, D.C.: Committee on the Judiciary, U.S. Senate.

Subcommitee on National Security Policy and Scientific Developments. 1970. *Background Information on the Use of U.S. Armed Forces in Foreign Countries.* Washington, D.C.: Committee on Foreign Affairs, U.S. House of Representatives.

Subcommittees on Human Rights and International Organizations and on Western Hemispheric Affairs. 1983. *U.S. Policy in Central America.* Washington, D.C.: Committee on Foreign Affairs, U.S. House of Representatives.

Suro, R. 1987. "Pope Lauds Those Who Aid Refugees of Latin America." *New York Times* September 14: 1. 11.

Tarrow, S. N.d. *Struggling to Reform.* Ithaca, NY: Center for International Studies.

Tilly, C. 1988. "Social Movements, Old and New." Pp. 1-18 in Louis Kriesberg and Bronislaw Misztal with Janusz Mucha (eds.), *Research in Social Movements, Conflict and Change,* Vol. 10. Greenwich, CT: JAI Press Inc.

Tolan, S. and C.A. Basett. 1985. "Informers in the Sanctuary Movement." *Nation* July 20-27: 40-44.

Tomsho, R. 1987. *American Sanctuary Movement.* Austin: Texas Monthly.

Vatican Congregation for the Doctrine of the Faith. 1984. "Instructions on Certain Aspects of the Theology of Liberation." *Origins* 14 (September 13): 185-205.

West, C. 1984. "Religion and the Left." *Monthly Review* 36 (July-August): 10-20.

Westhues, ,K. 1976. "The Church in Opposition." *Sociological Analysis* 37 (Winter): 299-314.

Williams, M. 1986. "Sanctuary: Liberation Theology and the INS." Paper presented at the Southwest Social Science Association, San Antonio, March.

Wilson, C. 1986. "International Law and the Sanctuary Movement." Paper presented at the International Studies Association, Anaheim, CA. March.

Wipfler, W. 1985. "Refugees and Human Rights." Pp. 109-117 in Gary MacEoin (ed.),
    Sanctuary. San Francisco: Harper and Row.
Wolf, P. and T. Smith. 1983. *Twelve Years on the Corporate Ballot*. New York: Interfaith
    Center on Corporate Responsibility.
Wright, S. 1986. "Fleeing for Life." *Amigos de Casa Marianella* 1 (November): 4-5.

STRATEGIES IN THE ITALIAN PEACE MOVEMENT

Carlo E. Ruzza

Social movements strive to achieve goals of different natures. Some movements address the polity, others press for changes in lifestyles. The theoretical tools that sociologists use to understand them do not often differentiate between these types of movements. Scholars who study movements seek general principles which can help explain movements pursuing different types of goals. Here I take issue with one such principle: the role of organization and strategy. These are often considered constant concerns of cadres in all social movements. I think we need examine to what extent this is so.

I will examine conceptions of strategy in the two kind of groups within the Italian peace movement: groups which seek to influence governments, and groups which seek to change elements of the lifestyles of individual persons in the community. The peace movement is particularly well suited to clarify if all leaders are equally concerned with the strategic pursuit and deployment of resources, since a variety of groups of different orientation

Research in Social Movements, Conflict and Change,
Volume 12, pages 111-138.
Copyright © 1990 by JAI Press Inc.
All rights of reproduction in any form reserved.
ISBN: 1-55938-065-9

coexist within it. Leaders of political movements seek to attain peace through institutional change and promote political processes and arms control. Leaders of personal movements believe in peace through individual change, and emphasize the modification of individual dispositions. My aim is to assess the centrality and meaning of each category of leaders conceptions of strategy, and to see whether these conceptions change in different contexts.[1]

In order to do so I shall identify indicators of strategic orientation. Through a content analysis of interviews, I will observe if cadres of all groups use these indicators and if there are regular variations between political and personal groups in the prevalence of strategic orientations. In order to examine whether strategic behavior is related to the characteristics of the environment which a movement addresses, I will score the debate section of activists' meetings and compare them to individual interviews.

I will develop the contrast between political and personal groups in my first set of analyses. However, I think it is necessary, in addition, to overcome what I see as a false dichotomy, supplementing this with further comparison with what, relative to this false dichotomy, are indistinguishable groups such as feminists and Catholics. My aim is to make clear the differences within the broad category of "personal," and thus redefine that dichotomy. Specifically, I shall examine if there are differences in conceptions of strategy between religious and secular groups.

My findings will indicate that political groups are more instrumental than personal groups. Personal groups are more likely to sacrifice instrumental effectiveness in the attainment of resources in order to remain faithful to their task of promoting change at the personal level. Among personal groups, while secular groups focus on interpersonal issues and orient their strategic efforts towards their community life, religious activists are more concerned with personal coherence than with effectiveness or with building a network of likeminded people. Furthermore I have found that movement goals, by affecting advocacy criteria and duration of commitment, influence the different rates of affiliation and disaffiliation of members of different groups, and issues relative to commitment and relative responsiveness to success and failure.

These results call for a redefinition of the category of strategy. I will reconceptualize strategy as existing within different ideological frames. In other words, extent and direction of cadres' instrumentality is directed by normatively defined goals which are sanctioned by the different organizational environments of social movement organizations. In this perspective a fundamentally instrumental strategic model is only applicable to political movements. Other groups place a value on the intrapersonal and interpersonal implications of processes of mobilization and not merely on its results. They do not necessarily subordinate one to the other. This reconceptualization addresses themes often discussed in the literature on social movements.

REVIEW OF THE LITERATURE

There is a vast literature which addresses issues of strategy, but relatively few, mainly historical, comparative studies of religious and non-religious groups. I consider the literature inadequate because it fails to address completely the contrast between political and personal groups, and does not consider differences between secular and religious groups.

The issue of cadres' tasks touches upon a controversial problem; that is whether collective action is best understood as guided by strategic considerations or whether it should be approached in terms of actors' motivations. While structural theories of social processes regard strategy as the main concern of movement cadres, normative accounts limit the centrality of strategy by pointing instead to the cultural tasks of leaders, particularly that of the formation of collective identity. The first approach, typical of resource mobilization theories, has been challenged for not satisfactorily explaining individual participation when this is not primarily instrumental.[2] The second, which is characteristic of theorists working on new social movements, is accused of glossing over structural conflict by psychologizing it.

The resource mobilization conceptualization of strategy selectively borrows from organizational theory. For resource mobilization theorists "Social Movements Organizations operate much like any other organization and consequently, once formed, they operate as though organizational survival were the primary goal." (McCarthy and Zald 1982, p. 1226). From this perspective movement leaders are conceived of as entrepreneurs who play a strategic game. Thus McCarthy and Zald (1982) remark that sociologists "largely have ignored the ongoing problems of strategic dilemmas of social movements." They shift the focus to an instrumental conceptualization of strategy asserting that:

> In the course of activism leaders of movements here and abroad attempted to enunciate general principles concerning movement tactics and strategy and the dilemmas that arise in overcoming hostile environments... The theories of activists stress problems of mobilization, the manufacture of discontent, tactical choices, and the infrastructures of societies and movements necessary for success (p. 1212).

In recent years the priority placed on strategic and organizational aspects has been doubted in relation to movement workers (cf. Knoke D. 1988), but not in relation to leaders. I will bracket the question whether non-introspective instrumental rationality is necessarily characteristic of large, successful movements, but I will suggest that the self understanding of activists does not bear sufficient resemblance to the resource mobilization approach (McCarthy and Zald), to justify continuing insistence that this is the best way to understand decisionmaking as it actually occurs, however useful it can be for ex post evaluations of effectiveness and conflict.

Some European theorists are proposing what is known as the "New Movements" or "Identity" approach, as an alternative to resource mobilization theory. The identity approach criticizes the focus on instrumental rationality. For instance, Eder says:

> Admittedly, this assumption of rationality is very restrictive. It reduces the rationality of protesting to the rationality of interest groups, to the ability to maximize the strategic accomplishment of interests in the given opportunity structure. Thus "rational motifs" which are of a genuinely social nature—for instance the establishment of a good and just society—are excluded. The idea of rational objectives is not susceptible of explanation by an assumption of rationality which restricts the rationality to the mobilization of resources for given objectives (Eder K. in Cohen 85, p. 885).

New Movements theorists dispute how much behavior can be explained by a measurement of costs and benefits. They argue tht focussing on the needs and values of members is more productive, and seek to identify new developments and put these in relation to changes in modalities of collective action. They propose a focus on identity as an alternative to strategy. The difference in outlook on this issue and its causes are well summarized by Jenkins:

> Most of the disputes in the field flow from this difference. Institutional change movements tend to conform to the basic resource mobilization model: rational actions oriented toward clearly defined, fixed goals with centralized organizational control over resources and clearly demarcated outcomes that can be evaluated in terms of tangible gains. The premise that social movements are extension of institutionalized actions is also plausible. The problem arises however, in applying this model to movements of personal change in which expressive actions are intertwined with rational-instrumental actions. In such movements goals tend to arise out of interaction; centralized control is tied to a charismatic leader or is weak; outcomes are diffused. Continuities between these movements and elementary collective behavior are more apparent (Jenkins 1983).

It could be argued that the indiscriminate application of instrumental rationality models was simply a carry over from the ideology of specific movements. An organizational emphasis was an integral part of the political change movements of the seventies. However the focus on identity also does not get at the issue of the differences that must be understood to characterize advocacy, duration and temporal reaction. In fact just as theories of social processes do not investigate the meaning of strategy for individual actors, limiting themselves to a broad assumption of instrumental rationality,[3] the normative paradigm shifts the analytical emphasis to different themes, and does not generally examine issues of strategy.[4] Thus the question of cadres' strategies is left largely unexamined. Yet the issue is important and raises a number of related questions, such as the relation between collective identity and actual decisionmaking. If leaders concentrated only on results, collective identity would be merely a prop to support mobilization, but if effectiveness is subordinated to doctrinal positions, normative factors would have a direct role in decisionmaking.

To clarify these issues it is necessary to focus on how the rules of the organizational environments of social movements are mediated within specific groups. This is important since groups ground their activism in larger institutional realms, such as the religious world for religious activists and the state for political groups. In this perspective it is important to determine which groups come to adopt which beliefs, and to relate these beliefs to the inducements of the environment. Social movement organizations are not primarily technical systems, but are systems that share common symbols and rules and are therefore part of environments normatively guided. Thus a focus on organizations as units of analysis in the study of social movements, together with a focus on the cultural dimensions of organizations, allows a framing of the issue of strategy in social movements. Strategies, as legitimated ways of pursuing sanctioned goals, can then be expected to vary according to the characteristics of environments. For instance, what is expected in the political system might well be seen as unacceptable by religious organizations because such organizations belong to different symbolic systems, and set goals differently. Without such a clarification the concept of strategy remains an empty box, accepted uncritically by some and ignored by others. In the next section I will examine the main institutional actors in the Italian peace movement, and the goals to which they subscribe.

HISTORICAL BACKGROUND:
THE ITALIAN MOVEMENT

In 1981, when Italian newspapers began to write about Cruise missiles and the Nato proposal to install them in Sicily, the whole subject of nuclear weapons took the Italian public by surprise (cf. Accame 1984). The peace movement suddenly and unexpectedly, became a prominent force. Some international developments fueled this resurgence. The most important of these were the German government's alarm about the new Russian SS20 and the project of massive rearming of the Reagan administration.

In Italy, the peace movement which was initially spurred by the PCI, was quickly joined by concerned citizens and supported by various groups on the left. On October 24, 1981 the first large march in Rome (330-500,000 people) took place as part of a day of mobilization held in other European capitals. Beside communists, the march gathered people from the new left and a few Catholics. For the next three years thereafter, flowered initiatives at all levels. With the condemnation of nuclear weapons by the conference of American Catholic bishops on November 21, 1981 the Church began to become involved. The year 1982 started with a reaction to the normalization of Poland, which threatened the credibility of Western pacifism, perceived as overly enthusiastic toward the state-sponsored pacifism of the Eastern block. The Communist party intervened to overcome this crisis by openly inviting militants to take part in peace initiatives. Other forces perceived this strategy as a process of colonization, and tensions began to develop. Many people abandoned the movement while more communist militants joined in.

The year 1983 saw the peak of mobilization, with a larger and somewhat more organized movement. In January there were the first cases of civil disobedience near Sicilian military bases, which have continued to this day. On October 22nd, the largest rally, with about one million participants, took place in Rome. The rally was extensively reported in all major newspapers, even if with skeptical tones. At the end of that year, two tendencies within the movement come into opposition to one another. The leftist political groups pushed for more organization. The decentralized wing, which included ecologists, feminists and nonviolents, criticized the concepts of hierarchy and forced homogeneity, and pushed for the dissolution of a short lived coordinating committee. The advantage of a coalition was not seen as being worth the price of organizational structures felt as confining for individual militants. The break did not occur between groups which had competing political projects since as far as the political arena was concerned, all groups shared the political agenda of halting missile deployment. The issues which precipitated contention were political styles and organizational structures.

Meanwhile the government proceeded to deploy the first cruise missiles despite the mounting protests. The movement, perceiving this as an irreparable defeat, began to lose vitality. The destruction of the South-

Korean jet liner by the Russians further reduced public support for the movement which was seen as naive in its trust of the Soviet Union's peaceful intensions.

The year 1984 was a year of crisis for the movement. A large part of the left abandoned the cause of peace. Many "committees for peace" closed down. There were no major protest actions. From 1985 to 1988 the leftist peace movement shrank to a fraction of its former size. While some committees were kept alive on paper, they lost their vitality and ability to attract new people. In 1988, in an attempt to revitalize the movement, a group of communist and independent leftist members of parliament founded a new organization, the "Association for Peace." Its purpose is to coordinate the efforts of individuals working on peace issues in an organization which includes regularly elected officials among its members and emphasizes competence and knowledge of disarmament issues. Although membership is individual and non-exclusive, a number of groups including the nonviolents, advised their members not to join to safeguard their independence. These groups accused the newly founded organization of excessive bureaucratization and a technocratic emphasis on experts. Thus as the movement declines, it remains divided on matters of priorities and political styles.

From this review two clusters stand out in the Italian Peace Movement: one with groups focussing on personal changes, and one concentrating on political change. The personal change cluster is divided into a Catholic and a non-Catholic component.[5] To examine whether these divisions result in opposite ways of conceiving the process of goal attainment, I gathered information on actors' intentions, using the methods described in the next section.

METHODOLOGY

Before beginning my field research I had acquired sufficient familiarity with groups in the antinuclear movement to classify them into one of three categories: political, secular-personal and religious-personal.

Beginning in the summer of 1987 I carried out in-depth interviews with cadres of different groups operating in the Milan area. Samples of the recordings of these interviews constitute my empirical material. I asked each interviewee for a history of his or her group, and of the peace movement since 1981. Then I asked questions concerning the choice and effect of action repertoires. I asked what forms of action were employed and why, who chose them, whether they were successful and why. Some interviews were recorded; in other cases I took notes. My interventions were as limited as possible. In the process of data collection my objective was to provide as much as possible an undistorted insight into activists definitions of the movement, hierarchies of priorities, and conceptualization of costs. For this reason I approached activists through personal connections and conducted the interviews in a relaxed and informal fashion.

In order to assess leader dispositions toward strategic and non strategic judgments, I identified three thematic areas in which these attitudes might be displayed. The variable strategy refers here, in syntony with resource mobilization theory, to the institutionalized rules of the political system. The negation of these rules was taken as indication of non-strategic emphasis. The thematic areas were: (a) the importance of mobilization, (b) attitude toward the movement's members, adversaries and audiences, (c) use of the media. Briefly a strategic attitude toward mobilization implied a stress on results rather than an emphasis on the educational outcomes of the process of participation. A strategic disposition towards adversaries, members and participants subordinated personal costs to effectiveness of participation. The media in one case was manipulated at will to achieve movement goals, in the other case such manipulation was rejected. Appendix A lists items considered in each category.

The recordings of the interviews were scored independently by two judges. Samples of two hours of recording were taken from each category. The samples were taken from recordings of 9 interviews for each category. Each sentence expressing one of these concepts was counted as a mention. Repetitions in the same sentence were not counted. The reliability between the two judges was 87 percent. Simple average was calculated. This procedure resulted in a list of strategic and non-strategic instances collected for the three types of groups and organized by theme.

Then I set to compare individual interviews to concepts utilized in the collective decision-making process. I went to several meetings of peace activists and formally compared four such meetings. One meeting had institutional actors, two non-institutional actors and one Christians. I recorded the debate of these meetings, then I defined and scored strategic mentions of organizational concerns according to the previous scheme, and noted which decisions were taken. I obtained a comparable set of activists public statements organized by type of group.[6]

In discussing the results I will begin by contrasting the personal and political clusters, and then address the Catholic cluster. First I will give examples of the different methods of institutional and personal change movements, then I will focus on their different conceptions towards members and media. In my presentation, to integrate the results and illustrate specific differences in collective identity. I used frequent excerpts from the interviews.

INTERVIEWS ANALYSIS

Methods: Education versus Organization

Personal change leaders consider movement method in a distinctive way, which is well illustrated by a national leader of the nonviolents. In the context of a history of their movement, he said:

> ...it is not possible to develop nonviolence if one does not act nonviolently, and so it is not possible to educate in the abstract but only within a strategy that conceives a nonviolent transformation and thus can directly face these themes, to educate the persons who act, to educate the adversaries, and to educate the people that see you. I believe that the most important thing is education. Let's say it's education and politics, but the political element is maybe less accentuated by us than the educational one.

Focussing on education, however, does not set his group apart from contentious groups. Distinguishing it from religious groups he said:

> I have always been furious with those that say "conscious objection is an act of witness." It is not an act of witness but a form of contention (lotta).

also:

> Strategy for me is not within the logic of numbers. Even if you accept the electoral moment, there must be also a moment of relation with the base, or else it is an elitist direction, and everyone now, from political parties to associations like Italia Nostra are totally elitist.

and:

> You set the problem in terms of power equal strength; the more we are the more power we have, which is a mechanical and quantitative approach, whereas if your objective is not to be many, but to be able to join the personal and the political element...then a quantitative discourse is not sufficient

In contrast a political leader said:

> The problem of the peace movement in Italy is that it was never organized. This is the crucial point. Why don't we have a peace movement in Italy today? Because it was never organized.

also:

> To build an association is the only way. An association for peace is the only way to
> do something, or else you have a movement without head or tail.

The choice of method also implies that different groups place a different
weight on the task of organizing. Groups differ in the way they employ
resources and the emphasis they place on durability of the organization.
These sentences of a feminist are pertinent to this latter issue:

> I believe that the (Peace) movement is not doing very well, but it is positive that there
> is a joining of efforts on other modalities of action in one's own city. Some (join) on
> the same theme, some not, some have become greens or anyhow antinuclear, ecologist,
> or they still work. For example there is a small group, some are Catholic, others are
> not, and they meet every Sunday and they remain silent for an hour in front of a nuclear
> base in Longare, near Vicenza. It is not a large base, but there are nuclear materials.
> It is only an hour and is done in a very unglamorous way, there are not the echoes
> of Comiso. And then maybe one changes, because at the personal and group level we
> have developed the need to work on other things, and other things have been found...I
> have the needs to find other situations on which to work...that concern other aspects
> of life...

In contrast leaders of the institutional group say:

> I would just feel like an academic if now I were to talk about military actions of
> NATO...because...,it would feel like the orchestra playing while the Titanic sank, which
> is a beautiful and noble gesture, but, it was not, so to speak, oriented to the problem.

and

> I am an insatiable reader, so I frame my metaphors in book terms. The peace movement
> has been a beautiful book, but now it is time to turn the last page. Maybe close the
> book and open a new exciting one. I am sure that there are plenty of exciting books
> to read.

Organization is seen instrumentally 7 times by personal activists out of
19 and 6 out of 7 times by institutional activists. Differences in the
movement's purpose also are related to views on organizational survival,
members' role, and the media.

Decisionmaking and Member's Role

Personal activists, reject the idea of dividing labor, especially when it leads
to manifest status stratification. A nonviolent said:

Young people seek forms where the collective component and the personal component can be joined... organization is created with the intervention of everyone, with a constant and creative participation, not something predetermined... parties kill spontaneous and anarchistic organization... by seeking to regulate the movement they suffocate it.

Concerning the gathering and organizing of activists a feminist said:

I was very critical of the demonstration of 10,000 in Comiso, because this little town was smothered, a dove on the ground drawn with chalk is not an invasive thing, whereas 10,000 people with 10,000 flags can be an invasion.

In these interview it is possible to see a non instrumental conceptualization of relationships. In contrast a leader of ARCI said:

The phases of political mobilization of the masses require big simplifications, this is one of the indispensable characteristics to assemble (richiamare) a lot of people in the squares.

also:

When you start thinking in terms of political struggle and long term strategy, and to contemplate on these problems (of mobilization) beyond the understandable emotions of the moment, you inevitably find that you are few and that it is difficult to make yourselves be heard and understand.

The advocating of consensual decisionmaking and emphasis on the importance of not forcing decisions on members, adversaries or bystanders recurs 18 times among personal activists. There are no instances of this theme in my sample of interviews with political activists. Political activists emphasize non-consensual decisionmaking twice; personal activists never do so. Concern with the role of members is more central to personal activists than to institutional activists.

Media

Personal change leaders are often willing to use the media instrumentally. For instance a leader of the Nonviolents said:

Actions done for the sake of newspapers are stupid, anyhow newspapers are brainwashed... whereas... yes we care that newspapers write about certain things, but to do actions for newspapers is decidedly wrong, whereas it is important to do actions both to involve and to transform the people that perform them, thus the action is in itself a source of information.

In contrast a leader of CGIL said:

> As for mass media, I share (the opinion) that on peace issues they are fugitives in the most manifest way, we should, constitute a specific organization "peace and Mass Media," as in Mondadori someone is considering doing, so that mass media are sensitized, forced, pushed, denounced when they give distorted information...

Another said:

> To use the mass media does not simply mean to succeed in getting a press release published, which however is an important and decisive thing...

While personal activists reject an instrumental use of the media 3 times, institutional activists never do so. In general from the interviews it appears that there are two well defined ideological tendencies. Strategic mentions appear relatively more frequent in the political group, that is, concern about organizational survival is more frequent. So also are attempts to mobilize crowds. Attitudes towards members are more instrumental, and media orientation is stronger. Personal activists stress consensus and the rights of internal minorities, and promote open debate. They are prepared to sacrifice efficacy for participation. Similarly, organizing efforts are subordinated to communication. Over all, among groups oriented to personal change, expressed strategic beliefs were 20 percent of all coded beliefs; among political activists they were 90 percent. This indicates a clear difference between these two types of groups in their emphasis on strategy.

However the question remains whether these principles are used in the decision-making process. To ascertain this, I turn to the analysis of the national meetings I recorded.

STRATEGY AND DECISION MAKING IN MEETINGS

The debate sections of the meetings provide a sample of activists engaged in decisionmaking. The three debates had a number of similar tasks which makes them comparable, but also some significant difference. Hence an explanation of the context of the meetings is necessary. The first personal-change meeting took place in Florence in April 1988. It was a northern Italian assembly of conscience objectors (Fiscal Objectors) to taxes going to the military. Although the objecting is carried out by individuals, various pacifist groups, such as the nonviolents, also participate in the meeting of this group. The money not paid to the state is put into a fund. Objectors in each of several cities choose representatives who meet two times a year to elect a committee that allocates money to various projects supported by the assembly. The assembly ratifies the projects and approves the major ones. Among the projects funded there are grants to farms based on biological agriculture and grants to support the development of alternative energy sources. Projects are presented and sponsored by cadres representing cities.

The second meeting was held in Comiso, Sicily in August 1987. Under the name Ecopax it attempted to gather both ecologist and pacifist forces. The pacifist component was dominant. Among the pacifists the majority were nonviolents and feminists. The third meeting, held in April 1988, was a convention of Milanese groups for peace. It gathered trade unions and leftist cultural associations such as ARCI. The event had been repeated every year since 1984, and had the purpose of planning new actions and serving as a forum for a debate. Each event lasted two days and scheduled an afternoon for open debating. The large majority of participants came from the Milan and Florence areas.

In general the meetings focussed on the state of a particular branch of the peace movement, proposed initiatives, and reported on local realities. There was an open debate with several participants at each meeting (Ecopacifist 15, LOC 19, Milano per la Pace 22). While one of the personal-change meetings (LOC) allocated significant resources, the political-change meeting and the other non-institutional meeting had only minor resources to allocate, such as space in publications and room for meetings. The task of allocating resources made the Florentine non-institutional meeting more controversial, and it was to be expected that these tensions were reflected in the debate. Would non-institutional cadres turn to institutional strategies, such as voting blocks, or would they attempt a consensual working out of differences as would be consistent with the expressed belief of members of these groups?

An analysis of the data reveals that both electoral and consensual strategies were employed, but that the electoral strategy was much stronger than in the interviews. However the choice was difficult and much debated. This complain during the LOC meeting expresses the concerns of the participants.

As for the issue of unanimity, consensual decisions etc., the only thing that I feel, and I feel strongly about it, is that we talk a lot about consensual decision making and then when we organize things, we organize them in an exactly opposite way...this is the element that worries me...of course decisions must be taken, but I believe in the possibility of consensus...and to reach unanimous decisions...if we think it out well, if we discuss and work well...probably to achieve these forms of unanimity, different organizational models are necessary, with more space for team work etc...Organizational models like the one we have do not allow it (3.2).

Despite this and other appeals to innovative organizing this meeting approached controversies in a strictly legalistic manner, with 16 motions presented and voted in addition to the project approvals.

Focussing on the debate section of each meeting, I counted mentions of strategic considerations using the same definitions employed in coding the interviews. I computed the frequency of emphasis on organization versus education, decisionmaking and members role, and attitude towards the media. Results are presented in Table 1. They show that the political meeting's (Milano per la Pace) statements were strategic 90 percent of the time. This is more than the conflictual personal meeting (LOC), which was strategic 65 percent of the times, and considerably more than the non-conflictual personal meeting (Ecopax), whose statements were strategic 16 percent of the time. The higher instrumentality of the LOC meeting shows that the extent of conflict over resources influences the frequency of strategic statements. However the political groups remain more strategic.

At this point one can begin to address the question: Why are activists addressing the polity more strategic and personal activists more solidaristic? Regardless of whether a political activist shares norms of group cohesion, organizational rules must cope with an environment where results are visible and rewarded. Political goods are scarce and efficiency in obtaining them is a must. Action tends to be framed in terms acceptable to the political system. Personal groups, however, are not subject to the same constraints. Their stated aim is to change people. This type of change is less clearly defined. The organization is certainly under the imperative of survival, but not as clearly under all the constraints of the political environment. Criteria of effectiveness are not as necessary, and cannot be objective, since the possibility of clearly interpretable results is lacking. Consequently success comes to be defined in terms of the confidence and good faith of movement participants and sympathizers, just as happens in other non-technical environments (cf. Meyer S., Scott, W. 1983, p. 40).

However in a situation of conflict over political resources, the Loc meeting participants reverted to the more suitable vocabulary of political strategy. In such cases the cultural paradigm of political groups is borrowed. This is possible both because a knowledge of that paradigm is widespread in electoral systems, and because movements are rarely completely focussed on one approach. More often the choice between a political and a personal approach is one of emphasis. Hence there is indication that different conceptions of strategy are used in the decision-making process. When political resources are at stake, the mode of the institutionalized political environment becomes more relevant.

In the context of movements addressing different institutional environments, it is important to notice that this can be done simultaneously. Action forms can have quite intentional meanings which are intended for different audiences at the same time. Theoretically, this problem has been framed by Habermas (1984). An action is seen as meaningful at three distinct levels at the same time: the instrumental, the normative and the expressive. With this perspective, different collective actions can emphasize one or the other level, but be meaningful and be intentionally employed at all three levels. Thus it is possible to examine which component is stressed in specific situations. Habermas' scheme is useful because it allows us to conceptualize the relationship between an actor, in this case an activist, and the environment.

In his scheme Habermas thematizes four types of action: (1) teleological action focused on bringing about a desired state, (2) normative action focused on complying with a norm, (3) dramaturgical action focused on stylizing the expression of one's own experience with a view to the audience, and (4) communicative action which integrates the other three and is focused on reaching discursive understanding (Habermas 1984, p. 93). While communicative action represents an ideal state of communication, the other three types refer to a difference of emphasis which can be used to describe social movements. In the peace movement the institutional cluster illustrates the position of "those who have only the realization of their own ends in view." As I will now show, the religious cluster illustrates "the consensual action of those who simply actualize an already existing normative agreement," and the personal-change cluster "the presentation of self in relation to an audience" (cf. Habermas 1984, p. 95). Thus the goals are respectively strategic, normative and interpersonal, with the last being used strategically in special circumstances.

The lack of a clear assessment of personal-change activism makes the category of strategy problematic, and makes possible a number of different criteria of evaluation, which are only limited by culturally mediated consensual agreements. Other institutional system conceptualize strategies for personal change in a different way. In the peace movement an important variation is provided by religious activists. They also focus on personal change, but their ultimate ends are different. To examine the differences I interviewed Catholic activists. Before analyzing the results, a brief historical background of the Catholic peace movement is necessary.

THE ITALIAN CATHOLIC MOVEMENT

The Italian peace movement is the only Italian mass movement largely supported by a Christian component which did not break with religion.

There have been other movements heavily influenced by the Christian component, but the component that remained attached to the Church was extremely small. In the peace movement, on the contrary, connections to the church have been maintained. While a continuity between religion and politics is typical of countries like the United States, where movements such as those supporting the civil rights, prohibition, and anti-pornography took to the streets without emptying the Churches, this is unusual in Italy.

When the peace movement re-emerged in the early eighties, the Italian Catholic dissent which had supported the new left was still alive, although not very active. For the first few crucial years the Catholic left failed to mobilize large Catholic support for the peace movement. In 1985, in a period of total disarray for the peace movement, a group of missionaries began a very vocal campaign linking the theme of peace with the exploitative relationship between industrialized and third world nations. Their effort was successful and brought together concerned Catholics in many regions. They received substantial support from some bishops and many monastic orders, but also strong opposition by conservative sectors of the hierarchy.

In the late eighties the Catholic component is the most active in the Italian peace movement. In a period of the movement's decline Catholics continue to organize conferences, vigils and protest actions. The Catholic component has a distinctive identity which separates it from the rest of the movement. It is different because Catholics' decisionmaking is oriented not only towards political institutions, but also toward the Church hierarchy. In recent decades Catholic doctrine has oscillated between retreat from politics and integralism (cf. Wertman in Berger 1982). After Vatican II, the Church retreated from direct political interventions in favor of specific parties and laws, but entered the national debate on social issues as an independent party. While some sectors kept an integralist position, other sectors, particularly on the left, renounced politics as Christians. They confined faith to the private domain, and entered politics on a secular basis, opposing the Christian party. This situation found an echo in the peace movement. The Catholics who joined political groups kept their religious commitment private until a specific Christian approach emerged.

The reasons why this Christian approach developed later and grew in a climate of public indifference are complex. It is possible that the Church, as a transnational organization, has slowly incorporated innovative positions from other local Churches. This might have resulted in a diminished repression of a Catholic peace movement which would have acted long before, had it not been for repression from the hierarchy. Also, a breakdown of Catholic networks in recent years might have contributed to Catholics being exposed to themes of the left.

Be that as it may, Catholic activism revived precisely when the larger peace movement had admitted defeat. It grew despite the hostility of a large part of the Catholic hierarchy, and the skepticism of older peace activists. Once started its duration and intensity have surprised many traditional pacifists. This poses a sociological question: What is different about Catholic pacifists that sustains such an intensity and durability of commitment? Unlike secular activists, who act in a complex social movement industry which allows for periodic changes of issues. Catholics are remarkably constant once a theme has been chosen. Yet they also act in a thematically rich multiorganizational field. What accounts for this? Different rates of joining and quitting could be related to activists' definition of success and their cost-benefits assessment, that is, to their conceptualization of strategy.

To explore this possibility I made an additional comparison with secular-personal activists, using the same methodology described above. In the next section I concentrate on Catholic activists whose main identification in the peace movement is religious. I interviewed priests and monks active in the peace movement, and lay activists who live in the Milan area.[7] I attended a conference of the religious organization Pax Christi. I scored the interviews for the same categories: importance of organization, attitude toward members and towards the media. The Catholics which I interviewed constitute a subset of the personal activists group. I did not consider Catholics working in political groups because a preliminary research showed that they are indistinguishable from other political activists. These Catholics confine their religious concerns to the non-political realm and in entering the political arena they completely accept the strategic models of the political system. Conversely Catholics that identify themselves as Catholics are generally concerned with personal change as a political factor. In the next section I will discuss my findings.

CATHOLICS' INTERVIEWS ANALYSIS

The interviews show that Catholics' reasons for mobilization are closer to the education pole of personal movements than the policy oriented pole of institutional change movements. Out of 25 mentions of objectives, 23 concerned education. The Catholic and personal-change collective identities are similar in rejecting the principle of representation and collectivistic strategies. They share a belief in the power of examples as the preferred method for social change. However there are significant differences. Table 1 illustrates the relationships.

From the Table it appears that Catholics are less strategic overall than other personal activists. Only 8 percent of their statements are strategic,

Table 1.   Proportion Instrumental Beliefs over Non-instrumental
Beliefs for Type of Movement and Setting.

Movement Type	Setting	%	N
Personal	Individual Interviews	20	40
	LOC[2] meeting	65	20
	Ecopax meeting	16	12
Total		31	72
Political	Individual Interviews	90	10
	Milano Pace meeting	90	20
Total		90	30
Catholic	Individual Interviews	8	25
	Pax Christi meeting	38	26
Total		23	51

Note: [2]LOC stands for Lega Obiettori di Coscienza

compared to 20 percent of those of the secular activists. Their meetings are more strategic, with 38 percent strategic items compared to only 16 percent for the Ecopax meeting and 65 percent for the conflictual LOC meeting. Thus the difference between individual and collective statements is larger than for other activists. Political activists show no difference between the two sets, secular-personal activists showed an average difference of 20.5 percent and Catholics 30 percent. Since all meetings have at least a minimum of instrumental goals, the more the ideology is anti-instrumental, as it is for Catholics, the larger is the cleavage between the individual and the public level. This happens regardless of other sources of variations which affect meetings, such as conflict over resources. To understand the difference between personal and Catholic activists it is necessary to examine both ideological differences and the characteristics of the different environments which they address.

Catholic groups are in strict relation with the Catholic church, as political activists are to the communist party. The ideological feature of these larger institutions become the common referent for these groups. This ideological dependency is reinforced by rewards granted in return for compliance. Thus, for instance, by "playing by the rules" of their institutional environment, political groups in this study could organize meetings in city hall and received public funds for advertising, while the Pax Christi meeting took place on church property. In this sense personal groups were disadvantaged since they could not tap from a resourceful organizational environment. However they also could use external organizational resources, such as those of certain environmental and feminist groups. These groups address civil society more than the political system, and have a specific vision ranging from the choice of action repertoires to participatory ideological elements. Thus the "Ecopax" meeting was held in a house normally used by a commune of ecologists who practiced biological agriculture. However the land had been purchased with donations of antinuclear activists. This shows the extent of the connections between organizations with similar collective identities. Just as the political and personal groups' ideological cohesion translated into typical strategic visions, so did that of Catholics. Consider the following metaphor used by a Christian activist:

> If you are climbing a mountain you care less about what is happening in the valley. Yes, it is true, there are more people in the valley, but you are climbing the mountain... Your objective is not the people in the valley, even if being in good company might be useful. Somehow you have already made your choice. You must climb to the top.

Here neither education nor mobilization is the most important thing, but rather a purely personal dimension which can be called prophecy or witnesssing. This is typical of Catholic thinking. This quotation illustrates the attitude toward strategies:

> In the Christian way one has the problem of taking one's responsibility here and now... the tradition of prophetic witnessing. That is to say that you are forty years ahead of others, but you don't care. It is likely that someone who does this (witnessing) is there at all times... I find that it (witnesssing) could sometimes be a limitation. You say "I do this thing" and you don't even think that you could build a strategy upon it—such as a strategy with the mass-media so that you give more effectivness to your actions. If more people came to know about actions of prophecy it would be better, but a quantitative logic has never been the Christian way, or at least it has been that in unhappy times... Anyway, if you have a prophetic mentality you are far less attentive to build alliances, (and) to the strategy of information. For instance consider the case of Pagani[8]... has had an influence his Christian faith... on his choice; it gives you a strong energy, a strong motivation, a strong acceptance of your responsibility,... and so you do it (actions) and you don't even think that it would be important to hear CGIL (trade union), inform the press, do grassroots work, consolidate the struggle, go here and there so that your case is discussed by the unions etc.

In this interview, as in many similar to it, activists' concerns are ultimately individual. At a general level the differences in goals which emerge from the interviews between personal-secular and religious movements appear to be that while religion is concerned with the actualization of ethical norms which concern the individual, groups that advocate peace in a community are concerned with interpersonal goals, that is the type and quality of relationships in networks. The interpersonal focus of the personal change group is bound to be reflected in a differential emphasis on community building. While community is a problematic issue for these activists, it is not so for Catholics, who take it for granted. They belong to a univeral religion which is very stabilizing. In fact, they cannot make community problematic without ceasing to be Catholic, because that would be to deny that they were part of a larger faith. Within that faith, the only residual question is the trueness of one's own faith. Thus, in this framework, they are oriented to personal affirmation, where members of the other group are community builders.

To test this analysis, I counted the mentions of community concerns in the interviews. The previously analyzed beliefs are generally related to finalities, or statements about the consequences of different orientations. I counted as a mention every occurrence of a belief related to the concept of community as a desirable goal. For instance, the nonviolent who advocates better communication among activists, the feminist who stresses the importance of her personal group and the nonviolent who wants actions to involve people together (coinvolgere), are all referring to ideal communities as desirable entities. On the contrary the Christian who wants to climb alone the mountain of wisdom, is not. Results of this analysis are presented in Table 2.

This table shows that while the self understanding of the personal change group is centered on the issue of self expression, a characteristic element is a community building orientation. Religious activists, on the other hand, are much less community oriented in the concrete sense of caring and working for advancing a sense of common belonging in the movement. To be sure, the clergy component of the movement refers on occasion to the abstract community of "the people of God," but this does not translate into an effort at communitarian integration. If we consider the clergy as a separate group, they appear even less concerned about organizational issues. Comparing two hours of recording of clergymen with two hours of Catholic laymen, one notes that clergy never mention organizational concerns, and limit themselves to supporting the movement's aims. To explain this some broader considerations concerning Catholic ideology are necessary.

Table 2.   Proportion of Mentions of Community as a Desirable Goal
           over Total Mentions of Community

	%	N
Personal Group-Individual Interviews	65	38
LOC	16	31
Ecopax	33	12
Catholics	12	25
Pax Christi	7	26

PROPHECY

Religiously inspired collective action is often as substantial and radical as
other types, yet it has distinctive characteristics. In the religious peace
movement the community is to be saved from the moral evil of war.
Conversely, in the institutional and personal branch of the movement, that
what is to be saved is a territorially defined community. In the former case,
this is effected through a modification of its institutional rules, in the latter
of its culture. The individuality of religious salvation makes strategy an
essentially personal pursuit. To understand this type of action it is useful
to consider the Catholic category of martyrdom.

Martyrdom is a Catholic ideal. It is grounded in admiration for a martyr's
traits, such as firmness. The martyr's sacrifice is often not efficacious in
furthering the religious institution, yet calculations are not made. Martyrs
do what they do, they withstand torture and death because they "have to,"
regardless of effectiveness. This moral imperative gives them a special
weakness and a special strength: the weakness of the ineffective use of
resources, the strength of a clear cut ideological stand which supports
motivation and, by not being tied to instrumental contingencies, is
particularly durable, and credible as an example.

Like martyrdom, actions or prophecy are more instrumental for achieving
salvation than accomplishing goals in the world. Their otherworldly
orientation protects believers from the doubts and constant revisions that
accompany political pursuits. This results in a non-negotiability of goals
but at the same time in their abstract specification. The eschatological
character of the goals promotes an expectation of total dedication to the
cause, regardless of personal costs. In fact, given the personal character of

salvation, personal costs have a value in themselves, regardless of results. This sets religious commitment apart from other social action. In religious movements goals are not negotiable, demands on activists' involvement are ideally limitless, and personal costs are intrinsically valued. Thus there is in religion a special class of individual rewards which can be conceptualized as selective benefits. The fact the goals are unspecified, allows the hierarchy to provide specifications which, because of the sacralized nature of the goals, tend to be unquestionable. The extent to which the hierarchy's recommendations are accepted is an historical variable. The more they are, the more religious activism becomes a powerful force at the disposal of those who set its rules. They operate in an institutionalized framework which has objective requirements for prospering. Prophecy comes to be interpreted in light of these requirements, and on occasions to be a tool for meeting them.

Prophecy is useful since it ensures commitment, but can be dangerous since it might engender a deterioration of the precarious balance between the charismatic and the traditional element, and between personal imperatives and general principles (cf. Haes 1972, p. 117). From an institutional viewpoint, while some slack is necessary to adapt to social change and to accommodate dissent without losing human resources, too much of it is dangerous since it weakens the ability to prevent schisms and control millenarian drives. Its methods can also be a hindrance for a Church that tries to come to term with the state. This ambivalence is reflected in the dynamic between church and activists. Activists must stretch the interpretation of the official documents to accommodate their views in order to ensure legitimacy. Their goal is to force the institution to accept their positions without being outlawed. If they are outlawed, they lose the support of the massive organizational resources of the Church; if they don't push enough they miss the opportunity to implement desired changes. Thus Catholic activists constantly act in a situation of organizational conflict.

These considerations help explain differences in instrumentality between the clergy and lay component. Clergy, being more controlled by the hierarchy, tend to eschew an openly political role. This fits well with the organizational need to divide labor, and to assign to a specialized class the task of being moral examples above political squabbles.[9]

In general the Catholics' double loyalty characterizes their activism. Since it is an activism rooted in organizational conflict, and is not nourished by results, one needs to ask how it comes about and develops, even before it can be self sustaining. While more research is needed, for the time being I propose with Susan Berger (1987) to conceptualize the Christian community as generally very receptive to morally motivated activism, but isolated in a network of Christian associations which regulate the appearance of themes and whose gatekeepers are the clergy. Once an issue penetrates the Catholic world, its reception is contingent upon its sacralization, which occurs through rituals. As action repertoires filter recruitment and maintain loyalties in secular movements, so ecclesiastical and protest ritualism channel devotion on specific themes.

To complete my analysis I would have to present my types historically, and to compare institutional types and Catholics. However, their collective identities are very different and such a task would require an articulated description of the secularization process in Italy. I can do that only very briefly. A good starting point is Martin's (1978) observation that Catholic societies illustrate well a transition from religion to politics, where hopes become fully secular. In Italy, communism acts as the available valve of discontent, while the Church situates itself to the right (cf. p. 66). This location undermines the possibility of using the whole repertoire of religious motifs and modes of expression for political protest. Traditionally the only exceptions were radical Catholics. For all the others the dream was militant secular politics.

In Italy however, Martin notes, the split is gradually closing. Recently it has become easier to borrow the languge of protest from religion. "Post-industrial" politics, including the activists of the personal change groups of the peace movement, fall into this category. However this is still not the case for the institutionally oriented who have long standing anticlerical roots. Thus while Catholics and personal activists share pieces of ideology and forms of action, relations between Catholics and political activists are hindered by the recent history of ideological context.

CONCLUSIONS

I shall now return to my original questions about whether the context of strategy changes in different contexts. My research demonstrates that cadres' instrumentality varies in different movement types. Within that type it varies with context and division of labor. In a situation of conflict over political goods, personal change activists limited their emphasis on consensuality and recurred to strategic decisionmaking. In different situations activists were non-strategic. The effect of the division of labor is best exemplified within the Catholic movement, where clergy took the role of non-strategic leaders. Thus the resource mobilization school is not correct in positing generalized instrumental concerns.

The normative approach is incorrect in identifying a paradigmatic difference between an old strategy orientation and new identity concerns, since institutional strategic dispositions are just as typical of new "postmaterialist" movements, which emerged in connection with new identity models. In a conflictual situation strategic dispositions increased in groups close to the new movement paradigm. Conversely, identity models are not just inconsequential ideology, as is argued by the resource mobilization approach. Decisionmaking is affected not only by organizational contexts, resources and structures. Collective identity also affects decisionmaking by defining goals and influencing the choice of action forms. For instance, the nonviolents, because of their opposition to elitism and criticism of electoral representation, did not join the Association for Peace, even though the Association would have provided access to important resources.

This points to a redefinition of the concept of rational pursuit of incentives in relation to collective identities. Rationality, in the sense of how activists make choices about what actions to undertake and the way they decide whether they have been successful, is related to the advocacy issue. My research indicated that activists' participation is contingent on cadres' perception of effectiveness, but the difference between them is that they have different visions of how they judge success. For many religious people activism is worthwhile if they can bear witness, and would be so on no other ground. Their commitment is largely self sustaining, and they see no reason to attend very much to worldly or empirical matters. Theirs is often a lifetime vocation. Some might eventually demobilize to some extent, but the tempo is very different. Thus they are on one end of the scale for political instrumentality.

On the other end are the instrumentalists whose aim is to alter government policies. They know that a mass following is crucial, whether it be knowledgeable or not, and their advocacy criteria is whether or not mobilization is happening. As soon as it appears to be waning, they might simply look for the latest social schism to continue their project of remaking society. Both of these are perfectly rational ways to behave, the first based on the assumption that there is an afterlife, the second that social engineering is possible. Similarly a good strategy for building a community is to incorporate people into networks of participation through the filtering of knowledge. Here commitment to long term goals is important in so far as it guarantees association.[10]

Thus, as resource mobilization argues, strategy is a generalized concern of social movements, but must be qualified by the pursuit of a hierarchy of resources which come from normative processes. Likewise all movements are rational, but it is their normative base that determines the standard of effectiveness and the criteria for joining and quitting. What varies are criteria of validation, which are a function of the organizational environments of different social movements and the goals of different groups. These criteria are precise for large movements which contend for political goods intermediate for those who seek to build networks of likeminded people, and more ambiguous for movements concerned with personal affirmation. Collective identities are therefore forced to meet varying standards of effectiveness.[11] Even with different standards of effectivness, all the environments of social movements are normatively oriented environments. They rely heavily on the elaboration of rules and requirements to which individual organizations must confirm to receive support and legitimacy. Collective identities and structural factors intertwine. For instance Catholic groups are very concerned about seeking endorsements from the hierarchy, political groups from major parties, and secular-personal groups from a network of smaller related organizations. They share organizational cultures and are rewarded for their allegiance.

Finally some considerations on the divisions of competencies among groups are in order. In this study groups have, to some extent, overlapping referents. Although the peace groups analyzed have a main referent in a specific organizational environment, they also address others. Both religious people and personal activists publicly comment on the political situation. Occasionally political activists invite prominent clergy to join in their activities, or focus on the psychological implications of different action repertoires. It is possible that transformations of groups' hierarchies of resources occur. Although any definitive answer is premature, it is useful to locate strategies along a time dimension of movement lifecycles. In this perspective movements start out from small numbers of conscience activists and progress to mass movements when cadres have the ability and desire to acquire and maintain a large following. Clearly many small groups behave in a non-instrumental fashion, since they have as yet no following. In a mature movement political instrumentality is a necessity, and the advantages of non-instrumentality are pursued through division of labors and separation of contexts, or else a price in effectiveness has to be paid. In this sense the emergence of post-materialist values might well have affected organizational choices, as new-movements theorists have argued. As many cadres have said, the peace movement could have had a greater political impact in many countries if more groups had tried to organize people in the society. It would be misleading, however, to exclude those that did not from the analysis, on the ground that they are not properly political. In Offe's terms "the actor makes some explicit claim that the means of action can be recognized as legitimate and the ends of action can become binding for the wider community" (Offe C. in Cohen J. 1985, p. 827). In this sense they are solidly in the political realm.

APPENDIX A

Organization: Non Instrumental / Instrumental

- Belief in individual / collective responsibility.
- Belief of negative / positive consequences of acting in large crowds
- Belief of negative / positive stratifying consequences of organizing (elitism)
- Belief of low / high motivation of organized groups
- Belief in low / high duration of organized activity
- Belief in (non-/legalism to solve controversies
- Belief in (non-)/legalism in decisionmaking
- Belief in consensus / majority in case of controversies

ACKNOWLEDGMENT

This project was supported by a predoctoral MacArthur grant.

NOTES

1. Strategy can be defined as a concern with the most efficient way of achieving goals, given specific resources.
2. For a discussion of the free rider problem in a perspective critical of rational actor models see Gross E., "The Rationality of Symbolic Actors," *The British Journal of Sociology*, v. 37, n. 2. Also Cohn 1982.
3. Rational actions are seen as those that involve a calculation of goals, and the benefits of various alternative means toward given goals.
4. Alain Tourain examines strategic questions. However he focuses on strategy because he wants to actively help the social movements which he studies, and not merely analyze them. The analytical focus is on identity. Conversely within resource mobilization theory there have been attempts to focus on meaning in the context of micromobilization. Actors' intentions, however, are not a focal concern.
5. The division between Catholics and non-Catholics is not salient in the political change cluster. See my analysis below to understand the absence of a Catholic political change movement.
6. I classified peace groups as follows:

- *Personal Change*
  Nonviolenti, Femministe Venete, Femministe Milanesi, La Ragnatela, Loc, Fiscal Objectors
- *Political Change*
  Arci, Democrazia Proletaria, Cudip, Radicali, Milano per la Pace, CGIL, CISL
- *Catholics*
  Cattolici di base di Verona, Cattolici di base di Como, Acli, Pax Christi, Mir

7. The priests were two parish priests who had supported and practiced objection to military tax, and three monks active in the peace movement. Catholic lay activists were from the Association of Christian Workers (ACLI).

8. Pagani is a worker in a weapon factory who protested and sued his boss because of weapon sales to South Africa.

9. At this point my research cannot indicate to what extent the social control issue and the division of labor issue contribute to the clergy's lack of instrumentality. Clearly from the interviews both components are present, but it would be misleading to attempt quantification since organizational loyalties clearly hinder the clergy's candor.

10. Thus the Nonviolents did not join the Peace Association because there is a hierarchy of resources. For those who care about community, it is not worthwhile to be lost in a multitude of uncommitted members in exchange for money from membership and a forum. However when money goes to local groups and does not carry with it other losses, they can act instrumentally.

11. In this study one can see a direct relation between these standards and the technical level of validation of the environment. However variations are possible. It would be impractical to have exacting standards for a movement whose goals are unverifiable, as it would be a losing approach not to have them when goals are clear. To cope with inappropriate collective identities organizations can define arbitrary goals and pursue them ceremonially. As an example of this, one could think of the extreme emphasis on the rational pursuit of organizational strategies matters by some new left groups of the seventies. There, a series of complex organizational strategies and complex bureaucratic structures had a largely ceremonial function in groups whose limited influence hindered real possibilities of effectiveness in the environment of the polity.

REFERENCES

Accame, F. 1984. *Pace e Sicurezza*. Milano: Franco Angeli.

Berger, S. 1982. *Religion in West European Politics*. London: Frank Cass Pub.

―――― 1987. "Religious Transformation and the Future of Politics," in Maier C., (ed.) *Changing Boundaries of the Political*. Cambridge, MA: Cambridge University Press.

Cassese, M. (ed.) 1987. *Religioni per la Pace*. Roma: Asal Pub.

Chiavacci, E. 1987. *Per una Teologia della Pace*. Roma: Borla.

Cohen, J. L. (ed.) 1985. "Strategy or Identity: New Theoretical Paradigms and Contemporary Social Movements" in *Social Research*. Vol. 52, N. 4.

Cooper, A. H. 1988. "'The West German Peace Movement and The Christian Churches: An Institutional Approach." *Review of Politics*. Vol. 50, No. 1, pp. 71-79.

Fierro, A. 1977. *The Militant Gospel*. New York: Orbis.

Habermas, J. 1984. (Transl.) *The Theory of Communicative Action*. Boston: Beacon Press.

Haes, R. 1972. *Pour une Theologie du Profetique*. Paris: Nauwelaerts.

Inglehart, R. 1988. *Generational Change and the Future of the Atlantic Alliance, PS, Summer 1984*.

Jenkins, J. C. 1983. "Resource Mobilization Theory and the Study of Social Movements." *American Review of Sociology* 9:527-553.

Kaltefleiter, W. and Pfaltzgraff, R. (ed.) 1985. *The Peace Movements in Europe and the United States*. London: Croom Helm.

Knoke, D. 1988. "Incentives in Collective Action Organizations." *American Sociological Review*, vol. 53, pp. 311-329.

Lodi, G. 1984. *Uniti e Diversi: Il Movimento per la pace in Italia, Milano.*
Martin, D. 1978. *A General Theory of Secularization.* New York: Harper and Row.
McCarthy, J. D. and M. N. Zald. 1983. "The Trend of Social Movements in America: Professionalization and Resource Mobilization.' General Learning Press.
————— 1982. "Resource Mobilization and Social Movements: A Partial Theory." *American Journal of Sociology* 6 1213-1241.
Melucci, A. (ed.) *Altri Codici.* Bologna: Il Mulino.
Meyer, J. W. and Scott, W. R. 1983. *Organizational Environments.* Beverly Hills, CA: Sage Pub.
Mion, R. 1986. *Per un Futuro di Pace.* Roma: Las Pub.
Opp. K. 1986. "Soft Incentives and Collective Action: Participation in the Antinulear Movement." *British Journal of Political Science* 16: 87-112.
Peachey, P. 1986. *Peace, Politics, and the People of God.* Philadelphia: Fortress Press.
Rochon, T.R. 1988. *Mobilizing for Peace.* Princeton, NJ: Princeton University Press.
Scott, R. W. 1987. "The Adolescence of Institutional Theory," in *Administrative Science Quarterly.* Vol. 32, pp. 493-511.
Tarrow, S. 1989. *Democracy and Disorder: Politics and Protest in Italy, 1965-1975.* Oxford: Clarendon.
Tilly, C. 1985. "Social Movements, Old and New," Working Papers, Center for Studies of Social Change, New School for Social Research, NY.
Weigel, G. 1987. *Tranquillitas Ordinis.* Oxford: Oxford University Press.

REBELS AND THEORISTS:
AN EXAMINATION OF PEASANT
UPRISINGS IN SOUTHERN PERU

Benjamin S. Orlove

INTRODUCTION

The final months of the year 1931 were troubled in the Peruvian province of Espinar, a region heavily involved in an expanding wool export economy. A group of men arrested an Indian peasant whose lands were claimed, with scanty legal justification, by a local estate-owner. They shot the peasant as he attempted to escape. A larger group of peasants soon massed at a hill named Molloccahua and killed two of the men. This event touched off violent clashes between landowners and peasants. Many peasants died in the police interventions that soon followed, and a number of landlords fled the region. These events resemble a rebellion that took place nearby ten years earlier, in which Indian peasants who protested the usurpation of communal grazing lands by estate-owners were attacked by government troops.

Research in Social Movements, Conflict and Change,
Volume 12, pages 139-187.
Copyright © 1990 by JAI Press Inc.
All rights of reproduction in any form reserved.
ISBN: 1-55938-065-9

The anthropologists and historians who study Latin America have noted other cases of similar associations between export economies and rural violence. Even the spatial remoteness and cultural distinctiveness of areas such as the Andean highlands are no longer presumed to isolate them from involvement in a world economy and its attendant social and political transformations. The broad consensus on these issues directs attention to other concerns. In examining the rebellions, how much weight should be placed on forces external to the region and how much on local conditions? Are the changes in Espinar best understood as one instance of a general process of proletarianization, or as a unique case reflecting many particular conditions? How directly are the rebellions linked to an export economy? Should the actions of individuals and groups be explained in terms of their objective interests or of their subjective perceptions?

The theme of economic and political change has attracted the attention of many social scientists, whose diverse approaches are difficult to categorize into a small number of discrete schools. To bring, or perhaps to impose, some order on this complex set of perspectives, I decided to focus on the works of a few specific authors. There was only one writer whose works were so appropriate in terms in topic and approach that they would not reasonably be excluded: the French historian Jean Piel, who discussed the 1921 Tocroyoc uprising in Espinar from a well-defined mode of production perspective (1967, 1983). I used several criteria in selecting other authors. In order to have some coverage of the broad intellectual terrain, I wanted them to be representative either of the same approach as Piel's or of a distinct one. In addition, they should offer coherent views, with both general theoretical statements and concrete empirical works, to permit an accurate depiction of their frameworks; they should not, however, adopt extreme or polemic positions, or restrict themselves to either theoretical or empirical works, since these limitations would lead to an overstatement, and therefore a weakening, of the contrast.

With these factors in mind, I selected two individuals, the British historian Eric Hobsbawm and the American anthropologist Eric Wolf. I was also influenced by the fact that they have both written about the Indian peasantries of Peru; I felt that I could speak with greater confidence about the explanations for the 1931 rebellion which might be offered by the approaches they represent. Hobsbawm has written on agrarian change for an area close to Espinar (1969) and elsewhere in Peru (1974); Wolf examines Andean Indian communities, including a brief discussion of rebellions, in *Europe and the People without History*, his study of the encounter between an expanding Europe and native societies (1982, pp. 145-149). I will take Hobsbawm as typifying the mode of production approach, which Piel also applies; Wolf represents the distinct, but related, political economy framework.

These writers advance plausible claims. Mode of production analysis has an immediate appeal for the Molloccahua rebellion. The fight over land can be seen as competition for control over productive forces. The timing of the events, soon after the economic collapse of 1929, suggests that they were linked to a major capitalist crisis. The state supported the dominant rather than the subjected class. The Molloccahua rebellion in Espinar can thus be viewed as a typical example of the consequences of capitalist expansion, strongly resembling cases of mobilization and repression of workers elsewhere in the world. An understanding of the capitalist mode of production would explain the timing and causation of the rebellion, and the composition of the opposed sides. As a more detailed examination of the rebellion will show, Wolf's political economy approach can also offer a reasonable account of the events; though recognizing the importance of conflicts stemming directly from market-oriented production, it would place greater emphasis on the local forms of economic, political and social organization and on ideological constructions of inequality.

THE TWO THEORETICAL APPROACHES

Mode of Production Approach

The general outlines of the mode of production perspective will be familiar to many readers: the notion that there are characteristic forms, called modes of production, in which human labor generates value; the composition of each mode by a base, in which forces and relations of production are located, and a superstructure of political and legal institutions and ideologies; the dynamism which emerges from the production of value and from contradictions between forces and relations of production, and between base and superstructure.[1] The specific details of the capitalist mode of production—changing composition of capital, overproduction, periodic crises, concentration of capital—are also well-known, as is the idea of the articulation of modes of production. Although current expositions of this view are less rigid than earlier ones, which held, for instance, to a universal sequence of modes of production, the adherents of this view still claim that the base determines the superstructure, and that concrete social formations illustrate the dynamics of modes of production. Hobsbawm (1965, 1971, 1984) offers an eloquent and undogmatic version of this approach.[2]

Hobsbawm's analysis (1969) of a rural economy in Peru illustrates the basic orientation of this approach. He discussed the hacienda system in La Convención from the first decades of this century through the early 1960s. This province was a remote lowland frontier area, whose agriculture included market crops, notably sugar cane, coca, coffee and cacao, and subsistence crops. Serf-like workers on large estates received wages well below market levels, and were tied to landowners by personal obligations. Accumulated tensions in this highly stratified area led to a major political conflicts in the 1960s. This case is germane, not only because it is so close to Molloccahua in time and space (La Convención and Espinar are both provinces of the Department of Cuzco), nor because it contains a large peasant movement, but because the theoretical perspective is so similar. Hobsbawm opts for explanations which rest exclusively on the mode of production approach:

> Though it may be tempting to explain the peculiar neo-feudalism of La Convención by the historic facts of the Spanish conquest, by the survivals of pre-Columbian forced labor, by the character of social relations between lords and dependent peasants, or in similar terms, there is no need for such explanations. It is perfectly possible to assume that (within a given framework of society) the development of this specific form of neo-feudal agriculture is a necessary consequence of the decision to undertake demesne cultivation under conditions of labour shortage and inadequate communications...La Convención allows us to observe the emergence of an agrarian system surprisingly similar to some of those of European feudalism...[I]t holds a final lesson for the student of capitalist development, though perhaps a familiar one. For it demonstrates once again that the very growth of the capitalist world market at certain stages produces, or reproduces, archaic forms of class-domination on the frontier of development (*ibid,* pp. 48-9).

Once again, he suggests, the forces of production determine the structure and trajectory of a system of social classes, despite his explicit warnings, offered in other works, against the mechanical application of simple schemes about the dynamic of capitalism (1971b). This determinism also influences Hobsbawm's views of politics and ideology. He adopts as a central theme and organizing principle of *Primitive Rebels* (a thoughtful and nuanced account of bandits, mafias, millenarians and other social movements) a strikingly simple, and class-based, distinction between reformist and revolutionary movements. "Reformists wish to create a society in which policemen will not be arbitrary and judges at the mercy of landlords and merchants; revolutionaries, though also in sympathy with these aims, a society in which there will be no policemen and judges in the present sense, let alone landlords and merchants" (1959, p. 11). (He appears certain that peasants cannot become revolutionaries because of their ownership of land and their distance from urban centers; for him, the central focus of Wolf's *Peasant Wars of the Twentieth Century*—"the idea of a *general* peasant movement"—to be "quite unrealistic" (1973, p. 11).) He examines "ritual in social movements" with great care (1959, pp. 150-174) but adheres throughout to a straightforward class analysis. His book *Inventing Tradition* (1983) documents that many cultural traditions, such as Scottish highland dress and British royal rituals, which are thought to be ancient, have in fact been invented quite recently; he presents as representative a number of instances in which he associates specific ideologies with particular class interests, and suggests that new ideologies were directly imposed to support elite domination.

The Political Economy Approach

Eric Wolf's books might appear to have a great deal in common with this mode of production approach. In *Europe and the People without History*, Wolf makes numerous references to Marx. The third chapter, which lays out his analytical framework, bears the simple title "Modes of Production." It consists primarily of Wolf's presentation of his own version of this concept, "a specific, historically occuring set of social relations through which labor is deployed to wrest energy from nature by means of tools, skills, organization and knowledge" (1982, p. 75). This discussion makes more explicit the view which is latent in his earlier works (1966a, 1969), that societies are characterized by segments and strata whose conflicts are linked to systems of production. There might be little internal evidence to suggest that Wolf would exclude himself from the mode of production approach. His treatment of his relation to the mode of production school occupies less than two pages; in this brief discussion, tucked away in the middle of his long section entitled "Bibliographic Notes," he registers intellectual debts and disagreements with roughly equal emphasis. The Marxist writers whom Wolf rejects most openly are Frank and Wallerstein, who themselves are not orthodox mode of production theorists. (Wolf criticizes their Eurocentric assumption that the forces of change, and the models for understanding that change, can be drived from an examination of European history; however, this rejection is potentially compatible with an emphasis on the articulation of modes of production.)

Nonetheless, Wolf differs fundamentally from writers such as Hobsbawm and Piel. Of primary importance is his unwillingness to reduce politics and ideology to economic roots—in other words, to subordinate the superstructure to the base. The concluding section of his theoretical chapter begins with the claim "our discussion should make it clear that the deployment of social labor has both an economic and a political dimension" (ibid, p. 99); this point is equally clear in the subsequent empirical chapters, which often accord political systems autonomy from economic bases. Similarly, Wolf explains differences in the outcomes of peasant-based revolution not only by economic differences between nations but also by variations in the nature of political parties and military institutions. The origins of these distinct patterns constitute a "question...which has no easy answer" (1969, p. 299) and presumably are not reducible in any simple fashion to economic conditions.

Wolf's treatment of ideology occupies a special place in the volume. It constitutes the main focus of his "Afterword." He sees these understandings of the natural and social order as stemming from underlying economic and political forces but, once established, as influencing them as well. Ideologies do not neatly correspond to social groups or classes, but rather have a more complex and active relation to patterns of alliance and conflict. He stated these ideas in earlier works as well: "the contact between the capitalist center, the metropolis, and the pre-capitalist or non-capitalist periphery is a large-scale cultural encounter, not merely an economic one" (1969, p. 278). As Wolf acknowledges (1982, p. 425), these views draw heavily from the works of Antonio Gramsci and Raymond Williams, writers who certainly are Marxists and just as certainly are not straightforward mode of production theorists.

Another difference is Wolf's insistence on a global scale of research and on the linking of local societies with this world order. Mode of production theorists would be unlikely to push global analysis as far back as Wolf does (he titled the second chapter "The World in 1400"), though they would agree with him that this period was pre-capitalist. Because they accord less distinctiveness and internal dynamism to local societies, they would also grant them less attention. Mode of production theorists tend to choose intermediate scale units—regions, nations or continents. Wolf's linkage of micro-level and macro-level phenomena, drawing on his earlier work on brokers (1966b), is distinct.

The term "political economy" seems an appropriate label for Wolf's approach, although he does not give this name, or any other one, to his framework. He does contrast the nineteenth-century study of political economy as a totality with the twentieth-century fragmentation of the different social sciences, approving of the former and lamenting the narrow reifications of the latter (ibid, pp. 7-19). He also uses the term in a descriptive sense (e.g., "the concept of mode of production calls attention to major variations in political-economic arrangements and allows us to visualize their effects" (ibid, p. 77).

In her review of trends in anthropology since the 1960s, Ortner (1984) uses the term "political economy" to refer to one of two Marxist schools, calling the other "structural Marxism." My distinctions resemble hers, but are somewhat different in part because she limits her review to anthropology. Her political economists draw on Marx, but also on the world-system theorists (Wallerstein, Frank) whom Wolf, and other writers such as Smith (1984), reject as too Eurocentric. Ortner also views the research of the political economists as having "taken the form of studying the effects of capitalist penetration" (*ibid*, p. 141); the group whom I label with the same term examines the interactions between capitalism and other systems. I would disagree with her claim that "the political economists... tend to situate themselves more on the ship of (capitalist) history that on the shore" (*ibid*, p. 143); the political economists, as I identify them, tend to emphasize that both Europeans and non-Europeans are in motion, rather than just one, and that their journeys are closely connected. I think that Ortner and I use the terms "structural Marxism" in the same way. Although there is considerable overlap between mode of production theorists and structural Marxists, the terms are not identical. Some structural Marxists such as Nicos Poulantzas are quite removed from the basic examination of modes of production; other modes of production theorists, such as Hobsbawm, do not engage in the formal abstractions of structural Marxists.

Two Comparisons of the Approaches

It would be possible to construct a reading of the mode of production and political economy approaches which would present them as similar. One could see them as cousins in an intellectual genealogy. They share strong family resemblances, both in specific traits (the use of terms such as "class") and in a more general character (the reliance on historical materialism). Their frequent squabbles, at times amiable, at times ill-tempered, over petty issues like explanations "in the last instance," do not prevent them from quickly joining ranks in an united front when faced with challenges from more distant kin or strangers. In conversation they often turn to the recollection of the family history, which they both consider illustrious. Troubled that they do not receive the admiration due them for their noble lineage, they discuss the significance of the many actions of their famous grandfather, and seek to find the clearest embodiment of his heritage in the tangled events of their parents' generation.

This article, however, proposes a second reading, in which the two approaches are quite different. At this point, the difference will be presented in terms that are both schematic and analytical; it will also be reviewed in a later section in more detail and in reference to the empirical cases of the rebellions. Phrased in simplest terms, this reading views the two as fundamentally disagreeing about the reducibility of political and ideological forces to economic ones; it understands the mode of production approach to be an instance of determinism, and the political economy approach to be a case of holism. The determinism of the former lies in its emphasis on the economic base, which shapes superstructures of political and ideological elements; in an ultimate sense, these elements do not play an autonomous role in history. The holism of the latter [3] sees politics and ideology as linked to economic forces, but as retaining some independence from these forces. The mode of production approach presents strong causal explanations in simple terms; the political economy approach offers weaker ones in more complex terms.

This difference can be expressed at both a macro-level scale of societal change and at a micro-level scale of individual action. The mode of production approach views the economic base as the underlying motor of history. The economic vitality of capitalism allows it to overwhelm the other modes of production which it meets in its expansion. With their less unitary view of causality, political economists see the outcomes of these encounters as more diverse and less easy to predict. In part because political economists have several dimensions along which to classify societies, they pay more attention to the specific units of analysis, whether region, nation or world-system.

To explain individual action, mode of production analysis move from the economic base, first to a view of society as composed of classes, then to a discussion of class interests, and finally to a examination of individual action in relation to these interests. Political economists typically have a less deterministic view of action. They begin with several sorts of forces, and therefore several groupings of individuals, which need not overlap neatly. The greater complexity of social structure makes the interests of each grouping less evident.

At first glance, it is difficult to decide which of these two approaches offers the most promise in analyzing the peasant rebellions in highland Peru. Both have had some notably successful applications in the general study of economic systems and political movements and in the more specific realm of peasant revolts. Turning to the writings of major representatives, books such as Hobsbawm's *Primitive Rebels* (1959), *Labouring Men* (1964) and *Industry and Empire* (1968) and Wolf's *Peasants* (1966a) and *Peasant Wars of the Twentieth Century* (1969) are widely acknowledged as classics. More recent works, *Inventing Tradition* (Hobsbawm and Ranger 1983) and *Europe and the People without History* (Wolf 1982), have also drawn considerable acclaim.

This article compares the approaches in two ways. The first contrast focuses on three aspects of the rebellions: their timing, the composition of the opposed forces, and the nature of the precipitating or antecedent factors which led them to take place. The second contrast examines the differences in the frameworks. Like other deterministic theories, the mode of production approach makes claims which are reductionistic, in that they seek to explain events through the operation of simple factors. Like other holistic theories, the political economy perspective makes claims which are interactional, in that their explanations involve combinations of multiple factors. The second contrast entails a judgment of the relative plausability of two sets of claims: those of the mode of production analysts to reduce some factors to others, and those of the political economists to combine factors. Both contrasts favor the political economy approach, though not without certain important reservations.

THE CONTEXT OF THE REBELLIONS

A judgment on the relative strength of mode of production and political economy approaches rests not only on their ability to account for the events of the two rebellions, but also on their effectiveness in locating them in the context of systems of production and the state. This section of the article contains summaries of local systems of production, of the links of these systems to the world-economy through wool exports, and of the connections between local society and the Peruvian state.

Agropastoral Production

Somewhat simplifying a complex pattern of land tenure, the province of Espinar between the nineteenth century and the 1969 agrarian reform can be divided into two sorts of units: communities of *comuneros* or freeholding peasants, and haciendas or estates owned by landlords known as *hacendados*. The permanent work force on the haciendas was composed of workers called peons. The comuneros and peons will be referred to both as peasants and as herders (Orlove 1977a). Although there were differences of wealth within each category, and the hacendados owned more property than the herders, virtually no herder was without land or animals.

The province of Espinar offers a harsh and unpromising environment to the people who inhabit it (see Figure 1). Its high elevation (3900 to 5200 meters above sea level) brings frequent severe frosts. The low annual rainfall is concentrated in the period from November to March. Herding of sheep, alpacas and cattle was and continues to be the most important productive activity, complemented by some agriculture and mining. During the rainy

Figure 1.

season, natural pasture is abundant, but in dry months the animals must go to the *bofedales*, where permanent water sources maintain vegetation for grazing. Herd-owners had to have access to land both in the bofedales and in the lower areas. Other aspects of herding also followed seasonal rhythms. Major activities (shearing, the slaughter of old animals, meat preservation) were limited to brief periods of the year; the herd-owners consequently required large work teams to perform these activities in a short period. This seasonality of labor demand meant that herd-owners needed both to assure a steady supply of labor throughout the year and to obtain additional hands in certain periods.

Comunero households obtained rights to pasture and agricultural plots by inheritance. Their membership in corporate groups, whether peasant communities or small kin groups, assured them lands on which to grow crops and to graze their animals, which were owned by individuals. Corporate access to pasture and the tendency of herds to increase compensated in part for some inequalities in wealth and landholdings among comunero households.

The organization of haciendas was somewhat more complex. Most haciendas had a small group of resident families of peons who cared for hacienda flocks and received rights to graze their own animals (*Waqchu*) on hacienda land. They raised some crops, retaining a part of the harvest for their own consumption and giving some to the hacendado. The hacendado would give peons occasional gratuities, but there was no regular form of payment. Some peon families lived on the haciendas for generations, but it was more frequent for comuneros to work on haciendas for shorter periods. Relatively poor comuneros would take such positions, transferring the increase in their herds to community pastures and leaving the haciendas when they had accumulated a sizeable herd of their own.

These peons performed the routine herding tasks on the hacienda and organized work teams through reciprocal labor exchange. Hacendados formed the large work groups by several other means. In some cases they hired comuneros as day workers, giving them wool, agricultural produce or occasionally cash. Others granted comuneros the right to use bofedales on the haciendas during the dry seasons in exchange for a cash rental and a labor contribution in these large work groups.

Hacendados controlled peasant labor not only because they dominated access to land, especially the bofedales, but also because they held the positions of political authority in the district[4] capitals, such as justice of peace and governor. Hacendados could charge a comunero with invasion of their property, alleging that the peasant had permitted his animals to stray onto hacienda land, and then confiscate the offending animal. Restitution would be made by working on the hacienda at a fixed daily wage to pay off a fine; both the fine and the wage were set by the authorities. In a strikingly similar fashion, an hacendado could seize a waqchu animal belonging to a peon, claiming it as compensation for damages due to willful negligence. Peasants were unable to register complaints against this and other practices, such as beatings or the extraction of unpaid labor.

Hence the relations of production of the comuneros and peons were more similar than the apparent difference between communities and haciendas, peasant subsistence and contract labor, might lead one to expect. Common features include the timing and location of productive activities, the technology, and the use of reciprocal forms of labor exchange. Both sets of individuals had direct experiences of work on the haciendas, and there was a movement of individuals between the two categories. In addition, the peasants, whether peons or comuneros, had certain labor obligations to the mestizo families resident in the small villages that were district capitals and in the provincial capital of Yauri. These duties included some domestic labor, house construction, and the maintenance of streets and plazas.

Wool Exports

A number of recent studies examine the expansion of wool exports from southern Peru in the nineteenth and twentieth centuries (Burga and Reátegui 1981; Appleby 1977; Jacobsen 1978, 1982, 1983, 1988; Bertram 1977; Orlove 1977b; Miller 1982a). Despite regional variations and differences in interpretation, some general features are clear.

British-based wool export firms were established in southern Peru in the nineteenth century. Table 1 indicates the volume and value of wool exports from the major southern Peruvian ports. In Espinar and other provinces, these firms purchased wool, often in return for credit, from local merchants. The growing demand for wool during the first decades of the twentieth century led to considerable competition for land and grazing rights. Despite the influx of commercial capital, though, there was relatively little investment in technological improvements. Capital improvements in herding were difficult to make in Espinar, as in many other parts of the southern highlands, because of the nature of production and the lack of credit facilities to herd-owners. Several individuals had grazing rights to any particular section of pasture. Hacienda and waqchu herds used hacienda land, while flocks belonging to different comuneros grazed on village pasture. This multiple access, which comuneros and peons staunchly defended, greatly reduced the profitability of any capital investment, discouraging the introduction of purebred animals and the attempts to

Table 1.   Wool Export Statistics for Southern Peru, 1897-1931

	Sheep Wool			Alpaca Wool			Total Wool	
Year	Volume in metric tons	Price in pence/kg	Value in pounds sterling	Volume in metric tons	Price in pence/kg	Value in pounds sterling	Volume in metric tons	Value in pounds sterling
1897	1,281	15.0	80.090	2.068	25.8	222,360	3,349	302,540
1898	993	15.4	63,710	2,087	25.1	218,304	3,080	282,014
1899	1,114	16.5	76,601	2,459	25.8	264,346	3,573	340,947
1900	1,203	17.0	85,224	2,168	25.8	233,086	3,371	318,310
1901	946	16.3	64,218	2,088	25.8	224,495	3,034	288,713
1902	939	15.9	62,209	2,453	27.3	279,040	3,392	341,249
1903	1,252	17.2	89,727	2,687	30.0	335,875	3,939	425,602
1904	1,363	19.0	107,904	2,034	29.5	250,012	3,397	357,916
1905	1,587	22.9	151,426	2,649	26.9	296,909	4,236	448,335
1906	1,266	22.3	117,632	2,544	27.6	292,560	3,810	410,192
1907	963	22.9	91,886	2,382	28.4	281,870	3,345	373,756
1908	915	21.6	82,350	1,944	31.5	255,150	2,859	337,500
1909	1,067	20.9	92,929	2,236	28.9	269,288	3,303	362,217
1910	1,370	22.5	128,415	2,059	29.1	249,654	3,429	378,069
1911	2,049	21.2	180,995	1,655	28.7	197,910	3,704	378,905
1912	983	22.5	92,156	2,448	25.6	261,120	3,431	352,376
1913	1,207	21.2	106,618	2,483	28.2	291,778	3,690	398,396
1914	1,681	24.9	174,435	2,413	27.8	279,457	4,094	453,892
1915	1905	26.9	213,569	2,807	32.2	376,655	4,712	590,224
1916	1,833	34.2	261,148	2,729	35.7	405,969	4,562	667,117
1017	2,561	51.1	545,178	2,747	48.5	555,118	5,308	1,100,296
1918	2,117	79.4	200,523	2,921	112.4	1,367,974	5,038	2,068,497
1919	1,929	70.1	563,655	2,040	94.1	799,746	3,969	1,363,401
1920	1,200	39.7	198,500	1,600	48.5	323,333	2,800	521,833
1921	577	19.8	47,868	1,061	39.7	175,446	1,638	223,014
1922	1,293	29.8	160,501	2,694	41.9	470,269	3,987	630,770
1923	1,975	30.9	254,285	2,672	38.6	429,771	4,647	684,056
1924	2,197	48.5	443,890	3,211	50.7	678,299	5,408	1,122,189
1925	1,434	33.1	197,779	2,349	37.5	367,105	3,783	564,884
1926	1,304	30.9	167,953	2,130	33.6	298,155	3,434	466,108
1927	1,605	35.3	236,090	2,615	41.9	456,553	4,220	692,643
1928	2,123	39..7	351,106	2,425	55.1	556,608	4,548	907,774
1929	1,197	35.3	176,007	2,708	65.0	733,357	3,905	909,364
1930	521	19.8	42,999	2,042	41.9	356,457	2,563	399,456
1931	1,133	17.7	83,304	2,111	30.9	271,788	3,244	355,092

Source: Jacobsen, 1982:824-825, 829-830.

Note: These figures represent exports from the major ports of Islay and Mollendo. These ports account
   for virtually all the wool exported from the department of Cuzco, in which Espinar is located.

increase the yield per animal through the use of veterinary medicine. The
artificial sowing of higher-yield fodder crops was also hindered by the

impossibility of fencing. However, some modest capital investments were made. A few hacendados introduced improved breeds of sheep, purchased medicine to eliminate parasites, or planted barley for the consumption of the animals. There were restrictions on the labor intensity as well as the capital intensity of production. Increases in labor would not generate higher yields, because of diminishing marginal returns of labor inputs and the seasonal bottlenecks of labor supply. Beyond a certain point, the addition of labor would not reduce the loss of animals due to predation and mortality, nor would it increase the amount of wool shorn from the animals at the beginning of the rainy season.

Since increased inputs of labor would not greatly raise productivity and inputs of capital were also problematic, the efforts of producers to raise their incomes led directly to attempts to increase the size of their herds, and therefore of the amount of the land to which they had access. This situation led to competition between many producers. Although some comuneros disputed inheritance claims and community boundaries, the intense conflicts tended to take place between haciendas and communities and between hacendados and peons. Although the rights of individual comuneros to land rested on their membership in kin groups and communities, individuals could sell their shares. Thus an individual who shared a bofedal with two siblings and seven cousins could receive a cash payment for his or her one-tenth of the grazing rights. Women who married into distant communities often received such payments (in cash, animals or other goods) from their kin. When hacendados obtained such shares in a set of lands, they sought, often with success, to drive out the other share-holders from part or all of the lands.

In many cases these sales were fraudulent, particularly since hacendados and officials spoke Spanish and the comuneros spoke Quechua. Some hacendados took land by force, in one case using armed men on horseback to drive peasants off their lands, but such instances were infrequent. Hacendados more often sought to acquire documented title of land. Within the haciendas, the hacendados tried to reduce the size of the waqchu flocks belonging to their peons, so that they could graze more of their own animals on the lands.

Political Processes and Events

Shifting our attention to national politics, we may begin our account by noting that military governments in nineteenth-century Peru were discredited by the Chilean defeat of Peru in the War of the Pacific (1879-1883) and by the disorder of subsequent regimes headed by military figures.

A constitutional government later developed; the period 1895 to 1919 is often called the "aristocratic republic," because of the limited size of the electorate which chose governments from a small number of conservative parties. Exports, particularly sugar, cotton, wool, rubber, copper and petroleum, grew during this period (Thorp and Bertram 1978). These governments were increasingly prone to factional and regional rivalries among the elites and to conflicts between the president and branches of congress (Miller 1982b). The newly emerging labor movements, divided among several tendencies, did not offer a serious challenge to the aristocratic republic, although they made several successful demands, most importantly for the 8-hour day (Blanchard 1982).

The creation of new administrative units was a common practice at the time. Since each province sent a deputy to congress, influential departments could increase their power by having new provinces formed. Dominant political parties could reinforce their control by creating new provinces where they had followers, thus increasing the size of their delegation in the Chamber of Deputies. This process also distributed government revenues into the interior and reinforced the influence of local elites. In one such case, the districts which make up the province of Espinar were separated from the province of Canas, to which they formerly belonged, in 1917, under the sponsorship of an hacendado who represented the department of Cuzco in the national senate. Yauri, the new provincial capital, gained a subprefecture and a court; it also attracted a notary public. Its status as a provincial capital allowed its residents to make additional claims on unpaid peasant labor, particularly for construction purposes.

Leguía, who had been president from 1908 to 1912, ran as an independent progressive candidate in 1919 with broad support. Fearing that he would not be allowed to assume office, he took power in a coup soon after the elections, dissolved congress, and established a strong rule partly on the basis of, and partly in violation of, his new constitution, promulgated in 1920. His rule from 1919 to 1930 is known as the *oncenio*. Cotler described it as the time of "consolidation of imperialist domination and emergence of popular anti-oligarchic forces" (1978, p. 185). Exports and foreign loans increased dramatically, giving the state resources to use to consolidate its control, but also requiring new forms of support from it. Leguía encouraged exports through fiscal and monetary policies, through the expansion of infrastructure, and through political reinforcement of export-linked groups. The manipulation, cooptation and repression of the new political forces remained possible throughout the prosperous 1920s. Leguía soon turned against the students and workers who formed part of his political base in 1919, and relied on support from other sectors.

The growth of cities, factories and plantations during the oncenio expanded the basis for left-wing movements. Political mobilization was also stimulated by student movements throughout Latin America and by the examples of the Russian and Mexican Revolutions. Two major political leaders emerged during the 1920s, Haya de la Torre and Mariátegui. They initially cooperated during the heady years of organization. The definitive break between the two men and their movements did not come until 1928, quite late in the oncenio. This fact is often forgotten, since subsequent Peruvian history has been marked by the rivalry between the parties which they founded (APRA in 1924 and the Peruvian Socialist Party in 1928, which was renamed the Communist Party in 1930 only after Mariátegui's death) and since the factors that led to the split, particularly Haya de la Torre's reformism and Mariátegui's commitment to Marxist thought, can be seen throughout the 1920s. These two parties were strong in student and worker organizations and pro-Indian movements in Cuzco during the 1920s; their members often collaborated, and showed some independence from their national leadership (Aranda and Escalante 1978). The shortness of the gap between 1928 and 1931 is of some importance to an understanding of the Molloccahua uprising.

Several specific programs and events of the oncenio influenced the province of Espinar. These include the imposition of corvée labor for roadbuilding, the reorganization of the police force, and changes in the status of Indian communities.

The *Ley de Conscripción Vial* or road-building act was promulgated in 1920, and formed part of Leguía's expansion of infrastructure. It required adult males between the ages of eighteen and sixty to work for six to twelve days each year without pay to build and maintain roads; those who failed to comply were fined. The law, administered on the provincial level, was put to private ends in a number of cases. In Espinar, the local hacendados dominated the *Junta Vial* which administered the act. They ordered the building of roads to connect their haciendas with Yauri. Comuneros and peons, unable to pay the fine, worked on the road gangs. The Junta Vial took advantage of existing infrastructure, including the principal roads linking the province with regional markets and the railroad, and four sturdy colonial bridges spanning the swollen rivers in the rainy season, relics of an earlier period when Espinar supplied labor, animals and other goods to distant silver mines.

The *Guardia Civil* or police force was founded in 1922. The new police force received more funds and training than the older and less effective gendarmeries. In Espinar, the police were all based in a single station in Yauri. They helped enforce the Ley de Conscripción Vial and often sided with the hacendados in claims against the comuneros and peons.

Indigenismo, a movement which sought to redress the injustices done to the highland Indian peasantry, appeared in the late nineteenth century and grew in the period 1910-1920. It drew support from left-wing intellectuals and professionals in departments with large indigenous populations such as Cuzco, as well as from Lima and other urban areas with smaller indigenous populations. It suggested that forms of inequality had not changed greatly since the time of Spanish rule, and indigenismo was often linked with more general populist, reformist and radical critiques of Peruvian social structure and politics.

In his attempts to achieve broad political support, Leguía made several concessions to the indigenistas. The most important one was the provision in the 1920 constitution which permitted official recognition of Indian communities (*comunidades indígenas*). Under this law, groups of families could collectively register their lands, which then could not be sold or mortgaged to outsiders. Such registration only began in 1926. By 1930, Espinar contained nearly 10 percent of all the officially recognized communities in Peru (see Table 2). Peasants also used another institution created by Leguía, the Guardianship of the Indian Race (*Patronato de la Raza Indígena*) to register complaints of abuses by officials and hacendados (Kapsoli and Reátegui 1972, p. 29).

Another major event was the *Congreso Indígena* (Indian Congress) held in Yauri in 1930 with about fifty delegates from different areas in the province. The Patronato de la Raza Indígena granted it official recognition. The Indian Congress wanted to promote schools in the communities, following the early experiment in the hamlet of Huayhuahuasi in the northern portion of the province. Such schools had been established in the neighboring department of Puno (Hazen 1974).

THE FIRST REBELLION: TOCROYOC 1921

Before turning to the Molloccahua uprising in detail, this paper examines a rebellion which took place ten years before in the same province. The two events show interesting similarities. Furthermore, Piel (1967) analyzed that earlier uprising through the mode of production framework, allowing a comparison of that perspective with a political economy approach.

The Tocroyoc Uprising

Piel's account of the Tocroyoc rebellion emphasizes the activities of Domingo Huarca, the *personero* or head of the community of Tocroyoc,

Table 2. Date of Official Recognition of Communities, 1926-1932

Year	Espinar	Rest of Cuzco	Cuzco Total	Rest of Peru	Peru Total
1926	6	34	40	18	58
1927	0	33	33	21	54
1928	18	25	43	55	98
1929	7	27	34	47	81
1930	0	3	3	28	31
1931	0	0	0	23	23
1932	0	0	0	11	11

Source: *Directorio de Comunidades Campesinas.* Lima: Sistema Nacional de Apoyo a la Mobilización Social, Oficina Nacional de Apoyo a la Mobilización Social, Dirección de Apoyo a Empresas, 1974.

in the district of Ocoruro. Having attended elementary school and served in the army, he could speak Spanish as well as Quechua. He petitioned the central government in the name of the community to recover lands which had belonged to his community but were now controlled by hacendados. In addition, he sought permission to have a weekly market established in Tocroyoc to supplement the one in Ocoruro. He thus wished to end the administrative and commercial domination of the district capital of Ocoruro as well as the control of the grazing lands by the hacendados.

The central government delayed in replying to his results. Displeased by the initiative of the peasants, the regional authorities forbade public assemblies in the area. Nonetheless, the peasants gathered in remote places. After a certain period of these meetings, the comuneros from a number of communities, including Molloccahua, invaded the village of Ocoruro and demonstrated in its streets. They drove away the petty officials and hacendados who previously held power. Peasants began to graze their animals on the hacendados' pasturelands and established a weekly market in the village of Tocroyoc. They ceased providing unpaid labor in the district capitals and in Yauri. Several weeks later, hacendados and other men from Yauri, with some government reinforcements from Cuzco, attacked Tocroyoc on a market day. The peasants, armed with slings, were no match for the mounted troops with their firearms. The rebels were dispersed, ending the uprising. Domingo Huarca was captured and killed, his body left exposed for months on the roof of the church in Ocoruro. Frightened by the possibility of further uprisings, the hacendados in the southern part of the province virtually halted the expansion of their estates.

The Mode of Production Analysis

Piel applies mode of production analysis in his discussion of the Tocroyoc uprising. Although he occasionally includes other sorts of explanation,[5] he tends to explain historical change in terms of the internal development of a system of different modes of production. In discussing the consequences of declining wool exports immediately after World War I throughout highland Peru, he states:

> Above all, everything depends on the essential modes of pastoral production: the *large capitalized estate* which is modernized; the *large archaic estate* which draws its living from a precapitalist rent which the tenants provide in the form of unpaid labor and goods; the *rural communities* of Spanish and pre-Columbian traditions, which were called "Indian communities," having free access to collectively owned pasture lands. (1967, p. 391; emphasis in the original, my translation)

Piel thus views the study of the highlands as the study of the articulation of three modes of production in a predominantly capitalist economy. The other two modes of production are dominated by capitalist production for several reasons. In some cases, precapitalist units of production have been replaced by capitalist units of production; in other cases, precapitalist landlords seek to convert themselves into capitalist ones (*ibid*, p. 394). Comuneros can potentially become bourgeois (*ibid*, p. 400). Finally, precapitalist producers support the capitalist mode of production by the cash sale of their wool. In these ways precapitalist modes of production are articulated with the dominant capitalist mode of production through their economic bases. Since the archaic estates and communities are not yet fully capitalist themselves, they are particularly vulnerable to economic fluctuations; capitalist units of production have greater reserves on which to draw. In a recent work, Piel extends this analysis to a number of regions in Peru (1983).

Piel's general analysis of capitalism reveals internal contradictions between the forces and relations of production which bring cyclical crises. A rebellion would be a general expression of these crises. Concrete details of the rebellion—its timing, the composition of opposing forces, the antecedents—can also be explained. According to Piel, the timing of the Tocroyoc rebellion coincided with the cyclical crises that occur in capitalism.

The general capitalist crisis which occurred after World War I (*ibid*, p. 394), led to declining wool exports after 1918, to a major crisis in 1920, and to the rebellion in 1921. The composition of the rebellion also emerges from the base rather than the superstructure. The relations of production divide individuals into social classes. Since capitalism had only incompletely penetrated the Peruvian economy, capitalist units of production co-existed with pre-capitalist ones. Because the former were more productive and more fully articulated with markets, they were less prone to suffer from the effects of crisis; the workers on capitalized estates constituted a sort of rural labor aristocracy, partially sheltered from the impact of crises. The groups most severely affected by the crisis were engaged in modes of production dominated by capitalism. Piel describes regions with large capitalized estates in this period, such as the central Peruvian highlands, as zones of "relative social calm" (1967, p. 362), in contrast to the areas of the rebellions, where capitalism was articulated with precapitalist modes of production. It was the laborers in the precapitalist modes of production—the peons and the comuneros—who rebelled, and they chose as their target their immediate exploiters, the hacendados. The rebellion was precipitated by conflicts over the control of the forces of production which remained latent during times of prosperity but emerged during crises. The disputes centered around control of land, of labor, and of the products of labor. The rebels sought to recover their lands, to end unpaid labor in the towns, and to have direct access to sale of their wool through the opening of a market in Tocroyoc.

THE MOLLOCCAHUA REBELLION

On 12 September 1931, five men on horseback rode out of Yauri (see Figure 2). Three of them, Monzón, Torres and Zanabria, were policemen from outside the area who were stationed in Yauri. The other two were from the province—Alberto Meza, acting governor of the district of Yauri, and Genaro Flores Meza, his cousin, who owned several haciendas in the area. The Flores family had made extensive use of the corvée labor to have roads built to their haciendas at Accocunca, Islaycocha and Santa Sofía, reaching the former in 1925 and the others soon after. Accocunca, with a good location near a road, was founded by the Flores family around 1914, and began to expand in 1927, when members of the family improved the square in the hamlet and sold plots of land around it. They had their peons build houses. There was also a weekly market at the hamlet. The Flores family was sufficiently powerful to meet the opposition of the hacendados in Pichigua, who did not want the competition for the market that met in that district. The prominence of the Flores family was furthered by the relative importance of the hamlet, which, despite its small size of a dozen or so houses, contained a chapel, a schoolhouse (opened in the late 1920s), and several administrative offices, such as a justice of the peace court and a civil registry, which all accompanied its status as an annex of the district of Pichigua. If the Flores family's hopes that Accocunca would become an autonomous district, to be named Alto Pichigua, had been fulfilled, their power on the local scene would have become still greater.

Olivares, the subprefect of the province of Espinar, had issued an order to the three policemen to arrest a peasant, Domingo Tarifa. The police were also looking in the same area for several other men, accused of stealing hacienda livestock, who had eluded capture on previous occasions; in addition they thought that seditious meetings might have been taking place. Genaro Flores stated that he had paid Tarifa for some land, but that Tarifa refused to turn it over to him. The notarial records in Yauri, which are complete for the preceding decade, contain no reference to the sale, although they register the sale, on 2 August 1928, of Guillca-Mayo, a plot of about 11 hectares of pasture owned jointly by Domingo Tarifa and his sister Lucía, to a cousin of Genaro Flores', Antolín Flores Macedo,[6] at which time Guillca-Mayo was surrounded on several sides by other properties of Antolín Flores Macedo.[7] The three-year delay and the differences in parties make it doubtful that this sale was the only basis of the charge. It is possible, though unlikely, that Genaro Flores bought either another plot from Tarifa or Guillca-Mayo from his cousin, but that he either failed to notarize the sale or notarized it in a more distant town. It is more likely that Genaro Flores' charge against Tarifa was based on other grounds—a verbal agreement, perhaps, or a dispute over livestock; he may simply have tried to exercise force without legal backing.

The five men rode down from the hills on which Yauri was located, crossed the Río Salado, and began to ascend the gradually sloping plains. They stopped in Accocunca to drink. Setting off again in the afternoon, they found Tarifa on his land with his wife. They shot Tarifa as he attempted to escape; he ran a short distance and died. Flores and Meza returned immediately to Yauri. The three policemen loaded his body on a horse and began the trip back to Yauri, where they intended to offer a report on their activities.

Tarifa's widow ran to the nearby community of Molloccahua and told several peasants what had happened. They agreed that the body should be returned to Tarifa's kin for burial. A group of peasants gathered on a sizeable hill close by, at the site of the pre-Columbian fortress of Molloccahua.[8] The policemen had made arrests in the community earlier in the year, and the peasants recognized them. The peasants ambushed them and made their

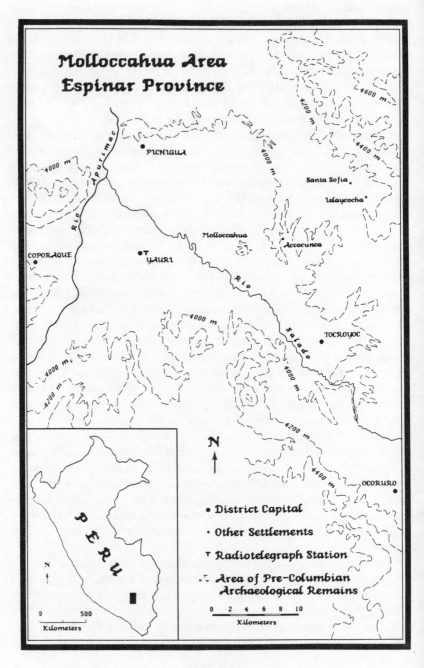

Figure 2.

horses rear. Only Monzón succeeded in escaping. A well-aimed shot from a sling killed Zanabria. The peasants captured Torres and beat him. Several men in the crowd, familiar with firearms from having served in the army, took the rifles and shot him. Both corpses were severely mutilated.

Monzón's story filled Yauri with panic. The inhabitants remembered the rebellion ten years earlier in Tocroyoc and the others that had occurred in intervening years in the adjcant department of Puno. Word of the killing of the police spread quickly around the province. The hacendados fled to Yauri, fearing that hordes of rebels would kill them if they stayed in the countryside. Even in town they were vulnerable, since only two policemen remained there..

On 13 September, the next day, the subprefect Olivares called a general meeting in the house of another relative, Flavio Meza, and organized the townspeople into a sort of militia. He collected the weapons in town and gave them to the young men, who took turns patrolling the streets at night. They also raided several houses to break up gatherings which they considered to be suspicious. Other men kept watch from the church tower, which had a good view of the surrounding countryside. They expected a mass of enraged Indians to attack the town. Many women spent the nights, not in their homes, but in the greater security of the church. The townspeople accused Francisco Arbuez Alvarez, the one landlord in the province who did not join them in their flight to town, of being a communist. He was virtually ostracized by other hacendados and by his family, although they later publicly apologized to him.[9] The parish priest, Hinojosa, gave strong support to Olivares in his mobilization of the town. He celebrated daily masses and permitted the church to be used as a meeting place. His sermons helped to rally support for the subprefect.

Olivares began a series of desperate telegrams to authorities on 12 September, immediately after Monzón returned. In his first message,[10] he requested the Minister of the Interior in Lima to provide troops and to order the subprefects of neighboring provinces to send men and weapons. He referred to the peasants as communists. Groups of civilians led by police officers, began arriving from neighboring provinces soon after. Thirty came from Chumbivilcas on 15 September, followed by thirty more from Ayaviri the following day and another group the day after from Sicuani. The residents of Yauri quartered them in their houses. The Ayaviri branch of the British commercial firm Gibson sent a truck with ammunition and other supplies.

There appears to have been little activity in the countryside at this time. Since Yauri had a radiotelegraph station, the rebels could not interrupt communications by cutting the lines. The messengers and trucks traveled with no threat of violence, possibly because several peasants kept Olivares informed of rebel plans, and possibly because the peasants did not anticipate the level of the reaction. Olivares' telegram mentioned a crowd of over one-thousand at the ruins of Molloccahua,[11] but his statements are likely to have exaggerated the situation greatly in order to gain rapid support from other provinces.

On 18 September the Yauri police and a number of local townspeople, reinforced by the groups from neighboring provinces, attacked the community of Molloccahua. They took several dozen prisoners and set fire to the pastures. The rains had ended in Espinar before May, and the grass was extremely dry. One peasant described to me how he fled across a gully to a point upwind of the ruins, from which he saw the houses and pasture burn. Over one-hundred of his kin and neighbors were roasted alive in the flames.

The townspeople located the bodies of Torres and Zanabria near the ruins. A widely-attended wake was held in the police station. The story that the policemen had been stripped of their clothes and forced to walk naked might be a result of Monzón's story or of popular imagination. Published descriptions[12] and the oral testimony of witnesses, however, coincide in a more reliable image of the two corpses: the eyes gouged out, the foreheads, noses, lips and genitals mutilated, gaping holes of charred flesh in the abdomens. A large crowd attended a service, at which the priest gave an impassioned sermon. The bodies were transported to Cuzco and were buried with military honors.

The conflagration of Molloccahua did not end the violence. Travelling in small groups, hacendados and townspeople raided peasant settlements throughout the province. They claimed that they were searching for communist agitators and for peasant rebels. A number of old disputes were settled in this fashion. These attacks were most common in the districts of Yauri, Coporaque, Pichigua and Ocoruro. About a hundred peasants were imprisoned and detained without food, in some cases for many days. Since the Yauri jail was so crowded, the Gibson agency at Ayaviri again lent its truck to transport prisoners to Cuzco. Peasants began to respond by thefts of hacienda animals and attacks on townspeople.

The local hacendado population remained in Yauri and the district capitals; they were afraid to return to the countryside. Groups of peasants continued to meet in the ruins of Molloccahua through remaining weeks of September and in October. Peasants started to graze their animals and to build houses on what had previously been hacienda land. The police became more cautious, travelling only in groups. Sporadic fighting continued in Espinar and in the neighboring province of Canas, where disturbances broke out in Langui and Layo on 20 November. Some hacendado families abandoned the province; others returned to their haciendas in time for the annual shearing. However, many of them lost control of some of their land to comuneros, or were less able to restrict the waqchu herds of their peons. Though tensions persisted in the countryside, there was little or no open violence by 1932.

Explanations of the Molloccahua Uprising

Hobsbawm's study of peasant land occupations in the central Peruvian highlands (1974) provides the best source for a mode of production account of the Molloccahua uprising, because he discusses invasions of haciendas which took place in the same year in the province of Huancayo, department of Junín. This region was quite similar to Espinar in ecological and economic terms, although the haciendas were larger and more capitalized. (In this article, Hobsbawm devotes more attention to the land invasions of the 1960s, which occurred in Cuzco as well as Junín, but he correctly notes that conditions in both departments were very different at that time than they had been thirty years earlier.)

The occupation of hacienda lands by community peasants is explained by economic forces, both long-term ones (widespread peasant opposition to landlords (1974, pp. 120-2)) and short-term ones (expansion of wool sale and of haciendas in the 1920s; commercialization of the regional economy; declining wool prices in 1921 and after 1929 (1974, pp. 134-5)). Hobsbawm mentions briefly the possibility that these forces may have led to internal differentiation within peasant communities, and suggests that members of a "new village bourgeoisie" (1974, p. 144) may have played an important part in the invasions. This view is consistent with other efforts of Hobsbawm's to link protest to economic forces. His essay "Economic fluctuations and some social movements since 1800" relates the "periodic and sudden expansions in the size, strength and activity of social movements" (1964, p. 126) to the rhythms of capitalist expansion and contraction.

Only two political variables are added to this otherwise economic explanation. A simple element of political culture, the great weight placed on written legal titles, allows peasants to make use of state entities otherwise oriented towards landlords, or, in Hobsbawm's word, "The peculiarities of the Latin-American situation must be mentioned, since they turn legalism in the strictest sense into a potent, if also limited, social force among the peasantry" (1974, p. 124). The second element is the tendency for divisions within the power structure to promote peasant mobilization;[13] these divisions allow outside political activists to bring to peasants the ideology and organization which they need for action but which they cannot provide for themselves. This "emergence of political agitation which reached into the countryside" (1974, p. 134), particularly by members of APRA, stimulated the invasions. (A quite similar sort of analysis, though one that rests more heavily on quantitative methods, can be found in the works of Jeffery Paige (1975, 1983); he shares with Hobsbawm an insistence on class to the exclusion of ethnicity, a tendency to subsume politics into economics, and a belief in the immediate comparability of cases from different continents (Burke and Goldfrank 1988).)

Hobsbawm makes careful use of these economic and political variables to trace the history of several communities which successfully oppose the expansion of important haciendas, particularly Laive and Tucle. He examines, for instance, the ambiguous position of old village leaders, who find that accepting hacienda domination can lead to some security for their communities and to personal benefits for themselves; when circumstances change in the 1920s, they are faced with acute dilemmas.

The mode of production approach leads Hobsbawm to neglect or omit other factors, however. His treatment (1974) of Leguía's rule focuses primarily on the expansion of roads and communication, which allow *apristas* to contact peasants. (He views the legal recognition of communities as a factor which takes on importance only after 1935 in the central highlands and even later in the south.)[14] No mention is made of the 1931 elections. He denies emphatically the importance of ethnic identity: "It will already have been observed that the classical land invasion is not specifically Peruvian, or even Indian. There are indeed plenty of exact equivalents elsewhere in Latin America" (1974, p. 129).

The dynamics of modes of production seem sufficient to account for the invasions, although perhaps some attention must be paid to the role of legal documents. But even these "peculiarities of the Latin-American situation" are not so fundamental in Hobsbawm's view; he cites several instances of European land invasions to conclude that "[t]hese scattered examples are at least sufficient to show that something very like the classical communal land invasion can be found in circumstances very different from those of the Peruvian highlands. They belong to the history not of Peruvian Indians or Latin America, but of peasant communities" (1974, p. 130-1).

In this sense, the Molloccahua uprising shares with the earlier one in Tocroyoc not only a general overall pattern and some specific details, but also the possibility of being explained through mode of production analysis. Such an account of the Molloccahua rebellion accords with Piel's recent treatment of agrarian crises in Peru (1983). Although the precise rate of expansion of haciendas is not known for Espinar, as it is for the southern highland province of Azángaro (Jacobsen 1982), notary records, accounts in local newspapers and local monographs show that haciendas acquired comunidad land during the 1920s.[15] Burga and Reátegui (1981, p. 185) document the sharp fall in wool prices after 1929. The poor harvest in the 1930-31 agricultural year, also documented in local newspapers,[16] would have exacerbated the tensions. This presentation would resemble Piel's analysis of the Tocroyoc rebellion: capitalist crises make more acute the contradictions between classes. At such times, landlords and peasants are likely to engage in violent encounters over the control of land, and the state will throw its support behind the landlords, ensuring their victory.

However, a political economy interpretation, by viewing the state and ideology as having more autonomy, and by placing Peru in a world-system context, has much to recommend it. It would not deny that the rebellions form part of the history of peasant communities, but would insist on locating them as well in the histories of Peruvian Indians and of Latin America. Such a view can be constructed, not only by reference to Wolf's general theoretical statements, but to his closer analysis of Indian communities after the Spanish conquest (1982, pp. 145-9) and to his general treatment of peasant movements in the twentieth century (1969). Although the latter book restricts its analysis to cases of national revolution, the analysis which it contains of the interaction of capitalism and pre-capitalist rural economies is sufficiently general to apply to non-revolutionary cases as well (Walton, 1984, pp. 1-33). For the convenience of exposition, I will treat the aspects of the rebellion—its timing, composition and antecedents—that I examined for the mode of production analysis. I will examine the factors which Hobsbawm neglects, particularly the policies of Leguía's regime, the impact of the 1931 election, and the nature of ethnic divisions.

One difference between Piel's work and a political economy approach lies in the explanation of the timing of the uprising. Though the latter would agree that the decline in wool prices after 1929 influenced the province of Espinar, it would insist less strongly in predicting the timing precisely. Instead, it would point to the 1920s as a decade of growing tensions and to 1931 as a year with some specific conflicts. Increasing class conflict and political mobilization took place throughout Peru during this period, as described in a previous section. The political economy approach would also look at the longstanding ethnic tensions in the region. To translate these time frames into Braudelian language, the ethnic tensions would be seen as the level of structures, the Depression and the growth of the Peruvian state as the level of conjunctures, and the 1931 elections as the level of events (Braudel 1972, 1973). Stern (1987) offers a similar application of these concepts to Andean peasant rebellions in the eighteenth century.

The role of the state at that period was complex; it went far beyond simple support of capitalist classes. The expansion of the state under Leguía introduced new economic and political resources for which different groups could compete. It whetted their appetite for such resources and thus led to increased conflict. In a situation of land conflict, hacendados and comuneros both sought to establish ties to the new government. The hacendados, who had received some political backing from earlier, weaker governments, established the first links, as shown by their successful use of road crews and the police force for their own ends. Later on, comuneros were also able to gain some measure of access to political power through the formation of Indian communities and the Indian Congress. It is important to note that the state offered resources to both parties, rather than only one.

Certain political circumstances in the months before the rebellion further increased tensions. The 1929 crash caused the prices of Peruvian export commodities to decline sharply, in turn leading to devaluations of the currency. Foreign loans, which had been easily obtained in the 1920s, were severely limited (Thorp and Bertram 1978). The ensuing reductions in national budgets led many groups to withdraw their support of Leguía. In this deteriorating economic and political situation, Sánchez Cerro deposed Leguía in August 1930 by a military coup with populist overtones. Faced with uneven backing, Sánchez Cerro in turn resigned in March 1931. A provisional government was installed and set 11 October 1931 as the date for elections, in which Sánchez Cerro was elected. In the months before the election, the new social and political forces which had built up in the previous decade found more open expression than had been possible under Leguía. Mass demonstrations were held on a scale which had never been witnessed before in Peruvian history (Stein 1980, pp. 122). The major contest was between Sánchez Cerro and APRA. There were two smaller coalitions, more resembling the older parties displaced by Leguía. The Communists did not run.

The general tension of the times reached even small, remote towns like Yauri. The presence for the first time in national elections of parties with strong mass bases concerned the hacendados, who had witnessed at close hand active indigenista politics. However, they were also struck not only by the newness of electoral politics, after a decade-long hiatus, but also by its familiarity. Political parties during the aristocratic republic drew their support on the basis of personal ties, rather than commitment to ideologies. Highland elections in this period were often occasions for competing factions of hacendados to attempt to seize control of patronage and local administration. (In this way, the 1931 election harked back not only to elections of the aristocratic republic but to the much longer period of competing *caudillos* or military strongmen in the nineteenth-century (cf. Wolf and Hansen 1967).) With little supervision of elections, fraud and violence during the aristocratic republic were common; the small number of electors also favored such abuses, since the shift of a few votes could change the outcome of a local election. Some of the most notorious incidents of this pattern took place in two provinces close to Espinar, Chumbivilcas in Cuzco and Cotabambas in the neighboring department of Apurímac. Open confrontation between opposed bands at the 1917 election left several hacendados dead in these provinces (Basadre 1963, pp. 3814-17).

The accusations that the peasants and that the hacendado Arbuez Alvarez were communists may have been seen differently in this context. The peasants had contacts with left-wing indigenista organizations, as shown by the large number of communities in the province which received official recognition and by the Indian Congress. They were unlikely to have been loyal followers of any specific party, though, since the formal break between APRA and the Communist Party was still quite recent in 1931; their links would have been with specific individuals or small organizations in the city of Cuzco whose own party affiliations were often less than firm (Valcárel 1981). It would be anacronistic to view Olivares as a red-baiter. By calling the rebels communists, he was suggesting that they were part of the tumultuous and dangerous politicization that affected Peru as a whole, rather than they were members of a uniquely odious party. It is virtually certain that Olivares had enough political sophistication to distinguish between the terms *comunista* and *comunidad*, but many of his listeners, less exposed to new political parties, may have assumed a closer connection between the party and the constitutional provisions than existed in reality.

The case of Arbuez Alvarez is somewhat distinct. The leading authorities of Yauri offered him a long apology, notarized in Yauri on 19 September 1931 and published in a Cuzco newspaper, *El Comercio*, on 30 September 1931. The apologies indicate that he was not a member of the Communist Party, that he did not participate in the uprising, and that he was in fact a member of the fairly conservative Decentralist Party.[17] Ironically, this party stood well to the right of Sánchez Cerro; it offered a nostalgic vision of a Peru less disturbed by the social turmoil which accompanied economic change. (The Decentralist candidate was José María de la Jara, an old follower of Nicolás de Piérola, whose presidency in 1895 inaugurated the aristrocratic republic. Lingering memories of Piérola's popularity among southern highland landowners and the Decentralist appeal to increase the budgets and power of local governments may account for the higher proportion of votes received by La Jara in the department of Cuzco than in Peru as a whole, and for the presence of Decentralists in Yauri (Rénique n.d.).)[18] The accusations that Arbuez Alvarez was a communist thus seem more likely a way to settle personal rivalries rather than to denounce class betrayal. It could be surmised that he was relatively isolated from elite kinship networks in Yauri on the basis of the fact that he shared neither his paternal nor his maternal surname with the other landowners, officials and notables mentioned in the documents.

Although the political economy approach accepts the importance of systems of production, it challenges a view of the opposed groups in the rebellion as being nothing more than classes rooted in system of production. Firstly, there were strong internal divisions among the landlords and among the peasants. Although the specific details of social organization in the two groups differ, ties among hacendados, as among peasants, were based on kinship, friendship and locality as much as on class loyalty, and the conflicts between different groups within the same stratum were strong. Some of this weakness stems from the competition for land in the poorly-capitalized pastoral production system. However, these divisions were exacerbated by the Peruvian state, as shown by rivalries between settlements for the status of district and provincial capital and between factions of followers of different political parties. In a similar fashion, the large number of *comunidades indígenas* in Espinar may show the weakness as well as the strength of the peasants.[19]

Secondly, personal ties between landlord and peasant cut across the class barrier. Arbuez Alvarez' capacity to remain on his hacienda suggests that he could count on his peons to warn him of danger, just as Olivares also had peasant informers. The hacendados often served as baptismal sponsors for the children of their peons, creating ties of compadrazgo. That the cross-class ties of kinship were not entirely on a ritual basis is shown by the wills of two hacendado members of the Flores family.[20] The illegitimate children for whom they legally recognized paternity in both cases outnumbered the children of their wives. The mothers of their illegitimate children have indigenous rather than Hispanic surnames; in the list of the six women for whose children Antolín Flores Macedo acknowledged extramarital paternity appear Marcela Tarifa and Sinforosa Tarifa, possibly related to the Domingo Tarifa who figured in the Molloccahua rebellion.

Finally, a consideration of ideology makes it difficult to see the groups exclusively in terms of class, and shows the importance of incorporating an understanding of ethnic identities into what one scholar has termed "a class analysis of the historical development of...highland villages" (Mallon 1983, p. 339). (Several recent works in Southeast Asia, where the lines of ethnicity, class and nationality cross-cut in even more complex a fashion than in the Andes, have shown the value of using these issues of ethnicity and ideology in the study of peasant movements (Stoler 1985, Scott 1985, Adas 1988).) The hacendados in Yauri and the peasants in the countryside shared an understanding that their society was composed of two strata whose differences were based not only on relations to land, labor and capital, but also on their inherent, and inherited, qualities—in short, on ethnicity. Numerous differences in language, dress and custom clearly distinguished them, and mobility between them, though not entirely absent, was infrequent. The rebellion could be viewed as a confict between Indians and mestizos, rather than between peasants and landlords. This ideology of ethnicity both reflected and reinforced the underlying tension between the two groups. The possibility of the outbreak of violence between them was always present, as the long history of rebellions in the Andes shows. Both groups had an awareness, a collective memory, of a chain of conflicts that stretched past the 1921 Tocroyoc rebellion back to the nineteenth-century uprising of Juan Bustamante, to the massive Tupac Amaru revolt of the 1780s, and ultimately to the Spanish Conquest itself (Rivera, 1986).

The peasants who gathered among the ancient walls of the fortress of Molloccahua gazed across the Río Salado to the town of Yauri, dominated by the towers of the colonial church in which the townspeople had assembled. The documents do not record, and informants cannot recall, the details of their speeches and prayers, in Quechua in the former and Spanish in the latter. The peasants may have been heartened by the recollection of ceremonies held by traditional ritual practitioners known as *layqas*, as the townspeople may have been cheered by the thought of the numerous masses celebrated in the church. It is certain, though, that each group believed that the spirits of the hills and the saints had powers to cure disease, to attack enemies, to defend themselves; however much the groups chose their locations on that September day for pragmatically strategic reasons based on topography, each must have felt, to some degree, the immediate presence of these supernatural forces. In other uprisings, there may not have been two stone structures to offer so simple a material image of the opposition as one between peoples rather than classes, but a similar sense was there. To the participants, these rebellions must have seemed in some measure not a moment in history but a moment outside history, one of the numerous battles in an opposition whose origin and definition lay in the distant era of conquest.

If the political economy explanations here differed from the mode of production approach in the analysis of the timing and composition of the rebellion, they vary even more greatly in terms of its antecedents and precipitating factors—the Braudelian levels of structure, conjuncture and event that the mode of production analysis tend to merge into a single dynamic. Although political economists would see the conflict over land as fundamental in the Molloccahua uprising, they would not claim that it was the only issue at work, and in the case of some other peasant uprisings, such as the ones in the department of Puno throughout the 1920s, even the main issue. The hacendados did not attack the peasants merely as part of their consolidation of economic control over land, but also as part of their political control over state agencies, to set an example for the peasants who organized themselves in communities and in the Indian Congress. They wanted to continue in their position as exclusive intermediaries between the peasant and the state. They opposed independent peasant access to the state, as shown by their resistance to the establishment of an autonomous district in Tocroyoc. The violence of the rebellion could also be seen not only as an expression of the struggle over land but also as a product of the tense political atmosphere in Peru less than a month before a key election. The police may have been as much concerned to weaken APRA and other left-wing groups as to defend a rural bourgeoisie against the peasants.

The long-standing ethnic element was also not lacking. It is interesting to note the importance of corpses to the peasants and the townspeople alike. The immediate goal of the peasants who attacked the policemen was to recover the body of Tarifa to assure his local burial in a manner that would permit the journey of his spirit to the afterworld. They were sure to recall the body of Domingo Huarca ten years earlier, which had been left on the roof of the Tocroyoc church for several months, unprotected from the weather and from vultures. The townspeople were concerned not only for their property, their safety and their lives, but also for the proper Christian burial of the policemen. The horror which they later felt at the mutilation of the corpses cannot be explained simply as their astonishment at the strength of the peasants as a class; their reaction in part was an expression of their sense of themselves as an essentially different and superior type of being. A funeral address delivered in Cuzco offers testimony to this mestizo view of Indians as uncivilized.[21] Although newspaper accounts clearly document that the two policemen were buried in Cuzco, the townspeople believe otherwise. A shrine-like structure was built inside the police station in Yauri, just to the right of the main entrance. It holds an electric light bulb and two skulls, believed to be those of Zanabria and Torres; any visitor, prisoner or policeman who leaves the station cannot fail to see it. Similarly, the vehemence with which the peasants attacked the dead bodies of the policemen cannot be seen solely as the release of long-pent fury or as a strategic move in a fight between two parties. The specificity of the attack on the bodies suggests a ritual treatment of enemies (Szeminski 1987). This view was also held by the wife of the subprefect, who mentioned to me in 1972 that she thought the tearing and cutting of the policemen's flesh had been done by men, the burning by women; whether or not she accurately presented the details of these acts, she was probably correct in viewing them as structured. They are likely to have derived from an established category of alien or opposed peoples, into which the policemen were placed.

COMPARISONS

Combination and Reduction

Like other applications of holistic theories, the political economy account of the Molloccahua revolt presents a combination of explanatory factors. Although this account does not utilize any precise formula for such combinations, it does follow the models offered by other such accounts, which emphasize the influence of ideology in shaping action and which treat as complex the relation between the state and social classes. Judged on the basis of its explanation of the timing, composition and antecedents of the rebellion, this account appears broader and more detailed, and therefore stranger, than the alternative mode of production view; particularly with regard to the composition and the antecedents, the political economy framework is more accurate as well.

Faced with this apparent success of the political economy approach, the mode of production approach can adopt the alternative open to other deterministic theories: to provide a reductionist account of the different factors which the political economy approach views as independent.[22] Much as the political economy approach does not offer guidelines for combination of factors, mode of production theory lacks an agreed-upon set of instructions for the reduction of superstructures to bases. In the case of the rebellions, there are three major elements which political economists treat as instances of independent political and ideological factors and which mode of production analysts seek to reduce to their economic determinants: state policy, pre-electoral tensions and ethnic divisions. Although it may be impossible to sort these into categories of reducible and non-reducible, or to evaluate precisely to what extent they are reducible, it is more feasible to rank them in terms of relative reducibility.

Of these three, state policy is the most amenable to reduction. One could hardly hope to find clearer instances of state support of capitalist interests than the conscription of peasants to road-building gangs and the use of police to support hacienda expansion, or of joint action by the state and capitalist firms than the transport of troops in trucks owned by a foreign export company. These examples support a narrowly instrumentalist view of the state as performing functions necessary to capitalist domination (Miliband 1969). Other instances of state policy, though, are more ambiguous. The *indigenista* legislation permitted official recognition of Indian communities, which encouraged local peasants to seek contacts outside the province. One could claim that this policy supported capitalism by diffusing class conflict through co-optation or through redirection of conflict to a bureaucratic realm, but such arguments appear somewhat forced, particularly for the case of Espinar. At best, one might try to explain indigenista policies as a capitalist effort to weaken opposing forces by offering a token reform to left-wing intellectuals and working-class movements in urban areas, who viewed the oppression of the Indian as a key element of the exploitative order in Peru. This alternative construction would still require a more detailed account of politics and ideology that the mode of production analysis offers.

Furthermore, the mode of production view sometimes misrepresents actions of autonomous political institution as stemming from economic forces. For example, Piel states that the formation of the province of Espinar in 1917 "confirms the increase in value" (1967, p. 388) in that region; in other words, the political change is a consequence of the economic change. It would be more prudent to emphasize the dynamics of the Peruvian congress, discussed earlier, since they led to the formation of other provinces where the "increase in value" was surely less. To pick only a few of the possible examples, Cutervo (in the department of Cajamarca) in 1910 and Aija (in Ancash) in 1936 were hardly centers of export growth comparable to Espinar in 1917.

For the other two cases, reduction is more difficult. To claim that the pre-electoral tensions in 1931 reflected the overall capitalist crisis, for instance, one would need to show a general correspondence between pre-electoral conflict and class conflict. These links are difficult to make. In certain regions and periods in Latin America, pre-electoral conflict is endemic, due to personalistic patron-client ties or to political culture. We have already mentioned cases of such violence from provinces close to Espinar in 1917, a prosperous year of rising rather than falling wool prices. Hobsbawm had limited success in relating high levels of electoral violence in Colombia to economic cycles (1986). In still other cases, such as Chile before 1970, pre-electoral violence was low, despite high levels of class conflict. It seems difficult to account for the level of tensions in the 1931 elections without examining the specific institutional history of Peruvian politics, of parties of the aristocratic republic, of the long rule of Leguía, of the coup; this history, in turn, is linked, though not reducible, to capitalist developments in Peru.

Ethnic divisions may well provide the hardest challenge to mode of production theorists. Ethnicity is a notorious problem for many versions of Marxists inquiry. One common line focuses on the issue of false consciousness, in which ethnic distinctions weaken working-class solidarity; this theme forms part of the explanation for the weakness of union movements in so industrialized a nation as the United States. For mode of production theorists, capitalist penetration should replace ethnic ties with those based on common class position, in Espinar as elsewhere. They might accept as ethnic the tension between Indians and mestizos, since it dates back to the Spanish Conquest and the colonial period, when Peru was not capitalist, at least in mode of production terms. The distribution of Indian populations in the more remote regions of Latin America in the twentieth-century might also support the mode of production view that capitalist penetration weakens rather than reinforces ethnic identity. Piel notes that the loss of ethnic identity in many portions of the Peruvian coast and highlands tended to follow the expansion of production of export crops (1975, pp. 310-313). He ignores, rather than explains, its general survival under the circumstances in the southern highlands and its specific role in the uprising.

More generally, the rebellions in highland Peru that stretched from the late nineteenth-century through the first decades of the twentieth varied greatly in the immediacy of their linkages to changing modes of production and, more specifically, to capitalist penetration. Puno, the department to the south and east of Espinar, was marked by many uprisings during the 1910s and 1920s; these events, whose timing shows no direct correlation with wool prices movements, occurred both in pastoral areas linked to export markets and in agricultural zones with little or no connection to export markets. Even Piel's accounts (1970, 1973) of the 1885 Atusparia revolt in Ancash document the weakness of the relation between capitalism and rebellion, despite the efforts by him and other mode of production theorists (Stein 1978) to fit it into their perspective. In that case, longstanding ethnic conflicts surfaced when tensions between rival military leaders weakened elite control. In much the same way, what made Espinar the site of two rebellions was not merely a conflict over land between hacendados and comuneros, but other tensions as well.

The Issue of Comparability

At this point, the two approaches might seem so different that they might not be directly comparable. To return to the genealogical metaphor, they might resemble two relatives who had long ceased talking to one another after a particularly bitter dispute. They might be brought into the same room by a third party bent on restoring, if not harmony, at least the appearance of polite conversation. However, such encounters would quickly turn to arguments. Because of the differences in their basic premises, the two parties could find no common ground. Perhaps the only point on which they could concur is that their disagreements were as fundamental as they had both suspected. Convinced of the futility of efforts at reconciliation, they would withdraw into stubborn silence. If two such relatives were asked about their views on any particular subject, they could not enter into the sort of dialogue proposed here. The Marxist family has many such pairs, such as the British social historian E. P. Thompson and the French structuralist Louis Althusser (Anderson 1980).

There are two areas of disagreement that might render incompatible the modes of production and political economy approaches, as exemplified by Hobsbawm and Wolf: their views of causality and of human action. The final paragraph of Hobsbawm's study of rural Cuzco opens, "We may conclude that the experience of La Convención does not tell us much about the problem of agrarian development under capitalism that we did not already know" (*ibid*, p. 48). By contrast, Wolf's research supports his view of the diversity of human history; he sees human action as "conveying in variable accents the divergent paths of groups and classes" (1982, p. 391). The mode of production theorists, committed to economic determinism, view the action of individuals as the automatic outcome of their position within structures. For the political economists, the complexity of economic, social and political structures often permit individuals distinct options, as does the existence of competing or internally inconsistent ideologies. There is a logical consistency between positions on these two issues: the mode of production theorists present both individual action and historical trends as readily predictable, and the political economists do not.

The mode of production theorists adopt a causal view more strongly than the political economists do. For instance, Hobsbawm states "the mode of production constitutes the structure which determines what form the growth of the productive forces and the distribution of the surplus will take, how society can or can not change its structures, and how, at suitable moments, the transition to another mode of production can or will take place. It also establishes the range of superstructural possibilities" (1984, p. 46). He does not think of this position as narrowly deterministic, noting that "even the more rigid proponents of historical materialism devoted lengthy discussions to the role of accident and the individual in history (Plekhanov)" (*ibid*, p. 43). However, the deterministic stance appears in his discussion of events as well as in his more analytical writings. In his discussion of the hacendados of La Convención, Hobsbawm claims that certain factors inherent in their class position (their lack of managerial skills, for instance, and their tendencies towards conspicuous consumption) "would inevitably lead" (1969, p. 43) them to place greater pressure on their tenants and sub-tenants. That this choice of language is not casual is shown by his critical remark of *Europe and the People without History*. Although he finds many pieces of it to be valuable, he calls it "a book about connections rather (than) causes" (1984, p. 46). He finds its underlying weakness to be its failure to explain—or even to seek adequately to explain—the rise of capitalism from pre-capitalist modes; for this reason, it cannot fundamentally treat the topic Wolf sets for himself, the relations of capitalist Europe and the other parts of the world.

Piel also adopts a causal stance. The most extreme instance is his account of a model sheep farm which the government established in 1917 to the east of the province of Espinar. This station was part of the efforts of pre-capitalist hacendados to introduce fencing which would permit the adoption of improved pasture and new sheep varieties, in short to develop the forces of production. The farm was established at the "peak of the levels of wool exports" (1967, p. 393); no additional explanation is required for the striking foresight of the semi-feudal hacendados, to whom Piel assigns the ability to detect in advance a decrease in exports. Armed with this knowledge, they could choose the most opportune moment for pressuring the state to support their entry into the capitalist mode of production.

By contrast, Wolf employs a much less causal vocabulary. The concept of mode of production is important, not for its predictive value, but because it "allows us to understand how the technical transformation of nature is conjoined with the organization of human sociality" (1982, p. 74). It "aims...at revealing the political-economic relationships that underlie, orient, and constrain interaction (among people)" (*ibid*, p. 74). The concept does not provide him with laws of history, but rather with the simple "axioms" (*ibid*, p. 73) of the human ability to transform nature through social action, axioms which are shared by many people with whom he might otherwise have little in common, such as sociobiologists. He states that "theoretically informed history and historically informed theory must be joined together to account for populations specifiable in time and space, both as outcomes of significant processes and as their carriers" (*ibid*, p. 21). His desire to "account for" rather to predict is reflected in his use of metaphors at critical points in his arguments. This choice of wording contributes to the content as well as the eloquence of his arguments. To state that "capitalism cut through the integument of custom" (1969, p. 279) is to avoid a precise statement of the nature and degree of causation. Even when he uses directly causative terms, he weakens their impact through metaphor: "as we unraveled the chains of causes and effects at work in the lives of particular populations, we saw them extend beyond any one population to embrace the trajectories of others—all others" (1982, p. 385). Wolf might well acknowledge Hobsbawm's claim that he avoids causal arguments. Even in *Peasant Wars of the Twentieth Century*, a book which searches for parallelism among distinct national histories and which seeks to link preconditions with outcomes, he is willing to discuss differences as well as similarities among his six cases.

Having argued the case for the fundamental nature of the understanding of causality, we can move to the related issue of human action. One could claim that mode of production theory sees in history the working of structures rather than of individuals, whose actions are determined by forces which they cannot control or even influence. By contrast, political economy offers much room for human choice to shape historical processes.

These positions are demonstrated not only in formal argument but in choice of words and exposition. Piel's various accounts of Peruvian peasant movements (1967, 1970, 1973) make very few specific references to individuals. In the most detailed case, a summary of the Atusparia revolt in the highland department of Ancash in 1885, he lists the successive national presidents and departmental prefects. In addition, precisely one member of each class which participates is named: an Indian mayor for the peasantry, a newspaper editor for the "petty bourgeoisie," a miner for an incipient working class (1973, pp. 311-3), and their actions reflect the interests of their class. In general, the actors are not individuals but classes, who are unified when strong, divided when weak. Similarly, Hobsbawm's discussion of La Convención presents classes as agents whose behaviors are determined by their interests, derived from their position in economic structures.

Wolf's position is much less deterministic:

The key relationships of a mode of production empower human action, inform it, and are carried forward by it. As Marx said, men make their own history but not under conditions of their own choosing. They do so under the constraint of relationships and forces that direct their will and their desires (1982, p. 386).

Though he rejects the analysis of human behavior in terms of rational decisionmaking (*ibid*, p. 391) because he finds that it divorces individuals from their contexts, he does recognize the existence of alternatives open to individuals, and the consequences of their selection among alternatives for the course of history. This perception draws on his earlier works on the importance of brokers as links between distinct social groupings (1966). His books contain many examples of the ambiguities which individuals face:

striking examples include not only categories (the *kurakas* or traditional Andean Indian leaders in the colonial period, caught between their communities and royal administrators (1982, p. 146-7); the jobbers or foremen in nineteenth-century textile mills in India, with a mesh of ties based on kinship, locality, caste, credit and market links (*ibid*, p. 289)), but also more detailed discussion of individuals (Johnny Kabes, an entrepreneur in seventeenth-century West Africa whose commercial activities linked the English and the Asante (*ibid*, p. 209); Pontiac, the leader of an eighteenth-century religious movement and military uprising against British expansion in the Great Lakes region (*ibid*, p. 174)). The different manner in which these authors present individuals does not reflect only expository style but also the logic of their arguments.

However, the appearance of disagreement is far greater than the actual disagreement itself. The two approaches share common ground in their views of causality and human action. The former can be found among political economists as well as mode of production theorists. Wolf makes numerous causal arguments, even if he does not use as explicitly a causal language as others do. Such views come most clearly in some of his comparative works, in which distinct societies, faced with a common pressure, respond in common ways. An early instance is his discussion (1957) of "closed corporate peasant communities," an organizational form which allows peasants to oppose elite efforts to take control of their lands. It would be difficult to deny causal status to his location of the origins and maintenance of this form in imperial penetration and colonial domination in two different regions, Mesoamerica and Indonesia. *Peasant Wars of the Twentieth Century* is another example; a single force, capitalism, caused similar responses in six quite distinct societies located on four different continents. Even *Europe and the People without History*, a book which focuses on diversity more than uniformity, discusses regularities in export economies and labor systems. Thus, though the mode of production approach may appear to provide law-like analyses, and political economy to offer merely narrative "accounts," both have sorts of causal explanations.

In a similar fashion, mode of production theorists examine human action, although in a more schematic fashion that political economists.[23] In *Labouring Men*, Hobsbawm shows the range of options open to individuals. He draws, quite successfully, on the nature of workplace and industrial organization and on overall economic conditions to explain the varying degree and form of mobilization of different British workers. He goes as far as to include detailed examples of political movements and ideologies whose leaders and supporters do not easily support a view of action based on class interest (1964, pp. 1-4, 231-238). Even when further from home, Hobsbawm presents, albeit in simple terms, the alternatives available to individuals; in his discussion of the central Peruvian highlands, for instance, he discusses a number of individual peasants. Their political behavior varies greatly, depending on many factors such as wealth, personal ties, experience with wage labor, migration history and exposure to radical ideologies.

The two approaches are thus not irreconcilable in a fundamental way; they do not lack the common ground, or common vocabulary, necessary to discourse and debate. In particular, they share explanations of causation and of human action, although each employs types of explanations quite different from those of the other.[24] They have not branched as far apart from their common Marxist roots as some others have; in particular, they continue to share an emphasis on economic forces. Wolf's efforts to "account" for world history does not represent an abandonment of causal explanation, but rather an effort to broaden it. Hobsbawm's and Piel's use of class interest to explain individuals and events retains some notion of the subjective basis of human action. (They are not as extreme in negating human agency as some structuralists, such as Althusser, who have been the targets of the more vitriolic attacks (Thompson, 1978). It should also be noted that Perry Anderson, also a strong critic of the structuralists, has praise for Hobsbawm's historical research (1983, pp. 24-25).)

CONCLUSIONS

The mode of production and political economy perspectives both offer analyses of the relations of economic, political and ideological phenomena. They may fruitfully be examined as examples of more general types of analytical theories, determinism and holism, in the ways that they differ on the reducibility of superstructures to bases. Their views on this issue provide them with analyses of historical causality at a societal level, and, with the use of the key linking concept of interest, of human action at an individual level.

Despite their differences, the two approaches are not incommensurable, in that they have enough in common to permit a comparison. An effort to apply them to particular cases, peasant rebellions in one part of highland Peru, reveals complementary weaknesses. Its deterministic claims notwithstanding, the mode of production approach offers no explicit directions on how to reduce ideology and politics to economic bases, much as the political economy framework does not indicate how to combine these different factors. This problem is mitigated for this specific case by the extensive writings from both perspectives on Latin America and on peasant movements. An analysis of the rebellion from both perspectives favors the political economy approach. Its holistic combination of factors gives a fuller, deeper and, in some aspects, more accurate presentation of the rebellion. The efforts of the mode of production approach to reduce politics and ideology to economic bases are less satisfactory.[25]

At this point we may return to the questions posed at the beginning of the article. External forces and internal conditions are involved in a complex interplay, in which the dynamics do not come exclusively from outside. The rebellions in Espinar bear strong connections to patterns of resistance to proletarianization elsewhere in the world, but also display important local characteristics. Objective class interests, though significant, do not manifest themselves in a transparent fashion. The mode of production approach is correct in asserting that fundamental transformations accompany the expansion of capitalism, in the Peruvian highlands and elsewhere; it is incorrect in asserting that no other patterns in the contemporary world are also fundamental. The development of capitalism in Espinar has to do with Espinar, as well with capitalism; by extension, the development of a world economy has to do with many local realities as well as with a single global one. The mode of production theorists misrepresent these developments by viewing them only as the product of world capitalism, which imposes itself on static non-capitalist systems. An examination of the history of Espinar from a political economy perspective challenges this portrayal. The events show the workings of local as well as global orders, impelled by political and ideological dynamics as well as economic ones. As the actors in the Tocroyoc and Molloccahua rebellions demonstrated, the encounter of highland Peruvian society and global capitalism is the meeting of a movable object and a resistable force.

ACKNOWLEDGMENTS

The field and archival research on which this article is based was supported by a grant from the Foreign Area Fellowship Program of the Ford Foundation. I would like to acknowledge the useful comments on previous versions of this article provided by: Arnold Bauer, Nancy Bonvillain, Daniel Calhoun, Jose Carazas, David Collier, William Davis, Henri Favre, James Griesemer, Gary Hamilton, Jim Hawley, Dan Hazen, Nils Jacobsen, Suad

Joseph, Karen Kraft, Hannah Lessinger, Tom Love, June Nash, George Primov, John Rowe, Pierre van de Berghe, Miriam Wells and Karl Yambert. I am very appreciative of Sharon Lynch's efforts in preparing a number of different versions of this manuscript. I would also like to thank Mary Beth Cunha, the cartographer who prepared the maps, for her many useful suggestions.

NOTES

1.   I am opting for a straightforward use of the concepts of base and superstructure, despite the extensive literature which examines their ontological and epistemological status. However, it is not for reasons of space alone that I do not address these concerns. The case which I am examining lends itself to a conventional use of these distinctions more than many others, such as the West African agrarian societies in which the allocation of kinship to base and superstructure has perplexed many analysts, whose writings Kahn ably summarizes (1981). In this article, I use the term 'economic' to refer to forces and relations of production on stylistic as much as theoretical grounds.

2.   Mode of production theorists sometimes disagree. This diversity stems in part from the lack of precise definitions in Marx' own work on mode of production and social formation which stimulated the different readings of *Capital* (Althusser and Balibar 1970). Since the terms "determination" and "domination," when used to refer to the relation of base to superstructure, are slippery ones (Foster-Carter 1978), the boundary which separates mode of production theorists from others can not be drawn precisely. Nonetheless, the individuals who follow the mode of production approach have used concepts in a sufficiently consistent manner to merit their inclusion under a single label.

3.   I chose the term holism to indicate the view that these elements are autonomous but interconnected. Alternative terms, such as emergentism, interactionism and vitalism, seemed more awkward and less specific. Nonetheless, for many people, particularly anthropologists, the notion of holism implies an understanding of systematically ordered wholes (Appadurai 1986); I do not wish to impute this understanding to political economists.

4.   Peru is divided into a three-tiered set of units for administrative purposes. Departments, the largest units, are divided into provinces which in turn are composed of districts.

5.   For example, Piel seems willing to accord ideology a certain degree of autonomy in his discussion of *indigenismo* (1967, p. 396). His more recent book (1975) shows a greater flexibility in his application of Marxist models to specific cases.

6.   Archivo Notarial Alvarez. 1927-1928 volume, pp. 265v-267. The Archivo Notarial Alvarez (ANA) in Yauri contains the records of all notarial acts recorded in the town from 1917 through the 1930s. There was never more than one notary active in the town at any given time, nor was there a gap in notarial records during this period. In 1972, when I consulted them, these records were housed in the notary office of Toribio Alvarez in Yauri.

7.   ANA, 1927-1928 vol., 266v. "...este fundo se halla rodeado en su mayor parte con la propiedad de nuestro actual comprador Florez Macedo."

8.   The site is almost certainly pre-Inca as well, probably dating from the Aymara-speaking Cana people who were conquered by the Incas around 1430. Like many other sites from immediately pre-Inca times, it is located on a defensible hilltop and is fortified. Some information on the site is available in an article (Pardo 1948) and in unpublished field notes

of Gustavo Alencastre, kindly made available to me by John Rowe. The site contains pottery and buildings in both local and Inca styles; the nature of the remains suggests construction by local builders who imitated prestigious imperial styles rather than by workers whom the Incas brought as part of an occupational force. It is thus unlike other Inca garrisons and administrative centers, built on unused ground, which were imposed in newly-conquered territories. I do not know whether local people, either in 1931 or in the present, were conscious of the Inca conquest, or whether they attributed all pre-Hispanic ruins to a single ancient people. Some recent research has examined the complexity of indigenous understandings of ruins (Salomon 1987).

9. El Comercio, Cuzco, 30 September 1931, "...el certificado expedido por las autoridades y principales vecinos de Yauri, en los que se prueba ampliamente la inculpabilidad del honrdo ciudadano don Francisco Arbuez Alvarez, que jamás ha sido miembro del Partido Comunista..."

10. Archivo Subprefectural Espinar. Libro: Diversas Autoridades. Principia en Mayo 1 de 1931 Termina en Abril 2 de 1932. 214. The Archivo Subprefectural Espinar (ASE), housed in the subprefectural offices in Yauri, contains a variety of documents of official business. The Libro: Diversas Autoridades. Principia en Mayo 1 de 1931 Termina en Abril 2 de 1932 (LDA) contains carbon copies, many of them partly illegible, of telegrams which the subprefect dispatched during the rebellion and correspondence with the police and other authorities.

11. ASE. LDA. 231.

12. El Sol (Cusco) 22 September 1931; El Comercio (Cusco) 23 September 1931.

13. Hobsbawm discusses this element in almost law-like terms; his language suggests that this tendency is a superstructural consequence of pre-capitalist modes of production. "...Peruvian experience shows, as experience elsewhere confirms, that if peasants do not have much concrete knowledge about the wider framework which encloses their little worlds, they are acutely conscious of the changes in that wider framework which appear to affect its indestructibility. If the power structure is firm and closed, they retreat into their usual posture of waiting. If it begins to open or shake, they prepare for action" (1974, pp. 137-8).

14. Hobsbawm states, "[t]he decision to acquire legal recognition evidently marks a stage in the development of communal political consciousness, those in the more advanced regions of Northern and Central Peru being in general quicker off the mark than those in the South" (1974, p. 136). This factual error reflects in part the limited documentary base available to Hobsbawm.

15. ANA vols. 1925-26, 1927-28, 1929-30 La Verdad (Sicuani) *Aspecto Jurídico de la Tenencia de la Tierra en la Provincia de Canas*, Tesis para obtner el grado de Bachiller en Derecho. Simeon Alencactre Ch. Universidad Nacional de San Antonio Abad del Cuzco. s.d.; *Kunturkanki: un pueblo del Ande*. Andrés Alencastre. 1965. Cuzco: Editorial Garcilaso.

16. El Sol (Cusco) 19 September 1931. This account of the fair held on 8 September in Ayaviri, the capital of the neighboring province of Melgar, discusses the lack of commercial activity due to poor harvests earlier in the year.

17. In contrast, Jacobsen argues that the Decentralist Party was progressive—"quite advanced," in his terms (1988:167). Additional research on this party may resolve such disagreements; in any case, Jacobsen's view is definitely supported by Decentralist plans for legislation to protect Indian comittees. This focus on communities may also account for the view that Arbuez Alvarez had been a communist.

18. The election results in Espinar were unusual, in that Sánchez Cerro received only 18 votes, while Haya de la Torre got 149 and de la Jara 105. Of all the provinces in Cuzco, it had the highest proportion of voes for APRA, the lowest for Sánchez Cerro, and the second highest (after neighboring Canas, also the location of rebellions) for de la Jara. Some of the

support for APRA may be due to the fact that it had the strongest anti-imperialist rhetoric of any of the parties represented in the election. Many local hacendados and merchants, already in opposition to the British-owned Southern Peruvian Railway which dominated wool transport, were strongly concerned by a proposal made in 1929 to the Peruvian government by the Peruvian Alpaca Company, a foreign firm. The company solicited an official monopoly on alpaca wool exports from southern Peru. It claimed that by fixing and stabilizing the price of wool, it would protect producers, encourage investment and improve quality. The threat to traders was immediate; landlords feared loss of control of their estates as well (Burga and Reátegui 1981; pp. 57-9; Jacobsen 1988: pp. 161-2). Though never established, this proposal may have influenced a number of votes. The most strongly aprista provinces were located in the high-elevation southern portion of the department of Cuzco, where the bulk of the department's alpaca herds were located. The votes which Haya de la Torre received in La Convención might also reflect the more commercialized agriculture in the region. Table 3, below, includes the percentages of total votes for these three candidates and a fourth, Osores.

19.   One informant described how Anansaya-Collana had been a single large community through the 1920s. It was composed of four sections or *ayllus*, named Phawsiri, Pumawasi, Oqebamba and Ch'isiqata, each of which had a leader or *personero*; the position of head *personero* rotated annually among the four. Tensions among the ayllus increased with the commercialization of wool, since some of them had better pasture and wished to restrict access to it. Each section also wished to establish schools. In 1928, all four sections achieved formal recognition as communities. Ch'isiqta took the name Anansaya-Collana; the other three sections were granted their ayllu names. Albó has shown this pattern of division to be common elsewhere in the Andean highlands, where he termed this contradictory peasant capacity for unity at some points and rivalry at others as "the...paradox [of] solidarity and factionalism" (Albó 1974).

20.   Antolín Flores Macedo, ANA, 1933-34, 21v-23v; José Angel Flores Jara, ANA 1936-38, 262-263v.

21.   The rebellion is described as "este horrible atentado de lesa humanidad, que no tenemos sino que calificar...como un hecho bárbaro, revelador de una incipiente cultura y digno únicamente de tribus salvajes, sin noción absoluta de los mas elementales principios de humanidad." El Comercio (Cusco) 23 September 1931.

22.   Several other alternatives are in fact available, but they appear much weaker. One could claim that the case on hand possesses certain unusual characteristics which allow the political economy approach to have an atypical instance of success. To have force, such a claim would need to be followed by a discussion, consonant with mode of production theory, of the nature of these characteristics; this task seems difficult, granted the close links of the rebellion to an export economy and a capitalist crisis. Still less satisfactory are the disgruntled claims that the mode of production account, though inferior in this instance, is still adequate, or that the large number of alternative cases in which the mode of production account is superior renders the political economy approach automatically suspect in this one.

23. The term "human agency" is trickier than many writers suppose. For example, Thompson uses it as part of his attack on structuralism (1978), typified for him in the works of Althusser. Anderson points out (1980, pp. 18-25) the ambiguities in his discussion, the most notable of which is his failure to distinguish between several distinct meanings of the term. For the purposes of the arguments which I am making here, it is sufficient to note that most writers use at least one of the three senses of the term which Anderson discusses.

24.   It should be noted that there are some writers, such as Geertz and Foucault, whose theories are in important senses non-causal, and others, like Althusser, whose notions of the behavior of specific human beings are arguably different from a view of individuals as actors.

Table 3. Voting Results in the 1931 Presidential Election

	Sánchez Cerro	Haya de la Torre	de la Jara	Osores	Total	% Sánchez Cerro	% Haya de la Torre	% de la Jara	% Osores
CUZCO	5,734	2,428	2,202	113	10,477	54.73	23.17	21.02	1.08
Cuzco	1,939	569	388	50	2,946	65.82	19.31	13.17	1.70
Acomayo	277	244	96	0	617	44.89	39.55	15.56	0.00
Anta	402	92	233	2	729	55.14	12.62	31.96	0.27
Calca	254	112	189	11	566	44.88	19.79	33.39	1.94
Canas	55	136	159	4	354	15.54	38.42	44.92	1.13
Canchis	697	286	411	3	1,397	49.89	20.47	29.42	0.21
Chumbivilcas	131	128	59	1	319	41.07	40.13	18.50	0.31
Espinar	18	149	105	0	272	6.62	54.78	38.60	0.00
La Convención	250	251	138	0	639	39.12	39.28	21.60	0.00
Paruro	217	43	52	28	340	63.82	12.65	15.29	8.24
Paucartambo	153	85	55	2	295	51.86	28.81	18.64	0.68
Quispicanchis	796	130	1300	5	1,061	75.02	12.25	12.25	0.47
Urubamba	545	203	187	7	942	57.86	21.55	19.85	0.74

Source: North 1973:257-268.

183

25. The choice between reductionism and holism may be made on other criteria as well. In this sesnse, the choice rests on a number of what some philosophers call "epistemic values" (Laudan, 1984). Some individuals have predispositions towards the one or the other, on fairly reasonable grounds. One may prefer reductionism because it is parsimonious or more readily generalizable, or find holism appealing because it is more complete, or closer to a frquently complex universe. These judgments about types of theories can be based on the examination of the relative success of many different theories on many different occasions, and are most apt when taking theories as wholes. They are less appropriate in evaluating the ability of two specific theories to account for specific phenomena.

REFERENCES

Adas, M. 1988. Market Demand versus Imperial Control: Colonial Contradictions and the Origins of Agrarian Protest in South and Southeast Asia. In Edmund Burke III, ed. *Global Crises and Social Movements.*Boulder, Colorado: Westview Press, pp. 89-116.

Albó, X. 1974. La Paradoja Aymara: Solidaridad y Faccionalismo? *Estudios Andinos.* 4:67-109.

Althusser, L. and E. Balibar. 1970. *Reading "Capital".* London: New Left Books.

Anderson, P. 1980. *Arguments within English Marxism.* Chicago: The University of Chicago Press.

Appadurai, A. 1986. Is Homo Hierarchicus? *American Ethnologist* 13: 745-61.

Appleby, G. 1977. "Export Monoculture and Regional Social Structure in Puno, Peru," in Carol A. Smith (ed.), *Regional Analysis.* Vol. II Social Systems. New York: Academic Press, pp. 291-307.

Aranda, A. and M. Escalante. 1978. *Lucha de Clases en el Movimento Sindical Cusqueño* 1927-1965. Lima: G. Herrera.

Basadra, J. 1963. *Historia de la República del Perú, Quinta Edición Aumentada y Corregida.* Lima: Ediciones Historia.

Bertram, G. 1977. Modernización y Cambio en la Industria Lanera en el Sur del Perú, 1919-1930: Un Caso Frustrado de Desarrollo, *Apuntes* 6:3-22.

Blanchard, P. 1982. *The Origins of the Peruvian Labor Movement, 1883-1919.* Pennsylvania: University of Pittsburgh Press.

Braudel, F. 1972. *The Mediterranean and the Mediterranean World in the Age of Philip II.* Vol. 1, New York: Harper and Row.

Braudel, F. 1973. *The Meditteranean and the Mediterranean World in the Age of Philip II,* Vol. 2, New York: Harper and Row.

Burga, M. and W. Reátegui. 1981. *Lanas y Capital Mercantil en el Sur: La Casa Ricketts, 1895-1935.* Lima: Instituto de Estudios Peruanos.

Burke, E., III and W. Goldfrank. 1988. Global Crises and Social Movements: A Comparative Historical Perspective. In Edmund Burke III, ed. *Global Crises and Social Movements.* Boulder, Colorado: Westview Press, pp. 1-10.

Cotler, J. 1978. *Clases, Estado y Nación en el Perú.* Lima: Instituto de Estudios Peruanos.

Foster-Carter, A. 1978. The Modes of Production Controversy, *New Left Review.* 107:47-77.

Hazen, D. 1974. 'The Awakening of Puno: Government Policy and the Indian Problem in Southern Peru, 1900-1955.' Unpublished Ph.D. thesis, Yale University.

Hobsbawm, E. 1959. *Primitive Rebels: Studies in Archaic Forms of Social Movement in the 19th and 20th Centuries.* Manchester: Manchester University Press.

Hobsbawm, E. 1962. *The Age of Revolution 1789-1848*. London: Weidenfeld and Nicolson.

Hobsbawm, E. 1964. *Labouring Men: Studies in the History of Labour*. London: Weidenfeld and Nicolson.

Hobsbawm, E. 1965. *Karl Marx: Pre-Capitalist Economic Formations*. New York: International Publishers.

Hobsbawm, E. 1968. *Industry and Empire*. (volume 3 of The Pelican Economic History of Britain), London: Weidenfeld and Nicolson.

Hobsbawm, E. 1969. A Case of Neo-feudalism: La Convención, Peru. *Journal of Latin American Studies* 1:31-50.

Hobsbawm, E. 1971a. Peru: The Peculiar "Revolution". *New York Review of Books* 17:29-36.

Hobsbawm, E. 1971b. From Social History to the History of Society. *Daedalus* 100:20-45.

Hobsbawm, E. 1973a. *Revolutionaries: Contemporary Essays*. London: Weidenfeld and Nicolson.

Hobsbawm, E. 19733b. Peasant and Politics. *The Journal of Peasant Studies* 1:3-22.

Hobsbawm, E. 1984. Marx and History. *New Left Review* 143:39-50.

Hobsbawm, E. 1986. Murderous Colombia. *New York Review of Books* 33:27-35.

Hobsbawm, E. and T. Ranger, eds. 1983. *The Intervention of Tradition*. Cambridge: Cambridge University Press.

Jacobsen, N. 1978. Desarrollo Económico y Relaciones de Clase en el Sur Andino (1780-1920): Una Réplica a Karen Spalding. *Análisis*, Vol. 5, pp. 67-81.

Jacobsen, N. 1982. "Land Tenure and Society in the Peruvian Altiplano: Azángaro Province, 1770-1920." Ph.D. thesis, University of California, Berkeley.

Jacobsen, N. 1983. Ciclos y Booms en la Agricultura de Exportacion Latinoamericana: El Caso de la Economía Ganadera en el Sur Peruano, 1855-1920. *Allpanchis* 18:89-146.

Jacobsen, N. 1988. "Free Trade, Regional Elites, and the Internal Market in Southern Peru" in Joseph L. Love and Nills Jacobsen, eds., *Guiding the Invisible Hand: Economic Liberalism and the State in Latin American History*. New York: Praeger. pp. 145-175.

Kahn, J. S. and J. R. Llobera. 1981. *The Anthropology of Pre-Capitalist Societies*. London: MacMillan Publishers Limited.

Kapsoli, W. and W. Reátegui. 1972. *El Campesinado Peruano 1919-1930*. Seminario de Historia Rural Andina, Lima: Universidad Nacional Mayor de San Marcos.

Laudan, L. 1984. *Science and Values: The Aims of Science and Their Role in Scientific Debate*. Berkeley and London: University of California Press.

Mallon, F. E. 1983. *The Defense of Community in Peru's Central Highlands*. New Jersey: Princeton University Press.

Miliband, R. 1969. *The State in Capitalist Society*. New York: Basic Books.

Miller, R. 1982a. The Wool Trade of Southern Peru, 1850-1915. *Ibero-Amikanisches Archiv* 8:297-311.

Miller, R. 1982b. The Coastal Elite and Peruvian Politics, 1895-1919. *Journal of Latin American Studies* 14: 97-120.

North, L. L. 1973. "The Origins and Development of the Peruvian Aprista Party." Unpublished Ph.D. thesis, University of California, Berkeley.

Orlove, B. 1977a. "Against a Definition of Peasantries: Agrarian Production in Andean Peru," in Rhoda Halperin and James Dow (eds.), *Peasant Livelihood: Studies in Economic Anthropology and Cultural Ecology*. New York: St. Martin's Press, pp. 22-35.

Orlove, B. 1977b. *Alpacas, Sheep and Men: The Wool Export Economy and Regional Society in Southern Peru*. New York: Academic Press.

Orlove, B. 1986. An Examination of Barter and Cash Sale in Lake Titicaca: A Test of Competing Approaches in Economic Anthropology. *Current Anthropology* 27:85-106.

Ortner, S. 1984. Theory in Anthropology since the Sixties. *Comparative Studies in Society and History* 26:126-166.

Paige, J. 1975. *Agrarian Revolution: Social Movements and Export Agriculture in the Underdeveloped World.* New York: The Free Press.

Paige, J. 1983. One, Two, Three or Many Vietnams? Social Theory and Peasant Revolution in Vietnam and Guatemala. *Theory and Society* 12(4):699-737.

Pardo, L. 1948. Dos Fortalezas Antiguas Poco Conocidas: Huaccrapucara y Molloccahua. *Revista del Instituto y Museo Arquelógico* 12:3-23.

Piel, J. 1967. A Propos d'un Soulèvement Rural Peruvien au Début du Vingtième Siècle: Tocroyoc (1921). *Revue d'Histoire Moderne et Contemporaine* 14:375-405.

Piel, J. 1970. The Place of the Peasantry in the National Life of Peru in the Nineteenth Century. *Past and Present* 46:108-133.

Piel, J. 1973. Rebeliones Agrarias y Supervivencias Coloniales en el Perú del Sigle XIX. *Revista del Museum Nacional del Perú* 39: 403-14.

Piel, J. 1975. *Capitalisme Agraire au Pérou.* Paris: Editions Anthropos.

Piel, J. 1982. *Crise Agraire et Conscience Créole au Pérou.* Paris: Editions du CNRS.

Rénique, J. L. n.d. *El Movimiento Decentralista Arequipeño y la Crisis del '30, Taller de Estudios Políticos, Programa Académico de Ciencias Sociales.* Lima: Universidad Católica del Perú.

Rivera, S. 1986. *Oprimidos Per No Vencidos: Luchas del Campesinado Aymara y Qhechwa 1900-1980.* La Paz: Hisbol.

Salomon, F. 1987. Ancestor Cults and Resistance to the State in Arequipa, ca. 1748-1754. In Stern, Steve, ed., *Resistance, Rebellion, and Consciousness in the Andean Peasant World, 18th to 20th Centuries.* Madison: University of Wisconsin Press. Pp. 148-165.

Scott, J. C. 1985. *Weapons of the Weak: Everyday Forms of Peasant Resistance.* New Haven, CT: Yale University Press.

Smith, C. A. 1984. Local History in Global Context: Social and Economic Transitions in Western Guatemala. *Comparative Studies in Society and History* 26:193-228.

Stein, S. 1980. *Populism in Peru: The Emergence of the Masses and the Politics of Social Control,* Madison: University of Wisconsin Press.

Stein, W. W. 1978. Town and Country in Revolt: Fragments from the Province of Carhuaz on the Atushparia Uprising of 1885 (Callejón de Huaylas, Peru). *Actes du XLII Congès International des Américanistes* 3:171-187, Paris.

Stern, N. J. 1987. New Approaches to the Study of Peasant Rebellion and Consciousness: Implications of the Andean Experience. In Stern, Steve ed., *Resistance, Rebellion, and Consciousness in the Andean Peasant World, 18th to 20th Centuries.* Madison: University of Wisconsin Press. Pp. 3-25.

Stoler, A. L. 1985. *Capitalism and Confrontation in Sumatra's Plantation Belt,* New Haven, CT: Yale University Press.

Szeminski, J. 1987. "Why Kill the Spaniard? New Perspectives on Andean Insurrectionary Ideology in the 18th Century" in Stern, Steve, ed., *Resistance, Rebellion, and Consciousness in the Andean Peasant World, 18th to 20th Centuries.* Madison: University of Wisconsin Press. Pp. 166-192.

Thompson, E. P. 1978. *The Poverty of Theory and Other Essays.* New York: Monthly Review Press.

Thorp, R. and G. Bertram. 1978. *Peru 1890-1977: Growth and Policy in an Open Economy.* New York: Columbia University Press.

Valcárel, L. 1981. *Memorias*. José Matos Mar, José Deustua and José Luís Rénique, eds. Lima: Instituto de Estudios Peruanos.

Walton, J. 1984. *Reluctant Rebels*, New York: Columbia University Press.

Wolf, E. R. 1957. Closed Corporate Peasant Communities in Mesoamerica and Central Java. *Southwestern Journal of Anthropology* 13:1-18.

Wolf, E. R. 1966a. *Peasants*. Englewood Cliffs, New Jersey: Prentice-Hall.

Wolf, E. R. 1966b. "Kinship, Friendship and Patron-Client Relations in Complex Society," in Michael Banton (ed.), *The Social Anthropology of Complex Socities*. New York: Praeger, pp. 1-22.

Wolf, E. R. 1969. *Peasant Wars of the Twentieth Century*. New York: Harper and Row.

Wolf, E. R. 1982. *Eruope and the People Without History*. California: University of California Press.

Wolf, E. and A. Hansen. 1967. *Caudillo* Politics: A Structural Analysis. *Comparative Studies in Society and History* 9:168-79.

CONFLICT OVER HOUSEWORK:
A PROBLEM THAT (STILL) HAS NO NAME

Marjorie L. DeVault

In social and political discourse, "the family" has typically been discussed and understood as a unified group, with shared interests and concerns. But new scholarship—the new social history of everyday life, feminist studies of women's experience, and research on household violence, for example—suggests a more careful attention to conflict within family groups. Feminist methods of analysis, which prescribe careful attention to gender and to everyday experience, reveal that men and women often have different interests within household groups and therefore, may have reason to struggle over issues of work and the distribution of household resources. Interests seem to diverge, for example, with respect to the household division of labor. In spite of the increasing participation of wives and mothers in paid work outside the home, women continue to be responsible for most household work as well, creating the situation that feminists refer to as the "double day" for working women.

Research in Social Movements, Conflict and Change,
Volume 12, pages 189-202.

Some analysts see this arrangement as constituting an objective conflict of interest, whether or not it is recognized by family members. Heidi Hartmann (1981), for example, argues that since men benefit from women's performance of housework, the family/household is inevitably a "locus of struggle." She suggests that women are beginning to "resist" inequitable arrangements at home: as women increasingly believe that economic security depends on their own paid work, they have begun to limit child-bearing and to do less housework. Hartmann reads these long-term trends in terms of the struggle which results as groups recognize their interests and construct lives in response to material conditions. She raises the issue of struggle, but leaves aside questions about the nature of women's resistance, and how conflict over household work is or is not expressed in everyday interpersonal relations.

In fact, argument about the division of household work is surprisingly rare. In one large survey study, over half of the wives responding reported no difference of opinion over who should do what, and only seven percent reported "a lot" of difference of opinion (Berk 1985, p. 188). When people are asked about the topics of family arguments, only three or four percent mention housework (Scanzoni and Scanzoni 1988). Apparently, most women accept a division of labor that gives them primary responsibility for housework, either because they believe it is fair or because they perceive an inequity but choose not to contest it. On the other hand, Rhian Ellis (1983) suggests that many incidents of domestic violence are triggered by men's complaints about the conduct of housework, and especially about the preparation and service of food. One reading of these findings is that women generally perceive a traditional division of labor as "fair," and that conflict arises largely from the complaints of a few "unreasonable" husbands. I wish to suggest a somewhat different reading, one which suggests that the family is a setting where men feel entitled to complain about housework, while women do not.

In this paper, I examine reports of conflict over housework (as well as reports of its absence) that were collected in the course of intensive interviews for a larger study of women's household work. The study focused on the activities of "feeding a family": planning, shopping, cooking, and conducting meals. Respondents were asked to describe their day-to-day routines in considerable detail; the aim was to examine the character of this often invisible and seemingly trivial work, primarily through careful attention to the language of respondents' reports.[1] Though conflict was not a focus of the study, I expected to hear about conflict; indeed, my interest in the topic grew in part from my own resentment of the inequities arising from the traditional expectation that feeding should be women's work. However, in spite of careful probing, I was surprised and a bit dismayed to find that very few of my respondents spoke about conflict over the division of labor: only two of the thirty women I spoke with discussed any sustained conflict about who would do the work or how it should be done. The others reported a variety of accommodations: some enjoyed cooking and described themselves as choosing to do the work themselves, some disliked the work but accepted the idea that they should do it, and some felt that they received "enough" help from their husbands or children (though women did a great deal more housework than anyone else in all but two households).[2] As I studied all of these women's accounts, I became interested in processes through which the family setting itself works to submerge potential conflict and suppress women's engagement in conflict. Below, I will examine some of the stories I collected about potential and (in a few cases) overt conflicts. These accounts suggest that while the household as workplace produces potential conflicts over women's efforts, the simultaneous construction of household as "family" (and the related construction of "wife" and "mother" as selflessly caring) tends to suppress both awareness and expression of these conflicts.

THE FAMILY SETTING

The family/household is a social setting with a dual character (Rapp 1982). Materially, it is the site of sustenance for a group of individuals, a terrain of material interdependence that supports consumption and necessary day-to-day maintenance. But it is also the place where individuals come together to create and sustain the groups we label "families." Such groups do not spring up "naturally"; they are constructed through the joint activities of family members. In modern industrial societies, the form of family that has developed is thought of as "private," a respite from activities outside the home (Zaretsky 1973). Women who are wives and mothers are expected to do most of the work of overseeing and managing "family life." For women, then, "family" is both workplace and venue for "personal life." As workers in the family setting, women's own interests are often challenged— both by the project of constructing "proper" families, and by the specific demands of other family members who benefit from the work and often express desires and preferences that require additional work.

Several features of household/family work in this setting are relevant to an analysis of the "disappearance" of women's complaints about housework:

1.   Much of the coordinative work of constructing family life is "invisible work" (Daniels 1987). It is easy to recognize the work of sweeping a floor

or chopping vegetables for dinner, but the work required to maintain a family also includes less easily recognized tasks such as organizing schedules, remembering what needs to be done or purchased, and promoting sociability among family members and kin as well.[3] Some of the work of "producing family" is simply not thought of as "work," even by those who do it.

2. Standards for household work are negotiated within particular households: the definition of the work varies from one household to another because it must be the work required to sustain a specific group of people within the constraints of a specific material situation. Cultural myth recognizes this feature of housework in the claim that a housewife is "her own boss," with the autonomy to organize her work as she wishes. What being one's own boss means, however, is that part of the work is to strategize about what needs to be done. The houseworker adjusts to multiple constraints, accommodating not only material circumstance but also the family members who make claims on her time.

3. Household work is strongly gendered and ideologically charged: though there is evidence of some (rather slight) change in attitude and behavior (Pleck 1985), women typically expect to do housework and men typically expect to be served. Many of the women I interviewed talked about cooking as a "natural" or "automatic" part of being "wife" or "mother," and expressed concern about preparing meals "appropriate for a man." And Anne Murcott's study of Welsh couples (1983) suggests that men feel a sense of entitlement to service: when their wives are not at home, they often eat with female relatives, quite comfortably, while women who receive such service talk of "being spoiled."

These features of the contemporary family, and household work within it, provide a context for an analysis of conflict (and its absence) over household work that emphasizes social interaction within a specific setting. In this view, individuals who define themselves as "family" organize their joint activities so as to produce the social relations they understand as constituting that setting. For women, I will argue, "family" is a setting that requires accommodation rather than conflict, and that provides few resources for individual claims-making.

ACCOUNTS OF "CHOICES": RE-DEFINING POTENTIAL CONFICTS

In their discussions of household routine, many of the women I talked with alluded to issues that might have produced conflict, and then dismissed them as untroubling, "nothing much" really. Fairly quickly, and seemingly automatically, most houseworkers develop adjustments to circumstance that are satisfactory enough to mute potential complaints. The boundaries that produce complaints from household members become requirements of the work, and those who do it find ways to manage around these fixed points. The perception that the routine that develops has been chosen provides an interpretive frame for redefining the adjustments that are made. One of my respondents, quite content with her household routine at the time of our interview, told a story from the early days of her marriage, of her first definitions of her work, an episode of resentment and its resolution:

> When we first got married, I played "Suzy Homemaker." I was young and stupid— what did I know? We lived in the suburbs and I worked in the city, and I had to get up at five every morning to get to work. And then on my days off, I'd get up to fix him breakfast, and you know, put on make-up, all that kind of thing. After a while my sister-in-law kind of pulled me aside, and told me I'd better cool it, or he'd get used to that kind of thing.
>
> I still remember, once I came home after a grueling day, and there was my old man, sitting in front of the TV with his potato chips. I said, "God, in my next life I hope I come back as a 26-inch Zenith, I'd get more attention!" That was probably our first fight. But it had been brewing for about four months. You know, we were just getting used to our differences.
>
> I like the way I do things, I'm used to it. I just get it all done on Monday and then I don't have to worry about it. If I don't do it, I'm a wreck by Wednesday. It's not that I like this kind of work, but you have to do it.

For this woman, the story is about something other than conflict over work: they were "getting used to [their] differences." She knows that she "has to do" housework, so she has found a way of doing it that she "likes," or at least, that she's "used to." Now, her husband goes to work before she's up; he has coffee and a doughnut, or buys something to eat on the job, and she sleeps until her daughter wakes up. She says, "If I'm in a pinch, my husband's not beyond doing the laundry, or washing a floor." But it is clear that she accepts responsibility for the housework: it is her domain, and although she would not say that she likes the work, she has accepted what seems to her a satisfactory compromise.

In some households, like this one, such compromises are negotiated with little overt struggle. Some men accept more responsibility, or are less demanding than others; some women are satisfied to take on the family work with little help. Sometimes accommodations cannot be found. What is quite typical in this account, though, is the definition of this kind of negotiation as something other than conflict.

Many other women spoke of doing work they did not enjoy, or think necessary, in order to please their husbands. However, very few of them expressed explicit discomfort about these efforts. As I analyzed their reports, I began to see how the organization of family work contributes to a sense that they have *chosen* responsiveness to husbands' demands. Most women have considerable flexibility in designing household routines, and they choose routines shaped to the idiosyncracies of those in the family. They find ways to adjust to special demands, and then take their adjustments for granted. The choices they have made, and the sense of autonomy that comes with making them, combine to hide the fact that they are so often choices made in order to please others.

Both deference and a sense that her deferential behavior has been freely chosen can be seen in this woman's comments, for example. Her husband is moody and unpredictable, difficult to please and quite openly critical when he does not like the meal she prepares. Although she told me several times that he is "not fussy," she also reported checking with him about every evening's menu before she begins to cook. I remarked that his preferences seemed quite important, and she responded:

> Yeah. I like to satisfy him, you know, because a lot of times I'll hear, oh, you don't cook good, or something like that.

The possibility of such criticism becomes part of the context within which she plans her work. She thinks ahead about what to prepare, but final decisions depend on his responses. When I asked what she would prepare the night of our interview, she could not answer:

> I haven't talked to him today, so I really don't know...
> [MD: Does he always know what he wants?]
> Well—I give him choices. Or he'll say "I don't care." So then it's up to me and I just take out something. Hopefully tonight—I would like to have the pot roast—so maybe he'll say yes. Because he actually bought it the other day, so he might want it.

She finds ways to build a routine that provides some shape for her work and still allows accommodation to his behavior. She explained, for instance, how she plans her shopping:

> Like I'll ask him, what do you want me to pick up? you know, what kind of meat do you want me to pick up? And he'll go through the paper, and he'll tell me, do this, get this. But as far as really making it out [a menu], I just don't. Because sometimes he might not be in the mood for it, he might not want it, or something like that. So I just leave it up in the freezer.

Her scheme sometimes involves an extra trip to the store:

> Then if he wants something, then I'll just go to the store and get what he wants. It's really kind of day by day. I find it easier that way. I couldn't sit there and write what I'm having for dinner every day. I just can't do that.

When I asked why not:

> I don't know, I figure maybe it's just me. I just can't sit there and write, well, we're going to have this and this and this. And then that day you might not have a taste for it. And then you'll want something else. That's the way I look at it.

She "finds it easier" to plan meals day by day, and she presents this as just her way, a personal inclination. It was clear to me that her strategy was shaped by her husband's demands, in response to his moodiness and in order to avoid his sharp words of criticism. Within the constraints of their relationship, she makes choices in order to avoid trouble. Further, though, she interprets her accommodations as choices freely made. She translates his peculiarities into a general observation: "you might not have a taste for it. And then you'll want something else." And finally she presents the result of her strategizing as her own belief: "the way I look at it."

Even when family members are not so demanding, the pattern of choosing to adjust to others is common. Another woman explained how she has chosen a breakfast routine that lets her sleep a bit later instead of eating with the family:

> During the week I usually get their food to the table and then I make a lunch [for her husband]. It's more pragmatic. I could get up earlier and do that, but I choose to stay in bed and avoid sitting at the table.

Such comments stress autonomy and choice; however, it is clear that these women's decisions are not so freely made as they suggest. When husbands decide to press their claims, these become the fixed points around which adjustments and "choices" are made. Another woman, for example, reported a more conflictual negotiation over the breakfast routine, and explained how she has adjusted her morning schedule to accommodate her husband's ideas about breakfast:

> Breakfast has turned into more of a social occasion than I perhaps would care for. For my husband it's a real social affair, and we got into huge fights years ago. He always from the day we got married expected me to get up and fix his breakfast, no matter what time he was going anywhere. Then we lived overseas and we had two maids, and

I couldn't see any point in getting up just to sit with him—I didn't even have to *make* the breakfast. Well, that was a dreadful, dreadful thing. Finally he got over that, and I don't mind getting up, you see, all right, that's a personal thing...So I usually fix breakfast for the two of us. Which is nice—but I would like to be able to read the newspaper, myself.

On this issue, her husband is adamant—it is a "dreadful, dreadful thing" not to have breakfast together—and she has adjusted to this "personal" preference. But she also describes her adjustment in somewhat contradictory terms: she "doesn't mind getting up," it's "all right," even "nice," but still, she would rather read the newspaper.

The choices that women talk about are not entirely illusory: in many ways, houseworkers can choose to do the work as they like. They adopt different general strategies: some maintain that they "couldn't live with" a regular routine, while others describe themselves as "disciplined" and "big on rules." To some extent, people even choose not to do the kinds of work they dislike. One woman, who would like to "just forget about" cooking, has simplified her food routine so that her work is quite automatic: she prepares meals that are "very easy to cook, and very quick also." And another, who enjoys cooking and prepares elaborate meals, thinks of her efforts as "compensation" for the cleaning that she does not enjoy, and often does not do. Still, these real choices—some of which certainly do ease the burdens of housework—seem also to provide a rationale for deference: women emphasize their freedoms and minimize their adjustments to others.

As women make choices about housework, their decisions include calculations about when to press their own claims and when to defer to others. The choice to do something in the way one prefers oneself is made to fit among the more compelling demands of others, especially husbands. The houseworker comes to understand her work in terms of a compromise that seems fair: since she is free to choose in some ways, it is only fair to defer in others. Most women seem only partly conscious of this logic. They, and others as well, notice the choices but not the deference. And the sense of having had the opportunity to choose makes it difficult for these women to press claims in their own interests.

ACCOUNTS OF "LOVE" AND "SELFISHNESS": THE COSTS OF RESISTANCE

When women do initiate conflict about housework, the process can be quite painful, at least partly because such an act carries so much emotional significance. Women who resist doing all of the work, or resist doing it as their husbands prefer, risk the charge—not only from others, but in their own minds as well—that they do not care about the family. When I talked with one woman, for example, she was engaged in an on-going struggle to get her husband to share the housework. She spoke eloquently of the injustice of her situation and her continuing frustration in two interviews, a year apart. But her account was also striking for its ambivalence. Her discussion was punctuated with assurances that she really did love her husband.

> In spite of all this, I love him. [Laughing, but then serious] No, I do love him, and I'm willing to make some sacrifices, but there are times when I really just go off half-crazy. Because the pressure is just too much sometimes. I just feel it's not fair. It's not a judicious way to live, a fair and equal way to live.

Her emphasis on her love for the family—and her willingness to make "sacrifices"—is important because it reveals her understanding of the meaning of a complaint: she is afraid that resisting housework will be heard as a lack of feeling and care.

Since household work is associated so strongly with love, it is quite difficult for women to continue to struggle with family members about the conduct of the work. Another woman I talked with had been married for over twenty years when I talked with her, and had experienced a long period of difficult change. She told the following story:

> There was a time when I was organized, did things on time, on a schedule. I cooked because I felt a responsibility to cook. I felt guilty if I didn't give my husband a certain kind of meal every day...When I made the transition it was hard. For me and him. And he's still going through some problems with objecting to it. But I felt that I had put undue pressure on myself, by trying to do what people used to do, you know...when the husband could pay the bills, and the wife took care of the house . . . told my family that there were certain things that I needed, which went neglected for many years. And when I recognized my own needs, there was a problem...I had given so much of my life to my husband and children, that he thought that I was wrong, not to give them that much time anymore. But I needed to go back to school, needed to improve myself, I needed time to myself...They've come to accept it now. Five, six years ago it was really rough. But now they accept, that you know. I'm a person. I am to be considered a person. I have rights, you know, to myself. It was a rough ride for a while. And I suppose it could have gone in another direction. But it didn't.

Things had changed by the time I talked with this woman: she was pursuing a degree and spent less time cooking elaborate meals. Her husband and children have not taken on much of the work burden, and typically do without meals when she is away from home in the evening—sometimes her daughters will prepare sandwiches—so she continues to be responsible for the bulk of the work, simply doing less than in the past. Yet when she talks about their struggles, she still worries about being "selfish":

> I do take that time now for myself. But I count my study time, and my class time, as my own, you know. You know, so that I don't—I try not to be selfish.

When I asked what "being selfish" meant, she replied:

> I make sure that I have time with them. If my stuff gets to be too much, whatever is necessary, whatever, whatever is important, I try to do. Because we still have the children to raise. So there must be some sharing. They're still there, I can't treat them as though they're not there. Even though they're pretty independent, on their own, they still require a lot of attention. So I have to be careful not to give too much to myself. Because you can fall into that. You know, studying too much. It's hard to describe.

It is, indeed, hard to describe. She claims that she has "rights," like any other person. Yet she will do "whatever is necessary" for her family, and must be "careful not to give too much" to herself. Her talk reveals quite different standards for evaluating her own needs and those of others. Raising such issues within the family requires this intense scrutiny of one's own desires.

This system for accounting her time was not unique. The other woman who was struggling with these issues reported considering her situation in similar terms. She identified two blocks of time as "hers," but both were hers in a rather ambiguous sense:

> I feel the only real time I have to myself is usually my lunch hour [at her job]. I consider that my time for myself.

She has to be firm to maintain even this break officially sanctioned by her employer. Her husband, who works at night and wakes up around noon, would like her to come home so that they could spend time together. But, she reported:

> I do kind of resist that, on any kind of a regular basis. Although, in order to keep a marriage going I should maybe not do that. It's hard for me. Because I know there's a need there, I feel that too. But this gets into all kinds of other issues, about him not helping. I feel that if he would help out more around the house, I'd be more willing to come home and spend more time with him. But you know, I feel like this is my own time for me.

On Sundays she and the family go to church, partly for the children, and partly because she and her husband enjoy the "social aspect," and she counts this activity as her own time as well:

> So Sunday morning is never a time when I can do chores or anything. And in a way,
> I mean, I count that as time for me, in a different sort of way.

These women have asserted to their families that they are people too, with rights (and it is surely striking that they feel a need to put forward such a claim). However, they still must calculate which time to claim as "theirs," and the logic of caring for others labels any too-active exercise of their rights as "selfish."

These women's stories help to show why there were only two of them in the group I studied, why conflict about housework is infrequent. They illustrate the force of the family context within which a mother's claims for time to pursue her own projects can so easily be framed as a lack of care, within which a mother's claim even to be "a person" may be taken as "selfish." If the act of pressing a claim for time off or help from others is so fraught with interpersonal danger, it is perhaps not surprising that so many women choose to accommodate to inequitable arrangements instead of resisting them.

CONCLUSION

Instead of focusing on conflicts that are common in family settings, I have been concerned with the "disappearance" of conflict over housework. In spite of considerable feminist attention to housework since Betty Friedan (1963) identified "the problem with no name," women still do most housework with relatively little complaint. I have suggested that it is still difficult for women to frame complaints about housework and to sustain conflict over the household division of labor.

Many women enjoy caring for their families and think of themselves as freely choosing to do housework for other family members. Yet when they assert their rights to pursue individual projects, at the expense of family service, they often discover the limits of choice and the force of cultural expectation. When women resist—by demanding help with housework or a respite from serving others—they challenge powerful consensual understandings about male and female activity in the family setting. The invisibility of the work that produces "family," the flexibility underlying perceptions of "choice" about the work, and the association between caring work and the supposedly "natural" emotions of a loving wife and mother all tend to suppress conflict over housework. Many women find that they can make enough choices and adjustments in some areas that accommodation in others seems preferable to sustained conflict. Those who insist on negotiating new household patterns must confront their own and others' sense that they do so out of "selfishness" or insufficient concern for those they love. Even as they struggle for more equitable arrangements, these women carefully ration ("count") the time and attention they give to their own needs, while attempting to provide "whatever" their families require. Their demands for themselves are painfully visible within the family, while their accommodations to others remain largely unacknowledged. For a woman to provoke and sustain conflict in the family setting is to risk the charge that she is unnatural or unloving. The costs of conflict are high. Conversely, when a husband complains, or even hints at complaint, his claims carry with them the weight of generations of traditional practice and a body of expert advice about housekeeping and family life based on the assumption that women will serve others.

Some researchers have suggested that women are less inclined than men to initiate or engage in conflict behaviors, or that conflict "avoidance" is characteristic of women—though the evidence is quite mixed, and other studies find no significant sex differences (for one review, see Womack 1988). I mean to suggest that such analyses, which define conflict behavior as a gender-linked "trait," suffer because gender is conceived abstractly, apart from any social context. I would argue instead that both "gender" and "conflict" are always constructed in particular settings, and that settings— and the social positions defined within them—provide actors with differential resources to bring into play in any conflict. Individuals are always "doing gender" (West and Zimmerman 1987), acting out specific versions of "male" or "female" appropriate to immediate, local settings. In family settings, women are expected to act as "wives" or "mothers." Their own and others' understandings of these categories include the idea that family service—doing things for others—comes "naturally" with being wife or mother. Given these understandings, "everyone knows" that a man enjoys a good meal, while a woman's resistance to providing it every evening is puzzling, and must be explained. And given such asymmetry in the construction of the "family" setting, it is perhaps unsurprising that conflict over the division of labor so often "disappears."

NOTES

1. These data were collected in 1982-83. I located households in several different neighborhoods, and then interviewed those household members who shared the work of feeding

the family (30 women and three men). All of the households studied included children, but they were ethnically diverse and included single-parent and two-paycheck families, as well as families of different classes. The individuals discussed here are all white or black women, and all but one, a professional woman, are from working-class/white-collar households. I do not believe that the pattern I discuss here is class-specific, though the nature of these data do not allow definitive evaluation of that possibility. In my attention to respondents' language, I have drawn on insights from Scott and Lyman (1968) on "accounts," and Mishler (1986) and Paget (1983) on the analysis of narratives in interviews. For more information about the study, see DeVault (1984, 1987). Portions of this paper have been excerpted from a book manuscript in progress.

2. Of course, since my sample is made up of couples who have chosen to stay together, it is possible that they represent a group whose experience is less conflictual than that of all couples who attempt relationships.

3. For development of this expansion of the definition of housework, see Davidoff (1976) and Luxton (1980), as well as DeVault (1987) on feeding, Di Leonardo (1987) on "kin work," and Papanek (1979) on status production.

REFERENCES

Berk, S. F. 1985. *The Gender Factory: The Apportionment of Work in American Households.* New York: Plenum Press.

Daniels, A. K. 1987. "Invisible Work." *Social Problems* 34:403-415.

Davidoff, L. 1976. "The Rationalization of Housework." Pp. 121-151 in Diana L. Barker and Sheila Allen (eds.), *Dependence and Exploitation in Work and Marriage.* London: Longman Group.

DeVault, M. L. 1984. "Women and Food: Housework and the Production of Family Life." Ph.D. Dissertation. Evanston, IL: Northwestern University.

————. 1987. "Doing Housework: Feeding and Family Life." Pp. 178-191 in Naomi Gerstel and Harriet Engel Gross (eds.), *Families and Work.* Philadelphia: Temple University Press.

Di Leonardo, M. 1987. "The Female World of Cards and Holidays: Women, Families and the Work of Kinship." *Signs* 12:440-453.

Ellis, R. 1983. "The Way to a Man's Heart: Food in the Violent Home." Pp. 164-171 in Anne Murcott (ed.), *The Sociology of Food and Eating.* Aldershot: Gower Publishing.

Friedan, B. 1963. *The Feminine Mystique.* New York: Dell.

Hartmann, H. I. 1981. "The Family as the Locus of Gender, Class and Political Struggle: The Example of Housework." *Signs* 6:366-394.

Luxton, M. 1980. *More Than a Labour of Love: Three Generations of Women's Work in the Home.* Toronto: The Women's Press.

Mishler, E. G. 1986. *Research Interviewing: Context and Narrative.* Cambridge, MA: Harvard University Press.

Murcott, A. 1983. "'It's a Pleasure to Cook for Him': Food, Mealtimes and Gender in Some South Wales Households." Pp. 78-90 in Eva Garmarnikow, David H. J. Morgan, Jane Purvis and Daphne Taylorson (eds.), *The Public and the Private.* London: Heinemann.

Paget, M. A. 1983. "Experience and Knowledge." *Human Studies* 6:67-90.

Papanek, H. 1979. "Family Status Production: The 'Work' and 'Non-work' of Women." *Signs* 4:775-781.

Pleck, J. H. 1985. *Working Wives/Working Husbands*. Beverly Hills: Sage Publications.

Rapp, R. 1982. "Family and Class in Contemporary America: Notes Toward an Understanding of Ideology." Pp. 168-187 in Barrie Thorne (ed.) *Rethinking the Family*. New York: Longman.

Scanzoni, L. D. and J. Scanzoni. 1988. *Men, Women and Change* (3rd edition). New York: McGraw-Hill.

Scott, M. and S. Lyman. 1968. "Accounts." *American Sociological Review* 33:46-62.

West, C. and D. H. Zimmerman. 1987. "Doing Gender." *Gender and Society* 1:125-151.

Womack, D. F. 1987. "Conflicts Between Women at Work." *Women and Language* 11:47-50.

Zaretsky, E. 1973. *Capitalism, the Family and Personal Life*. New York: Harper.

THE SUDANESE SETTLEMENT:

REFLECTIONS ON THE 1972

ADDIS ABABA AGREEMENT

C.R. Mitchell

One of the most interesting examples of recent international conflict management was the process which led to the signing of a peace agreement at Addis Ababa in February 1972. This settlement was made between representatives of the Sudanese government and of the South Sudanese Liberation Movement (SSLM), itself representing an amalgamation of smaller secessionist and guerrilla movements from the southernmost three provinces of that country.

The Agreement brought to an end (even if only temporarily) a complicated, sporadic but increasingly bitter civil war between "Arab" northerners and "African" southerners (although many southerners had remained part of the northern dominated political regime in Khartoum); a conflict which many dated from 1955 but which only involved sustained military activity on the part of southerners from 1962. It established a

Research in Social Movements, Conflict and Change,
Volume 12, pages 203-243.
Copyright © 1990 by JAI Press Inc.
All rights of reproduction in any form reserved.
ISBN: 1-55938-065-9

considerable degree of regional autonomy for the south (although it fell short of a classic "federal" solution); made arrangements for southerners to have continued representation in central government institutions in Khartoum; and established terms for economic assistance from the north to the traditionally impoverished and underdeveloped south. The Agreement also made arrangements for a ceasefire and a subsequent integration of the military wing of the SSLM (the Anya Nya) into the Peoples' Armed Forces (PAF) of the Sudan. It proved to be one of the main foundations of Sudanese President Nimiery's regime during the following decade and of that decade's peace and stability between the northern and southern regions of the Sudan, a stability that lasted until the terms and the spirit of the Agreement were unilaterally undermined by one of its main architects, Jafaar al Nimiery.

FEATURES OF THE AGREEMENT

Civil wars and secessionist struggles are the most notoriously difficult of all forms of large scale, violent human conflict to terminate successfully, short of outright "victory" for one side or the other.[1] Hence, the Addis Ababa Agreement is a relative rarity; a negotiated settlement of a major case of "civil strife." Aside from this a-typical success, the settlement negotiated at Addis Ababa in early 1972 was unusual in four other respects (and it might easily be argued that such special characteristics make it a unique and unrepeatable case of successful "peacemaking.")

For one thing, it represented a successful solution to a conflict in which the main issue increasingly became the survival of an existing political system, or its division into two separate systems via the secession of a part of the geographical "periphery." This type of domestic dispute is particularly intractable to any form of management. Usually, "solutions" involve the outright victory of the status quo party and the preservation of unity (as in the case or Nigeria or Kantaga) or, less frequently, the victory of the revisionist party and the final splitting up of the system (as in the civil war between West and East Pakistan). Resistance to compromise and the pursuit of all or nothing solutions are particularly the case when the previous behavior of the adversaries has been violent, widespread and long-lasting as had, indeed, been the case in the Sudan.

Secondly, the process of arriving at a final agreement involved a successful mediation by a number of external organizations and governments all of whom helped (in a variety of ways) to bring about the final meetings and the eventual settlement. The successful involvement of outsiders in high-level civil strife is a further rarity. Such disputes are normally highly resistant to outside peacemaking if only because of the barriers posed by doctrines of state sovereignty or non-interference in the domestic affairs of other countries—doctrines usually employed by political incumbents to avoid conferring any recognition or status to "rebel" movements, no matter how well supported.

Thirdly, the conventional wisdom about leaders who make peace usually being new replacements for those who have initiated and conducted the war does not seem to hold good in the Sudanese case. It could be argued that the regime of President Nimiery had only been in power since the military coup of May, 1969, and was thus in a position to repudiate previous failures and repression, especially that carried out under the military government of General Abboud. However, examination of the final peacemaking process does reveal clearly that it represented a major switch of policy from that pursued by the Nimiery regime between May 1969 and July 1971.

Finally, there is the familiar argument that a successful negotiation or compromise must rest on the unquestioned ability of the leadership of *both* adversaries to conclude an agreement that can be sold to their supporters (and forced upon any dissident elements) and that this, in turn, depends upon firm control of their organizations and on an unchallenged position of predominance by both leaderships. Again, this did not seem entirely applicable in the Sudanese case. In the north, Nimiery had barely survived an attempted military take-over by members of the Sudanese armed forces connected with the Sudanese Communist Party (SCP). In the south, Major-General Lagu, the military commander of SSLM, was still engaged in building up his leadership position (to the extent of not having it generally and formally recognized until May, 1971) even while southern representatives were conducting preliminary exchanges with representatives of the Khartoum Government. Given all these particular, features of the conflict,[2] can it seriously be argued that the process of peacemaking within the Sudan and the solution eventually hammered out at Addis Ababa constitute a "model" of anything connected with the conflict termination process, whether for Africa or any part of the world facing divisive disputes over unity and territorial integrity? The problem with trying to answer such a question is that the term "model" itself has been subjected to a great deal of abuse in the social sciences, and can take on a wide variety of meanings according to who is using it. Strictly speaking, a "model" is some formal representation of a system or a process in the real world such that a formal language of the model (usually mathematical) is used to map features of that part of the real world in such a way that the relationships in the model are formally equivalent to those in the system or process under study. No attempt will be made to produce such a model here.

A less formal definition is "an example for imitation or emulation" and this is the sense in which the term will be used in this paper. The Sudanese solution will be examined to see whether it might serve as an "example for emulation" in three senses. The first of these concerns the unilateral problem confronting the decisionmakers of parties in conflict who have to decide if (or when) a balance of factors make it "reasonable" to try to achieve a compromise solution rather than continuing the conflict in the hope of attaining victory. In this respect, is the Sudanese peacemaking process in any way typical of a class of conflict termination problems, making it usable (at least) as a source of general propositions about such decision-making dilemmas?

The second sense in which the Sudanese case might serve as a "model" adopts the standpoint of the outsiders attempting to ameliorate, and possibly conciliate, situations of widespread and violent civil strife. Does the Sudanese case offer any lessons about appropriate processes which can be initiated in such circumstances, or practices which might well be used in other, all too numerous, situations of intractable domestic conflicts?

Thirdly, the actual settlement itself might well be regarded as a potential "example for emulation," in that it represented a guide for solutions appropriate for other countries in Africa—or elsewhere—that confront problems of internal, colonially imposed boundaries, major regional differences, and a political community significantly divided along linguistic, religious or ethnic lines. In such situations, traditional answers based upon the conception of a unified national-state may be wholly unsuitable. The need to develop political forms to cope with such divided social systems is undeniable and urgent, given the colonial legacy in Africa and elsewhere. Can the Sudanese settlement, perhaps, provide some pointers to the kind of political arrangement that might prove a viable alternative to complete centralization, a federal structure or periodic efforts to secede?

THE CIVIL WAR IN THE SUDAN

Before attempting to examine the final settlement constructed in Addis Ababa in 1972, it is helpful to outline the main features of the civil war brought to an end by that Agreement. This section, therefore, attempts a brief sketch of the conflict, emphasizing a number of factors in the struggle which seem important for understanding both the difficulties of achieving any final, mutually satisfactory settlement and the processes which finally led to the meetings at Addis Ababa and the conclusion of such a settlement. Anyone interested in a detailed history of the conflict should consult the works mentioned in the bibliography (especially Eprille 1974; Beshir 1968; and Wai 1973).

The conventional date for the outbreak of "hostilities" between the Arabised North of Sudan and the "African" South (represented by the heterogeneous peoples of the three southernmost provinces in the country) is August, 1955, four months before the county formally achieved its independence. On that occasion, southern troops of the Equatoria Corps stationed in Juba mutinied on the rumor that they were to be moved North after independence. After killing several of their officers and a number of northerners and then looting the town, they disappeared into the bush, where for a number of years they formed roving, bandit-like groups pursued with little success by the Sudanese army. The mutiny is held by many to have highlighted and emphasized the ethnic, religious and cultural division between the northern and southern regions of the country, the mistrust between the leaders involved and the effects of a traditional British policy of administering the two areas separately and very differently, at least until after the Second World War. Whether it also marks the beginning of a sixteen-year struggle between southern political movements and the Khartoum Government—a struggle which led UNHCR to estimates of 176,000 Sudanese refugees in neighboring countries by 1970 and estimated deaths of 500,000 southerners—is another question. Organized, as opposed to sporadic, military resistance to northern troops only really began in the South in 1962, a process symbolized by the guerrillas' successful capture in September 1963 of an army post at Pacalla after a three-day battle. The new guerrilla organization was entitled the "Anya Nya." One of its leaders was Colonel (later Major-General) Joseph Lagu, a regular officer in the Sudanese army who had joined the guerrillas in the bush in Equatoria Province, and started to organize them into a force which could systematically harass northern security forces in the South. Guerrilla attacks and organization continued to grow, although development of the campaign was handicapped by external indifference to the regional struggle in Sudan and a consequent lack of arms and resources. The problem was somewhat alleviated in 1965 by acquisition of arms from the defeated "Simba" rebels in the neighboring Congo (Zaire) and later, in 1969, by Israeli willingness to supply arms and instructors via Uganda. This latter development materially assisted Lagu to extend his hold upon the southern guerrilla organizations and his rise to prominence in the southern leadership.

The vigor with which the military aspects of the conflict were prosecuted by the Khartoum Government varied with the regime in power at the time. The accession to power of Sudan's first military regime, that of Major-General Abboud, produced a policy of sustained repression of southern leaders and politicians, amounting to an attempt to wipe out completely what was always a small elite; and of repression and punitive sanctions by the army pursuing the anti-guerrilla struggle in the South. The civilian regime of Sir al Khatim el Khalifa, which replaced Abboud's government following a civil uprising in Khartoum in 1964, pursued a policy of conciliation. It was during this initial period of return to civilian government that the Round Table Conference of northerners and southerners to consider the regional problem was held (March, 1965). Tragically, this Conference collapsed without finding any settlement to the problem, one (but only one) of the stumbling blocks to agreement being the Khartoum Government's inability to control the behavior of the military in the South, who continued to pursue a bloody campaign against the guerrilla forces. Following the elections in June, 1965, the new government of Mohamed Mahgoub ushered in a new period of repression and anti-southern policies causing many southern leaders to flee into an exile from which some had only just returned. The subsequent government of Sadiq al Mahdi pursued a similar policy towards the southern problem when it came to power in 1966. It was not until the military again intervened in national politics in May, 1969, with Ja'afar Nimiery's coup, that any great change in official northern attitudes to the southern problem was clearly noticeable. Although there were internal differences within the new regime over southern policy, the military government in June, 1969 issued a declaration recognizing that historic differences did, indeed, exist between the North and South of Sudan, and putting forward a proposal that the South should be granted some unspecified degree of local autonomy. The offer had no immediate, direct effect upon the course of the struggle, however. It was not until over a year later that serious and continuous negotiations began between representatives of the Khartoum government and leaders of the southern political movement. In the end, it was not until October, 1972 (by which time Nimiery had survived an attempted, Communist-supported coup, the World Council of Churches (WCC) and All Africa Conference of Churches (AACC) had become involved as intermediaries, and prior agreements of mutual non-interference concluded between Khartoum and the Emperor of Ethiopia) that delegations from the rival parties to the conflict met to begin formal negotiations to end the dispute.

One factor which contributed to the longevity of the termination process was the continuing inability of the southern leaders to form a unified political movement to represent—even agree upon—southern aspirations, goals and tactics. This inability to overcome the divisions among southerners themselves had been a feature of southern politics thoughout the entire period of the civil war. It had bedevilled northern efforts both to produce a coherent policy towards the southern problem and to find a representative body with which to negotiate once northern policy had swung from repression to conciliation. The complex sources of division within the ranks of southern leaders, frequently based upon tribal and personal antagonisms, require a major analysis to do them any justice.[3] For our purpose, it is enough to note that they were important in determining whether educated southern leaders remained to work (when they could) with the government in Khartoum—that is, remained "insiders"; whether they went into exile and formed Sudanese movements (and sometimes governments) in exile—that is, became "outsiders"; or whether they remained in the country but operated in the southern bush with one of the guerrilla forces—that is, became "inside-outsiders."

The dilemma for members of the southern elite became acute following Aboud's army take-over in 1958, and many went into exile in Leopoldville to form the Southern African Closed Districts Union (SACDU), which later became the Sudan African National Union (SANU) based in Kampala. With the overthrow of Abboud, one wing of SANU returned to take part with the newly-formed "Southern Front" in Sudanese politics again and participate in the Round Table Conference. Another wing remained in exile, subsequently splitting over personal and other rivalries into the Azania Liberation Front, the Sudan African Liberation Front and SAUC. Even the subsequent period of northern intransigence under Mahgoub and el Mahdi failed to bring southerners together. In spite of a convention held at Angrudi in Eastern Equatoria in August, 1969 to set up a South Sudanese Provisional Government, the southern movement continued to remain splintered and divided. Such divisions were exacerbated by the willingness of prominent southern leaders, especially in the Sudanese Communist Party, to work with the northern government of General Nimiery when it came to power in 1969.

It should be emphasized that divisions within the southern political movement lasted right up to (and, in some cases, even beyond) the process of negotiation that preceded the Addis Ababa meetings. It was not until 1970 that most of the southern organizations amalgamated into the South Sudan Liberation Movement (SSLM). Even then, there was a residue of leaders and organizations in exile who remained separate from the SSLM. Moreover, it was not until May, 1971 (when contacts between Khartoum and SSLM were well advanced) that Lagu was able to call a conference in Upper Nile Province; firmly establish the SSLM as representative of the southern movement with Anya Nya as its official military wing; amalgamate other guerrilla groups into Anya Nya; and have his role as Commander-in-Chief generally acknowledged. The SSLM had thus only recently acquired its fragile unity when its representatives finally travelled to Addis Ababa to negotiate about a settlement on behalf of the south.

It is obviously impossible to cover the complexities, the shifts of policies and tactics, the changes in alignments and attitudes, that make up a period of at least ten years' violent civil war in a country as diverse and complicated as the Sudan. All that is attempted above is to draw out a number of themes which were important in their effects upon efforts to terminate the conflict and particularly upon the final process that began at the start of 1970. To recapitulate, emphasis needs to be placed upon four factors:

a. The historical roots of the division between northern and southern regions of the country, a division reinforced by both imperial administrative and missionary practices.

b. The relative "insulation" of the struggle from much external involvement, although some intervention took place towards the end of the war. Concerned individuals and groups in London referred to the conflict in Sudan as "the unknown war" and are said to have named their regular periodical on the problem "The Grass Curtain" to symbolize the lack of information on (or outside interest in) Africa's longest running civil war.

c. The relative instability of politics and hence regimes in the northern region of the country, such that, after independence in 1956, four civilian and two military regimes followed one another in rapid succession.

d. The lack of unity of the southern political movement in general, a lack which reflected uncertainties over the basic position of southerners; whether to work within a unified Sudan and hence press for some form of regional autonomy, or whether to attempt to secede and set up a separate and sovereign state, quite apart from the northern region and its alien-dominated government.

THE ADDIS ABABA AGREEMENT

The process by which the parties to the Sudanese conflict reached a stage of face-to-face negotiations in Addis Ababa and, finally, a workable agreement, was a complex one.[4] Initial contacts between the Khartoum

Government and the SSLM's representative in London began as early as August, 1970, originally under the auspices of the Movement for Colonial Freedom (MCF). By January, 1971, Colonel Lagu's and the SSLM's decision to accept some settlement "... within the framework of one Sudan..." had been communicated to Khartoum, although the nature of this offer did not become generally known in government circles until April, shortly before the attempted anti-Nimiery coup by the SCP. In May a WCC/AACC delegation had agreed with members of the Khartoum Government that it would try to contact southern leaders with a view to arranging formal negotiations, and when the delegation returned to Khartoum in October, 1971, it was able to report that southern leaders, having consulted among themselves (an extended process given the geographical "scatter" of southern groups and leaders), were ready to discuss preliminary negotiations for autonomy.

Unfortunately, when these preliminary talks took place they ended in failure, in spite of the fact that, a few days before the talks, President Nimiery and Emperor Haile Selassi had agreed to stop aiding each others' "rebels" in Eritrea and the southern Sudan, thus increasing pressure on the South for a settlement. The southerners objected to the Khartoum Government's view of the nature of "regional autonomy" and the war resumed. However, private meetings continued between SSLM representatives and members of Nimiery's government to try to work out acceptable meanings of "autonomy" and "federation," and on 28 January the WCC announced that new talks had been arranged for 15 February under the auspices of the AACC, with the Emperor of Ethiopia acting as formal mediator in the conflict. A few days later the Khartoum Government announced the convening of a conference of aid agencies to discuss humanitarian aid to the South. This was to begin six days after the start of the Addis Ababa negotiations.

In the event, the negotiations took slightly longer than six days, but a draft agreement was finally initialled on 27 February at the Addis Ababa Hilton. The date for final ratification was set for 12 March, but this was preempted by President Nimiery, who announced ratification at a public rally in Khartoum on 3 March. Ratification for the southerners was a more difficult matter. Colonel Lagu had to request an extension of the time permitted when 12 March arrived. President Nimiery announced a (mainly successful) ceasefire on that day, but when Lagu arrived in Addis Ababa for final ratification on 26 March, he brought with him several amendments to the original agreement which had been insisted upon by one or other of the southern leaders not directly involved at the original negotiations. However, when it came to the point of renegotiating and running the risk of an impasse, or retaining the original terms, the SSLM representative chose the latter course. The Addis Ababa Agreement was finally ratified on 28 March, 1972.

The settlement which emerged from Addis Ababa negotiations and the final period of intra-party politicking up to 28 March was a serious attempt to reconcile northern goals of retaining a unitary (or at least united) state with southern fears regarding safety and security, as well as desires for a considerable degree of autonomy. For some southerners, this last goal took the form of a demand for a separate state for the three southern provinces (although Colonel Lagu, after the agreement was concluded, specifically denied that this had ever been his personal goal). The preliminary communique announcing the Addis Ababa talks of 27 February had spoken of "...the fraternal desire of both parties to preserve the unity of their country and to safeguard the aspirations of the Southern Region...", and the final Agreement reflected this initial bargaining position.

The main provisions of the Agreement dealt with the nature of the autonomy that would be enjoyed by the South following a ceasefire and a brief (at most eighteen-month) interim period of rule by an Executive Council for the South, initially appointed by President Nimiery. The three southern provinces were to be regarded as a distinct "region" in the Sudan, with a Regional Assembly to be elected by universal adult suffrage within eighteen months of ratification of the agreement. The Assembly would recommend appointments to a Regional Council and choose its own Regional President as head of that council, although formal appointment of both would remain in the hands of the President of Sudan. The Regional Council was to control all aspects of southern policy except defense, foreign affairs, currency and finance and overall social and economic planning, the latter remaining under the control of the central government in Khartoum, in which the South would also be represented. (Under the Southern Provinces Regional Self-Government Act of 1972 it was later agreed that the Regional Assembly could ask the President to defer the entry into force of any central government legislation applying to the South. The President was also to be responsible for good relations between central Government ministries and members of the southern Council.) The Addis Ababa Agreement also stated that, while Arabic would be the official language of the Sudan, North and South, English would be the "common language" of the South and would be taught in schools. Finally, the last of the major provisions of the Agreement dealt with arrangements for the Anya Nya, the southern guerillas in the bush. These (estimated—incorrectly as it subsequently became apparent—at 12,000) were to be incorporated in the Sudanese army's Southern Command, which would, for a transitional term, be under the command of a commission of northerners and southerners) until the south had set up its own machinery for maintaining law and order, which was to consist of an armed police force and between 2,000 and 3,000 frontier guards.

The settlement therefore tried to satisfy the southerners by offering a considerable degree of regional autonomy, plus continued participation in central government decisionmaking and the national army. It provided for the gradual transfer of southern security into southern hands, both as regards control and direct implementation. It provided opportunities for rank and file members of the SSLM to become part of the national army. It safeguarded the position of English as the regional *linqua franca* and ensured that this would be used for both regional education and administration. In return, the agreement signalled the abandonment of any further effort to take the south permanently out of the Sudan, and maintained " ...the unity of their country..." for both northerners and southerners.

That the arrangement did not fully "...safeguard the legitimate aspirations..." of at least some of the southerners is indicated by the difficulties Lagu experienced in getting agreement to these terms prior to ratification, and by the list of amendments that were suggested between 27 March and 28 March, only to be finally abandoned by him at Addis Ababa on the latter date. Individual southern leaders denounced both the preliminary agreement to negotiate within a framework of a single Sudan and the eventual Agreement ratified at the end of March. Gordon Mortat Mayen denounced the former as an 'Arab fraud" from Kinshasa and was promptly expelled by an irate President Mobutu. Similar feelings were expressed by some southerners when the terms of the final Agreement were known. Nonetheless, at the time, the Agreement was generally welcomed by southerners and, although its short-term implementation was not without problems and difficulties, it did form the basis of a period of peace and stability in the three southern provinces.

ASPECTS OF PEACEMAKING: (1) CUTTING LOSSES

The brief review of the events leading up to the Addis Ababa Agreement and that Agreement itself lead to the question of whether it is possible (or proper) to use the Sudanese case study as, in any sense, a model for the process of conflict termination between powerful and strongly opposed adversaries. The question of whether it is "proper" is basically a methodological one. Can one ever derive "lessons" or principles from a single (apparently very unusual) example, or place any reliance upon generalizations arrived at without a systematic comparison of many cases?

The methodological justification for our approach derives from the theory-generating rather than the theory-testing end of the overall theory building process. There is no sense in which a single case can be used as *a test* of a general theory or hypothesis, but such a case can be used to generate an analytical framework or a set of hypotheses. The crucial questions are whether the model used in our present case study helps (a) to provide a coherent account of the Sudanese peacemaking process and (b) to generate hypotheses that can be carried over and checked in other cases, thus moving towards a general theory of peacemaking.

In other words, the Sudanese case will be used as a source of fruitful ideas or hypotheses about three aspects of the complex process of peacemaking. Such ideas are presented as starting points for further investigation of the topic. Our use of the term "model" should therefore also be understood as implying a heuristic function for the three aspects of: (i) problems of pre-negotiation decisionmaking, especially those associated with leaders' calculations about termination and cutting losses; (ii) features of successful intermediaries in widespread and violent intra-national conflicts; and (iii) the structure of regional settlements that are likely to be acceptable to parties in conflict over issues of regional autonomy or secession. More formally, it could be argued with Lijphart[4a] that the present work is partly an example of an *interpretative* case study, using generalizations to illuminate the ending of the first Sudanese Civil War; but more particularly of a *hypotheses-generating* case study which starts with "...a more or less vague notion of possible hypotheses ..." and then attempts "...to formulate definite hypotheses to be tested subsequently among a larger number of cases..."[4b]

The first heuristic use of the Sudanese case study thus focuses on the circumstances under which decisionmakers are likely to consider the option of conciliation and negotiation as opposed to that of continuing the conflict by coercion and violence. What influences leaders in their calculations about the costs and benefits of alternative courses of actions? What, on occasions, persuades them to cut their losses and attempt to make peace with an adversary? In what circumstances *can* a leader consider the option of seeking peace rather than prosecuting the war?

One of the first clues offered by the case of the Sudan to any general answer to this question is that by the beginning of 1971 the struggle had clearly reached a position of stalemate and, furthermore, a stalemate that was generally perceived to be one of long duration. This is not to say that the balance of forces (or even balance of advantage) between government and guerrillas was anywhere near equal. The Anya Nya did not "control" most of the South any more than government forces had succeeded in "pacifying" all key areas. However, while it was true that Sudanese Government forces could move anywhere in the region if in reasonable strength, it was also true that the Anya Nya (and hence the SSLM) had a wide measure of popular support from the local population and continued to be able to attract recruits into its ranks and to arm them. As John Howell emphasises,

> ... In guerrilla war, parity is reached not necessarily by equality of armed strength, but at a point where the superior conventional force of the counter-insurgent is unable either to eradicate the insurgent, or prevent his continued recruitment of men and continued access to weaponry; and the insurgent is unable to wrest control in areas which the counter-insurgent is determined to hold and is unable to destroy the political will of the counter-insurgent to defend ... (Howell p. 426).

It seems clear that the war in the South had reached something like this position by 1971. The guerillas could not "win" in any convincing sense, while the government could not eradicate the influence of the Anya Nya.

The perceptions and expectations of decisionmakers on both sides are more speculative but, given that neither party fundamentally misperceived the nature of their relationship, it seems unlikely that Nimiery and the leadership in Khartoum failed to recognize that they were confronting a long, drawn-out, frustrating and highly expensive struggle in the South. Similarly, Lagu and the Anya Nya leadership were equally aware that, unless the Khartoum government's will to continue the conflict collapsed completely, there was no hope of rapid success in achieving their objectives, either of autonomy or secession, by military means[5]. In other words, for all the involved leaders, the future seemed to offer a process of increasingly costly struggle, with little prospect of final, unequivocal[6] success, so that likely sacrifices and costs far outweighted likely gains.

In such circumstances, an added importance must be given to the manner in which the leaders of both sides perceive and evaluate each other's commitment and determination to continue in the pursuit of their goals; their unity and intransigence; and their level of previous commitment to and sacrifice in pursuit of their goals that underlie the conflict. If new leaders have come to power within an adversary, to what degree do they appear committed to the goals and strategies of their predecessors, and what public statements have they made that tie them to a continuance of coercion? If the commitment is not strong, what are the adversary's likely terms and conditions, and how firm is his initial bargaining position likely to be? Such questions arise in the Sudanese case because of the fact that President

Nimiery's regime in Khartoum was of relatively recent establishment, thus being able to distance itself from its predecessor's aims and behavior. Similarly, unchallenged leadership of the Anya Nya and—by implication—a key position in the SSLM had only recently come into the hands of Colonel Lagu and his associates and was, indeed, only finally confirmed while the initial peacemaking process was under way. As for likely terms, it should have been clear to southern leaders that Nimiery's "new strategy," announced in June, 1969, at least recognized differences between north and south as well as holding out some hopes for a form of regional autonomy, although its nature remained ambiguous. To southern leaders, the main obstacles to any serious consideration of some rapprochement (aside from the dynamics of an on-going guerrilla war) must have remained in the Sudan Communist Party's prior conditions of the development of some new, "...broad socialist orientated democratic movement in the south..." (Howell p. 422), an obstacle that was only removed following the purge of powerful SCP members from Nimiery's regime[7] after the abortive coup in 1971. In short, the Sudanese case suggests that among the key factors that influence parties' decisions to seek some negotiated settlement (as opposed to continuing the conflict through struggle and coercion) are complex *inter-party* factors, quite apart from the obvious one of the perceived position of both strategic and tactical advantage and the way what may be termed "success on the battlefield" changes over time. Inter-party factors include decisionmakers' evaluations of the likely long-term gains and costs of continuing the struggle as against any likely settlement they might be offered by the adversary; evaluations of sacrifices already made in pursuit of the party's goals, which tend to make it more difficult to abandon the struggle and sacrifice previous "investment" of effort, resources and (in many cases) people's lives; evaluations of the extent to which public commitments have tied their own and their adversary's hands over particular courses of action, removing some from realistic consideration; and evaluations of the internal condition of the adversary and particularly the leaders' unity, level of intransigence, room for maneuvre and the interests of dominant factions or groups within that leadership. All of these played a part in the Sudanese parties' considerations of whether, when and how to seek a negotiated settlement as opposed to a victory, and appear not unlikely to be important in other cases.

However, *inter-party* factors are not the only ones which are important in affecting decisions to seek a negotiated end to a conflict. The Sudanese case suggests that attention must also be directed towards at least two other sets of factors which potentially play a major role in any decision to carry on or to cut losses and negotiate. These are *intra-party* factors and *inter-*

ally factors. Both appear to have played a major role in the decisonmaking of both parties in Sudan and it seems reasonable to argue that the right combination of all three groups of factors must exist if any peacemaking process is to succeed in getting under way, let alone move towards a settlement.

One of the striking things about the intra-party situation for the adversaries in the Sudanese case was the way in which a number of internal conflicts and dilemmas had to resolve themselves before any realistic settlement effort could be made. For the Khartoum Government, the failure of the SCP coup in 1971 and the earlier (March, 1970) removal of a serious threat posed to the regime by the Ansari sect had left President Nimiery in (at least) a temporary position from which he could contemplate a settlement with the southerners which could only be presented as a compromise rather than as victory. Nimiery's power base was, for the time being, relatively secure. The influence of some dangerous factions within the regime had been removed although no new allies had been won over and future threats seemed inevitable. The internal cohesiveness of the Khartoum Government had been temporarily brought to the point where a settlement could be sought (without too much immediate danger of intra-party repudiation), sold to northern interests and made to "stick." Moreover, the northern leader was also astute enough to realize that, by concluding a reasonable settlement with the South, southern fortunes would be tied to those of the northern regime which had arranged and guaranteed the settlement. In a paradoxical sense, the regime's power base would be extended to include its erstwhile adversaries in the south. Not only would reconciled southern leaders develop an interest in remaining Sudanese, they would also develop some level of dependence upon the Nimiery regime and an interest in its survival.[8]

Viewed from Khartoum, the readiness of the southerners to negotiate realistically and the chance of concluding a workable agreement acceptable to all southern factions must have seemed problematical, given the divisions within the SSLM and its heterogeneous structure. However, the crucial feature of intra-southern politics during 1970-72 was the gradual and timely emergence of a leadership that could (just) speak and negotiate for the vast bulk of southern factions and an organization that could reasonably claim to be able to implement any "satisfactory" agreement that might be reached. In many ways, one of the most fascinating aspects of the Sudanese settlement was the race between processes of inter-party peacemaking and of intra-party coalition-building and coalition-maintaining. In the event, the dominance of the military wing of the SSLM under Colonel Lagu proved crucial, although the disagreements which wracked the SSLM after the initialling of the draft Addis Ababa Agreement and its final unaltered ratification by Lagu indicate how nearly the southerners had come to reverting to a set of rival factions with whom it was impossible to negotiate systematically and with any finality.

The Sudanese case thus indicates that, in any conflict, the decision-making process that precedes the initiation of any attempt to negotiate a solution is likely to be significantly affected by circumstances within the adversaries as much as the relationship *between* them. The former could pose serious obstacles to beginning to make peace, as well as to concluding such a delicate procedure. At the very least, attention in future cases might profitably be directed to such considerations as the overall intra-party balance of forces and factions; the interests of dominant factions or groups as well as the personal interests of individual leaders; the level of the leadership's public commitment to "victory"; the level of intra-party cohesion and organization, both of which affect the leaders' ability to control any anti-settlement back-lash; and the level of intra-party support for the personnel, policies and achievements of the existing leadership.

Finally, the Sudanese case emphasized that few conflicts can remain wholly isolated from what might be termed "extra-system" influences. In many cases, others become involved in the struggle as patrons or supporters of one or the other party. Paradoxically, the level of external involvement in the Sudanese civil war remained relatively low.[9] However, examination of the peacemaking process indicates that this involvement did bring a third set of factors into consideration when the major adversaries began to contemplate compromise and negotiation, namely relationships between the parties in Sudan and other governments or organizations that had intervened in the conflict. On the southern side, the outsiders most directly involved in helping were the Israelis—particularly after 1969—whose patronage consisted of supplying arms for the struggle and whose (apparently mistaken) choice of Lagu's faction as the main conduit for arms did much to help that group become predominant within the southern forces. The objectives of the Israelis appear straightforward. Their aid for the Anya Nya was both a part of their attempt to undermine or divert potential members of an Arab or Islamic anti-Israeli bloc and of their drive to win friends and influence in sub-Saharan Africa. While never substantial, Israeli aid and its continuation was undoubtedly an important factor in the southerners' ability to continue the fight. Equally, its severance would have seriously undermined the Anya Nya's ability to continue the struggle, at least at the level achieved by 1971.

Paradoxically, the Israelis' ability to continue to aid the Anya Nya depended upon the connivance of the Ugandan Govenrment and this, in turn, depended upon Kampala not discovering any mutual interests with Khartoum. However, this was one of the results of the overthrow of Milton Obote by Idi Amin, for Obote later was able to concentrate exile forces across the Sudanese border in Equatoria, thus posing a threat to Amin's survival. The mutuality of interests between Amin and Nimiery thus led to a situation in 1971 whereby, in return for Sudanese Government promises to abandon support for Obote's forces in Equatoria,[10] Amin agreed to undermine the Anya Nya's outside links via the Israelis in Uganda. He did this by expelling the Israeli mission in Uganda, partly on the grounds that previous efforts to curtail its pro-SSLM activities had been evaded. Both the action and the knowledge that one of their few sources of outside support had been removed must have put some pressure on the SSLM finally to endorse the draft settlement.[11]

In a similar manner, Nimiery was also able to sever the SSLM's links with the Ethiopian Government, who had been using the Anya Nya to counter-balance the aid offered tacitly (or inadvertently) to the Eritrean Liberation Front (ELF) by Sudanese regimes. Again, this relationship involved the Israelis as arms suppliers to the Anya Nya in Upper Nile province, while, on the other side, the ELF used the Sudan for refugees, base areas and gun-running into Eritrea itself. By the end of 1970 this source of supply and support had both helped to consolidate the guerrilla activities and organizations in the south of the Sudan, thus tending to make the leaders more rather than less intransigent, while at the same time becoming more dependent for that unity upon continued Israeli support. However, in March, 1971, the Sudanese and Ethiopian governments signed an agreement to stop support for one another's "rebel" forces, while a visit to Ethiopia by President Nimiery in November of that same year appears to have had a major effect of stopping the flow of weapons and equipment to the Anya Nya in the Upper Nile—supplies upon which the guerrillas had come increasingly to depend.

The interpretation outlined above suggests how vulnerable parties (even in such relatively "insulated" conflicts as that in the Sudan) can become to changes in the goals and behavior of external patrons and suppliers of resources. It also suggests that, to some degree, willingness to take a decision to seek a negotiated settlement can depend upon the vulnerability of one's external patrons to pressure or blandishments from the adversary. Had the Israeli connection not proved vulnerable, the willingness of the southerners to conclude a final compromise settlement might not have been high.[12] Hence, a final set of factors to include in any analysis of decisionmaking preceding (or accompanying) conflict termination initiatives should include such items as the changing interests and level of commitment of the external

Figure 1.

Factors Affecting Decisions to Seek A Settlement	Northern View	Southern View
A. Inter-Party		
1. Perceived position of relative tactical advantage over adversary.	Stalemate: recognition of inability to crush Anya Nya.	Stalemate: recognition of P.A.F.'s ability to deny Anya Nya towns, communications centres etc.
2. Evaluations of own sacrifices made by parties and (especially) current leadership.	Nimiery regime not committed by sacrifices of its predecessors.	Considerable sacrifices but not all directly at behest of new SSLM.
3. Evaluation of public commitments already made by other leadership.	Uncertain, but by Oct. 1970 Lagu had been willing to accept a solution "within framework of one Sudan…."	Uncertain: June '69 Declaration of new policy towards South "based on autonomous rule" but inspired by SCP.
4. Perception of likely long term gains from continuing v. long term costs.	Long drawn out drain on resources against gains in S. support from an acceptable peace.	Gains of peace and aid from N. against sacrifice of increasingly improbable independence.
5. Perception of internal state of adversary (unity, intransigence, level of commitment etc.)	South committed to rejection of unified Sudan, but otherwise disunited on goals/in organization.	Northern intransigence diminished by S. efforts, but also because of new regime.
6. Perception of adversary's likely terms (level of concessions etc).	Unclear: some in S. possibly willing to remain in a federalist Sudan, in view of need for aid, relief, development but q. of separate security force.	Unclear: N. gvt might be willing to concede internal self government but not independence.

220

B. *Intra-Party*

1. Personal interests of elite decision-makers.	Peace would enhance external reputation of regime and offer new potential source of support in S.	Highly varied and dependent on factional in-fighting among S. movements/leaders.
2. Interests of dominant groups and factions.	Timely agreement with south but price of abandoning Sudan's move into Arab sphere.	Again, varied according to views and positions of factions.
3. Balance of intra-party political forces.	Nimiery dominant, but this could rapidly change.	Lagu and Anya Nya finally dominant in SSLM and could determine whether war continued or not indep. of external political leaders.
4. Level and longevity of leaders' public commitment to "final victory".	Low and never as absolute as previous regimes.	Long and firm, but nature of "victory" open to interpretation.
5. Intra-party cohesiveness and level of control by hierarchy.	High, if only temporarily: state hierarchy still firmly in existence.	At its highest level, if only temp., for entire period of war.
6. Level of intra-party support for policies/personnel of incumbent elite.	Unsure, but immediate threats to regime had been surmounted.	Unsure, but Lagu undoubtedly dominant in internal forces & SSLM had estab. (temp.) unity among S. factions.

(continued)

Figure 1. (*continued*)

Factors Affecting Decisions to Seek A Settlement	Northern View	Southern View
C. *Extra-System*		
1. Attitudes and level of commitment of external patrons.	No help from USSR following SCP coup. Egyptian help sporadic, uncertain.	Pragmatic: Israeli support dependent on continued nuisance value of war in Arab-Israeli confrontation: Ethiopian aid dependent on N. help for ELF.
2. Perception of likely shifts in external support.	New sources of support unlikely.	Weakening of Ugandan (hence Israeli) assistance.
3. Vulnerability of patrons to pressure from adversary.	No real leverage available to SSLM should new patrons assist N. gvt.	Ugandan tolerance dependent upon N. manipulation of Obote threat to Amin Ethiopian help vulnerable to deal over N. help for ELF.
4. Change in external support and approval enjoyed by adversary.	Start of interest in Europe in war, but African states still unlikely to act to help S.	No major condemnation of N. policy or activities: still "the unknown war" in Africa.

patrons themselves (whether national govenments or other organizations); the sensitivity of external patrons to pressure from other third parties; and the vulnerability of external patrons to direct pressure from adversaries.

In summary, the Sudanese case clearly indicates three broad types of influence upon the process of parties mutually deciding to cut their losses, abandon the struggle (at least temporarily) and begin an exploration of the possibility of a negotiated solution; (i) inter-party relationships, (ii) intra-party circumstances and (iii) relationships between the adversaries and any patrons that may be assisting in the dispute.[13] While not claiming that this simple tripartite classification is any more than a starting point for enquiry, it can serve as a useful guide to other situations of conflict and other decisions for or against termination. Fleshed out, as in Figure 1, it might help to pinpoint sets of circumstances where settlement processes might begin, as well as those where a successful start is unlikely. Moreover, an understanding of such circumstances might materially aid the correct timing of peace initiatives by third parties and help to answer longstanding questions about appropriate timing of peace feelers, whether these are unilateral or made by third parties.

ASPECTS OF PEACEMAKING:
(2) THE INTERMEDIARIES

A second major set of lessons that might usefully be provided by the Sudanese "model" concerns the nature of the mediation process itself and the type of third parties that might be able to operate successfully in similar cases of intense civil strife. In this second sense, the use of the Sudanese case might well be particularly illuminating, for widespread, lethal, domestic conflicts involving the possibility of secession are the most difficult to conciliate. Negotiated settlements, as opposed to a victory/defeat outcome, are a rarity. To outsiders such conflicts present major problems of access, for no government in such a situation can tactically afford any suggestion of legitimacy or equality to its adversary. Moreover, the sheer physical problems of establishing and maintaining contact and credibility with insurgents are considerable, particularly when the latter are split into factions by major cleavages and intra-party frictions.

In such circumstances a number of fundamental questions about third-party activities arise. These mainly concern problems of the acceptability of intermediaries and mediatory activities to parties who are engaged in a conflict over the survival of some territorially-based political system. Typically the most baffling questions concern: (i) who might realistically be able to act as a mediator in such circumstances; and (ii) what procedures might maximize the chances of achieving some satisfactory negotiated solution. Given that such a settlement did occur in the case of the Sudanese civil war and that, as indicated above, the Sudanese parties (or at least some parts of them) had come independently to the conclusion that an acceptable negotiated settlement was a possibility,[14] what light can the case throw on these two crucial questions?

Before attempting to tackle these two questions, it is necessary to deal with a preliminary query: who acted as an intermediary in the complex process that led to the meetings in Addis Ababa and the final conclusion of the settlement agreement in March, 1972? An immediate answer would be that the major roles of *go-between,* establishing contact and communication between the various parties, and of *convenor and moderator* of both preliminary (November, 1971) and substantive negotiations (February, 1972) were fulfilled by delegations and personalities from the World Council of Churches (WCC) and its regional adjunct, the All Africa Council of Churches (AACC).[15] Certainly, much of the credit for helping to arrange the final settlement was justifiably assigned to these bodies, and particularly to Kodwo Ankrah (the WCC's Secretary for Africa) and Canon Burgess Carr of AACC. However, it is also the case that other organizations played a role in bringing about both final meetings and agreement.[16] As already noted, a preliminary attempt to make contact between the Khartoum Government and SSLM representatives in London was undertaken in the summer of 1970 by the Movement for Colonial Freedom and, even though this effort had proved abortive by the end of the year, the preliminary contacts it established planted the immediate possibility of a negotiated settlement in the minds of key northerners and southerners.

Other organizations affected the overall process productively, but in a rather different manner. For example, while there is evidence to the effect that, as early as December, 1970, the WCC was contemplating a scheme to bring the Sudanese Government and the Anya Nya to a negotiating "round table" and that a high-level WCC/AACC delegation to pressure the Khartoum Government towards such an idea was planned,[17] the preparatory meetings held in Addis Ababa in January, 1971 were ostensibly concerned largely with humanitarian isues rather than mediation. Publicly, the main task was seen as finding some means of channeling humanitarian aid to the south of the Sudan. One reason for this stance may have been a feeling within the AACC that there should be a clear adherence to the OAU's principle of non-interference with the internal affairs of African countries. However, later in March the WCC was replying to a group of southern supporters at Makerere University that its own proposed fact-finding mission to the Sudan also planned to contact southern leaders apart from those working with the Khartoum Government, so that the WCC was then manifestly thinking of something more than a humanitarian function for its mission.

Moreover, when the WCC/AACC mission arrived at Kampala in March, its intention to explore the possibilities of a mediatory role were probably reinforced by meeting two organizations that had been active in Uganda in support of the SSLM, the Kampala Committee and the Makerere Group. The latter had been established by SSLM sympathizers at Makerere University and was channeling aid into the Anya Nya held areas of the south to help in the setting up of civil administration there. The former organization had been established by the Church Missionary Society and Anglican and Catholic church organizations to co-ordinate the provision of medical, educational and agricultural aid for the south. Both regarded the WCC/AACC's (ostensible) purpose of sending a mission to the Sudan to explore routing aid via the north as misguided. Both set out to persuade the WCC/AACC to undertake a mission of reconciliation, having first clarified what the Khartoum Government's offer of "regional autonomy" might mean in practice. In addition, the groups in Kampala attempted to persuade the WCC/AACC to consider approaching a much wider range of southern opinion than had initially been the intention and to switch the emphasis of their exploration from southerners inside the Sudan to those in exile and representing more "extreme" southern opinion, such as the groups in Ethiopia, Zaire and Kenya, as well as in Uganda. Thus, both the Kampala Committee and the Makerere Group's views must have reinforced any previous intentions of the WCC/AACC to undertake an intermediary rather than a purely humanitarian mission, and had some influence on both the nature of the final WCC mission and the form it took.

While it is true, therefore, to say that the main intermediaries in the process of setting up and conducting peacemaking in the Sudan were the WCC/AACC, other organizations played some role as *advisers and pathfinders* particularly in the early stages of the process. What is noticeable about all these third parties however, is their unofficial and informal nature as regards the normal conduct of international politics. This may provide both a clue to their success in the Sudanese case and an indication of the advantages that such "unofficial diplomats" might enjoy in similar domestic conflicts. One of the outstanding features of efforts to find solutions for widespread domestic conflict and civil strife is the ease with which formal intermediary initiatives from other governments or from regional or international organizations can be blocked or aborted. Often, other governments are unacceptable as intermediaries, either because they are perceived to have direct interest in the outcome of the struggle or because allowing them to act as intermediaries would confer some benefit in terms of recognition. Equally, international or regional organizations have often tied their own hands as potential intermediaries by taking a stand on the particular case in question, or upon some general principle that directly affects many such cases. Doctrines of non-interference and domestic sovereignty are usually invoked by incumbents to head off unwanted peace initiatives that might confer recognition in some substantive, moral or legalistic sense. Quiet diplomacy by some international body is usually difficult in today's world of instant communication, global news coverage and the transistor radio. Hence, one lesson of the Sudanese settlement might well be that appropriate third parties to assist in achieving such solutions frequently have to be unofficial, low profile and, above all, private.

However, even intermediaries of this type must still fulfill a variety of requirements commonly cited as necessary for mediators before their activities will be either acceptable or credible to parties involved in the struggle. It is commonplace that mediators must be seen to be impartial (or, at least, as balanced in their partialities) and must somehow manage to maintain this perception throughout a process which is almost structured to guarantee a rapid loss of such perceived impartiality.

Many writers (Lall, Young 1967) have argued that successful intermediaries must be independent from the parties, possess prestige and authority as well as knowledge, skill, flexibility and access to independent resources and services. On all these dimensions, the position of the WCC/ AACC in the Sudanese peacemaking process presents something of a paradox. Certainly the church leaders possessed no overtly political axe to grind within the Sudan and few seem to have doubted their genuine disinterest in efforts to achieve a peaceful solution for its own sake. However, in other ways they were thoroughly "involved" in the Sudanese situation. One of the major concerns of the Khartoum Government, for example, was that the churches had been an important element in maintaining and strengthening the divisions between north and south and hence were, to a degree, "responsible" for southern separatism.[19] Again, the position of the AACC on African intra-state conflicts was well-known to southern leaders, both in exile and in the Sudan. More immediately relevant to the SSLM's suspicion of Church involvement in any peacemaking initiative—and especially the WCC/AACC's initial proposal for a goodwill mission to the Sudan in 1971—was a previous AACC Report resulting from a "goodwill mission" made in 1966. This had somewhat uncritically adopted the Khartoum Government's version of affairs and, especially in the eyes of southern leaders whom the church mission had not approached, damaged the southern cause considerably. Over-identification with the views, goals and positions of one of the parties to a dispute can be fatal to any intermediary initiative. (It was this that wrecked the MCF's initiative in the autumn of 1970, when one of its members published an article in the *Nile Mirror* which virtually adopted the position of Khartoum's Minister for Southern Affairs while also alleging that members of the SSLM were instruments of the CIA!) In the case of the WCC/AACC, the suspicions of both northerners and southerners seem almost to have balanced each other out, and to have been seen as minor obstacles when compared with the likely benefits of making contact and opening discussions about a negotiated solution. Furthermore, the WCC's decision to provide aid to the guerrilla organizations in southern Africa certainly seems to have raised that body's prestige in Khartoum and suggests that an intermediary's reputation and acceptability can be helped (as well as hindered) by actions taken over issues apparently remotely connected with the situation being mediated. Reputation (and hence acceptability) can be affected by diverse factors. That the WCC itself may have doubted its own position and credibility with the parties can be seen by its efforts to involve other, prestigious African figures in the overall peacemaking process including President Kaunda and, later, the Emperor of Ethiopia.[20]

What can the actual pattern of events and actions in the Sudanese case tell us about processes of successful mediation in civil wars? A recent work (Mitchell 1981) has suggested that the overall mediation process might fruitfully be viewed as one of an intermediary proceeding to play a number of roles in rough sequence depending upon the stage reached by the peacemaking initiative. Four major stages were identified: *initiatory, bilateral contact, face-to-face discussion,* and *implementation.* Each involved a variety of functions to be carried out by a third party (see Figure 2). Certainly many of these functions can be identified in the Sudanese peacemaking process, although they were not necessarily carried out by a single third party in this case. For example, a frequently enacted role consists of some third party fulfilling what might be termed a *synchronizing* function by ensuring that the parties to the conflict are equally ready to contemplate the possibility of a negotiated settlement and, hence, are prepared to engage in some form of realistic dialogue. It is unarguable that the WCC/AACC intermediaries carried out this role, particularly once their contacts in Kampala and elsewhere indicated in March, 1971 that the SSLM was willing to consider a negotiated settlement and that explorations of the willingness to consider negotiation in Khartoum should be undertaken. The main intermediary *took over* a synchronizing function as well as that of acting as a go-between and fulfilling a *communicating and informing*

Figure 2.   Stages of Mediation

Mediation states	Intermediary functions
1. Initiatory	Delaying
	Synchronising
2. Bilateral contact	Defining
	Communicating
	Informing
3. Face-to-face discussion	Providing a forum
	Suggesting ideas
(a) Confrontation	Initiating
	De-committing
	Substitute-proposing
(b) Negotiation	Excusing
	Providing resources
	Encouraging
	Managing
4. Implementation	Supervising and securing
	Guaranteeing
	Legitimising

function, partly through the encouragement of other interested third parties and partly because of the support received from the adversaries themselves. The WCC/AACC were helped in this *bilateral contacts* stage by the fact that the Khartoum Government had responded favorably to the overtures made from Kampala and, earlier in their *initiation stage,* by the fact that the aborted MCF initiative had already occurrred, thus focusing both SSLM and Khartoum leaders' attention upon the possibilities (and hence the details) of a dialogue with the adversary. In this sense, the WCC/AACC were the heirs of the MCF and also benefited from the thinking and activities of the Makerere Group and the Kampala Committee.

In all its roles[21] during the two initial stages of the peacemaking process the WCC/AACC had an inestimable advantage over many other potential intermediaries, both "public" and "private", both resourceful and resourceless. This was the degree of access to both African and non-African leaders provided by the church network throughout Africa. This even extended to the Sudan itself, in spite of the expulsion of missionaries from the southern provinces. Church leaders, both Catholic and Protestant, were able to make contact with key African leaders and governments, with the

Sudanese guerrilla organizations and exile groups, and with the Khartoum Government itself. In many ways, this multi-level, multi-functional church network seems to have proved an ideal entry point for peacemaking initiatives in the Sudanese case, while the level of legitimacy provided by church sponsorship for the peacemaking initiative seems to have been vital, not merely in the initiatory and bilateral contacts stage, but also in helping to provide a forum for the talks and setting them up under the aegis of an African elder statesman who was a neighbor as well as as having a direct interest in ending the conflict via negotiation.[22]

Once the third stage of *face-to-face discussion* had been reached, and a forum for that discussion found, the WCC/AACC's role as intermediary became a typical one of helping to "manage" meetings successfully, so that deadlocks were avoided or removed, discussion proceeded smoothly and suitable wording found for points of disagreement. At the preliminary talks in November, 1971[23] the four church representatives were twice called in to resolve serious deadlocks, in particular one over whether the main talks should take place within the formula of a single Sudan. At the final negotiations in February, 1972 (a bilateral discussion took place in London during December, 1971) the meeting was chaired by the AACC representative, Cannon Burgess Carr (the Emperor had implicitly declined to act as chairman), although he took on the title of "Moderator" rather than Chairman. Available accounts indicate that the meetings were by no means easy, with both parties negotiating hard, determined not to give way on vital issues, although both had obviously prepared initial bargaining positions from which retreat was possible and not wholly unexpected. However, some issues proved particularly intractable, including the powers to be afforded by the President of the Sudan and the question of security and the armed forces in the south. The latter issues revolved around the question of what proportion of northern and southern troops in some future integrated force should be stationed in the south, and this question was eventually referred to the Emperor Haile Selassi himself for determination,[24] thus bringing in another direct intervention from a further intermediary.

Whatever difficulties were encountered during the fourteen days of negotiation, a final draft peace agreement was produced by 27 February, 1972, signed in the ballroom of the Addis Ababa Hilton Hotel by all delegates except the leaders (who merely initialled it) and witnessed by the church leaders and the Emperor's official representative. However, as suggested above, there is usually a fourth stage to any peacemaking process, in which intermediaries can play a role—that of *implementation,* and the Sudanese case proved no exception. Of the many possible "follow-up" functions that can be performed by an intermediary, perhaps the most important are to do with initially *legitimizing* and *selling* any final agreement to leaders and factions not directly involved in the negotiations. Later, third parties might have the functions of *supervising* or *guaranteeing* the terms of an agreement, but first it is frequently necessary to have it fully accepted by the parties themselves. Often this is no easy task and so it proved with the Addis Ababa Agreement. Between the announcement of the Agreement in February and its final ratification in March, 1972, much third party activity was directed towards persuading factions within at least one party— the southerners—to accept the agreement's provisions.

Efforts both to publicize and legitimize the agreement began almost as soon as agreement had been reached in Addis Ababa. The Emperor made a speech publicly congratulating all concerned immediately after the signing ceremony and a reception was held at OAU headquarters, thus simultaneously signifying the approval and support of Africa's elder statesman and of the relevant regional organization. However, while such action may have helped to legitimize the settlement on the regional and world stage, a much harder task lay in convincing many of the harder line leaders of the SSLM factions that the agreement was the best that could be gained at that time and with the existing levels of sacrifice. In many ways, the most important actions in persuading doubting or recalcitrant southerners that the agreement should be accepted came from the third parties that had originally persuaded the WCC/AACC to undertake an intermediary role. Many members of the Makerere Group, for example, were active in trying to persuade southerners to accept what one of them has described as "an acceptable, if imperfect, settlement...." (Pirouet p. 141).[25] The Group underlined the warning that, if the agreement were to be rejected, then relief and other aid would no longer be forthcoming, while if it were accepted, a massive aid program in the south would not merely assist recovery but involve a large foreign presence in the area helping to guarantee the settlement. Similarly, the Kampala Committee threw its weight behind efforts to make SSLM see the sense of accepting the agreement, writing directly to Colonel Lagu and then making transport available to him so that he could contact groups within the southern provinces more easily and persuade them to accept the settlement.

In spite of such efforts, when Lagu arrived in Addis Ababa in late March, 1972 to ratify the agreement, he brought with him a large number of amendments which southerners wished to make to the settlement. It was only after the Emperor had used his own personal prestige to reassure the southern leader that the Agreement was finally ratified unchanged. In the event, most southerners outside the Sudan accepted the Agreement thus ratified as the best that could be hoped for, although a few of them rejected it as a sell-out and continued to hope for some improvement in southern fortunes—international intervention or major new sources of supply—that would provide the opportunity for independence. Such dissent was not widespread, however, and this fact must be partly attributable to the strenuous efforts put in by third parties, both governmental and private, to "sell" the agreement to southerners, but also to northerners within the Sudan.

One major lesson regarding the role of intermediaries emerges from the Sudanese case, in addition to the customary important factors such as access, impartiality, acceptability and an initial willingness of the parties to consider dialogue. This is that potential intermediaries must also be in a position to avoid conferring public recognition of any sort by their activities on either of the adversaries, otherwise their activities might become part of the tactical interplay, the gaining of advantages at the expense of the adversary that signals the continuation, rather than the termination, of a conflict. A second lesson appears to be that, while the list of potential intermediary functions mentioned above is not wildly inaccurate as far as the Sudanese settlement is concerned, it is a mistake to believe that all functions must necessarily be carried out by the same party. In the Sudanese case, the functions listed above were, in fact, carried out by a number of organizations, some of whom were regarded as impartial by both main adversaries, but some of whom quite clearly were not. The WCC/AACC in its role as a go-between, conciliator and arranger of contacts might well have been viewed as basically impartial by northerners and southerners. The same could hardly be said of the Makerere Group, or of the MCF, or even—in spite of its commitment to "humanitarian" relief—of the Kampala Committee. (In strict power politics terms, any aid to the southerners which removed Khartoum's pressure to bring about a surrender was highly "political.") Nonetheless, it was such directly committed third parties that fulfilled many of the necessary follow-up functions that ensured the final ratification of the agreement and that the settlement worked out at Addis Ababa would, at the very least, be given a trial by the adversaries.

ASPECTS OF PEACEMAKING: (3) THE SETTLEMENT

The final sense in which the ending of the Sudanese civil war might well be considered (in some sense) a "model" relates to the nature of the settlement itself, its terms and provisions and the manner of its implementation. Of the three senses in which we have used the settlement as a "model," this last is possibly the most interesting and important, not least for the fact that the Addis Ababa Agreement of 1972 represents an all too rare example of the manner in which conflicts between a central government and a regionally-based movement for some form of "self-determination" or "independence" might be settled without either secession or annihilation of the insurgents. It is in this sense, then, that the agreement and its implementation might well be taken as a preliminary "model" for regions of the world prone to conflicts which, if mishandled, frequently threaten both the survival of existing political entities and the peace of the region.

The Terms

At one level of analysis, the lessons offered by the Sudanese settlement concern how it might be possible to cope wtih three of the major dimensions that customarily lie at the heart of regionally based struggles for self-determination: the degree of independence that can be obtained consonant with the retention of the minimal level of national unity and integration desired by the central government; the means of achieving a desired level of regional security (i.e., from the potential dangers posed by the agents of the central government to local interests and even survival) which does not wholly undermine either national unity or national security; and the extent to which the system devised by the settlement can manage residual and new conflicts as they emerge, both between central government and new region and within the region itself.[26]

In a superficial sense, the first question involves whether a settlement to a conflict maintains a unitary state at one extreme, sets up some federal system or, at another extreme, results in complete secession. In the case of the Sudanese settlement, the negotiated compromise was a system of "regional autonomy," although some observers have argued that what was actually agreed was a federal system under another name. However, the symbolic title of the system established is less important than the practical degree of independent decisonmaking enjoyed by whatever regional governmental body or bodies are established. This question involves three broad aspects: (i) the degree of central government influence over regional political processes; (ii) the level of administrative independence enjoyed by the region; and (iii) the level of economic and financial autonomy for the region established by the settlement. The first of these can, to some extent, be gauged by the formal powers handed over to the regional authority and those retained by the central government, but also by the degree to which the central government is subsequently able to influence political processes and outcomes at the regional level. The second is closely linked with the first, but largely involves questions of administrative autonomy at a regional level. (Where does responsibility for appointment, promotion or posting of regional personnel lie, to what extent are administrative practices in the region subject to central government edict, or how much are regional administrative systems open to being swamped by central government appointees?[27] The third involves questions of (i) the ability to raise local taxes rendering the region no longer (or much less) dependent upon central government funds; (ii) the right not to levy centrally imposed taxes or impostes; and (iii) the ability not to be overly dependent upon central government loans and grants for capital development and economic growth.

The actual terms of the Addis Ababa Agreement provide some clues as to how such matters were dealt with, at least in an initial effort to implement some systems of "autonomy" in the South. A large degree of freedom of action was, in fact, handed over to southern leaders by the Agreement which, following transitional arrangements, gave to a regionally elected Assembly the power to recommend to the national President a High Executive Council which would be responsible for all southern affairs, except defense, foreign affairs, currency and finance, and national economic and social planning. The Regional Assembly would also select its own Regional President, who would head the HEC as chairman, and recommend the appointment to the national President. (The Regional Assembly also had the power to recommend the Regional President's dismissal!) Affairs in the south were further formally insulated against influence from the north by the Regional Assembly's ability to ask the President to defer entry into force of central government legislation as it applied to the south. At least on paper, this range of provisions gave the south a high degree of insulation from interference by both central government and northerners in general, while also guaranteeing southern representation in central government, planning and administration. Some northerners were quick to point out that the south enjoyed a privileged position not available to other Sudanese and there were some fears that similar regional concessions might be demanded by other groups within the remainder of Sudan. However, the key question of whether northern presidents would invariably implement the recommendations of southern assemblies exercised some southern minds even in 1972.

Similar problems arose of how much independence a settlement could attain in administrative and economic fields, especially in view of the relative poverty of the south and the level of disruption caused by the civil war. At the time of the settlement, a large potential sacrifice for the SSLM was the dismantlement of grass roots structures of administration, health and education that had been painfully built up, especially in the last years of the guerrilla struggle—although the quid pro quo in the form of famine relief and development planning was considerable. However, the replacement of even this system by a formal, regional one could inevitably lead to problems of boundary demarcation between central and regional administrations. The question of efficient centralized administration clashed with the need to mark out clearly that area of essentially southern activity that was delineated by an inevitably ambiguous agreement. Problems of relations between central and regional economic planning, of postings out of the south in services that are nationally based, of promotions and educational qualifications, inevitably arise in any arrangement where a system has been established, containing two centers of power and two administrative structures. Events soon after the 1972 settlement showed that such difficulties do arise and have to be offset against advantages offered by the semi-autonomous, two-tier system of administration.

While the practicalities of administrative independence inevitably prove tricky in any regionally devolved settlement, those concerning economic independence are also likely to prove troublesome, and the Sudanese settlement illustrates some problems likely to confront similar solutions to regionally-based conflicts. Complete and sovereign economic independence is a myth, even for separate countries. In the case of regions of previously integrated countries, even limited economic autonomy is likely to prove difficult to arrange. This is true even in countries like the Sudan, where the absolute level of economic exchange between regions has never been great. The problem for creating any genuine form of southern economic autonomy, apart from the initially low level of development and the devastation of the war, was that the south was almost wholly dependent upon (i) the central government and (ii) outside aid for economic growth. This proved to be the case even for finances to run administration and government in the south at a minimal level.

The Addis Ababa Agreement guaranteed that the central government would provide revenue and finance for the region in a variety of ways, as well as development funds from a "Special Development Budget." However, the very fact that the "autonomous" southern region was to be so dependent upon the central government for its finances emphasized one of the difficulties likely to attend attempts to establish systems of regional autonomy as solutions to regionally-based conflicts. Poor regions seeking regional autonomy are likely to have to accept continued dependence upon, and influence from a richer center, while rich regions (Katanga, Biafra) are likely to have their efforts to achieve autonomy of any description fiercely resisted by a center determined not to lose control of a rich source of revenue and resources. This became a key issue in Sudan once oil deposits had been discovered in the Southern Region.

As far as the security requirements of any settlement are concerned, the first of these obviously involves immediate questions of a ceasefire or armistice which does not appear to imperil the security or survival of either side. However, in the longer term it is frequently the case that a major issue becomes one of actual physical security for the insurgent region, once the insurgent forces have agreed to lay down their arms. How is it possible to ensure that one has not merely turned over the region and its people to a vengeful central government, at the same time as the central government is reassured that a minimum amount of security and law and order (in a conventional sense) is maintained and that the region ceases to be a direct military threat to national security and survival?

In principle, security solutions can range from a wholly integrated national army and security forces at one extreme (in which case, the security fears of any minority regional group will be exacerbated to the degree that the army represents the dominating majority) to a wholly separate regional force, regionally based and with its own local command structure (in which case the central government is likely to see this arrangement as lessening rather than increasing national security). Between these two extremes lies a wide variety of theoretically possible arrangements, involving separate commands, independent regional units, regionally based, mixed forces with separate units, mixed forces with integrated units, or some balance of regional and extra-regional troops stationed in the autonomous region. In all such arrangements the key questions are likely to be: How many troops in the region, with what balance between locals and outsiders? Are the units separate or integrated? Who is in command and with what powers and responsibilities? Who appoints regional commanders and how? What safeguards are there against destabilising postings into and—equally important—out from the region? Even in the longer term, these problems usually prove to be crucial to be maintenance of any agreed settlement. In the immediate aftermath of a civil war, with recent antagonists in a guerrilla/security forces campaign involved in some peacetime security "mix", solving the problem of both regional and national security is likely to prove intractable.

The military aspect of the Addis Ababa settlement called for a separate "Southern Command" of 12,000 men, half of which were to be drawn from the ranks of the Anya Nya. The recruitment, deployment and eventual integration of the forces was to be in the hands of a Joint Military Commission, which was to carry out its task with the difficult objective of ensuring "... that an atmosphere of peace and confidence shall prevail in the Southern Region ...." How this was to be accomplished was by no means clear, given the level of mutual distrust prevailing, the need to preserve some mutual balance of forces as a perceived guarantee to southerners and an implied agreement that units in the south would, at some later stage, become integrated under both northern and southern officers. The length of time before any moves towards the unit-level integration were to be attempted indicated the sensitivity of the security issue to southerners[28] and the difficulties thought likely to accompany any attempt by a central government to provide security and law and order in a previously disaffected region.

The Structure of the Settlement

An alternative way of analysing the Addis Ababa settlement and examining any final lessons it might have for similar situations is to abandon detailed consideration of the terms and ask what kinds of advantages the agreement offered to the parties in the dispute, and how various factions and individuals in each party might have come to regard the agreement as preferable to a continuation of the armed conflict. Naturally, the benefits available were not equally shared by all northerners or all southerners, but the crucial feature of the Agreement seems to have been that if offered "enough" to a wide enough range of individuals and factions to make it sufficiently acceptable to ensure at least its initial implementation.

First and most obviously, the agreement offered peace and an end to violence for both northerners and southerners. For the latter, moreover, it offered a chance of return and resettlement both for leaders in exile and for the large number of refugees that had fled the southern Sudan into neighboring countries. Hence, the support from those packed in refugee camps for this (and almost any other peaceful) settlement was hardly surprising. On the other hand, for southern leaders in exile, the agreement offered a genuine chance of political power and of participating in effective decisionmaking about the future of their own region. It is true that the agreement fell short of complete independence, but in its draft form it was undoubtedly perceived as offering a chance for southern leaders to put their ideas into effect in the south, and to obtain the political influence and status that they had been seeking. Moreover, the proffered two-tier system provided a considerable number of decision-making and administrative roles for southern leaders (both "insiders" and "outsiders," although friction was likely between the two groups) who would be able to make careers and fulfill ambitions at either regional or national levels. For the leaders in the north (those, that is, who were not tied to old intransigent policies, and thus convinced that the southerners would reject the agreement and enable the conflict to continue) the settlement represented an end to a divisive conflict and a potential new basis for support among southerners who would undoubtedly see that the continuation of the settlement depended very much upon the continued existence of the Nimiery regime in Khartoum. For the members of the regime, although the regional settlement was a gamble risking (at least) elite criticism in the north, the success of the peace process ensured a greater solidity and international status that accrues to those who have successfully made a domestic peace. Its failure might, in the longer term, have left them more vulnerable to their remaining enemies in the north.

It is often easy to see the benefits brought by peace to leadership and elites, in the form of political status, power, opportunity and support. Usually, it is less easy to see what rewards peace brings to rank and file followers. This is frequently because such aspects are not dealt with directly by the settlement. Followers achieve their reward by a cessation of violence and physical destruction and thus are the benefits of peace conveyed to them. However, the Addis Ababa Agreement was interesting in that it set out quite explicitly to make available direct benefits to the rank-and-file of the Anya Nya, thus giving them a stake in the settlement. Deliberately, provisions were made to bring what were estimated to be the bulk of the guerrilla forces into the settlement by guaranteeing them roles in the newly-founded Southern Command of the PAF. In other words, benefits were built into the agreement not merely for elites but also for followers—and moreover for armed followers who might otherwise have been able to disrupt the peace process. In the event, far more guerillas proved to be available for recruitment than the estimated 6,000. Over 15,000 had to be accommodated. The strain upon meager southern resources was considerable, but 4,000 taken into the police and prison services somewhat eased the burden.[29]

Lessons that such aspects of the Sudanese settlement appear to teach, then, are that successful solutions must include at least some benefits at all levels if they are to be sufficiently acceptable in the initial stages and thus have some chance of survival in the medium and longer term. Not only must elites be satisfied and perceive that the settlement fulfills at least some of their salient goals. Rank-and-file followers, middle echelon administrators, and other key groups in the parties must see that their ends are, to some considerable degree, served by cutting losses and compromising and not by wrecking the agreement and trying to continue the fight onward to victory. In this and other respects, the Addis Ababa settlement appears to offer some useful guidelines for all countries with a geographically concentrated "subnational" community striving for some degree of autonomy, and potentially able to translate that endeavor into overt and violent conflict.

CONCLUSION

All of the foregoing may appear to be "academic" in two senses of the word—irrelevantly hypothetical in the light of the subsequent failure of the Agreement to hold, and of no current interest in view of the completely changed situation in Sudanese politics. The Agreement ultimately failed to ensure long term stability within the Sudan, or peace between the northern and southern halves of the country, for longer than ten years. Its provisions were steadily undermined by rivalries and cleavages within the ranks of southern leaders themselves, and the resultant failure of the regional government structure to govern effectively. The discovery of considerable wealth in the south in the form of oil led to divisions and disputes over the sharing of benefits from that discovery, symbolized by the struggle over the siting of a planned oil refinery either in the south near the wells or at Port Sudan on the Red Sea coastline at the end of a lengthy pipeline. The fragility of the South's political autonomy was revealed by President Nimiery's decision to restructure the southern political system into three separate provincial systems in place of the southern regional system established at Addis Ababa ("repartation"); and underlined by decisions to transfer southern troops out of the region to posts in northern Sudan. The fragility of social and cultural autonomy was amply and finally demonstrated by President Nimiery's decision to impose the full rigors of Muslim Law (shariya) throughout the entire country, irrespective of the sensibilities of non-Muslim southerners or the spirit of the Agreement that he had helped to achieve in 1972.

The southern response was another army mutiny and the formation in 1983 of new and radical resistance movements in the south, one of which took on the name (Anya Nya II) and secesionist objectives of previous southern movements, while another, the Sudan People's Liberation Movement and its army (the SPLA), posed a more radical threat to the regime in Khartoum by seeking to become the leaders of a new, democratic and socialist regime for the entire country. Under the leadership of Colonel Dr. John Garang, the SPLM became Khartoum's main adversary in a second civil war which, by 1988, had; (1) engulfed the southern region of the country and left the "rebels" in far firmer control of all save a few strategic towns than even Anya Nya I in 1971; (2) contributed to the overthrow of Nimiery himself and the coming to power of a civilian regime under Sadiq al Mahdi; and (3) resisted all efforts to get northerners and dissident southerners to negotiate a solution to the renewed conflict, in spite of indirect contacts and even direct talks between Garang and al Mahdi.

The breakdown of the 1972 settlement was, by 1988, so obvious that it must seem perverse, at the least, to argue that it could serve as a model of anything, let alone "successful" conflict termination. At best, surely, it might be regarded as a temporary truce in a long drawn out, episodic struggle likely to end, if it does come to any definite conclusion, (and prolonged stalemate is not impossible) with secession of the southerners or the eventual, forcible re-imposition of rule from Khartoum. Even if the Agreement lasted for a decade, its ultimate breakdown surely argues an inherent flaw in the *content* of the settlement (even if not the process of arriving at it) to do with the settlement's inherent fragility, its lack of robustness when facing subsequent political stresses. A political arrangement as fragile and as easily overturned as the 1972 settlement cannot be deemed a success to be used as a "model"?

Two points may be made against this conclusion. The first is the practical point that one of the major demands of the southern dissidents once again fighting in the bush has been that the country should return to the arrangements for regional autonomy (or something very like them) agreed in 1972, together with a call for a democratic decentralized and non-military national government presumable to ensure that new arrangements are not overturned on the personal whim of a non-elected, non-responsive military leader. The fact that one of the parties to the present struggle has, as a prime object, a return to the type of settlement reached in 1972 argues that some merit was and is perceived in the nature of that settlement.

The second point is a less practical one, and raises the issue of the definition of "success." For a conflict termination process to be characterized as a success, is it necessary for it to produce some set of arrangements that lasts for several generations or stands some other test of time to demonstrate a most unusual permanence and robustness? Admittedly, it would be pleasant if the arrangements made at Addis Ababa in 1972, at the end of a long civil war, proved to be long-lasting and able to withstand the shifting stresses and strains of Sudanese national politics for decades thereafter without giving way in some fashion. However, all political systems are fragile, and nowhere more so in countries that contain major cleavages of a religious, ethno-linguistic and class nature. It should not be surprising that the strains finally placed upn the Addis Ababa arrangements arising from such a society finally proved too much. In terms of longevity, then, the 1972 Sudanese settlement may not have been a success. However, the point needs to be made that, with conflict termination processes, there are degrees of success. Some such processes never manage to get the parties into dialogue, let alone to agree to a cessation of fighting. Others reach dialogue but fail to find any possible agreement. Still others—the Anglo-Irish Treaty of 1921 comes to mind—achieve agreement, only to see it repudiated. Still others rapidly break down at the implementation stage and the process ends in recrimination and accusations of bad faith. In these terms, and bearing in mind previous comments about the difficulty of finding any compromise solution to intense civil strife involving the survival of a country, an argument can be made that the Addis Ababa process and Agreement itself were relatively a successful example of conflict termination, and therefore might have lessons to teach—perhaps even to those currently seeking an end to the second Sudanese civil war.

In short, I would argue that the Agreement concluded at Addis Ababa in February-March, 1972 can be seen as a "model" solution for a not untypical problem in contemporary politics, that of a major conflict caused by a desire for regional independence in a divided society. The settlement provides a model for a peace-making process[30] and for a solution which was, at the time, acceptable because it offered considerable benefits to most sections of the minority without weakening the position of the majority in national affairs or in the country's role in regional and international politics; which decentralized, without losing complete control of regional affairs, while at the same time offering genuine participation in decisonmaking on regional affairs to regional elites; which offered considerable security to the regional minority, without weakening the security of the remainder of the country; which preserved important cultural, religious and linguistic values in a region again without diminishing the dominant cultural pattern in the majority's area or without, in the event, weakening national identity; which afforded real, concrete and immediately recognizable benefits to both leaders and rank and file, especially within the regional minority; and which established a system which did nothing to infringe the formal sovereignty and unity of the country in question, while both avoiding the formal implications of a federal system and providing some of the informal benefits of decentralized decisionmaking appropriate to a large country with under-developed communciations.

The format of the final settlement achieved at Addis Ababa is thus one which merits considerable respect for its appropriateness, and for the fact that it managed to achieve at least ten years of relative inter-regional peace in a country which had experienced little of that commodity since independence. In spite of the settlement's ultimate failure, the Addis Ababa settlement might well serve as a starting point for considering solutions to similar situations, both in Africa and the rest of the world.

ACKNOWLEDGMENTS

This paper originated as part of a study of conflict termination processes carried out by the Conflict Management Research Group at The City University, London. I am very grateful for helpful comments on earlier drafts of this paper by Dr. Peter Woodward of the University of Reading and Dr. Hezekiah Assefa, and for other research help by Katherine Kennedy at City University and Jack Hope at Center for Conflict Analysis and Resolution at George Mason University.

NOTES

1. See the analyses contained in Rosenau (1964) and Eckstein (1964).

2. Another unusual feature of the civil war, which may account for the way in which it remained relatively insulated from major external intervention by outside governments and political movements, is the fact that it failed to develop any clear-cut ideological features— at least, in the sense that the parties involved fell clearly on to some conventional left-right, or east-west dimensions. Other countries did intervene—Israel and Uganda to help the southerners, and Egypt, the USSR and, later, the CPR to assist Khartoum—but never at a high level and never as part of any world-wide ideological struggle.

3. See John Howell; *Political Leadership and Organisation,* Unpub. Ph.D., Reading University, 1978.

4. This is necessarily a sketchy and incomplete account of the events leading up to the final settlement. For more detailed descriptions readers should consult Pirouet (1976) and Howell (ibid).

4a. See Arend Lijphart "Comparative Politics and the Comparative Method" *American Political Science Review* 65 (2) 1971, pp. 682-694.

4b. Lijphart. ibid. p. 692.

5. It is something of an over-simplification to treat relevant decisionmakers as falling into two clear-cut and separate "leadership," especially given the overlapping of interests and views, exemplified by such individuals as Abel Alier.

6. As Howell points out, the southerners (especially Lagu) recognized both that "...the rebels were never likely to be able to overrun a major Sudanese army garrison or take over any sizeable town for anything more than few days..." (p. 426) and that the campaign for African and international recognition of the SSLM had failed totally (Howell 1978).

7. The SCP supported Nimiery's government and provided both key ideas and key personnel (including the Minister of Southern Affairs, Joseph Garang) between June, 1969 and July, 1971.

8. The realism of these calculations was illustrated in the Libyan-backed coup which failed in July, 1976. The southern response to the events in Khartoum was to prepare to send elements of the Sudanese forces stationed in the south (both northerners and southerners) northwards to put down the uprising—although this proved unnecessary in the event.

9. It is possible that both sides in the Sudanese civil war saw that any major internationalization of the conflict would involve them in major costs to offset any advantages—such as greater external interference, loss of control, freedom of action and autonomy and the detrimental tying in of the local Sudanese conflict to regional and global confrontations.

10.   In March, 1972, immediately after the signing of the Addis Ababa Agreement, Obote's forces were moved from their Sudanese government camps in Equatoria to others further north—much further away from the Ugandan borders. In June, 1972 they sailed from Sudan to Tanga in Tanzania.

11.   The Israeli expulsion from Uganda was ordered on 24 March, 1972, the day on which Colonel Lagu left Kampala for final talks on ratification in Addis Ababa.

12.   Equally, however, the Khartoum Government had the foresight to realise that even cutting off outside resources from the SSLM did not mean that "victory" would be achieved in the short term, and that the SSLM's outside links might easily be restored by a sudden shift in the region's volatile coalition patterns.

13.   Patrons do not, of course, help through altruism. Frequently conflicts can change their nature as the interests of patrons come to dominate those of clients. Local conflicts, such as that on Cyprus, become bound up with Turkish-Greek disputes over the Aegean and over questions of Turkish military security. They also—usually—become more intractable.

14.   Many observers of mediation and conciliation in both international and domestic disputes argue that this is a *necessary* but not necessarily *sufficient* condition for the initiation of a successful mediatory process.

15.   Haile Selassi had agreed to act as official mediator for the meetings to be held from 15 February, 1972.

16.   Among other activities the Apostolic delegate in Khartoum, Monsignor Calabresi, held a meeting in February, 1979 with President Mobutu of Zaire and requested him to undertake the role of mediator in the Sudanese dispute.

17.   H. Assefa. personal communication.

18.   The OAU's commitment to the preservation of the territorial status quo of its member-states has effectively tied its hands as an "impartial" mediator in many African intrastate conflicts, beginning with that in the Ethiopian Ogaden and being most apparent during the Nigerian Civil War.

19.   This argument, plus the alleged direct support and encouragement given by the churches to southern separatists and guerrrillas, underlay the expulsion of Christian missionaries from the south of the country in 1964.

20.   It has been suggested that the Emperor stayed aloof from the peacemaking process— even to the extent of allowing his Foreign Minister to act as host to the February, 1972 talks in Addis Ababa—for fear of becoming involved in discussions that might widen to include Eritrea (Pirouet p. 135).

21.   It might, with truth, be argued that the WCC/AACC performed an intensely practical *equalizing* function during the peacemaking process by providing SSLM leaders with financial support for fares, accommodation, administrative services when attending conferences and for legal and constitutional advice (in the form of Sir Dingle Foot).

22.   The fact that the WCC/AACC felt that they needed to rely upon the prestige of an African elder statesman or leading political figures indicates that church leaders were still unsure of their own ability to provide a necessary level of legitimacy to their efforts and any settlement that might possible emerge. Hence their initial efforts to involve President Kaunda and their final move to hold talks in Addis Ababa, both Haile Selassi's capital and the headquarters of the OAU.

23.   This meeting was attended by Dr. Leopoldo Niilus, director of the WCC's Commission on International Affiars, Kodwo Ankrah and Canon Burgess Carr, Secretary of AACC.

24.   The Emperor suggested a solution through a parity agreement; an equal number of southern and northern troops to be stationed in the three southern provinces.

25.   Some important individuals in the Group had serious doubts about accepting.

26.   Dealing with this problem would require a review of Sudanese politics over the past decade and must be the subject of another paper.

27.   In the Sudanese case, for example, clashes subsequently arose over who controlled appointments and postings of the police in the South, and over the extent to which the head of the southern police force was responsible to the Regional Assembly as opposed to the national police commissioner in Khartoum. Again, some criticisms have been made of the retention of the British colonial style of Provincial and District Commissioners in the south who report directly to the President's Office and are responsible to the President himself.

28.   Note the disturbances that occurred on two occasions when efforts were made to integrate PAL and ex-SSLM units, one at Juba in 1974 and the near mutiny at Aboko in 1975.

29.   The HEC decided to employ the remainder as road workers or agricultural/forestry assistants, but the bill for so doing came to £3 million in the first eighteen months of peace, and in 1973-74 payment for even a number reduced by offering three months' severance pay as bonus amounted to more than all locally raised revenues for the region (Kasfir 1977, pp. 155-6).

30.   It is also an interesting example of an agreement embodying transitional arrangements difficult to reverse once started (even without President Nimiery's pre-emptive implementation of the ceasefire and the agreement) yet not putting either party in a position of overwhelming disadvantage at any particular stage should the agreement break down.

REFERENCES

Assefa, H. 1987. *Mediation of Civil Wars: Approaches and Strategies - The Sudan Conflict.* (Boulder, CO: Westview Press.)

Bell, J.B. 1975. "The Conciliation of Insurgency; the Sudanese Experience." *Military Affairs* 39 (3): 105-113.

Beshir, M.O. 1968. *The Southern Sudan; Background to Conflict.* London: C. Hurst.

Eckstein, H. (ed.) 1964. *Internal War.* New York: Free Press.

Eprile, C. 1974. *War and Peace in the Sudan; 1955-72.* Newton Abbot: David and Charles.

Howell, J. "Horn of Africa; Lessons from the Sudan Conflict." *International Affairs* 54 (3): 421-436.

Kasfir, N. 1977. "Southern Sudanese Politics since the Addis Ababa Agreement." *'African Affairs.* Pp. 143-166.

Lagu, J. 1972. "A Southerner's View of the Sudan Settlement." *New Middle East* 49: 17-18.

Lijphart, A. 1971. "Comparative Politics and the Comparative Method." *American Political Science Review* 65 (2): 682-694.

Mitchell, C.R. 1981. *The Structure of International Conflict* London: Macmillan.

Pirouet, M.L. 1976. "The Achievement of Peace in the Sudan", *Journal of East African Research and Development* 6 (1): 117-145.

Rosenau, J.N. (ed.) 1964. *International Aspects of Civil Strife.* Princeton: U.P.

Wai, D.M. (ed.) 1973. *The Southern Sudan; The Problem of National Integration.* London: Frank Cass.

GENOCIDE AND SOCIAL CONFLICT:

A PARTIAL THEORY AND A COMPARISON

John L.P. Thompson and Gail A. Quets

Despite the importance of the topic, and recent rising interest, the sociology of genocide remains relatively underdeveloped. The most widely accepted definition, which is contained in the 1948 United Nations Genocide Convention, is problematic (Drost 1959; International Commission of Jurists 1979; Kuper 1982, chapter 2; Whitaker 1985). A comparative literature is emerging (Kuper 1982, 1988; Chalk and Jonassohn 1988; Harff and Gurr 1988), but it incorporates little detailed examination of less extreme and negative cases. There is almost no specification of the relationship between genocide and other types of social conflict (Wallimann and Dobkowski 1987), and little sociological theory of genocide, in the sense of a set of propositions specifying the relationships among a set of factors which together help account for it. We are thus little enlightened on the questions of how genocide emerges from nongenocidal situations, and why some conflicts become genocidal and some do not. This paper addresses these issues. It seeks to incorporate previous work, while avoiding some of

Research in Social Movements, Conflict and Change,
Volume 12, pages 245-266.

its problems. We provide a definition of genocide, a multidimensional conception of conflict which allows the relationship of genocide to social conflict to be explored, an embryonic theory of genocide, and some comparative evidence from two cases, the Holocaust and the Northern Ireland conflict.

DEFINITION

While a variety of definitions of genocide have been proposed, most share a core element, the destruction of a social group. We take this as our starting point, and assess whether various refinements and restrictions which have been offered are defensible.

In the United Nations definition genocide is the destruction of a national, ethnic, racial, or religious group.[1] Political groups are excluded from the definition. For this to be justifiable, two conditions must be met. One is empirical: that "political" groups do not overlap with ethnic, racial, national or religious groups. In fact the national, ethnic, racial, and religious groups which are the victims in genocide are often politically organized, and a clear separation between them and "political" groups is impossible (Kuper 1982, pp. 93-4).[2] The second condition is conceptual: that it makes sense to say that the destruction of some groups constitutes genocide and that of others does not. No adequate argument to this effect has been advanced: the restriction arose as a political compromise necessary to obtain passage of the Genocide Convention (Kuper 1982, chapter 2).

The United Nations definition also directly incorporates intent: it declares genocide to be constituted by a listed set of acts "committed with intent to destroy" the four types of groups mentioned above. This reflects the origin of the concept within a legalistic framework. (Raphael Lemkin, its principal drafter, was a jurist.) Where the goal is to prosecute leading architects and planners of genocide, this orientation is cogent. For sociological purposes, however, it is ill-advised. Our argument here is not that the sociology of genocide should neglect intent, but only that including it in the definition is unnecessary and has undesirable consequences. The nature of the latter can be illustrated by referring to another sociological field, that of social stratification. Research in this area focuses at times on actions committed with the intention of bringing about systematic socioeconomic advantage or disadvantage for a collectivity. But like any large-scale social phenomenon, social stratification is the product of ranges of different actions. Sometimes their consequences for stratification are intended or anticipated by those who engage in them, sometimes not. Often there is great ambiguity. Given this, a definition of stratification as constituted by actions committed with the intent to produce it would be quite inappropriate. It would mean that even where one social collectivity was known to have been systematically disadvantaged by the actions of another, if it could not be shown that these actions were committed with the intent of producing stratification as such, we would be unable even to claim that stratification had occurred.

Since genocide is also a large-scale composite social action involving multiple actors and multiple actions, these considerations apply to it. If anything they hold with greater urgency because in no field is there greater motivation for actors to hide and deny their intentions. However, because the United Nations definition has held sway, even when groups have been entirely destroyed by coordinated social action, the occurrence of genocide has frequently been denied on the grounds that the intentions fall outside the specifications of the United Nations definition. No consistent research tradition with agreement as to when genocide occurs has developed under this definition, and it is hard to see how it could. An effective solution is to treat genocide as the destruction of a group by purposive action, and emphasize that this leaves us free to explore the role of intentional action in any way that is found useful.

Other definitions suggest other restrictions to the basic concept of destruction. Chalk and Jonassohn (1988, p. 40) require that genocide be unilateral as opposed to reciprocal. Again, the fact that this distinction is important does not mean that it should be included as an aspect of the definition. Treating unilateral and reciprocal destruction as two subtypes of genocide which can then be compared seems preferable to defining one as genocide and excluding the other. Another modification is to include restrictions regarding agency. Thus some (e.g., Horowitz 1976) treat state involvement as a defining feature of genocide, at least in the twentieth century. This is an effort to deal with the prominence of the state in contemporary genocide—in the Holocaust, as well as in the genocide of the Turks against the Armenians (another paradigmatic twentieth-century case) and in many other instances. It leads to major difficulties, however. One is that the destruction of groups by agents other than the state (Clay 1988) is not recognized as genocide. A second is that it ignores the fact that we can establish which agents contribute to genocide, and to what extent, only empirically, not by definition. As a result it tends to discourage investigation of many crucial matters, such as the relative contributions of state and non-state actors, which vary; the extent to which some populations or social-structural arrangements are more amenable to state-sponsored genocide than others; and the extent to which the state requires popular support for genocide, can create it, or simply acts independently of it. At worst this facilitates a projection of responsibility for genocide entirely onto the state. A less problematic way of taking account of state involvement is to treat it as a causal factor which greatly increases the severity of genocide. Both its independent impact and its relationship to the other factors can be investigated empirically.

In short, given the problems which arise from restrictions, we define genocide as the destruction of a group by purposive action. This allows the role of intentional action to be explored, different subtypes of genocide to be compared, and the impact of different factors on genocide to be examined empirically.

A final point concerns the conceptual status of genocide. Both in everyday speech and in the language of research the tendency to treat genocide as a dichotomy—in any given situation, genocide either occurs or does not—is deeply ingrained. No doubt this partly reflects the desire to express moral disapproval of genocide. In fact, however, the destruction of a group or category of people is a matter of degree: technically, the underlying concept of interest is a continuous variable.[3] Given this, dichotomous conceptions of genocide tend to generate disputes as to where "the" boundary between genocide and "not-genocide" falls. Recognizing genocide as a matter of degree avoids these debates, which are inherently insoluble, and encourages the development of theories which explain movements from less to more genocidal behavior, and vice versa. Rather than thinking in terms of one boundary between genocide and not-genocide, we think in terms of a continuum from no group destruction to complete destruction.[4] Societies are pushed shorter or longer distances along it by different causal factors. In empirical terms, the task is to develop models which account for variation in the level of destruction. Another analogy to the field of social stratification may be helpful here. Blau and Duncan's (1967) reconceptualization of social stratification as the process of status attainment stimulated detailed study of how this process differs for different racial and ethnic groups (Duncan 1968; Kelley and McAllister 1984), men and women (Roos 1985), different segments of the labor market (Beck et al. 1978) and different classes (Robinson and Kelley 1979). It also allowed social stratification as a whole to be broken down into the component processes which produce it, and the relationships among them to be established empirically. We are in effect suggesting a parallel reconceptualization of the study of genocide as the study of the process of social destruction. This too will allow study of how this process differs for different groups, and will also permit the decomposition of the genocidal process into its component elements.

GENOCIDE AND SOCIAL CONFLICT:
A MULTIDIMENSIONAL APPROACH

Genocides frequently emerge in the context of other types of social conflicts, such as civil war, ethnic conflict, colonial expansion, and the struggle for political power after colonial withdrawal (Kuper 1982). Yet not all such conflicts become genocidal. This poses a series of vital questions about the relationship between genocide and other types of social conflict. How does genocide differ from other conflicts? What factors push conflict in or away from a genocidal direction? Students of genocide are aware of these issues, but have been hampered by the absence of a definition which facilitates the study of the emergence of genocide as a process, and a lack of attention to negative cases. The sociology of conflict has also failed to address these questions. General definitions of conflict and violence usually include the destruction of another party either explicitly (e.g., Mack and Snyder 1957, p. 218) or implicitly (Eldridge 1979, p. 1), but substantive discussions and research on conflict usually omit it. Schellenberg (1981), for example, does not discuss genocide, massacre, the Holocaust, or National Socialism. One obstacle is the breadth of the concept of social conflict, which has long been a target for complaint.[5]

In seeking to open up the question of the relationship between genocide and other conflicts our strategy will be to differentiate among different dimensions of conflict, of which genocide is one. As an initial step we distinguish between two dimensions of social conflict: social competition, defined conventionally as a striving for scarce objects under rules which limit the damage competitors can inflict on each other (Weber 1978, p. 38; Mack and Snyder 1957, p. 217; Stigler 1968, p. 181), and social destruction, i.e., genocide as we have defined it. Social competition ranges from noncompetitive harmony to maximal between-group competition; social destruction from zero to total. The two dimensions are conceptually distinct, and empirically they seem to be highly independent. Given conflicts may be highly competitive but not particularly destructive, and vice versa, or they may display both elements to a substantial degree. Specific cases can be located statically within this conceptual space, or tracked as they move through it. This multidimensional conception of conflict permits theories which identify factors which push conflicts in more or less destructive directions to be proposed and ultimately tested.

THEORY

Although there is no developed theory of genocide, a series of explanatory factors are found in the literature. We begin by considering three which constantly recur. One is the state, whose prominence we have noted. Another is advanced technology, which clearly facilitates mass slaughter (Arlen 1975, pp. 243-4; Kuper 1982, pp. 101-2; Smith 1987, pp. 32-6). The third is modern bureaucracy, whose affinity for the genocidal enterprise many have emphasized. It distances people from actual killing, routinizes the work which supports it, and is uniquely suited to the administration of cruelty without passion which was the hallmark of the Holocaust (Bauman 1988; Browning 1983; Hilberg 1985; Milgram 1974). While these factors are often highly significant, an adequate general theory of genocide can not be developed from them alone, for at least two reasons. One is that most states, and even most bureaucratized and technologically advanced states, do not commit extreme genocide: and much severe genocide is committed in societies which are not technologically advanced or highly bureaucratic.[6] A second problem with these three factors is their historical specificity. The phenomenon of genocide (although not the term) is ancient (Kuper 1982, p. 11; Smith 1987, p. 28). Since the state, bureaucracy, and advanced technology are all features of modern social organization, they can not contribute to a theory of genocide outside the modern period. Additional specification of what sometimes makes these elements effective contributors to genocide, and why genocide can occur even when they are not in play, is therefore required.

A fourth factor provides the type of specification missing in the first three, and for that reason will be the main focus of our attention. It suggests that the normative climate plays a significant role in promoting or inhibiting genocide. Many analyses of genocide have advanced this perspective in one form or another. Fein (1979) emphasizes that victims in modern genocide are defined by perpetrators as beyond the circle of moral obligation. Kuper (1982, pp. 84-100) starts from the premise that the existence of societies presupposes the existence of moral restraints on destructive conflicts. He then identifies a range of ideological factors which help override them. Lifton (1986) examines how under the Nazis one specific aspect of the normative order, the healing ethic of medical doctors, was transformed into a killing ethic which was then proclaimed a moral good.

In the most general terms, a moral climate conducive to genocide may arise in three ways. One is that the prohibition against it may simply not exist. Smith (1987, p. 28) suggests that before approximately the sixteenth century this was the case. "[I]t is only within the past few centuries that genocide has produced even a sense of moral horror, much less been thought of as 'criminal'." Genocide was then routine behavior, for example in the slaughter of conquered enemies. Alternatively, the prohibition against destruction may exist, but become attenuated by other ethical imperatives or displaced by the approval of genocide as a moral good. It is often difficult to identify the boundary between these last two mechanisms. Since the shift noted by Smith, however, genocide has come to be seen as the most illegitimate conceivable collective violence, and one or other of them, or some combination, has become almost essential if genocide is to occur. Hence the appeal to students of modern genocide such as Drost (1959, frontispiece quotation) and Kuper (1982, p. 100) of Pascal's observation that men never engage in evil with more joyous abandon than in the service of a good conscience.

When related to the first three factors the normative explanation suggests that it is not only the organizational resources of bureaucracies and states and the destructive capability of advanced technology which are relevant, but also the prevailing ethical ambiance. Once the appropriate normative climate is created, then given the great resources which these three factors constitute, they can have a major impact on genocide.[7]

Before considering some evidence bearing on this explanation, we will consider a fifth. This is nonrecognition. Nonrecognition by perpetrators, i.e., denial, seems to be almost universal.[8] Nonrecognition by bystanders (Morse 1968; Laqueur 1980; Staub 1988) and even victims (Fein 1979, pp. 314-6) is also widespread. The latter in particular is on an utterly different moral level from perpetrator denial, its exact opposite in terms of motivation, and causally secondary to it, since it can not occur if perpetrators do not engage in genocidal actions in the first place. Nevertheless, nonrecognition by bystanders and victims can not be explained simply as an artefact of the success of perpetrator denial. Each requires explanation in its own right. Some of the problems discussed above, such as the exclusion of some groups and the use of a dichotomous definition of genocide, facilitate nonrecognition: but beyond this genocide by its nature seems to inhibit the human ability to acknowledge that it is occurring. We do not, however, need to be able to explain why nonrecognition occurs in order to note that it is widespread and study its consequences. In general, nonrecognition facilitates genocide, in the sense that if movement in a genocidal direction is occurring but unrecognized, attempts at prevention will not be undertaken. It should be treated not as an aberration which can be neglected by theory but rather as an important causal mechanism.

A COMPARISON

We turn to a comparison of two cases which differ substantially in destructiveness, the Holocaust and the Northern Ireland conflict. Figure 1 records their approximate locations in terms of our two dimensions of conflict. The Northern Ireland conflict is more competitive, in that the society is dominated by a deep cleavage between two ethnic groups (Darby 1976; Rose 1971; Stewart 1977). And, with some 2900 fatalities since 1969, it is of course far less destructive. Nevertheless it does display an incipient genocidal element.[9] Precise behavioral indicators of social destruction in our sense are not well developed, although efforts to create them are under way (Thompson 1988). We take the view, following Kuper (1982, p. 191), that killing members of a group without regard for their individual characteristics or behavior constitutes a behavioral movement in a genocidal direction. In the Northern Ireland conflict acts committed by both Protestants and Catholics have met this criterion on more than a few occasions.[10] Three examples will suffice (more could be given):

- In early 1976 a minibus carrying twelve workmen was stopped by a group of armed men. The passengers were asked whether they were Protestant or Catholic, and the one who gave the "right" answer, in this case Catholic, was told to leave. His colleagues were shot to death, except for one victim who survived eighteen bullet wounds (Kelly 1986).
- Seventeen people were killed by a bomb placed in a Catholic bar by members of a Protestant paramilitary organization in December 1971 (Hamill 1985, p. 81).
- On a Sunday in November 1987 a bomb exploded by the IRA at a Remembrance Day celebration, a religious service, killed eleven people and injured 63, many of them seriously (Moloney 1987).

Given this genocidal element in the Northern Ireland case, our comparison focuses on two issues. Is there evidence indicating first that a normative transformation facilitated the Holocaust, and second that some similar transformation might account for the genocidal element in the Northern Ireland conflict? We also suggest some constraints which may operate in the latter case.

The extent of the campaign to pervert the nongenocidal moral order in Nazi Germany is well documented:

A systematic propaganda campaign to break down superego values was directed at the entire population, including children. A ghastly example is a widely used school

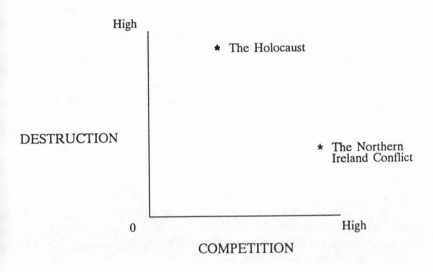

Figure 1.   Two Dimensions of Social Conflict

book on applied mathematics, on the high school level, entitled *Mathematics in the service of National-Political Education* [*1*]. The choice of problems in this mathematics book was designed to break down the taboo against mass killing, as when (on page 75) pupils were asked to compute how much phosgene would be needed to poison a city of a certain area and of a specified population, with special attention to the average rate of breathing in relation to the atmospheric concentration of gas. The book also attacked normal and desirable compassion for the sick and crippled by setting problems in terms of distorted statements of the cost of their proper care and rehabilitation, asking, for instance, how many new settlement houses could be built and how many marriage-allowance loans could be given to newly-weds for the amount of money it cost the state to care for the crippled, the criminal, and the insane (Alexander 1948, p. 173).

Overall, the Nazis' efforts were highly successful. The organization of daily life under their regime displayed many of the characteristics of a relatively secure and accepted prevailing moral order. As in most ongoing social systems, in everyday life the nature of the established moral order, and its implications on a given topic (in this case, genocide), were not matters of much remark or collective examination (Engelmann 1986). Transgressors were few, and received little or no social support, positive indications of the effectiveness of the established normative order. Arendt (1963, p. 134) observes:

> [J]ust as the law in civilized countries assumes that the voice of conscience tells everybody 'Thou shalt not kill,' even though man's natural desires and inclinations may at times be murderous, so the law of Hitler's land demanded that the voice of conscience tell everybody: 'Thou shalt kill,' although the organizers of the massacres knew full well that murder is against the normal desires and inclinations of most people. Evil in the Third Reich had lost the quality by which most people recognize it—the quality of temptation. Many Germans and many Nazis, probably an overwhelming majority of them, must have been tempted *not* to murder, *not* to rob, *not* to let their neighbors go off to their doom (for that the Jews were transported to their doom they knew, of course, even though many of them may not have known the gruesome details), and not to become accomplices in all these crimes by benefiting from them. But, God knows, they had learned how to resist temptation.

It can be argued that much of the conforming impulse reflected not so much moral reconstruction as a realistic fear or retribution. But the two elements are not exclusive. A normative order is typically underpinned by concrete sanctions against nonconformity, but these do not nullify its existence or invalidate its character as a normative order. The genocidal moral order under the Nazis was no exception. Although violent punishment was applied for the failure to do evil, that failure was condemned in thoroughly moralistic terms. An example is provided by a Nazi general who spoke to occupying troops in Serbia about the need for their participation in the hangings, burnings, deportations and hostage-shootings which were sufficiently extensive to exterminate the male Jewish population in the region:

> Anyone who wishes to rule charitably sins against the lives of his comrades. He will be called to account without regard for his person and placed before a court-martial (Browning 1985, p. 46).

Turning now to the Northern Ireland conflict, there is evidence of an incipient transformation of the moral order in a genocidal direction which can reasonably be interpreted as having facilitated its genocidal component. As so often, each side shows great sensitivity to the outrages committed by the other, and less to those emanating from its own camp.[11]

One element is the *denigration of out-groups either as subhuman or by metaphors of disease.* There is a consensus that this provides moral license for genocidal destruction. Dehumanization is one of the processes by which the usual moral inhibitions against violence become weakened (Kelman 1973, pp. 48-9). Metaphors of disease imply that social "afflictions" must be destroyed if the "host body" (society itself) is to survive. Hence the special appeal of the cancer image, implying particular malignancy and the obligation to perform the most radical "surgery."[12] The vigorous use of these symbols by Hitler and other Nazis (Jäckel 1981, pp. 58-9; Browning 1985, p. 27) is well known. They are also employed in Northern Ireland:

[Concerning the murder of a politician and his female companion] "It was a godsend to get rid of vermin like that."

"Even our own Protestant defence forces have seemed unwilling to walk that extra mile and stamp out themselves the cancer which has been eating away at the very bowels of Ulster."

"When the cancer within the human body lies deep, the surgeon must cut accordingly." (All three examples from Dillon and Lehane 1973, pp. 285-6.)[13]

These examples are from the political crisis of 1972, when the Protestant-dominated parliament had been suspended, and the IRA bombing campaign and activities of Protestant murder gangs were at their height. Such imagery has not passed away, however. Figure 2 reproduces a "cartoon" from a magazine available on public sale in central Belfast in 1985. A Protestant politician, Mr. George Seawright, made a public endorsement of the incineration of Catholics at an Education and Library Board meeting in May 1984, when members of the Board were discussing objections by Catholic parents to the playing of the National Anthem at school concerts:

Seawright said he viewed their attitude with disgust ...[he] went on to criticize Catholic priests for indoctrinating their people and suggested that the board should acquire an incinerator and "burn the lot as they are all Fenian scum" (*Irish Times* October 31, 1984, p. 6).

Mythologies of world conspiracy have often been available to those who, in a context of societal threat, seek to legitimate genocidal destruction. The most astonishing example is the belief in a Jewish world conspiracy (Cohn 1967), which was heavily utilized by the Nazis. Iranian hostility to the Baha'is is also fueled by a belief in their involvement in an international conspiracy (Kuper 1985, p. 152). Some fundamentalist Ulster Protestants have a firm belief in a Catholic attempt to dominate the world, and certainly Northern Ireland. The interviewer of a veteran Orangeman reports (Burns 1985, p. 11):

Figure 2.

As a child he had a Catholic wet nurse. "She lived near my mother and these two women were very close for years and years. Well when she was dying she told my mother 'you know if the priest told me to kill you I would have to do it, I would have no choice.' That is how they are. It is authoritarian and they have no freedom."

Since even a "good" Catholic such as the woman in question is powerless to resist the dictates of her Church, the conspiracy myth facilitates the belief that it is necessary to take steps against Catholics in general, and that doing so would be both patriotic and morally righteous. While the IRA is at considerable odds with the Catholic Church,[14] the two are viewed, in the conspiracy interpretation, as being in league. This is apparent in the following extract from what is ostensibly the oath of loyalty taken by members of Sinn Fein (the political wing of the IRA). These oaths are quite widely circulated: this particular version was published "to show people the true reasons behind the IRA's war of genocide against the Loyalist[15] people of Ulster":

I swear by Almighty God, by all heaven, by the holy and blessed prayer book of the Roman Catholic Church, by the holy Virgin Mary, Mother of God, by her bitter tears and wailings, by Saint Patrick, our blessed and most adorable Host, the Rosary, to fight until we die wading in the field of red gore of the Saxon tyrants and murderers of our glorious nationality, and, if spared to fight until not a single trace is left to tell that the holy soil of Ireland was trodden in by these heretics.

Also, these Protestant robbers and brutes, these unbelievers of our faith, will be driven, like the swine they are, into the sea, by fire, the knife or by poison cup, until we of the Catholic faith and the avowed supporters of the Sinn Fein action and principles clear these heretics from our land...." (*Irish Times* September 14, 1985, p. 6.)

The *creation of lists of potential victims* is a familiar precursor of organized genocide (Arendt 1963, pp. 102-106; Hilberg 1961, p. 124). In the 1972 crisis, a leading Protestant politician made a series of speeches before large assemblies of uniformed men in which he referred to the need to "liquidate the enemy" if the politicians failed, and declared that "[i]t is important that we get on with speed in compiling dossiers on known IRA supporters" (Dillon and Lehane 1973, pp. 62-63). It is significant that the reference is not to IRA members, but to the broader and less precise category of their supporters. Recent IRA statements also refer to lists:

Over the past few months our intelligence personnel have compiled accurate and extensive dossiers on all those involved in building or refurbish work for the security forces. As a result of this intelligence, we are now in a position to take effective action if builders do not henceforth desist from playing an active role in support of the Crown Forces (*Irish Times* August 21, 1985, p. 1, quoting an IRA statement in *An Phoblacht*.)

The assumption that statements such as these are effective incitements towards genocide presupposes some receptivity to them among their audience. Evidence of this and more comes from Thompson's field study of a Protestant paramilitary group.[16] Members of the group conducted lengthy conversations in which they speculated on the nature of the "message" being sent to them by public figures in statements to the press or on the radio. Two members of the group were, in the researcher's judgement, predisposed to the killing of Catholics. They frequently promoted the interpretation that officials (for example, the British Secretary of State) were "really" asking Loyalists to "take action" which British Army personnel were unable to take because "their hands are tied."

Open approval for genocidal measures clearly indicates a redefinition of the moral order. In Northern Ireland an underlying enthusiasm for genocidal killing comes into the open at times. In May 1974, during a Loyalist strike organized by the UWC (Ulster Workers' Council) which brought down a power-sharing government in Northern Ireland, Loyalist paramilitaries set off bombs in the South, including one which killed civilians walking to a train station in central Dublin.

> ... Sammy Smith, 'minister of propaganda' [of the UWC] and a man who believed in a ritual cleansing by violence, delivered himself of one short, terrible comment: 'I am very happy about the bombings in Dublin,' he said. 'There is a war with the Free State and now we are laughing at them.' Perhaps more chilling than Smith was the loyalist politician—a well-known, generally respected figure ... who played a part in the UWC strike. He said he had seen the effects of bomb injuries on television programs and could not condone such things. But outside humanitarian feelings, he suddenly added, his reaction to the Dublin bombings had been: "Slap it into you fellahs—you've deserved every bit of it" (Fisk 1975, pp. 80-81).

An example of the destruction of restraints against genocidal behavior is a stress on the *absence of personal hostility* as a motive for violence. Among Nazis, Adolph Eichmann had little "personal" hostility to Jews. He was not an anti-Semitic fanatic, and he had Jewish friends, including a Jewish mistress (Arendt 1963, pp. 23, 26-7). It is also a familiar theme of Provisional IRA ideology that their conflict with the British and Protestants is "nothing personal." This is presented, and often interpreted, at least in the IRA case, as a benign feature. But as the Eichmann example reminds us, it is highly malign, and an aspect of the "cruelty without passion" which Smith noted as a hallmark of the Holocaust. In violent conflict which is not genocidal, extreme personal hostility, based for example on knowledge of a victim's personal or alleged responsibility for dreadful deeds, is usually expected as a justification for violence against members of a collectivity.

The removal of this normative requirement inhibits the usually effective constraints against genocide, and vastly expands the number of potential targets.

A significant element providing positive urges to genocide, as opposed to removing inhibitions against it, is the process of *"universalizing the target."* The Holocaust featured a vast battery of devices for collectivizing victims for destruction (Browning 1985; Gilbert 1985; Hilberg 1985). In Northern Ireland there is substantial public opposition to the killing of civilians. This reflects a commitment to a nongenocidal moral order which is deeply rooted in most of the population. There is evidence of this both in survey data,[17] and in behavior such as fierce political opposition to killings which are perceived as crossing new moral boundaries (Kuper 1982, p. 204; Thompson 1985). But the commitment to maintaining the nongenocidal moral order is not universal, as we have seen. One way in which the IRA has attempted to further subvert it is by gradually redefining the concept of the legitimate target so that it becomes more comprehensive. This has been done by identifying functional relationships to the security forces and announcing that individuals who engage in them merit the death sentence. Once this process has begun, it is extended, logically enough, by the simple addition of ever more distant functional relationships. A struggle takes place in the political arena over the *morality* of each attempt at extension.

If we chart this process by examining IRA press releases, we find that it has advanced a long way. Some time ago, explicit Provisional IRA declarations of "legitimate targets" began to include hoteliers and traders who catered for the security forces, and contractors and workers involved in the construction of police stations. With the more recent (August 1986) announcement that anyone engaged in work for the government is a legitimate target, the formula has been expanded to embrace a very large proportion of the population.[18] A genocidal calculus has been constructed, even though its genocidal character is, as usual, publicly denied.[19]

To summarize the comparative analysis, in Nazi Germany overwhelming state power was directed to the extermination of an ethnic subsection devoid of martial tradition. A thorough transformation of the normative order in a genocidal direction facilitated this. In Northern Ireland there is a genocidal element in the conflict. This is partly explained by the fact that a transformation of the moral order in a genocidal direction has proceeded some way. It is also facilitated by the fact that it is widely denied by perpetrators and generally ignored by bystanders.

Since the two cases differ greatly in the level of destruction, some attempt to explain this is in order. Three possible causes can be suggested. One is the role of the state. Unlike in the Holocaust, in the current outbreak of violence in Northern Ireland the state is not the main agent of killing (see note 10). The social foundation of the conflict is the aspiration of two indigenous ethnic groups to incompatible conceptions of a homeland. Given the destructive proclivities and behavior of some of the members of the paramilitary groups which each community sustains, the fact that these groups lack control of the resources of a state is a *restraining* factor.[20] A second restraint is the relatively equal balance between the two sides, and a third is the substantial public opposition to the killing within each ethnic group. The difference in the severity of the killing between the two cases, and the restraining factors in Northern Ireland, must be borne in mind, but they should not lead us to ignore the progress in a genocidal direction which has occurred there.

SUMMARY AND CONCLUSION

We have sought to contribute to the sociology of genocide in four areas.

1. *Definition.* Our broad definition of genocide as the destruction of a group by purposive action avoids arbitrary restrictions and facilitates comparative analysis. The exclusion of explanatory elements from the definition allows their impact to be established empirically. Our treatment of genocide as a continuous variable allows justice to be done to extreme cases without diminishing them, and less extreme cases to be recognized without exaggeration. It also encourages the study of the emergence of genocide as a process. All of these features lay the foundations for the construction of theories of genocide which account for variation in the level of destruction in different cases.

2. *A multidimensional conception of social conflict.* The nature of the relationship between genocide and social conflict must also be established empirically rather than by definition. To explore it we have discriminated among different dimensions of conflict, treating social destruction (genocide) as one of them. As a starting point we have distinguished between two dimensions, destruction and competition. This approach allows the development of theories which explain how genocide emerges from other types of conflict, and why some conflicts do not become genocidal.

3. *Theory.* In an effort to move towards a developed theory of genocide we have considered five interrelated explanatory factors. The first is the transformation of the normative order in a genocidal direction. This

facilitates the emergence of genocide and helps explain how three other factors—the state, bureaucracy, and advanced technology—can contribute to it. It also explains how genocide can occur when these three factors are not in evidence. A fifth contributing factor is nonrecognition, which facilitates genocide by precluding preventive action.

4. *Comparative analysis.* Our substantive discussion found that just as in Nazi Germany a transformation of the normative order in a genocidal direction facilitated the Holocaust, so in Northern Ireland it has progressed some way, and helps account for the genocidal element in the killing. Further escalation in Northern Ireland has been prevented by the lack of control of the state by the paramilitary organizations which do most of the killing, the relatively equal size of the two ethnic groups, and the opposition to the paramilitary groups within each ethnic community.

These results do suggest the particular importance of normative transformations in explaining not only the emergence of genocide in general, but also why some conflicts move towards destruction rather than remaining competitive. We would emphasize, however, that the utility of our approach goes beyond the merits of any single explanatory factor. The increasing interest in genocide has yielded a series of typologies and partial explanations which are often insightful but whose logical status and relationship to each other is frequently far from clear, as a recent review shows (Charny 1988). Since our definition of genocide is not tied to any particular theory, it permits a wide range of hypotheses about the genesis of genocide to be differentiated, tested, and ideally synthesized. The conception of genocide as a continuous variable opens up for investigation other significant issues, such as the extent to which the dynamics of genocide are similar at different levels of severity. The multidimensional approach to conflict encourages precise specification of whether an explanation accounts for severe conflicts in general, or only for their genocidal components. This facilitates investigation of the question of what exactly causes "normal conflict" to become genocidal, which has not received the attention it deserves. Finally, the multidimensional conception of conflict itself can be further developed. For example, as a third possible dimension of conflict we might suggest anarchy, i.e., the extent to which conflict is not conducted under established rules. Anarchic conflict may or may not involve destruction, and the extent to which, or conditions under which, genocide emerges out of anarchic as opposed to competitive situations is of interest. In various ways, therefore, our approach may contribute to the development of a vital emerging field.

ACKNOWLEDGMENTS

This is a substantial revision of a paper read at the Meetings of the American Sociological Association in Chicago 1987 under the title "Redefining the Moral Order: Towards a Normative Theory of Genocide." We are grateful for comments on previous versions to Israel Charny, Lee Clarke, Randall Collins, Tormod Lunde, Tom Mayer, Susan Opotow, Robert V. Robinson, Joseph Schwartz, Roger W. Smith, Jennifer Todd, Robert White, and Everett L. Wheeler. The research was supported by the Harry Frank Guggenheim Foundation.

NOTES

1. The UN definition is reproduced in Appendix 1 of Kuper (1982).
2. A recent empirical study which seeks to distinguish between genocides and politicides is obliged to recognize a group of mixed episodes (Harff and Gurr 1988, p. 368, Table 2).
3. This holds even if only dichotomous or other ordinal indicators are available.
4. Bauer (1984) and Staub (1989) also conceive of genocide in terms of a continuum. Bauer excludes political groups from the rubric of genocide; Staub does not.
5. For example: "'[c]onflict' is for the most part a rubber concept, being stretched and molded for the purposes at hand. In its broadest sense it seems to cover everything from war to choices between ice-cream sodas or sundaes" (Mack and Snyder 1957, p. 212). For more recent complaints see Eldrige 1979, p. 1 and Turner 1986, pp. 403-4.
6. For many examples see Kuper (1982, 1985) and Harff and Gurr (1988).
7. Although not the only sources of this moral climate, the three factors may themselves help generate it. Bauman (1988) and Rubenstein (1975, p. 22), for example, analyze how bureaucracy facilitates the crossing of the moral barriers to genocide.
8. Smith (1989) provides a particularly comprehensive study of denial by the Turkish government of the genocide against the Armenians.
9. Since Protestants and Catholics in Northern Ireland are ethnic groups and politically organized, their destruction would constitute genocide under either the narrow UN definition or a broader one including political groups. Kuper (1982, chapter 10) provides a pertinent discussion of Northern Ireland as a non-genocidal society. For a general overview of the political conflict in the society see O'Malley (1983).
10. The political violence in Nothern Ireland is most usefully seen as a three-way interaction between Protestants, Catholics and the security forces. Despite their much greater firepower, between 1969 and 1986 the security forces killed a smaller proportion of the victims (12 percent) than did the Protestant and Catholic paramilitaries (27 and 55 percent respectively) (New Ireland Forum 1983, p. 7; the killers of seven percent of the victims could not be ascertained). For a more detailed discussion and time-series analysis see Thompson (1989).
11. The following discussion of mechanisms of normative transformation makes no claim to exhaustiveness. For a discussion of moral exclusion in general and a list of processes which constitute it see Opotow (1988).
12. Sontag (1978, p. 33) suggests that "the concept of disease is never innocent. But it could be argued that the cancer metaphors are in themselves implicitly genocidal." See also Kuper's discussion of the Kelman and Sontag articles (Kuper 1982, pp. 87, 90-91).

13. Thompson conducted a series of interviews in 1972 with members of a Protestant paramilitary group in Belfast, some of whom routinely referred to the IRA and their supporters as "animals." Survey evidence (O'Donnell 1977, pp. 189, 195) confirms the use of this term by both Protestants and Catholics.

14. Despite this, Catholic religious conceptions permeate the world-view of the Provisional IRA and their supporters (O'Brien 1986).

15. Loyalists are "Queen's Rebels," Protestants whose loyalty to the Crown is often coupled with defiance of British governments (Miller 1978).

16. See note 13.

17. For example, in the Irish Mobility Study of 1973, seventy percent of respondents from Northern Ireland (N = 2402) selected the response "Disagree very much" to the statement "Overall, violence is a legitimate way to achieve one's goals." (Tabulation by the current authors.)

18. Thus, after planting a fire bomb in a hotel in Kesh, county Fermanagh (it was defused) the IRA claimed that the hotel catered for members of the security forces and warned of further attacks if traders continued to serve soldiers and policemen (*Irish Times* October 15, 1984, p. 7). In Lisnagelvin, a mainly Protestant housing estate in Derry, they said that the builders of a police station would be considered "legitimate targets" unless they stopped work on the site (*Irish Times* June 22, 1985, p. 22). In Strabane, they threatened to kill municipal workers who collected garbage from the police station. For the extension to all government workers, and condemnation of it by trade union leaders, see Clines (1986).

19. For the salience of denial in the Northern Ireland conflict see Thompson (1986).

20. This is not to deny that on occasion the Protestant paramilitary groups have at times exploited connections to the security forces to deadly effect. They do not, however, control these forces, which have moved against them in recent years. The IRA's lament is that they have been unable to persuade the Irish state to deploy its resources in support of their activities. The implication is that the nearer either paramilitary force comes to control of the state, the greater the probability of further movement in a genocidal direction.

REFERENCES

Alexander, L. 1948. "War Crimes: Their Social-Psychological Aspects." *American Journal of Psychiatry* 105: 170-177.

Arendt, H. 1963. *Eichmann in Jerusalem: A Report on the Banality of Evil.* New York: Viking.

Arlen, M.J. 1975. *Passage to Ararat.* New York: Farrar, Strauss and Giroux.

Bauer, Y. 1984. "The Place of the Holocaust in Contemporary History." *Studies in Contemporary Jewry* 1: 201-224.

Bauman, Z. 1988. "Sociology after the Holocaust." *British Journal of Sociology* 39:469-497.

Beck, E.M., P. Horan, and C.M. Tolbert III. 1978. "Stratification in a Dual Economy: A Sectoral Model of Earnings Determination." *American Sociological Review* 43: 704-30.

Blau, P.M. and O.D. Duncan. 1967. *The American Occupational Structure.* New York: Wiley.

Browning, C.R. 1983. "The German Bureaucracy and the Holocaust," Pp. 145-149 in Grobman, A. and D. Landes (eds.) *Critical Issues of the Holocaust.* Los Angeles: Simon Wiesenthal Center and New York: Rossel.

Browning, C.R. 1985. *Fateful Months: Essays on the Emergence of the Final Solution.* New York: Holmes and Meier.

Burns, J. 1985. "Just an Old Fashioned Orangeman." *New Hibernia* 2 no. 7 (July): 11.

Chalk, F. and K. Jonassohn. 1988. "The History and Sociology of Genocidal Killings." Pp. 39-58 in I. W. Charny (ed.) *Genocide: A Critical Bibliographic Review.* New York: Facts on File.

Charny, I.W. (ed.) 1988. *Genocide: A Critical Bibliographic Review.* New York: Facts on File.

Clay, J. 1988. "Genocide: An Activist's Views of Academic Research." Paper presented at the Annual Meeting of the International Studies Association, St. Louis, April.

Clines, F.X. 1986. "I.R.A. Broadening Its Death-Threat List in Ulster." *New York Times* August 9 p. 24.

Cohn N. 1967. *Warrant for Genocide.* New York: Harper and Row.

Darby, J. 1976. *Conflict in Northern Ireland: The Development of a Divided Community.* New York: Barnes and Noble.

Dillon, M. and D. Lehane. 1973. *Political Murder in Northern Ireland.* Harmondsworth: Penguin.

Drost, P. 1959. *The Crime of State II–Genocide.* Lyden: A.W. Sythoff.

Duncan, O.D. 1968. "Inheritance of Poverty or Inheritance of Race?" Pp. 85-110 in D. P. Moynihan (ed.) *On Understanding Poverty: Perspectives from the Social Sciences.* New York: Basic Books.

Eldridge, A.F. 1979. *Images of Conflict.* New York: St. Martin's.

Engelmann, B. 1986. *In Hilter's Germany: Everday Life in the Third Reich.* New York: Pantheon.

Fein, H. 1979. *Accounting for Genocide: National Responses and Jewish Victimization during the Holocaust.* New York: Free Press.

Fisk, R. 1975. *The Point of No Return: The Strike Which Broke the British in Ulster.* London: André Deutsch.

Gilbert, M. 1985. *The Holocaust: A History of the Jews of Europe during the Second World War.* New York: Holt, Rinehart and Winston.

Hamill, D. 1985. *Pig in the Middle: The Army in Northern Ireland 1969-1984.* London: Methuen.

Harff, B. and T.R. Gurr. 1988. "Toward Empirical Theory of Genocides and Politicides: Identification and Measurement of Cases since 1945." *International Studies Quarterly* 32: 359-371.

Hilberg, R. 1961. *The Destruction of the European Jews.* Chicago: Quadrangle Books.

Hilberg, R. 1985. *The Destruction of the European Jews.* Second edition. New York: Holmes and Meier.

Horowitz, I.L. 1976. *Genocide: State Power and Mass Murder.* New Brunswick, NJ: Transaction Books.

International Commission of Jurists. 1979. *The Trial of Macias in Equatorial Guinea.* A Report by Alejandro Artucio. Geneva: International Commission of Jurists.

Jäckel, E. 1981. *Hitler's World View: A Blueprint for Power.* Cambridge: Harvard University Press.

Kelley, J. and I. McAllister. 1984. "The Genesis of Conflict: Religion and Status Attainment in Ulster, 1968." *Sociology* 18: 171-190.

Kelly, M. 1986. "Service to Mark Kingsmills Massacre." *Irish Times* January 4 p. 17.

Kelman, H.C. 1973. "Violence without Moral Restraint: Reflections on the Dehumanization of Victims and Victimizers." *Journal of Social Issues* 29: 25-61.

Kuper, L. 1982. *Genocide: Its Political Use in the Twentieth Century.* New Haven: Yale University Press.

Kuper, L. 1985. *The Prevention of Genocide.* New Haven: Yale University Press.

Kuper, L. 1988. "Other Selected Cases of Genocide and Genocidal Massacres: Types of Genocide." Pp. 155-171 in I. W. Charny (ed.) *Genocide: A Critical Bibliographic Review.* New York: Facts on File.

Laqueur, W. 1980. *The Terrible Secret: Suppression of the Truth about Hitler's "Final Solution."* Boston: Little Brown.

Lifton, R.J. 1986. *The Nazi Doctors: Medical Killing and the Psychology of Genocide.* New York: Basic.

Mack, R.W. and R.C. Snyder. 1957. "The Analysis of Social Conflict—toward an Overview and Synthesis." *Journal of Conflict Resolution* 1: 212-248.

Milgram, S. 1974. *Obedience to Authority.* New York: Harper and Row.

Miller, D.W. 1978. *Queen's Rebels: Ulster Loyalism in Historical Perspective.* Dublin: Gill and Macmillan.

Moloney, E. 1987. "The Most Expensive Own Goal." *Fortnight* December, pp. 6-7.

Morse, A. 1968. *Why Six Million Died: A Chronicle of American Apathy.* New York: Random House.

New Ireland Forum. 1983. "The Cost of Violence Arising from the Northern Ireland Crisis since 1969. Dublin: The Stationery Office.

O'Brien, C. C. 1986. "Ireland: The Mirage of Peace." *New York Review of Books* 24 April: 40-46.

O'Donnell, E.E. 1977. *Northern Irish Stereotypes.* Dublin: College of Industrial Relations.

O'Malley, P. 1983. *The Uncivil Wars: Ireland Today.* Boston: Houghton Mifflin Company.

Opotow, S. 1988. "Outside the Realm of Fairness: Aspects of Moral Exclusion." Meetings of the American Psychological Association, Atlanta, August.

Robinson, R.V. and J. Kelley. 1979. "Class as Conceived by Marx and Dahrendorf: Effects on Inequality and Politics in the United States and Great Britain." *American Sociological Review* 44: 38-58.

Roos, P.A. 1985. *Gender and Work: A Comparative Analysis of Industrial Societies.* New York: State University of New York Press.

Rose, R. 1971. *Governing Without Consensus: An Irish Perspective.* Boston: Beacon.

Rubenstein, R. 1975. *The Cunning of History: The Holocaust and the American Future.* New York: Harper and Row.

Schellenberg, J.A. 1981. *The Science of Conflict.* New York: Oxford University Press.

Smith, R.W. 1987. "Human Destructiveness and Politics: The Twentieth Century as an Age of Genocide." Pp. 21-39 in Wallimann, I. and M. N. Dobkowski (eds.) *Genocide and the Modern Age: Etiology and Case Studies of Mass Death.* New York: Greenwood.

Smith, R. W. 1989. "Genocide and Denial: The Armenian Case and Its Implications. *Armenian Review* 42:1-38.

Sontag, S. 1978. "Disease as Political Metaphor." *New York Review of Books,* 23 February: 29-33.

Staub, E. 1988. "The Psychology of Perpetrators and Bystanders." *Political Psychology* 6:61-85.

Staub, E. 1989. *The Roots of Evil: The Origins of Genocide and Other Group Violence.* New York: Cambridge.

Stewart, A.T.Q. 1977. *The Narrow Ground: Aspects of Ulster 1609-1969.* London: Faber.

Stigler, G.J. 1968. "Competition." *International Encyclopedia of the Social Sciences* 3: 181-186. New York: Macmillan and The Free Press.

Thompson, J.L.P. 1985. "Crime, Social Control, and Trends in Political Killing." Paper presented at the Annual Meetings of the Sociological Association of Ireland, Belfast, March.

Thompson, J.L.P. 1986. "Denial, Polarization, and Massacre: A Comparative Analysis of Northern Ireland and Zanzibar." *Economic and Social Review* 17: 293-314.

Thompson, J.L.P. 1988. "From Conflict to Genocide." Paper presented at the Annual Meeting of the International Studies Association, St. Louis, April.

Thompson, J.L.P. 1989. "Deprivation and Political Violence in Northern Ireland 1922-1985: A Time-Series Analysis." *Journal of Conflict Resolution* 33:676-699.

Turner, J. 1986. "Toward a Unified Theory of Ethnic Antagonism." *Sociological Forum* 1: 403-427.

Wallimann, I. and M.N. Dobkowski. 1987. *Genocide and the Modern Age: Etiology and Case Studies of Mass Death.* New York: Greenwood.

Weber, M. 1978. *Economy and Society.* Berkeley: University of California Press.

Whitaker, B. 1985. *Revised and Updated Report on the Question of the Prevention and Punishment of the Crime of Genocide.* United Nations Economic and Social Council, Commission on Human Rights. (E/CN.4/Sub.2/1985/6, 2 July 1985).

PERSONAL SECURITY, POLITICAL SECURITY:

THE RELATIONSHIP AMONG CONCEPTIONS OF GENDER, WAR, AND PEACE

Terrell A. Northrup

This paper addresses the relationship between conceptions of gender and conceptions of war and peace. I will argue that masculinity, as it is socially constructed, to a significant degree is related to conceptions of war, while femininity is related to peace. The thread which is interwoven between these concepts of gender and war/peace is that of security. I will make the case that, in Western industrialized cultures at least, there is an inter-connection between personal security as it is related to gender and as it is related to beliefs about prescriptions for international security.

Masculinity and feminity are not just ideas; they involve socially constructed training in the nature of a gender system which is manifested on multiple levels of human relationship. Research (described below) has

Research in Social Movements, Conflict and Change,
Volume 12, pages 267-299.
Copyright © 1990 by JAI Press Inc.
All rights of reproduction in any form reserved.
ISBN: 1-55938-065-9

shown that masculinity is defined, at least in part, in terms of assertiveness, competitiveness, and dominance—predominantly a concern with the promotion of the self. Femininity, characterized by caretaking, nurturance, and warmth, involves concern for others. More important, not only are masculinity and femininity defined differently, but they are differentially valued. While maleness and masculinity are overvalued, femaleness and femininity are underemphasized, even devalued. This has implications for the nature of relationships. Within this gender system relationships tend to be characterized by dominance and submission, assigning men to the former of these roles and women to the latter (see Flax 1987).

Both women and men learn the nature of masculinity and femininity (as they are socially constructed), and both learn that maleness is more highly valued then femaleness. However, through socialization masculinity is integrated into the identities of males (in large part as self-concern), while females learn to identity themselves as feminine (in the sense of other-concern). Although the focus of this discussion is on differences between women and men, this is only because they are the recipients of training in masculinity and femininity. The purpose of this analysis is not to generalize about women and men but, on the contrary, it is to make clearer the socially constructed nature of gender. I do believe, however, that the different training women and men receive tends to result in two different constructions of reality, partially due to definitions of gender and partially because of the experience of differential status.

In a sense, naming these clusters of characteristics "masculinity" and "femininity" masks their social origins and discriminatory nature by implying biological origins. The current gender system essentially restricts both women and men from participating in whole arenas of human experience (for example, men from homemaking and women from holding positions of power) and as signs differing status to these arenas. Further, I will argue that there is a negative or "hyper" masculinity and a negative or "hyper" femininity. In Western industrialized cultures masculinity and femininity become constructed as being *opposed* to each other. When they are experienced as being in opposition, the negative aspects of masculinity become fused with the positive, for example, assertiveness is associated with aggression and dominance. An equivalent process occurs in relation to femininity; caretaking becomes associated with vulnerability and submissiveness.

The fusion of negative and positive serves to maintain the system. The hypermasculine view of the world maintains that to take care of the self requires aggression; since femininity/caretaking is associated with weakness, it is at best devalued and at worst feared. Coupled with the devaluing of other-concern and femaleness, this process results in a rejection of things associated with femaleness, including connectedness and care for others. For women, assertiveness (taking care of themselves) has implications of harmfulness, since it is associated with dominance. For women, being nurturing means giving up part of the self; for men it means making oneself vulnerable and weak. (See DeVault in this volume for a discussion of how for women "care of family" becomes fused with deferential behavior and the suppression of conflict in the home).

These hyper-masculine and hyper-feminine views are distortions of reality. Effective caretaking involves both "masculine" and "feminine" characteristics, both nurturance and assertiveness, as any parent of a two year old or a teenager knows. Similarly, being effective at more stereotypically male tasks, such as management and organization, requires awareness and understanding of the people and things being managed.

It is because of these socially constructed distortions that the concepts of masculinity and femininity are postulated to be related to the concepts of war and peace. Negative masculinity, which fuses assertion with dominance and which rejects femininity (othercare), results in war-like behavior and a militaristic outlook. Peace, in the sense of dynamic, interdependent relationship building, is related to positive femininity, other-concern which is blended with self-concern.[1]

The questions which this paper raises, then, are the following: Could war to some extent be a product of a socialized "hyper-masculine" or self-oriented system of thought? Is a feminine, or caretaking, system of thought in some way correlated with peace? In order to investigate these questions, a research project was conducted which compares the relationship between the meanings of war/peace and masculinity/femininity held by males and females. Women and men were compared because they are the most likely groups to have integrated femininity and masculinity (respectively) into their self concepts. It is important to note again that these differences are viewed as socially constructed distortions which carry with them restrictions on human experience and possibilities for behavior.

The following sections discuss the concepts of masculinity and femininity, their relationship to war and peace, and the implications for ideology concerning gender and militarism. The research investigating the gender war/peace relationship is described, and the results and their implications are discussed.

MASCULINE AND FEMININE:
THE SELF-OTHER CONTRAST

There is a vast literature on sex-role research which supports the contention that both men and women conceptualize "masculinity" and "femininity" as being different, and there is general agreement on how they are different (e.g., Broverman et al. 1972; Chafetz 1978; Heilbrun 1981; Williams and Bennett 1975). Typically, sex-role investigators report two clusters of characteristics and behaviors which are attributed differentially to men and to women (by both female and male subjects): a "competency" cluster and a "warmth-expressiveness" cluster. The masculine cluster includes such descriptors as aggressiveness, competitiveness, independence, strength, non-emotionality, dominance, and self-confidence. The stereotypical feminine pole includes nurturance, gentleness, awareness of others' emotions, warmth, passivity, and expressiveness of tender feelings. More generally, "masculinity" can be described as part of a self-concept which is to some degree centered around traits that are "self"-oriented rather than "other"-oriented, while "femininity" can be described as being part of a self-concept involving, at least in part, characteristics which are oriented toward care for others.

Bakan (1966) conceptualizes masculinity as self-concern or "agency," defined as the tendency for individuals to take care of and promote their own interests. Other-concern or "communion" is viewed as more typically feminine, referring to the participation of individuals in a larger "organism" or system of which they are a part. More specifically,

> agency manifests itself in self-protection, self-assertion, and self-expansion; communion manifests itself in the sense of being at one with other organisms. Agency manifests itself in the formation of separations; communion in the lack of separations. Agency manifests itself in isolation, alienation, and aloneness; communion in contact, openness, and union. Agency manifests itself in the urge to master; communion in noncontractual cooperation. Agency manifests itself in the repression of thought, feeling, and impulse; communion in the lack and removal of repression (Bakan 1966, pp. 14-15).

As Bakan's description suggests, one of the central contrasts of human existence is that between a concern with the survival of the self and a concern with relationship. The tension between self and other has its foundation in the fact that what is good for or desired by the self is frequently in conflict with the needs and hopes of others. The relationship is rarely simple, of course, since we are free to interpret this conflict in many ways. One person might believe that the greater good of the community is what is best for the individual. Another person might adhere to the principle that we are all responsible only to ourselves. An alternative view is that we must balance the needs and goals of self and other and make behavioral choices which are appropriate to each situation.

A central idea of Bakan's is that there are dangers in both self-concern and other-concern if either is *unmitigated* by the other. This reasoning has two important implications: there are both desirable and undesirable aspects to each, and the undesirable aspects are decreased when agency and communion coexist. One might argue further that mere coexistence is a necessary but not a sufficient condition for the elimination of pathological manifestations of agency and communion. Indeed, the ideal is to have the ability to blend concern for self and other in such a way that decisions concerning action may emphasize either or both. Taking care of an infant would seem to require a different combination of agency and communion than defending oneself against a mugger.

Bakan (1966) also suggests that, if agency and communion are not integrated and one is predominant, there are pervasive implications for personality. Unmitigated agency may result in rigid, hostile, self-serving behavior, the goal of which is to dominate others. In fact, others may be viewed as objects to be mastered, or worse, destroyed. Unmitigated communion, on the other hand, in its most pathological manifestation, would result in debilitating dependency and the ability, or even the desire, to be manipulated and dominated.

SECURITY AND THREAT:
THE CONNECTION BETWEEN
GENDER AND WAR/PEACE

Whether agency/masculinity and communality/femininity reach "pathological" levels in any one individual or not, it seems clear that women and men as groups are socialized to adopt the sex-role "appropriate" characteristics and behaviors. Further, existing social, political, and economic structures tend to reinforce the maintenance of this gender system. For example, women's significantly lower earning power compared to men encourages women to be, at the least, economically dependent, while encouraging men to emphasize the role of "breadwinner" and deemphasize parenting and homemaking roles.

Consequently, men spend more time and energy thinking, acting and relating in an agentic fashion, while women focus on communality. It seems likely that these two approaches or "realities," when either is predominant (unmitigated), will result in different definitions of security and of danger. Carol Gilligan (1982), in her work on moral development, suggests that the agentic "reality" defines security in terms of individualism, separation, and achievement, while danger is perceived in intimacy. Within the communal "reality," security is defined in terms of connection and caring, and danger in terms of separation.

The idea that motivated the current research was that these contrasts of agency-communion and masculinity-femininity are also related to the contrasting concepts of war and peace. Could war to some extent be a product of a socialized "masculine" or self-oriented system of thought, of an agentic manner of construing events that is unmitigated by communality? Is a "feminine" or communal system of thought in some way correlated with peace? In a very broad sense, war may be thought of as the ultimate social act of separation, of expansionism, and the attempt to control others (and not be controlled by others). If "normal" training in masculinity involves learning a fear of intimacy and a distrust of the motivations of others (unmitigated agency), then it would not be surprising for men to put much of their energy into defending against and outdoing others. The combination of a need to win, a distrust of others, and a tendency to aggress seems to be a recipe for war-like behavior and attitudes.

Peace, on the other hand, implies cooperation with others in the context of interdependent coexistence. If women are trained and socially reinforced to be caretakers, to be aware of the needs of others, and to think in terms of the needs of a group, then this training in femininity may also be training in peace behavior. Further, if separation and isolation are perceived as threatening, then women are likely to feel an impetus to maintain, if not work to improve, relationships. In a sense, "normal" training in femininity results in communality mitigated by agency.[2] Defined in this way, war and peace have a conceptual relationship to agency/masculinity and communion/femininity.

In a recent critique of the American obsession with competition, Alfie Kohn (1986) discusses the potential destructiveness of competitive behavior, a behavior which is stereotypically masculine. He outlines the process through which competition leads to the breakdown of relationships. Competition in its essense, he says, implies that

[o]ne person succeeds only if another does not. From this uncluttered perspective, it seems clear right away that something is drastically wrong with such an arrangement. How can we do our best when we are spending our energies trying to make others lose—and fearing that they will make us lose? What happens to our self-esteem when it becomes dependent on how much better we do than another person? Most striking

of all is the impact of this arrangement on human relationship: a structural incentive to see other people lose cannot help but drive a wedge between us and invite hostility. (Kohn 1986, p. 9).

There is evidence that competition interferes with empathy and care for others in the context of sports (Kroll and Petersen 1965; Olgilvie and Tutko 1971) and in children's relationships with each other (Barnett and Bryan 1974; Barnett, Matthews, and Howard 1979; Johnson and Johnson 1983; Rutherford and Mussen 1968).

Not only does competition inhibit empathy, Kohn contends, it creates hostility and fear between competitors, primarily because self-esteem becomes dependent upon winning. In this process opponents become objectified.

> ...competition entails a perverse interdependence: our fates are linked in that I cannot succeed unless you fail. Thus I regard you merely as someone over whom to triumph. Because you are my rival, you are an 'it' to me, an object, something I use for my own ends...But competition takes objectification a step further since I not only use you but try to defeat you. (Kohn 1986, p. 138).

One might argue with Kohn's total rejection of competition as too extreme. When competition is integrated into negative masculinity described earlier, however, elements of connectedness that might occur within the context of competition are eliminated. Losing is not interpreted in a positive way, for example, as respect for the opponent's skill or determination to improve one's own skills. Rather it is experienced as defeat, as a threat to self-esteem. When we want to use a particularly demeaning put-down, we frequently call someone a "loser." Competition as a part of unmitigated agency involves hostility and mistrust and interferes with relationships. The obsession with winning and "being better than," the development of mistrust and hostility, and the dependence of security on winning, are closely related to war-like behavior.

> The *reductio ad absurdam* of competition is war, and it is here that we find antagonists most thoroughly negating the humanity of others in order to be able to kill them. One fires on Krauts or gooks, not on people. (Kohn 1986, p. 138)

Negative masculinity contrasts significantly with the lessons women learn, particularly in their role as mother. In an analysis of the relationship between mothering and peace, Sara Rudnick (1983) states that the traditional association between women and peace has a basis in the practice of mothering. Maternal practice, she suggests, involves a particular kind of thinking which is "incompatible with military strategy but consonant with pacifist commitment to nonviolence" (p. 233). In contrast to our conventional views of what constitutes achievement in public life, achievement as a mother involves preserving, supporting, and shaping the development of children, the social activity of what Ruddick calls "preservative love." One central characteristic of preservative love is peacefulness.

> By 'peacefulness' I mean a commitment to avoid battle whenever possible, to fight necessary battles nonviolently, and to take, as the aim of battle, reconciliation between opponents and restoration of connection and community. I will call this the 'pacifist commitment'... Military strategy is opposed to pacifist commitment in that it accepts violence to achieve causes deemed good or advantageous and values victory over reconciliation. (Ruddick 1983, pp. 239-240).

By preservative love, Ruddick does not mean a feeling, but rather an activity, an activity which involves caring for and supporting the growth of other humans who are vulnerable to risk. This activity of care, as well as the recipients of care, are endangered by military endeavors. Nonviolent "battle" aimed at conciliation is seen as sharply contrasting with violent pursuit of victory. Inherent in the role of mothering, then, is not only the valuing of life and growth, but also of the maintenance of relationships.

GENDER, WAR-PEACE, AND IDEOLOGY

If the values and at least some of the skills of peacemaking already exist, why then are we in our current state of nuclear armament? Feminist theorists emphasize that not only are masculinity and femininity socially constructed as different, but they are also differentially valued. The argument which draws a connection between gender and war/peace attitudes seems to be compatible in many ways with recent feminist theory concerning gender and issues of peace and militarism (e.g., Abzug 1984; Elshtain 1982; Enloe 1983; McAllister 1982; Reardon 1983; Swerdlow 1984). Many feminist writers agree that militarism, as well as the actual potential for the occurrence of war, are significantly related to the positive value that Western culture (among others) places on traditional masculine, agentic qualities, and the low regard held for traditional feminine qualities (see especially Adcock 1982; Brock-Utne 1985; Enloe 1987; Kokopeli and Lakey 1982; Leghorn 1982; Reardon 1983; Tobias 1984; Warnock 1982; Zanotti 1982). Indeed, sociological and psychological research has found evidence that "maleness" and the masculine role are more highly valued in our society (e.g., Dinitz,

Dynes, and Clarke 1954; McKee and Sheriffs 1957, 1959). For example, Gallup (1955) found that 5 to 12 times more women than men had wished they were of the opposite sex at some time in their lives. When Broverman et al. (1972) asked subjects to indicate the most desirable characteristics for an adult, sex unspecified, both men and women identified stereotypically masculine characteristics. In other words, it was the socially desirable, stereotypical masculine characteristics which were identified as ideal for *all* adults.

Interestingly, Broverman and her colleagues (Broverman et al. 1970) found in another study that psychotherapists produced a similar list of traits which they characterized as being descriptive of a "mentally healthy" adult female (submissive, emotional, easily influenced, sensitive to being hurt, excitable, dependent, non-competitive, unaggressive, and unobjective) and a list of traits of a "mentally healthy" male (aggressive, independent, self-sufficient, non-emotional, competitive). What is most salient is that when asked to describe a healthy *adult*, sex unspecified, therapists produced the list of descriptors which was almost identical to the list identified by subjects in the Broverman et al. (1972) study as being characteristic of *males*.

In a more recent study, (Baumgartner 1983) schoolchildren (grades 3 through 12) were asked what their lives would be like if they were the opposite sex. Both boys and girls showed an awareness of not only what the socially acceptable differences were, but also of the differential valuing of these characteristics. Boys, when considering their lives as girls, stated that they would have to be more reserved and quiet, less active, and more restricted. They said they would have to worry more about their appearance, would be treated more as sex objects ("I'd have to watch out for boys making passes at me"), would worry about violence against them, and would perform different duties at home (babysitting, ironing). As boys, girls expected to be more assertive, show less emotion, have more freedom, have to think less about their appearance, be freed from treatment as a sex object, and perform different chores at home (taking out the garbage). It was clear from girls' statements that they were quite aware of the greater ability they would have to take care of themselves if they were boys. Boys, however, almost never mentioned the positive, caretaking aspects of the female role. In fact, grammar school age boys frequently made statements like "If I were a girl, I'd kill myself." Clearly, children get the message that there is something undesirable about femaleness.

Adults show a bias towards maleness in a series of studies which ask subjects to evaluate the quality of various products and qualifications. Subjects evaluated the same product (such as a professional article) or description of qualifications (a resume) as better when it was identified as having been written by (or descriptive of) a male (see Deaux, 1984 for a review).

The feminist perspective that a masculine or self-oriented perspective is overemphasized in our culture, and a feminine, caretaking orientation is underemphasized, finds some theoretical support in the work of Miller (1976) who has developed a theory for a psychology of women. Miller argues that current psychological theory and practice are based on a male view of the world. This male-oriented psychology serves in some ways to maintain a status quo that views "'mankind' as basically self-seeking, competitive, aggressive, and destructive" (p. 69). A new psychology, she continues, would provide "a greater recognition of the essential cooperative nature of human existence" (p. 41).

More recently, Gilligan (1982) has suggested that Kohlberg's (e.g., 1958, 1969, 1976) well-known stage theory of moral development is based on a male perspective of morality, one that is legalistic and abstract. Kohlberg interpreted his research findings to indicate that women are frequently unable to achieve the highest stage of moral development. Gilligan, however, offers a reformulation of this position, proposing that there is a *different* kind of morality which is more typical of women, one that is based on caring and connection with others. It is interesting that in studies of children's game playing behavior (e.g., Piaget 1965) girls are often found to start a game over or switch to another game if there is a disagreement over the rules. This has been interpreted as a weakness in girls, for example, as an inability to negotiate successfully. As Kohn (1986) suggests, however, an alternative interpretation is that for girls adherence to abstract rules is much less important than maintaining relationships. Devaluing the girls' priorities as a weakness may simply be a case of assuming that the male "reality" is the best reality.

Indeed, several feminists suggest that this overemphasis on "masculinity" (as agency), and an underemphasis on "femininity" (as communion), is reflected not only in individuals, but also in our social structures and our politics.[3] In an incisive analysis, DiStefano (1983) identifies masculinity as an *ideological structure* "with specific cognitive and perceptual tendencies" (p. 634) which has important political implications. She considers this masculine ideology as a "deep structure" in the sense that it is "comprised of systematically interrelated elements" which are not necessarily manifested explicitly in theoretical discourse, but which nevertheless have a significant impact on social and political behavior.

Tickner (1988), in a feminist reformulation of Morgenthau's principle of political realism, argues that the language and content of foreign policy are decidedly masculine. She suggests that the concept of national security has historically been associated with military strength and the defense of nations against outside threats. This "realist" position deemphasizes, if not displaces, cooperative and community building efforts. While not denying the existence of power politics, a feminist view of international relations, according to Tickner, would also focus on "a more global perspective which appreciates cultural diversity but at the same time recognizes a growing interdependence which makes anachronistic exclusionary thinking fostered by the nation-state system" (p. 437).

One relatively invisible result of the current predominance of a self-oriented ideology is the *rejection* of the alternative ideology which is other-oriented, the "female" reality. On a personal level, not only are caretaking and conciliation devalued, but femophobia is created. This has important political manifestations as well. Several political commentators have noted the tendency on the part of politicians to reject "femaleness" in foreign policy decisionmaking. This rejection is evident in reports of discussions between leaders which were made public in the Pentagon and the Nixon tapes, for example (by Fasteau 1976; Steinem 1974; Stone 1974). What is clear in the words of these leaders is their great fear of being seen as feminine. Fasteau (1976) in particular discusses the "cult of toughness" evident in foreign policy decisions throughout the Viet Nam War. Reardon (1985) suggests that this pairing of "proving masculinity" with "war behavior" is apparent in leaders' ambivalence about arms control and arms negotiation.

Political reporter Richard Barnet (in Steinem 1974) provides an inside view of what he dubs "bureaucratic machismo." He states that national security managers in Washington are taught that toughness is viewed as a highly valued virtue in decisionmaking. While managers who recommend the use of violence are lauded, those who suggest more conciliatory measures such as taking an issue to the United Nations or seeking negotiations are quickly labeled as "soft." "To be soft," Barnet states, "that is, unbelligerent, compassionate, willing to settle for less—or simply to be repelled by homicide, is to be 'irresponsible.' It means walking out of the club" (quoted in Steinem 1974).

SEX DIFFERENCES: A REVIEW OF RESEARCH

The previous analysis suggests that some differences found in people's conceptions of war and peace are mediated by gender. Although no previous research appears to address the relationship between masculinity/femininity and war/peace, there is a substantial body of evidence across a broad range of research areas which reveals significant sex differences in war/peace attitudes, opinions, values, and conceptualizations. As will be seen in this section, females are consistently reported to be more "peaceful" in their attitudes than are males, in the sense that they show less approval for violent means of resolving conflict or dealing with social problems. In this review of the literature relevant research regarding attitudes, opinions, and conceputalizations of violence, war, and peace will be examined.

Public Opinion Research

Public opinion polling has consistently found differences between men's and women's responses to questions related to violence. In a study by Baker and Ball (1969), a large sample of men and women was polled on attitudes toward the use of interpersonal violence. The investigators found that 25 percent of the males polled, compared to 14 percent of the females, exhibited a high degree of approval for high-level violence (e.g., a parent beating a child, a teacher beating a student, a teenager knifing another teenager, an adult shooting a spouse).

A recent review of pubic opinion polling (Smith 1984) examined poll questions concerning attitudes toward violence across a wide range of social conditions, including foreign affairs, (e.g., defense spending, military action), social control (e.g., the use of capital punishment), and interpersonal relations (e.g., hitting children, violence between men and women or between husband and wife). Smith analyzed 285 data points from polls conducted from 1937 to 1983. He found that men were more supportive of a violent or forceful option in over 87 percent of the cases. In only five percent of cases did women favor the violent option more than men. A 1984 survey (Yankelovich and Dobel) reported tht American women are more likely than men to urge accommodation with the Soviet Union and to favor peaceful coexistence.

Attitude Research

In reviewing attitude studies related to war and peace, Zur (1984) states, "The notion that men are more militaristic than women is reflected in most of the studies of attitudes toward war" (pp. 96-97). Porterfield (1937), Stagner et al. (1942), and Stagner (1942) all reported more militaristic attitudes in men and more pacifistic attitudes in women. In a study which investigated national and international images, Rosenberg (1965) found that men were less prone to acknowledge apprehension over the risk of war than women. He also stated that men are "prone to accept the strategic use of the threat of war, and are more ready to credit the idea that under extreme circumstances actual recourse to war is acceptable or even desirable" (pp. 305-306). In relation to political behavior, Greenstein (1961) states that women have been found overall to be less willing than men to support policies and candidates they perceive as more warlike and aggressive.

In a study of 1,200 college students, Putney and Middleton (1962) found consistent sex differences in war attitudes as measured on three separate scales. Results indicated that males were significantly more accepting of war on all three scales. Regarding their images of war, males were more certain that nuclear weapons would be used, were more hopeful that the United States would win, expected fewer casualities, and were more confident that they would survive and would want to survive a nuclear war.

There is also evidence that women value peace more highly than men in relation to other important values. In a well known study, *The Nature of Human Values*, Rokeach (1973) asked subjects to rank order a list of 18 "terminal values" (e.g., a comfortable life, a world at peace, inner harmony, national security) and 18 "instrumental values" (e.g., ambitiousness, courageousness, lovingness, and responsibility). Women's rankings of several values were significantly higher than men's: a world at peace, happiness, inner harmony, self-respect, wisdom, lovingness, cheerfulness, and the ability to forgive. Men rated other values more highly: an exciting life, a sense of accomplishment, freedom, pleasure, social recognition, ambitiousness, capability, imaginativeness, and logic. In general, these differences in values seem to be consistent with the findings of sex-role research which show men to value self-oriented competency more highly, while women value communality.

Political Socialization Research

A series of fascinating political socialization studies seems to have tapped into the ways in which war and peace are differentially conceptualized by boys and girls. Cooper (1965) conducted a study which attempted to investigate the development of children's conceptions of war and peace based on Piaget's stage theory of intellectual development. The children were asked to write down verbal associations to the words "war" and "peace," a definition of war, their ideas about nuclear war, the circumstances that might provoke a war, the justification for war, and the moral and psychological effects of war. It was found that at all ages the word "peace" prompted fewer responses than "war." It is also interesting to note the four major categories of responses to "war": weapons, fighting/killing/dying, negative emotions, and people and countries. The major categories of associations for the word "peace" were inactivity, lack of war, respite from war, and reconciliation from war/means of avoiding war.

Several sex differences were found. Across age groups girls made less mention of concrete aspects of war (e.g. weapons and related objects) and more mention of dying, fighting and killing. More boys than girls believed that war is justifiable and necessary. Girls, however, were more "provocable" under circumstances in which the family was in danger. Girls to a greater extent than boys believed that war was likely and that death was unlikely during war. In a similar study, Rosell (1968) found that girls mentioned more about the consequences of war (e.g. death, suffering, destruction) and less about war processes (e.g., the use of weapons, actions or soldiers, the occurrence of battles) than did boys.

In another study which built upon Cooper's and Rosell's work, Haavelsrud (1970) reported that girls gave more positive attributes to peace than boys did, and a negative conceptualization of peace was somewhat more prevalent among boys. This evidence supports the notion that boys and girls construe the meanings of war and peace in fairly different ways.

Existing research has provided fairly consistent evidence that females appear to be less accepting of war and violence than males. I hypothesize in this paper that at least some of this difference is caused by the social construction of gender. Little research has been performed as yet, however, which considers the relationship between conceptions of masculinity and femininity and conceptions of war and peace. The current research was designed to explore this relationship.

RESEARCH HYPOTHESES

The overarching hypothesis of this research is that women and men, as groups, are socialized to develop different meanings concerning war and peace as a result of the social construction of gender. This hypothesis is grounded in the personal construct personality theory of George Kelly (1955). The central tenet of personal construct theory is that every individual erects a representational model of the world (which includes the self) in order to anticipate events. Personal constructs are organized into relatively coherent systems which allow us to understand our experiences. An important aspect of Kelly's theory is its treatment of the varying types of personal constructs and the relationships among them. For example, constructs may be subordinate or superordinate to each other. A construct such as good-bad would probably occupy a superordinate position in many people's construct systems, subsuming many other constructs (such as goods, clothes, works of art).

Especially salient to the current discussion are two categories of constructs, core constructs and constellatory constructs. Core constructs are superordinate constructs which are of particular importance for organizing a person's approach to life and the roles he or she plays, in other words, the sense of self. According to Kelly (1955), they govern our basic maintenance processes, i.e., they enable us to maintain a sense of identity and of continuing existence. Most important, they cannot be changed in any way without threatening the very roots of our existence. "Threat" is defined as a state which is unfavorable to the formation of new constructs. If an individual comes upon new information which elicits a disconfirmation of constructs regarding the core sense of self, it is likely that the new information will be rejected or redefined in order to fit the existing, rather impermeable, constructs, which define an individual's sense of security.

Stereotypes are considered to belong to the category of constellatory constructs. This type of construct is one which allows its elements to belong to other realms, but which fixes those realms. For instance, a constellatory construct is expressed in the statement, "Anyone who is a woman must also be... (e.g., passive,loving, weak, gullible)."

A person for whom concern with self rather than others is a core construct would exemplify Bakan's notion of unmitigated agency. For such a person, behavior related to caring and empathy would pose a threat to the core sense of self. In contrast, the person for whom concern with others rather than the self is a core construct would exemplify unmitigated communality. For this person, threat would involve separation from others and focusing on and taking care of oneself. (This is not to say that core constructs could not encompass both self- and other-concern.)

This formulation was used to develop two major research hypotheses. These hypotheses are based on the overarching hypothesis that men and women, because of differential socialization and social experiences, tend to develop different construct systems concerning war, peace, and security. With the assumption that gender is a relatively core construct for most individuals, it is reasonable to presume that women and men will construe the self differently in some significant ways that are consistent with sex-role socialization. They will, however, both construe masculinity and femininity in very similar ways, although they will identify themselves with the sex-role which is consistent with their biological sex. In order to test the relationships among constructs, a method developed by Osgood and his colleagues (Osgood, Suci, and Tannenbaum 1957) was used. This method is used to compute relative distances between concepts and to represent concepts as they cluster in "semantic space."

Hypothesis 1: Conceptions of War and Peace. For women, then, the construct peace was expected to have a constellatory association with certain other elements, all of which reflect caring for and cooperation with others. These were expected to be primarily female-valued concepts, such as family, community, and cooperation. Men, however, (in addition to some of these female-valued concepts) were predicted to associate some negative concepts with peace (for instance, boredom, passivity, and "wimpishness"), since peace should be construed by males as passive, feminine, and therefore "not-self."

Associations for war were expected to show a similar pattern. For women, war was expected to have negative associations like death, defeat, and isolation, all reflective of separation from others. Men, on the other hand, were predicted to show some male-valued, positive associations of war (in addition to the negative concepts listed for females), for example, honor, patriotism, and adventure. In addition, for both men and women the concept of masculinity, compared to femininity, was hypothesized to be closer in meaning to war, and femininity was expected to be closer to peace.

Hypothesis 2: Conceptions of Security. The second hypothesis is related to the earlier discussion concerning women's and men's differential definitions of security. Specifically, men were expected to define security in terms of masculinity and other agentic concepts related to achievement, winning, and individuality. Women, on the other hand, were predicted to define security in terms of femininity and communal terms, such as cooperation, compassion, and community. More specifically, the concept security was expected to be found nearer the peace/femininity cluster for females and closer to the war/masculinity cluster of concepts for males. Further, because war is theorized to be conceptually related to masculine/ agentic constructs (aggression, competition) and peace to feminine/ communal constructs (caring, cooperation), it was predicted that the concept of war would be located closer to the concept of security for males while peace would be closer to security for females.

RESEARCH METHOD

As stated above, the hypotheses were explored using a technique developed by Osgood, Suci, and Tannenbaum (1957) for investigating "cognitive maps." This technique seemed particularly appropriate because of its similarity to personal construct theory. Osgood developed a statistical method, to be used in conjunction with his semantic differential scale method, which makes it possible to plot several concepts showing their relative distances from key concepts. The result, according to Osgood, is a conceptual structure, "a kind of map, a bit of 'semantic geography,' which provides an objective picture of subjective meaning states" (Osgood, Suci, and Tannenbeaum 1957, p. 96).

A sample of 205 subjects, 101 female and 104 male undergraduates, was asked to rate 22 concepts along 10 semantic differential scales. The 10 scales consisted of 4 *evaluative* scales (good-bad, fair-unfair, honest-dishonest, and useful-useless), 3 *potency* scales (strong-weak, tenacious-yielding, and hard-soft), and 3 *activity* scales (hot-cold, fast-slow, and active-passive). These scales are standard ones used frequently for semantic differential measures, and they have been found to reliably load onto the three factors of evaluation, potency, and activity.

The 22 concepts were chosen because they were hypothesized to be related conceptually to the constructs of war-peace and masculinity-femininity. For heuristic purposes these concepts were divided into 4 categories, feminine-related, masculine-related, negative, and neutral. The groupings of concepts are as follows:

- Feminine-related:

  femininity
  peace
  negotiation
  cooperation
  community
  compassion
  family

- Masculine-related:

  masculinity
  adventure
  pride
  freedom
  bravery
  victor
  patriotism
  honor

- Neutral:

  security

- Negative:

  boredom
  defeat
  death
  isolation
  war
  wimp

Mean evaluation, potency, and activity scores were computed for each concept, and several specific tests were performed based on a priori hypotheses related to the two major hypotheses. In addition, distances between concepts were computed, and relative distances of all of the concepts from several key concepts were examined (war, peace, security, masculinity, femininity). Significance tests were performed to look for differences in distances between concepts for male and females. Finally, clusters of concepts around the major concepts of war and peace were estimated for males and females separately, and the clusters were compared.

Results and Discussion—Hypothesis 1. The first hypothesis regarding differential conceptualizations of war and peace by females and males was explored in two ways. First, males' and females' clusters of concepts around War and Peace were compared. Second, relationships between the meanings of War, Peace, Masculinity, and Femininity were examined.

In order to examine females' and males' concept clusters, concepts were plotted in two-dimensional space in relation to War and Peace for males and females. The clusters for females, shown in Figure 1, are quite similar to the predicted clusters. A negative concept cluster, containing the concepts Death, Isolation, Wimp, and Boredom, is located closest to War. A cluster of primarily feminine-related concepts is closest to Peace. This "feminine" cluster includes Femininity, Community, Negotiation, Compassion, Family, and Cooperation. Contrary to prediction, two masculine-related concepts are also found in this cluster, Honor and Freedom. A separate cluster of primarily masculine-related concepts is located between the "feminine" cluster and the negative-concept cluster. This "masculine" cluster is closer than the "feminine" cluster to War.

All but two of the concepts in the feminine cluster are either significantly closer to Peace or significantly further from War (or both) for females (including 5 of the 6 feminine-related concepts: Femininity, Negotiation, Family, Compassion, and Community) (see Tables 1 and 2). This is consistent with the hypothesis that "communal," feminine-related terms are, for women, closer in meaning to the concept of peace and further in meaning from the concept of war.

Clusters which were formed from males' scores (see Figure 2) look somewhat different than those hypothesized. The predicted location of the "negative" concepts of Isolation, Wimp, and Boredom nearer to Peace for males did not occur. There was no significant sex difference in the distance of these concepts from Peace (see Table 2). The prediction that several masculine-related concepts would be closer to War for males was only partially supported. Honor, Bravery, and Adventure were significantly

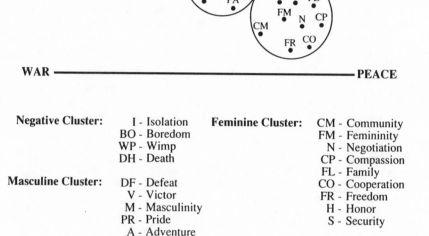

<table>
<tr><td>Negative Cluster:</td><td>I - Isolation
BO - Boredom
WP - Wimp
DH - Death</td><td>Feminine Cluster:</td><td>CM - Community
FM - Femininity
N - Negotiation
CP - Compassion
FL - Family</td></tr>
<tr><td>Masculine Cluster:</td><td>DF - Defeat
V - Victor
M - Masculinity
PR - Pride
A - Adventure
PA - Patriotism
BR - Bravery</td><td></td><td>CO - Cooperation
FR - Freedom
H - Honor
S - Security</td></tr>
</table>

Figure 1.   Female War-Peace Cluster

closer to War for males. Distances from War for the concepts Pride, Victor, Patriotism, and Freedom were not significantly different (see Table 1).

It appears, in fact, that the males' and females' clusters are remarkably similar, at least in terms of the location of concepts in relation to each other. Both males' and females' ratings produced three clusters: a feminine concept cluster nearest to Peace, a negative-concept cluster nearest to War, and a masculine-concept cluster between these two. There are few significant

Table 1.   Distances of Concepts from "WAR" for Females and Males

	Females			*Males*	
Concept	*Mean*	*A priori Category*	*Concept*	*Mean*	*A priori Category*
1 Isolation	8.093	-	1 Victor	8.617	M+
2 Death	8.519	-	2 Masculinity	8.696	M+
3 Defeat	8.804	-	3 Isolation	8.802	'-
4 Masculinity	8.804	M+	4 Pride	8.942	M+
5 Boredom	8.901	-	5 Death	8.959	-
6 Victor	9.358	M+	6 Boredom	9.172	-
7 Pride	9.744	M+	7 Adventure	9.291	M+
8 Wimp	9.756	M−	8 Defeat	9.320	-
9 Patriotism	9.943	M+	9 Patriotism	9.421	M+
10 Community	10.176	F+	10 Community	9.487	F+
11 Adventure	10.289 *	M+	11 Security	9.549	+
12 Bravery	10.512 *	M+	12 Bravery	9.693	M+
13 Security	10.991 *	+	13 Honor	10.072	M+
14 Honor	11.059 *	M+	14 Wimp	10.088	M−
15 Femininity	11.127 *	F+	15 Femininity	10.249	F+
16 Negotiation	11.216	F+	16 Negotiation	10.431	F+
17 Cooperation	11.494 *	F+	17 Cooperation	10.606	F+
18 Freedom	11.778	M+	18 Family	10.837	F+
19 Family	11.962 *	F+	19 Compassion	10.922	F+
20 Compassion	12.080 *	F+	20 Freedom	11.141	M+
21 Peace	12.911	F+	21 Peace	12.051	F+

Notes: *Significant sex differences:

Security	p < .001	Female > Male
Family	p < .01	Female > Male
Compassion	p < .01	Female > Male
Adventure	p < .05	Female > Male
Bravery	p < .05	Female > Male
Honor	p < .05	Female > Male
Femininity	p < .05	Female > Male
Cooperation	p < .05	Female > Male

differences in distances of concepts from either War or Peace for the masculine cluster. In contrast, all but one of the feminine-related concepts are either closer to Peace or further from War (or both) for females compared to males.

Another way to investigate the relationship between sex-role identification and war-peace attitudes is to look at the relationships between the meanings of these words by both males and females. Several post hoc hypotheses were generated which were consistent with the hypothesis that masculinity is conceptually related to war and femininity conceptually related to peace.

Table 2. Distances of Concepts from "PEACE" for Females and Males

	Females			Males	
Concept	Mean	A priori Category	Concept	Mean	A priori Category
1 Compassion	5.393 *	F+	1 Cooperation	5.785	F+
2 Cooperation	5.429	F+	2 Family	5.937	F+
3 Negotiation	5.591 *	F+	3 Freedom	6.039	M+
4 Freedom	5.674	M+	4 Community	6.084	F+
5 Family	5.686	F+	5 Compassion	6.272	F+
6 Honor	5.887	M+	6 Negotiation	6.370	F+
7 Family	5.915 *	F+	7 Honor	6.504	M+
8 Community	6.049	F+	8 Family	6.585	F+
9 Security	6.292 *	+	9 Security	6.917	+
10 Patriotism	6.748	M+	10 Patriotism	7.143	M+
11 Adventure	6.966	M+	11 Pride	7.248	M+
12 Bravery	7.130	M+	12 Adventure	7.261	M+
13 Pride	7.184	M+	13 Bravery	7.433	M+
14 Victor	7.555	M+	14 Masculinity	7.484	M+
15 Masculinity	7.754	M+	15 Victor	8.064	M+
16 Defeat	8.968 *	-	16 Death	9.514	-
17 Death	9.931	-	17 Defeat	9.804	-
18 Isolation	10.521	-	18 Boredom	10.434	-
19 Wimp	10.627	M-	19 Isolation	10.455	-
20 Boredom	10.868	-	20 Wimp	10.813	M-
21 War	12.911	F-	21 War	12.051	F-

Notes: *Significant sex differences:

Compassion	p < .01	Male > Female
Negotiation	p < .05	Male > Female
Family	p < .05	Male > Female
Security	p < .05	Male > Female
Defeat	p < .05	Male > Female

First, it was hypothesized that the distance from Masculinity to War would be smaller than the distance from Femininity to War for both males and females. This was confirmed (Females: $t(100) = 5.29$, $p < .0005$; Males: $t(103) = 3.55$, $p < .0005$). Similarly, the Femininity-to-Peace distance was expected to be smaller than the Masculinity-to-Peace distance for both males and females. This hypothesis was also confirmed (Females: $t(100) = 5.41$, $p < .0005$; Males: $t(103) = 2.41$, $p < .01$). In addition, it was expected that Masculinity was closer to Peace than to War (since it seems safe to assume that most subjects would interpret the concept of Masculinity in the sense of "positive masculinity"). This hypothesis was also confirmed for both females and males (Females: $t(100) = 2.19$, $p < .01$; Males: $t(103) = 3.0$, $p < .005$).

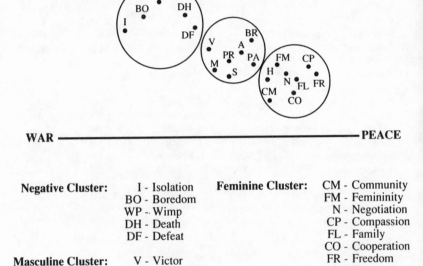

WAR ————————————————————————————— PEACE

Negative Cluster:	I - Isolation	**Feminine Cluster:**	CM - Community
	BO - Boredom		FM - Femininity
	WP - Wimp		N - Negotiation
	DH - Death		CP - Compassion
	DF - Defeat		FL - Family
			CO - Cooperation
Masculine Cluster:	V - Victor		FR - Freedom
	M - Masculinity		H - Honor
	PR - Pride		
	A - Adventure		
	PA - Patriotism		
	BR - Bravery		
	S - Security		

Figure 2.   Male War-Peace Cluster

Discussion.   These findings are supportive of the hypothesis that men's and women's conceptualizations of war-peace and masculinity-femininity are to some extent representative of two "realities" or world views (one the "agentic" or self-oriented reality and the other the "communal" or other-oriented reality). The evidence seems to point to the idea that each of these "realities" is relatively internally consistent, at least when the specific 22 concepts chosen for this research are considered.

Hypothesis 1 stated that women and men would manifest clusters of concepts around War and Peace which are alike in some ways and different in others. Both males and females were predicted to manifest a cluster of feminine-related concepts nearest the concept of Peace. This hypothesis was for the most part supported. All six of the concepts identified as feminine-related appeared in this cluster for both males and females (including Femininity, Negotiation, Community, Cooperation, Compassion, and Family).

Also as predicted, males' evaluations produced a cluster of masculine-related concepts which was located closer (compared to the feminine cluster) to War. All but 2 of the 8 concepts identifed as masculine-related appeared in this cluster (including Masculinity, Victor, Adventure, Bravery, Patriotism, and Pride). No prediction was made concerning where females' evaluations would place these concepts, but their location was similar to the males'. In addition, as predicted, both sexes' evaluations located the negative cluster of concepts (Death and Isolation) nearest War. The order of appearance of these three clusters along the War-Peace dimension, for both males and females, was the negative cluster closest to War, the masculine cluster in the middle, and the feminine cluster closest to Peace.

It was also predicted that males and females would differ in the location of three negative concepts in relation to War and Peace. Specifically, Boredom, Wimp, and Defeat were expected to be located near Peace for males, and near War for females. For both sexes, all of these concepts were in or near the cluster of negative concepts nearest War, along with Death and Isolation.

Figure 3 illustrates the relative location of the three clusters in semantic space for both males and females. It can be seen that the clusters are consistent with the hypothesis that femininity is conceptually related to peace. Indeed, significance tests showed that for both males and females all but one of the feminine-related concepts were both closer to Peace and further from War than the concept of Masculinity. Further, Femininity is significantly closer to Peace than War for both sexes.

The hypothesis that males' evaluations would provide a cluster of masculine-related concepts *around* War was not clearly supported since these concepts are actually on the Peace side of the War-Peace continuum. It is consistent with the hypothesis, though, that masculine-related terms are closer to War than the feminine-related terms.

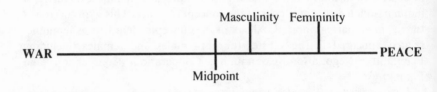

Figure 3.   Masculinity and Femininity on the War-Peace Continuum

These results provide some support for the hypothesis that femininity is conceptually related to peace. They do not, however, support the contention that masculinity is conceptually related to war, since neither Masculinity nor any of the masculine-related concepts are closer to War than to Peace, as shown in Figure 3. That Masculinity is significantly closer to Peace than to War may be accounted for in part by the fact that both males and females tend to evaluate masculinity, femininity, and peace positively (on the average, 5.3 or greater on a 7-point scale), but evaluate War negatively (2.4 or less). It seems likely that subjects conceptualized both Masculinity and Femininity as positive rather than negative.

The masculinity-war relationship can be described relative to the concepts of femininity and peace. For example, Masculinity, compared to Femininity, is significantly further from Peace and closer to War for both males and females. In addition, 4 of the other 7 masculine-related concepts are significantly closer to War than the concept of Femininity is to War (including Adventure, Pride, Patriotism, and Victor, but not Honor, Freedom or Bravery).

It appears, then, that femininity is conceptually related to peace to a much greater degree than masculinity is related to war. What can be said about masculinity from these results is that it appears to be more related to war, and less related to peace, than femininity. In addition, some sex differences suggest that males experience some ambivalence about war compared to females. For example, males evaluate war more positively and peace less positively than females do. It should be remembered that most of the concepts used in this study were related to positive aspects of masculinity and femininity. Since the argument is that *unmitigated* or negative masculinity is related to war, future research of this kind should include concepts related to negative masculinity.

Results and Discussion—Hypothesis 2. Hypothesis 2 postulated that males and females conceptualize security in different ways. The most striking finding which supports this hypothesis is in the differential placement of the concept Security in semantic space for males and females. As shown in Figures 1 and 2, the concept Security is located in the masculine-concept cluster for males and in the feminine-concept cluster for females. This is consistent with the statement that men and women define security differently in terms of sex-role consistency. In fact, the distance from Security to Masculinity is significantly greater for females than males (t (203) = 2.56, $p < .01$). Means and significance tests are shown in Table 3. Similarly, the distance from Security to Femininity is significantly greater for males than females, as expected (t (203) = 3.10, $p < .002$). As predicted, the concept Security is significantly closer to War for males than for females (t (203) = 3.53, $p < .0005$), and the distance from Security to Peace is significantly smaller for females (t (203) = 2.04, $p < .04$).

Discussion. These findings provide some evidence that males and females do tend to hold quite different meanings of the concept of security. Females' and males' differential placement of the concept Security is not unexpected, since security can be presumed to be related to sex-role consistency. These findings are consistent with Kelly's (1955) notion of core constructs, and with the assumption that gender is a relatively core construct. In essence, it appears that subjects have located their conception of self within the cluster of same-sex concepts.

The finding that the distance from War to Security is greater for females than for males suggests that males find war to be less threatening to their security than females do. (It should be noted that this finding has to do with an abstract notion of war; if males were asked to evaluate participation in war as a soldier, results might be quite different.) Similarly, Peace is significantly closer to Security for females. In a way, females' sense of security is more conceptually related to peace than males' sense of security.

Table 3. Distances of Concepts from "SECURITY"
for Females and Males

	Females			Males	
Concept	Mean	A priori Category	Concept	Mean	A priori Category
1 Honor	5.297	M+	1 Adventure	5.261	M+
2 Patriotism	5.319	M+	2 Pride	5.285	M+
3 Pride	5.496	M+	3 Community	5.308	F+
4 Freedom	5.640	M+	4 Honor	5.352	M+
5 Femininity	5.659 *	F+	5 Masculinity	5.412	M+
6 Cooperation	5.678	F+	6 Bravery	5.528	M+
7 Community	5.712	F+	7 Patriotism	5.559	M+
8 Negotiation	5.714	F+	8 Cooperation	5.560	F+
9 Bravery	5.763	M+	9 Victor	5.599	M+
10 Victor	5.768	M+	10 Freedom	5.771	M+
11 Adventure	5.806	M+	11 Family	5.839	F+
12 Compassion	5.823	F+	12 Negotiation	6.177	F+
13 Family	5.824	F+	13 Compassion	6.383	F+
14 Masculinity	6.202 *	M+	14 Femininity	6.644	F+
15 Peace	6.292 *	F+	15 Peace	6.917	F+
16 Defeat	8.156 *	-	16 Death	8.562	-
17 Death	8.953	-	17 Defeat	9.251	-
18 Isolation	9.473	-	18 Isolation	9.532	-
19 Boredom	10.128	-	19 War	9.549	F-
20 Wimp	10.188	-	20 Boredom	9.883	-
21 War	10.991 *	F-	21 Wimp	10.665	M-

Notes: *Significant sex differences:

Femininity	p < .01	Male > Female
Defeat	p < .01	Male > Female
Peace	p < .05	Male > Female
War	p < .001	Female > Male
Masculinity	p < .05	Female > Male

It is not surprising that Femininity is closer to Security for females, and Masculinity closer to Security for males. This finding provides evidence that sex-role identification is tied to security, and it supports the contention that gender is a relatively core construct (however flexible or rigid it may be), at least for the sample measured.

Another interesting finding is that the concept Defeat is significantly further from Security for males (t (203) = 2.56, p <.01). One interpretation is that defeat is more threatening to males than to females. This is consistent with Kohn's (1986) argument and with the feminist contention (e.g., Miller

1976) that men's sense of security is tied in with success and that self-esteem is threatened by defeat. A related finding is that the concept of Wimp is further than War from Security for males, while the reverse is true for females (Females: t (100) $= 1.95$, $p < .05$; Males: t (103) $= 2.7$, $p < .01$). This could be interpreted to mean that for males weakness (Wimp) is further in meaning from security than war. To the extent that wimpishness is equivalent to non-masculinity (weakness) and war is the most extreme case of non-nurturance (while also consistent with the aggressive element of masculinity), this finding is supportive of Gilligan's formulation of differing definitions of security for men and women.

These results concerning the concept of security are especially salient since the notion of "security" is so central to both intrapersonal functioning and international relations. An orientation which focuses on characteristics such as self-sufficiency, separation, winning, power over others, fear of closeness, and a fear of others is likely to result in very different behavior (both personally and in relation to foreign policy attitudes) than one which focuses on connectedness, empathy, and fear of separation. This is particularly true if these notions not only take on meaning as intellectual beliefs but are also deeply experienced as *requirements for survival*, i.e., are basic constructs about the core nature of human experience.

The results of the semantic differential scales are suggestive of future research. The fact that women and men do indeed appear to define security in quite different ways (and to see danger in different circumstances) supports theory concerning the psychology of women proposed by Miller (1976) and Gilligan (1982). Future research might be aimed more directly at examining the ways in which sex-role identification affects conceptualizations of security. It would also be of interest to study whether and how differing conceptualizations of security are related to particular attitudes concerning foreign policy positions, particularly positions laden with security implications. For instance, one might expect different definitions of security to be related to different opinions on how peace should be achieved and maintained (e.g. peace through strength versus peace through common security).

CONCLUSION

Although the focus of this analysis has been on masculinity and femininity, the purpose of the research is not to spotlight sex differences. The superordinate principle is that differential socialization can result in groups which hold two alternative constructions of reality, two different systems for construing the world. The "realities" of self-orientation and other-orientation, when unmitigated by each other, can produce strikingly different perceptions concerning what events are threatening and what events are safe.

Feminist theorists have drawn a connection between sex-role identification as a psychological process and as a part of social processes and social structures. They argue that a culture which overemphasizes the importance of agency, the "masculine" reality, is a culture which also leaves unexamined, if not entirely unrecognized, the usefulness of the "feminine" reality. The kind of individual who is produced by such conditions is one who is

> self-possessed and radically solitary in a crowded and inhospitable world, whose relations with others are unavoidably contractual and whose freedom consists in the absence of impediments to the attainment of privately generated and understood desires. [He] bears the tell-tale signs of a masculinity 'in extremis:' identity through opposition, denial of reciprocity, a constitutional inability/refusal to recognize what might be termed dialectical connectedness (DiStefano 1983, p. 643).

The above discussion points again to the importance of several polarities that seem to be central to the notion of a hypermasculine/self-concerned ideology: men versus women, agency versus communion, self-concern versus other-concern, war versus peace, dominators versus victims. If a "hyper-masculine" approach is predominant in foreign policy decisionmaking, Reardon (1985) and others argue, the result may be a foreign policy based on a belief system which presumes that winning, dominating and maintaining superiority is *always* the best way to achieve security. If alternative world views go unrecognized, or worse, are criticized as "wimpish," foreign policy decisionmakers are less able to be flexible and less able to be open to interpreting international events in nonrigid ways.

Etheredge (1978) suggests that in international crisis situations which are ambiguous, that is, for which there is little information available, leaders are more likely to base their decisions on what they "know," or believe they know (i.e. their personal constructs). In a sense, he says, an ambiguous political situation is basically a projective test, a situation on which leaders will project their own constructs as if they were reality. The potential for error is great under these circumstances. Truly conciliatory gestures on the part of one superpower, for example, may be dismissed as posturing, and an opportunity for arms reduction may be missed or concessions may be construed as wimpish and as showing a lack of will to defend if necessary. It is likely that better leaders, and citizens, would be those whose construct systems were more permeable, allowing them to be sensitive to definitions of security and threat other than their own.

In a recent review of psychological research on foreign policy, Tetlock (1983) notes tht there is a substantial body of research which suggests that foreign policy makers' decision-making processes are significantly affected by personality factors and the protection of preconceptions in spite of contrary evidence (e.g., Christiansen 1959; Etheredge 1978; Janis 1986; Terhune 1970; Tetlock 1981; Tetlock et al. 1981). Etheredge (1978), for example, found a strong relationship between the personality characteristic of interpersonal dominance in major American policymakers and their willingness to use force in several international crises. He also studied contemporary policymakers and found that those who exercised dominance over their subordinates were much more likely to prefer military responses to international crises.

DiStefano's (1983) analysis of masculinity as an *ideological structure* points to some important political implications of the current research. This masculine ideology is not necessarily explicit in theoretical discourse, but it still may have a significant impact on policy formation and political behavior. In its most extreme form this ideology is "hypermasculine" (the equivalent of unmitigated agency), and it includes elements such as the need to dominate and exert power *over* others, the fear of femininity, and projection of hostility onto other men. DiStefano suggests that although these elements do not manifest themselves in apparent or obvious ways, they do exert a powerful influence on political theory and decisionmaking. The significance of this analysis is that it points to the *unexamined nature* of a salient underlying influence on political behavior, including foreign policy decisions. This ideology remains unexamined because it is deeply embedded in our individual, social, and political lives, and is therefore experienced as "reality" rather than as one of several ways of viewing the world. In particular, world views which distort reality by fusing negative aspects of masculinity with positive aspects, that is, dominance with assertion, seem particularly dangerous. Further, as long as positive and negative femininity are fused, i.e., caretaking is associated with submission, then the fear of being dominated may guide policy formation, unmitigated by an awareness of interdependence and an appreciation of cultural diversity.

NOTES

1. Hooks (1984) makes a case for an alternative interpretation and definition of power from a feminist perspective, one which views power as competence rather than domination

over others. One might argue that this conception of power is essential to the definition of positive peace.

2. This statement should not be interpreted to mean that women are presented with no difficulties in behaving agentically. Because of the hierarchical nature of gender relationships, there are many circumstances under which women are negatively reinforced for powerfulness or are simply not allowed power. In circumscribed situations,such as those involving caretaking (which itself is devalued), women are allowed to be agentic.

3. See Andersen, 1988, for a discussion of the dichotomies of meaning of male/public and female/private as they relate to political thought and behavior.

REFERENCES

Abzug, B. 1984. *Gender Gap: How Women Will Decide the Next Election.* Boston: Houghton Mifflin.

Adcock, C. 1982. "Fear of 'Other': The Common Root of Sexism and Militarism." Pp. 209-219 in *Reweaving the Web of Life: Feminism and Non-violence,* edited by Pam McAllister. Philadelphia: New Society Publishers.

Andersen, K. 1988. "No Longer Petitioners: Women's Political Involvement in the 1920s." Unpublished paper presented at the annual meeting of the Midwest Political Science Association, Chicago.

Bakan, D. 1966. *The Duality of Human Existence.* Chicago: Rand McNally.

Baker, R. K. and S. Ball. 1969. *Mass Media and Violence. A Report to the National Commission on the Causes and Prevention of Violence.* Washington, D.C.: U.S. Government Printing Office.

Barnett, M. A. and J. H. Bryan. 1974. "Effects of Competition with Outcome Feedback on Children's Helping Behavior." *Developmental Psychology* 10:838-842.

Barnett, N. A., K. A. Matthews and J. A. Howard. 1979. "Relationship Between Competitiveness and Empathy in 6- and 7-year-olds." *Developmental Psychology* 15:221-222.

Baumgartner, A. 1983. "'My Daddy Might Have Loved Me': Student Perceptions of Differences Between Being Male and Being Female." Paper published by the Institute for Equality in Education, Denver.

Brock-Utne, B. 1985. *Educating for Peace.* New York: Pergamon Press.

Broverman, I.K., D.M. Broverman, F. E. Clarkson, P. Rosenkrantz and S.R. Vogel. 1970. "Sex-Role Stereotypes and Clinical Judgments of Mental Health." *Journal of Consulting Psychology* 34:1-7.

Broverman, I.K., S.R. Vogel, D.M. Broverman, F.E. Clarkson and P.S. Rosenkrantz. 1972. "Sex-Role Stereotypes: A Current Appraisal." *Journal of Social Issues* 28:59-78.

Chafetz, J. S. 1978. *Masculine, Feminine, or Human?* Itasca, IL: F. E. Peacock Publishers.

Christiansen, B. 1959. *Attitudes Toward Foreign Affairs as a Function of Personality.* Oslo: Oslo University Press.

Cooper, P. 1965. "The Development of the Concept of War." *Journal of Peace Research* 1:1-17.

Deaux, K. 1984. "From Individual Differences to Social Categories: Analysis of a Decade's Research on Gender." *American Psychologist* 39:105-116.

Dinitz, S., R. R. Dynes and A. C. Clarke. 1954. "Preference for Male or Female Children: Traditional or Affectional." *Marriage and Family Living* 16:128-130.

DiStefano, C. 1983. "Masculinity as Ideology in Political Theory: Hobbesian Man Considered." *Women's Studies International Forum* 6:633-644.

Elshtain, J. B. 1982. "Women as Mirror and Other: Toward a Theory of Women, War and Feminism." *Humanities in Society* 5:29-44.

Enloe, C. 1983. *Does Khaki Become You? The Militarization of Women's Lives.* Boston: South End Press.

————. 1987. "Feminists Thinking abut War, Militarism, and Peace." Pp. 526-547 in *Analyzing Gender: A Handbook of Social Science Research*, edited by Beth B. Hess and Myra Marx Feree. Beverly Hills: Sage.

Etheredge, L.S. 1978. *A World of Men.* Cambridge, MA: MIT Press.

Fasteau, M. F. 1976. *The Male Machine.* New York: McGraw-Hill.

Flax, J. 1987. "Postmodernism and Gender Relations in Feminist Theory." *Signs* 12:621-643.

Gallup, G. 1955. *Gallup Poll.* Princeton: Audience Research.

Gilligan, C. 1982. *In a Different Voice: Psychological Theory and Women's Development.* Cambridge, MA: Harvard University Press.

Greenstein, F. 1961. "Sex-related Differences in Childhood." *Journal of Politics* 23:353-371.

Haavelsrud, M. 1979. "Views on War and Peace Among Students in West Berlin Public Schools." *Journal of Peace Research* 7:99-120.

Heilbrun, A. 1981. *Human Sex Role Behavior.* Elmsford, NY: Pergamon Press.

hooks, b. 1984. *Feminist Theory: From Margin to Center.* Boston: South End Press.

Janis, I. L. 1986. "Problems of International Crisis Management in the Nuclear Age." *Journal of Social Issues* 42:201-220.

Johnson, D. W. and R. T. Johnson. 1983. "The Socialization and Achievement Crisis: Are Cooperative Learning Experiences the Solution?" In *Applied Social Psychology Annual 4*, edited by Leonard Bickman. Beverly Hills: Sage.

Kelly, G. 1955. *A Theory of Personality: The Psychology of Personal Constructs.* New York: W. W. Norton and Co.

Kohlberg, L. 1958. *The Development of Modes of Thinking and Choices in Years 10-16.* Unpublished doctoral dissertation, University of Chicago.

————. 1969. "Stage and Sequence: The Cognitive-development Approach to Socialization." Pp. 347-480 in *Handbook of Socialization Theory and Research*, edited by David A. Goslin. Chicago: Rand McNally.

————. 1976. "Moral Stages and Moralization: The Cognitive Development Approach." Pp. 31-53 in *Moral Development and Behavior: Theory, Research and Social Issues*, edited by Thomas Lickona. New York: Holt, Rinehart, Winston.

Kohn, A. 1986. *No Contest: The Case Against Competition.* Boston: Houghton Mifflin.

Kokopeli, B. and G. Lakey. 1982. "More Power Than We Want: Masculine Sexuality and Violence." Pp. 231-240 in *Reweaving the Web of Life: Feminism and Nonviolence*, edited by Pam McAllister. Philadelphia: New Society Publishers.

Kroll, W. and K. H. Petersen. 1965. "Study of Values Test and Collegiate Football Teams." *The Research Quarterly* 36:441-447.

Leghorn, L. 1982. "The Economic Roots of the Violent Male Culture." Pp. 195-199 in *Reweaving the Web of Life: Feminism and Nonviolence*, edited by Pam McAllister. Philadelphia: New Society Publishers.

McAllister, P., ed. 1982. *Reweaving the Web of Life: Feminism and Non-violence.* Philadelphia: New Society Publishers.

McKee, J. P. and A. C. Sherriffs. 1957. "The Differential Evaluation of Males and Females." *Journal of Personality* 25:356-371.

McKee, J. P. and A. C. Sherriffs. 1959. "Men's and Women's Beliefs, Ideals, and Self-concepts." *American Journal of Sociology* 64:356-363.

Miller, J. B. 1976. *Toward a New Psychology of Women*. Boston: Beacon Press.

Ogilvie, B. C. and T. A. Tutko. 1971. "Sport: If You Want to Build Character, Try Something Else." *Psychology Today* October:61-63.

Osgood, C. E., G. J. Suci and P. H. Tannenbaum. 1957. *The Measurement of Meaning*. Urbana, IL: University of Illinois Press.

Piaget, J. 1965. *The Moral Judgment of the Child*.New York: Free Press.

Porterfield, A.L. 1937. "Opinions About War." *Social and Societal Resources* 22:252-264.

Putney, S. and R. Middleton. 1962. "Some Factors Associated with Student Acceptance or Rejection of War." *American Sociological Review* 27:655-667.

Rapoport, A. 1964. *Strategy and Conscience*. New York: Harper and Row.

Reardon, B. 1983. "A Gender Analysis of Militarism and Sexist Repression." *International Peace Research Newsletter* 22:3-10.

_____. 1985. *Sexism and the War System*. New York: Teachers College Press.

Rokeach, M. 1957. *The Nature of Human Values*. New York: Free Press.

Rosell, L. 1968. "Children's Views of War and Peace." *Journal of Peace Research* 5:268-276.

Rosenberg, M. J. 1965. "Images in Relation to Policy Process: American Public Opinion and Cold-war Issues." Pp. 278-336 in *International Behavior*, edited by Herbert C. Kelman. New York: Holt, Rinehart and Winston.

Ruddick, S. 1983. "Preservative Love and Military Destruction: Some Reflections on Mothering and Peace." Pp. 231-262 in *Mothering: Essays in Feminist Theory*, edited by Joyce Trebilcot. Totowa, NJ: Rowman and Allanheld.

Rutherford, E. and P. Mussen. 1968. "Generosity in Nursery School Boys." *Child Development* 39:755-765.

Smith, T. W. 1984. "The Polls: Gender and Attitudes Toward Violence." *Public Opinion Quarterly* 48:384-396.

Stagner, R. 1942. "Some Factors Related to Attitudes Towards War, 1938." *Journal of Social Psychology* 16:131-142.

Stagner, R., Brown, J. F., Grunlich, R.H. and White, R.K. 1942. "A Survey of Public Opinion on the Prevention of War." *Journal of Social Psychology* 16:131-142.

Steinem, G. 1974. "The Myth of Masculine Mystique." Pp. 134-139 in *Men and Masculinity*, edited by Joseph H. Pleck and Jack Sawyer. Englewood Cliffs, NJ: Prentice Hall.

Stone, I.F. 1974. "Machismo in Washington." Pp. 140-144 in *Men and Masculinity*, edited by Joseph H. Pleck and Jack Sawyer. Englewood Cliffs, NJ: Prentice Hall.

Swerdlow, A., ed. 1984. "Peace, War and Women in the Military." [Special issue]. *Women's Studies Quarterly* 12.

Terhune, K. 1970. "The Effects of Personality on Cooperation and Conflict." In *The Structure of Conflict*, edited by Paul G. Swingle. New York: Academic Press.

Tetlock, P. E. 1981. "Personality and Isolationism: Content Analysis of Senatorial Speeches." *Journal of Personality and Social Psychology* 41:737-743.

_____. 1983. "Psychological Research on Foreign Policy." *Review of Personality and Social Psychology* 4:45-78.

Tetlock, P.E., F. Crosby and T. Crosby. 1981. "Political Psychobiology." *Micropolitics* 1:191-213.

Tickner, J. A. 1988. "Hans Morgenthau's Principles of Political Realism: A Feminist Reformulation." *Millenium* 17:429-440.

Tobias, S. 1984. "Toward a Feminist Position on the Arms Race." *Women's Studies Quarterly* 12:20.

Warnock, D. 1982. "Patriarchy is a Killer: What People Concerned About Peace and Justice Should Know." Pp. 20-29 in *Reweaving the Web of Life: Feminism and Nonviolence,* edited by Pam McAllister. Philadelphia: New Society Publishers.

Weingarten, H. R. and E. Douvan. 1985. "Male and Female Visions of Mediation." *Negotiation Journal* October: 349-357.

Williams, J. and S. Bennett. 1975. "The Definition of Sex Stereotypes via the Adjective Check List." *Sex Roles* 1:327-337.

Yankelovich, D. and J. Doble. 1984. "The Public Mood: Nuclear Weapons and the U.S.S.R." *Foreign Affairs* 63:44-50.

Zanotti, B. 1982. "Patriarchy: A State of War." Pp. 16-19 in *Reweaving the Web of Life: Feminism and Nonviolence,* edited by Pam McAllister. Philadelphia: New Society Publishers.

Zur, O. 1984. *Men, Women and War: Gender Differences in Attitudes Toward War.* Unpublished doctoral dissertation, Wright Institute, Berkeley, CA.

REDISTRIBUTION AND INCOME INEQUALITY IN INDUSTRIAL DEMOCRACIES

Erich Weede

In the 'democratic class struggle' perspective, democracy, strong unions and / or strong socialist parties contribute to the redistribution of income from the top to the bottom of the income pyramid. By contrast, a radical interpretation of some public choice theories makes you expect that democracy does not prevent the poor from losing the rent-seeking and redistribution game. While empirical support for the 'democratic class struggle' approach crucially depends upon the exclusion of Japan from the analysis, the fate of the radical public choice view is not tied to either the inclusion or exclusion of Japan. Age of democracy and another rent-seeking indicator are negatively related to the income shares of lower class people, in particular of the poorest quintile. It is argued that unequal levels of information and unequal opportunities for collective action between classes provide the most plausible explanation of this finding.

Research in Social Movements, Conflict and Change,
Volume 12, pages 301-326.
Copyright © 1990 by JAI Press Inc.
All rights of reproduction in any form reserved.
ISBN: 1-55938-065-9

301

THEORETICAL ISSUES

The purpose of this paper is to outline two positive theories of redistribution, to derive some testable implications from them and to confront these propositions with data from contemporary industrial democracies. According to the 'democratic class struggle' line of reasoning (Hewitt 1977; Korpi 1983; Lenski 1966; Lipset 1960), the lower classes can improve their income shares by collective action. Workers should band together in unions. Lower class people should join socialist parties. By strikes the workers can force their employers to pay better wages. By voting socialist politicians into legislative and executive offices, the lower classes can tax the rich and spend public money for their own benefit. The distribution of income is thereby somewhat equalized. The workers and the lower classes enjoy a latent strength in numbers that is exploitable in a democracy. The 'democratic class struggle' line of thought leads to the following expectations: The higher the degree of lower class mobilization, the stronger the unions and socialist parties, the better off the lower classes are, the larger the piece of the pie going to the poorest strata of society.

'Public choice' offers a competing line of reasoning that generates rather different expectations. Downs' (1957) economic theory of democracy is a first important component of the public choice perspective. Downs agrees that the lower classes command a majority of votes and that the lower classes would enforce some redistribution of income in their favor, if they were fully informed about politics and if they were not affected by uncertainty in their calculations. These are big 'ifs.' In practice, many voters are quite poorly informed and they suffer from considerable uncertainty. Thereby, the egalitarian impact of majoritarian democracy is very much reduced. Adherents of a 'democratic class struggle' perspective may admit this Downsian insight, but add that unionized workers or socialist voters at least do not suffer from 'false consciousness' or lack of information and therefore can effect equalizing reforms. From a Downsian perspective some political pressure towards equalization has to be admitted, but it is mitigated by the need to recruit the median voter to the winning party or coalition[1] and by the inequality in the distribution of information within the electorate. By and large, the privileged classes are better informed than the lower classes (Nie and Verba 1975). This provides room for political 'compromises' such as the lower classes imposing progressive taxes and the privileged classes getting their tax loopholes.

Another component of the public choice approach is Olson's (1965) logic of collective action. In Olson's view, large groups such as the working or lower class find it much more difficult to organize themselves and to procure public goods for themselves than elite interests. While members of large groups could certainly benefit from collective action and the procurement of public goods, such as higher wages for workers or welfare benefits for the lower classes, individual members of these latent interest groups face incentives to freeride. Where employers grant benefits to unionized and non-unionized workers alike, selfish workers hope that fellow workers fight for the common cause and let them freeride. In Olson's view, selective incentives and coercion may overcome this freeriding tendency. But there remains a difference between large or lower class interest groups and small or elitist groups. The latter find it much easier to combine, to collect resources, and to lobby within the political system than the lower classes do.

Once you combine Downsian uncertainty with Olson's headstart for privileged groups in the procurement of public goods for themselves,[2] once you realize that the possession of adequate information may be an intermediate public good for latent groups, you can no longer confidently expect that majorities will win the political redistribution game. Instead it becomes conceivable that small privileged groups mobilize to become active distributional coalitions first, that they propose and lobby in favor of programs which concentrate benefits on themselves at the expense of a much wider part of the tax-paying electorate. As long as the losers suffer from a lack of information or rational ignorance, because each individual suffers so little from each single program for the benefit of special interests, democracy may be compatible even with regressive redistribution, i.e., redistribution from the bottom up.

Under pressure to gain the confidence and the votes of 'moderate,' but largely 'rationally ignorant' voters, even socialist parties may become an easy prey of special interest groups, including some from the middle and, possibly, upper classes. Given unequal levels of organization and information, democracy may still produce the rhetoric of equality, but without ever delivering egalitarian results.

It should be added that many actions of interest groups cannot easily be classified according to their egalitarian impact. If some group of specialized workers unionizes and succeeds in controlling access to its job market and in getting inflated wages, this may (slightly) narrow the wealth and welfare gap between themselves and their employers, create an income gap between themselves and less fortunate workers, contribute even to involuntary unemployment (Hayek 1960; McKenzie and Tullock 1978, p. 256; Olson 1982, p. 201), and imply some transfer from consumers to producers. On the face of it, some of these effects increase equality, others inequality. It seems much more straightforward to predict inefficiencies and lower productivity as a result of interest group action (Olson 1982;

Buchanan, Tollison and Tullock 1980) than to make any specific prediction about the impact of political action on the distribution of income.

According to the 'democratic class struggle' line of reasoning, redistribution of income by governments is good, at least if administered by socialists who ensure that the redistribution goes from the top to the bottom of society. In the public choice approach, the ideological colors of politicians, parties and governments are often neglected. Instead it is disputed "that almost all the redistribution of income that occurs is the redistribution inspired by egalitarian motives, and that goes from the nonpoor to the poor. In reality many, if not most, of the redistributions are inspired by entirely different motives, and most of them have arbitrary rather than egalitarian impacts on the distribution of income ..." (Olson 1982, p. 174). Similar views about the arbitrariness of contrived transfers can be found elsewhere, too (Albert 1978, p. 148; Bernholz 1977; Jackman 1986; Tullock 1983).

So far it looks *as if* the 'democratic class struggle' approach and the 'public choice' approach to redistribution differ only in their predictions about the distributional impact of trade unions, socialist parties and governmental interference with the economy. While they certainly differ in this respect, a more radical interpretation of the public choice approach in general and of Olson's (1982) theory about 'the rise and decline of nations' is conceivable. Olson (1982, p. 175) himself provides the starting point where he hypothesizes: "There is greater inequality ...in the opportunity to create distributional coalitions than there is in the inherent productive abilities of people." Unfortunately, however, Olson himself does not systematically elaborate on the implications of this proposition.

The radical interpretation of Olson's theory has first been proposed by Steve Chan (1987a, 1987b, p. 138) in his work on East Asian societies. According to Chan, "there seems little doubt that (Olson's, E. W.) theory would predict in general a negative relationship between the strength and number of distributional coalitions in a society and its level of socioeconomic equity. The poor, the uneducated, and the unemployed lack the skills, the time, the information, and the selective incentives that make collective action possible. In contrast, as suggested by implication 3 of Olson's theory (1982, p. 41), 'members of "small" groups have disproportionate power for collective action.' In addition to small size, collective action is facilitated by social homogeneity or cohesion, frequent interaction, and selective incentives—all of which tend to favor the privileged or socially-entrenched groups in efforts to redistribute income for the benefit of their members at the expense of the disadvantaged, the disorganized, and the more numerous underclass ... The lobbying and collusion efforts of such minorities of special interests create what can be described as 'reversed welfare' for the powerful and well-to-do."

Olson's (1982) theory is primarily concerned with the price distortions and inefficiencies generated by distributional coalitions. One of Olson's (1982, p. 77) major propositions is "that countries that have had democratic freedom of organization without upheaval or invasion the longest will suffer the most from growth-repressing organizations and combinations." Here Olson hypothesizes a lawful relationship between the age of democracy which permits the accumulation of distributional coalitions and 'institutional sclerosis' on the one hand and low growth rates on the other hand. If Chan's (1987a, 1987b) explication of Olson's theory is accepted, we may add another hypothesis, according to which older democracies should suffer from higher inequality than younger democracies.

The public choice theories referred to (Downs 1957, Olson 1982) should be put into a rent-seeking perspective (Buchanan, Tollison, and Tullock 1980). According to Tollison (1982, p. 577), rent is defined as "a payment to a resource owner above the amount his resources could command in their next best alternative use," where the alternative use refers to a competitive market. Since excessive payments, or rents, are always desirable for those who get them, there is a strong incentive for resource sellers to induce or compel buyers to pay an excessive price for the resource. Rent-seeking is competition for such contrived transfers. Where such competition and distributional struggles are on the rampage, we refer to rent-seeking societies.

Monopolies or cartels are examples of successful rent-seeking. Monopolists or cartels usually maximize profits by selling smaller quantities at higher prices than would prevail in competitive markets. This implies three different effects. First, some people become worse off without anybody making a corresponding gain. Those who simply stop buying over-priced goods from a monopoly or cartel suffer a welfare loss, because they no longer can buy the goods at lower competitive prices. But not even the monopolist or cartel can exploit those who refuse to buy.

Second, there is some transfer of income from the buyers to the sellers of the good or service in question. Since monopolists and owners of cartelized businesses are usually richer than the buyers of their products, this transfer almost always is regressive. It is not even clear whether cartels of workers or trade unions ultimately result in progressive or regressive shifts in the distribution of income. Of course, workers are poorer than their employers. Where unions succeed in getting higher wages *at the expense of their employers,* the transfer is progressive. Where the employers succeed in passing the increased wages on to consumers, the net effect on the distribution of income depends on the relative standing of the cartelized or unionized group of workers. If they make more money than the average consumer of their products does, the ultimate effect of unionization on the distribution of income is regressive. If the unionized workers belong to the poorest people, the final effect is progressive.

Rent-seeking theorists argue that regressive income shifts are more likely than progressive ones. Olson's (1965, 1982) greater ease of organization of small, privileged or elitist groups compared with large groups of ordinary people is one reason behind this expectation. The necessity of government support of or, at least, acquiescence in rent-seeking behavior is another reason. Governments could destroy many monopolies or cartels—most of which exist at the national level, not at the global level—by abolishing all barriers to international trade. Or, they could outlaw cartels. In order to gain or retain political support, they do not do it. For affected interest groups, whether unionized workers, the farm lobby, or business leaders, notice any harm to their special interests, whereas the general public of voters, tax-payers and consumers largely suffers from Downsian (1957) uncertainty and rational ignorance. Therefore, politicians tend to be more responsive to organized special interests than to general interests. Given the headstart of privileged interests in organization, this lopsidedness of political responsiveness tends to favor inegalitarian trends in democratic societies.

Finally, monopolies and cartels have a third effect. If successful, they elicit imitation; i.e., the rent-seeking society is contagious. The more interest groups succeed in effecting contrived transfers, the more they teach others the lesson that monopolization, cartelization, and political protection of restrictive practices instead of productive work are the fast track to higher incomes. While this may be true for some special interest groups, in particular small ones, the economy as a whole gets impoverished, the more people divert effort from production towards attempts to gain transfers.

Mainstream public choice theorists, like Bernholz (1977), Downs (1968), Olson (1982) and Tullock (1983), warn us against exaggerating the egalitarian impact of democratic politics and governmental redistribution. In general, they pointed to the heavy losses in efficiency created by attempts to 'correct' market allocations of incomes. As the poor are also affected by slower economic growth, they might be net losers of the redistribution game, *even if* they were to win it in the sense of getting a larger piece of the pie. In Chan's (1987a, 1987b) radical interpretation of Olson's work, the lower classes lose twice: first, by unnecesarrily slow expansion of the pie; second by getting smaller pieces of the pie in the political redistribution game than they could get in competitive markets. Such an interesting idea certainly deserves an empirical test.

DATA AND ANALYSES

The dependent variables of this paper refer to the distribution of income. I shall focus on the income shares of the lowest 20 percent, the lowest 40 percent, the lowest 60 percent, and the lowest 80 percent,[3] as reported by the World Bank (1987, p. 253). These data refer to "total disposable household income accruing to percentile groups of households ranked by total household income" (World Bank 1987, p. 280), i.e., to income shares after taxes. Inequality data refer to different years ranging from 1973 to 1982 for the industrial market economies investigated here.

Explanatory or independent variables are derived from the 'democratic class struggle' and 'public choice' approaches. Korpi (1983, p. 40) provides five indicators of "patterns of working-class mobilization and political control", i.e., percentage unionization, left votes as percentage of the electorate, working class mobilization,[4] weighted cabinet share,[5] and proportion of time with left representation in cabinet.[6] The last mentioned three variables are rating scales where Korpi merely distinguishes between three levels of working class mobilization and control. Here I have coded high as 2, medium as 1 and low as 0.

Since such rating scales are easily afflicted by political bias, I should point out that Korpi is a true believer in the benefits of Swedish-style social democracy and intellectually rather distant from the public choice school of thought. If "working-class mobilization and political control" puts *effective* equalizing pressure on income distributions, as the adherents of the democratic class struggle line of reasoning contend, then these five indicators should correlate positively with the four income shares analyzed here.

Of course, there is room for controversy within the 'democratic class struggle' perspective about the relative importance of which aspect of working class power, whether it is unionization, or votes, or only socialist partnership in or control of government that counts. Since my purpose is to find out whether the 'democratic class struggle' or the 'public choice' perspective is more promising rather than to refine the democratic class struggle approach, I shall not discuss the conceivable or actual controversies within this school of thought in any detail.

Cameron (1984, p. 160 and 165) provides a second set of independent variables: the control of government by leftist parties which itself is the product of the percentage of cabinet portfolios held and the percentage of minimum parliamentary majority held by leftist parties[7]; percentage unionized; organizational unity of labor, where the highest scores are given to nations with a single confederation and a small number of industrial unions (i.e., to Finland, Sweden, Norway, Denmark, West Germany); confederation power in collective bargaining (rather than component union ability to call strikes independently) where the highest scores are given to Sweden and Norway; scope of collective bargaining, where economy-wide bargaining as in Finland, Sweden, and Norway produces the highest scores; and works councils and codetermination in order to assess worker participation on the plant floor and company boards. Sweden, Norway, Denmark, Netherlands and West Germany score highest on this scale.

Conceptually, there is some obvious overlap betwen Korpi's (1983) and Cameron's (1984) measures in variables such as unionization. While Cameron provides rather detailed information about unions and collective bargaining together with an aggregate measure of leftist political power, Korpi disaggregates various aspects of political power, but does not comment so much on industrial relations. Moreover, the two sets of measures differ in their temporal frame of reference. Korpi's variables refer to the 1946-76, Cameron's to the 1965-82 period, i.e., *Korpi* refers to working class power during the three decades *before* the measurement of *income shares,* whereas *Cameron* refers to working class power *more or less at the time* of income inequality assessment.

The 'public choice' perspective is represented by three independent variables all of which are related to the power of narrow interest groups and distributional coalitions whose purpose is price-distortion and rent-seeking. First, there is the age of democracy or, more exactly, the number of years of *uninterrupted* democracy within *unchanged borders* before 1965 (from Weede 1984, p. 366).[8] This particular operationalization has been chosen, because it follows Olson's (1982, p. 77) own cues for operationalization rather closely, because the expectation that the age of democracy might be negatively related to income inequality is derived from Olson's (1982) work and Chan's (1987a, 1987b) interpretation of it, and because it has been applied successfully in cross-national studies of economic growth rates (Bernholz 1986, Weede 1984, 1986a, 1986b). Although this is my own and favorite indicator of distributional coalitions and the damage they do, it suffers from some obvious shortcomings. The measure is rather indirect and refers to a putative background condition of the formation of distributional coalitions rather than to the coalitions themselves. Moreover, the measure does not assess at all the qualitative features of distributional coalitions, whether they are more or less encompassing. In Olson's (1982) view, encompassing interest groups do much less damage to the economy than exclusive ones do.

Second, there is Pryor's (1984, p. 160-161) classification of nations into three categories. His 'predicted winners' are scored '0' and refer to societies least affected by rent-seeking. His 'predicted losers' are scored '2' and refer to societies worst affected by rent-seeking. The intermediate category is scored '1'. The advantage of Pryor's rating scale[9] is that it takes the narrow or encompassing character of distributional coalitions explicitly into consideration. The disadvantage of the measure is that rent-seeking is assessed after its effects are already observable. Since the negative effects of rent-seeking on growth are theoretically more commonly accepted than the negative effects of rent-seeking on equality, the conceivably tautological element in Pryor's measure (which I criticized in Weede 1987) is not as worrisome in the context of the analysis of income shares below as it is in Pryor's (1984) own analysis of growth rates.

Third, there is Choi's (1983, p. 70) index of institutional sclerosis.[10] According to this index the accumulation of interest groups dates back to the 'consolidation of modernizing leadership,' i.e., to 1649 in the British case at one extreme and to 1868 in the Japanese case at the other extreme. The pattern of accumulation of interest groups is assumed to follow a logistic curve. But the index is adjusted for major disruptions, such as revolutions, totalitarian governments, lost wars and foreign occupations. The very complexity of the index as well as its extremely high correlation with (reduced) growth rates makes me suspicious about it.[11] Moreover, the index does not really refer to the accumulation of distributional coalitions within *democracies*. If you make something approaching universal(male) suffrage part of your definition of democracy, then even Britain became a democracy only in the twentieth century. In the case of Germany, too, modernizing leadership dates much further back than democratic government. But since much testing of Olson's theory has used Choi's index, I feel that I should find out how it does here, too.

Income inequality might not only be affected by working-class mobilization and power or by distributional coalitions and rent-seeking, but also by the level of economic development. It has been argued that there is a curvilinear relationship between the level of economic development on the one hand and income shares of the lower classes at the other hand (Kuznets 1963; Lenski 1966).[12] In this view, early development increases inequality, but later development decreases inequality again. In cross-national studies no other proposition about inequality receives as robust support as this one (for example: Ahluwalia 1976; Paukert 1973; Weede 1980).[13] Since this paper investigates industrial democracies only, a non-monotonic relationship is no longer to be expected. Here I shall use three alternative indicators of the level of economic development: gross national product per capita (henceforth GNPC) in 1965 (taken from Taylor and Hudson 1972, p. 314-320), logged GNPC, and purchase power parity adjusted GDPC data for 1970 from Kravis, Heston, and Summers (1978, p. 236-237).

Both the 'democratic class struggle' perspective and the 'public choice' approach should lead one to expect that the impact of democracy or socialist strength on inequality is somehow mediated by government action or, more concretely, by taxation, expenditure and particularly by social security transfers. Here, I shall use current receipts of government, total outlays of government and social security transfers—always as a percentage of GDP (from OECD 1984, for the average of the 1960-82 period)—as conceivable influences on incomes shares.

Outside of the communist orbit most industrial societies are OECD members. This gives us 24 cases. Unfortunately, Portugal and Spain became democracies only rather recently so that their income distributions need not reflect either democratic class struggles or rent-seeking *within a democracy.* Similarly, the fairly recent interruptions of democratic development in Greece and Turkey blur the effects which class struggles or rent-seeking in these unstable democracies may have had. So, we are down to 20 cases. Since the World Bank (1987) does not report inequality data for Austria, Iceland, and Luxembourg we lose another 3 cases. Sometimes data for New Zealand are missing, too. So, the correlations to be reported below refer to either 16 or 17 cases only. (Tables 3 and 4 below list the nations.)

Since the measures of working class mobilization and political control, of the level of economic development, of government taxation and expenditure should all correlate positively with low 20 to low 80 income shares, since the measures of distributional coalitions and rent-seeking, however, should correlate negatively with income shares for theoretical reasons, the use of one-tailed significance tests seems justified. Unfortunately, the number of unexpected signs in the correlation matrix below counsels against such a procedure. Therefore, I shall use two-tailed tests. Given the extremely small number of observations (16 or 17) I shall apply a rather loose threshold of significance, i.e., the 10 percent level. Of course, my significance threshold is identical to the more usual 5 percent level in one-tailed tests.

There are five indicators of working class mobilization and political strength from Korpi (1983) and another six from Cameron (1984). Therefore there should be 11 times 4 or 44 positive correlations between these indicators of union and socialist strength on the one hand and income shares on the other hand. But 16 of these 44 correlations expose the wrong sign. Another 20 positive correlations are not significant. Only 8 out of 44 correlations are positive and significant. If these 44 correlations had been generated by a random process, about 2.2 out of 44 correlations should be positive *and*

Table 1. Product-Moment Correlations between Income Shares
and Conceivable Explanatory Variables

	Low 20	Low 40	Low 60	Low 80
Korpi % unionization 46-76	0.04	0.01	−0.05	−0.15
left votes as % of electorate	0.03	−0.11	−0.18	−0.28
working-class mobilization	0.01	−0.11	−0.17	−0.22
left (weighted) cabinet share	−0.13	−0.10	−0.08	−0.10
time with left cabinet representation	0.22	0.36	0.37	0.26
Cameron leftist government control 65-82	0.08	0.04	0.05	0.05
% unionization	−0.05	−0.01	0.00	−0.03
organizational unit of labor	0.10	0.24	0.37	0.39
confederation power in collective				
bargaining	0.33	0.44	0.45	0.35
scope of collective bargaining	−0.01	0.16	0.23	0.22
works councils and codetermination	0.25	0.33	0.35	0.27
age of democracy	−0.49	−0.46	−0.43	−0.40
Pryor's rating scale for rent-seeking	−0.62	−0.63	−0.62	−0.51
Choi's institutional sclerosis	−0.27	−0.23	−0.14	−0.04
GNPC	−0.50	−0.37	−0.19	−0.10
logged (ln) GNPC	−0.52	−0.39	−0.21	−0.11
purchase power parity GDPC	−0.36	−0.25	−0.10	−0.05
government revenues/GDP 60-82	0.08	0.18	0.21	0.16
government expenditures/GDP	0.15	0.20	0.17	0.12
social security transfers/GDP	0.27	0.33	0.32	0.20

Notes: Underlined coefficients are significant in two-tailed tests at the 10% level. N is 17, except for rows 6 to 11 and 18 to 20, because of missing data for New Zealand.

significant. So there seems to be a kernel of truth in the assertion derived from the democratic class struggle perspective that lower class mobilization and political power affects the size distribution of income. But the kernel looks rather small.[14]

Moreover, none of the correlations of union or socialist strength with low 20 percent income shares actually jumps the significance threshold (although confederation power in collective bargaining comes very close). The effectiveness of unions and socialist parties in helping the poorest stratum of society is even more in doubt than their effectiveness in increasing the share of those a little bit higher up in the class structure. Strangely, unions and socialist parties come closest to demonstrating effectiveness in redistribution where we focus on the low 60 percent rather than on truly deprived groups. From a public choice perspective we can easily accomodate the finding that unions and socialist parties do best where they help a broad group of people including not necessarily the median voter but his 'brother,' i.e., the median income receiver.

One should also look rowwise at the upper part of Table 1 in order to find out which aspects of working class mobilization and power contribute most to some egalitarian redistribution of income. Here, confederation power in collective bargaining stands out. Time with left cabinet representation does rather well, too. While the organizational unity of labor produces two significant correlations, their location is slightly disturbing, because unity of labor is not related significantly to either low 20 or low 40 percent income shares.

All of the 12 correlations between indicators of distributional coalitions and rent-seeking at least demonstrate the expected sign. Whereas less than one (i.e. 0.6) correlation should be negative and significant, if generated by some random process, we observe 8 out of 12 such correlations. Moreover, the pattern of correlations read columnwise from left (low 20) to right (low 80) poses no problems. Rent-seeking seems to hurt the poorest strata as much *or more* than better-off strata—of course with the exception of the top income receivers who actually gain from rent-seeking. While age of democracy and Pryor's rating scale beautifully support the public choice perspective, Choi's (1983) index does very poorly. Why?

Like my age of democracy, Choi's index does not even try to assess the more or less encompassing character of distributional coalitions, but attempts to get at some supposed background condition of the increase in the number of interest groups over time. In contrast to the age of democracy index, Choi's index lets the accumulation of interest groups start before the democratization of polities. The age of democracy index treats universal manhood suffrage combined with regular and fair elections and an accountable government as a constitutional revolution that effectively devalues any organization, access and support that particularly interest groups may have achieved before democracy. As constructed, the age of democracy index also assumes a more devastating impact of totalitarianism, lost wars and foreign occupation than Choi's index does. Therefore, I am inclined to reject Choi's index of institutional sclerosis for not giving adequate weight to all kinds of revolutionary change, whether the introduction of democracy itself or its temporary suspension by totalitarian rulers or foreign armies of occupation.

Olson's (1982) theory does not only comment on the negative effects of distributional coalitions but also qualifies these effects by the more or less encompassing character of interest groups. Cameron's (1984) 'organizational unity of labour' and 'confederation power in collective bargaining' assess the encompassing character of the labor movement. In Olson's theory, encompassing interest group desist from a lot of harmful actions and accept limits in the negative-sum game of rent-seeking. So, the positive correlations between an encompassing labor movement and low 20 to low 80 income shares constitute little problem from a public choice perspective. Less rent-seeking should help the poor.

The consistently negative correlations between indicators of economic development and low 20 to low 80 income shares constitute the greatest surprise within Table 1. After all, it was established about as well as anything else in cross-national studies (Weede and Tiefenbach 1981) that more developed countries tend to be or become more egalitarian over time. Inspection of the scattergrams does not provide an easy explanation, much less an 'excuse' for the unexpected findings. Moreover, the pattern of correlations should also be noticed. In more highly developed countries the poorest groups seem to suffer worst from getting a shrinking piece of the pie. The correlations between the level of economic development and income shares seem to support the fears of those who forecast economic development as leaving some people further and further behind.

Governmental taxation and expenditure, in particular transfer payments, are the obvious means of redistribution. While these variables consistently correlate positively with larger shares for the lower and middle classes, none of these correlations is significant. Social security transfers just fail to jump the threshold for the low 40 and low 60 percent groups. On the background of the rather poor performance of taxation, spending and transfer indicators, the performance of the age of democracy indicator as well as of Pryor's rating scale look all the more impressive. Who would have expected that the inegalitarian impact of aging democracies is stronger than the egalitarian impact of social security transfers?

In cross-national studies of industrial societies the inclusion or exclusion of Japan is a contentious issue which often matters. Recalculating the correlations after Japan has been eliminated produces somewhat different results. First, Korpi's time with left cabinet representation now correlates significantly and positively with low 20, low 40, low 60, and low 80 percent income shares. The order of magnitude of these correlations now is about the same as for age of democracy or Pryor's indicator of rent-seeking. Second, while Cameron's leftist government control and his percent unionization remain unrelated to all income shares, his four indicators of union power now correlate more strongly than before with income shares. Again, the order of magnitude of the correlations is about the same as for age of democracy or Pryor's index and income shares. Third, while age of

Table 2. Product-Moment Correlations between Income Shares
and Conceivable Explanatory Variables, *Japan eliminated*

	Low 20	Low 40	Low 60	Low 80
Korpi % unionization 46-76	0.16	0.09	0.01	−0.11
left votes as % of electorate	0.05	−0.10	−0.18	−0.28
working-class mobilization	0.04	−0.10	−0.16	−0.21
left (weighted) cabinet share	−0.03	−0.03	−0.02	−0.06
time with left cabinet representation	0.45	0.55	0.52	0.36
Cameron leftist government control 65-82	0.25	0.16	0.15	0.11
% unionization	0.16	0.15	0.13	0.05
organizational unity of labor	0.34	0.44	0.54	0.52
confederation power in collective bargaining	0.53	0.60	0.58	0.43
scope of collective bargaining	0.35	0.49	0.50	0.42
works councils and codetermination	0.48	0.51	0.49	0.36
age of democracy	−0.42	−0.40	−0.37	−0.36
Pryor's rating scale for rent-seeking	−0.56	−0.58	−0.58	−0.48
Choi's institutional sclerosis	−0.22	−0.04	0.03	0.09
GNPC	−0.38	−0.25	−0.08	−0.01
logged (ln) GNPC	−0.36	−0.24	−0.06	0.01
purchase power parity GDPC	−0.30	−0.19	−0.04	−0.01
government revenues/GDP 60-82	0.42	0.45	0.44	0.32
government expenditures/GDP	0.50	0.47	0.38	0.26
social security transfers/GDP	0.50	0.51	0.46	0.28

Notes: Underlined coefficients are significant in two-tailed tests at the 10% level. N is 16, except for rows 6 to 11 and 18 to 20, because of missing data for New Zealand.

democracy and Pryor's index become slightly weaker correlates of income shares, Pryor's index still remains the strongest correlate of low 20 percent income shares among twenty variables. Fourth, the exclusion of Japan makes government revenues, expenditures and transfers stronger correlates of income shares than before or in Table 1.

Obviously, the inclusion or exclusion of Japan affects the bivariate evidence concerning the 'democratic class struggle' perspective much more strongly than the radical public choice perspective. By and large, you have to eliminate Japan, if you want to argue the effectiveness of unions or socialist parties in the redistribution game. And you absolutely depend on excluding Japan in order to make a case for socialist redistribution actually reaching the poorest quintile. But age of democracy or Pryor's index are hardly affected by the Japan issue. At most their correlations are depressed by 0.07. Support for the radical reinterpretation of Olson's (1982) theory by Chan (1987a, 1987b) seems rather robust. As the public choice approach to inequality looks better supported by Table 1 than anything else, I want to display the relationship between my age of democracy indicator and Pryor's rating scale on the one hand and income shares on the other hand in some more detail.

Since Pryor's (1984) rating scale of rent-seeking in industrial societies classifies nations into three categories, one may easily compute the average shares for groups of income receivers and the three subsets of nations. As can be seen in Table 3, societies less afflicted by rent-seeking and distributional struggles give somewhat larger shares to the poorest 20, 40, 60, or 80 percent than other societies do. By and large, the important difference between groups of nations concerns Pryor's winners who suffer from little rent-seeking and the other two groups, whereas the difference between the intermediate category and those most afflicted by rent-seeking matters less.

Age of democracy is a continuous variable. Nevertheless, the trichotomization displayed in Table 4 is not entirely arbitrary. After all, the victorious armed forces of the Western allies established or reestablished democracy within a rather short period of time in many West European countries and Japan. This gives us our first category. The other cut-off point distinguishes between truly old democracies which achieved universal manhood suffrage[15] even before World War I and those who did it during or after the great war. Again, we get the expected results. The older the democracy, the smaller the share of the low 20, low 40, low 60 and even low 80 percent groups of income receivers. While the difference between rather young democracies and the intermediate category is between small and negligible, the truly old democracies demonstrate the least egalitarian pattern. Definitely, democracy does not prevent the top 20 percent from winning the distributional struggles and the rent-seeking game.

The negative relationship between the age of democracy and equality is likely to be received with disbelief by those social scientists who do not belong to the public choice school of thought. An obvious strategy to call the findings in Table 4 into question is to challenge the validity of operationalizing the age of democracy only in terms of *uninterrupted* democracy. Hewitt (1977, p. 457) is not only the data source for my own efforts to assess the age of *un*interrupted democracy, but he also supplies us with an alternative indicator of the age of democracy.

Hewitt's measure 'years of full democracy' is counted from the first year in which a secret ballot, responsible government and universal adult male

Table 3.   Average Income Shares for Pryor's Grouping of Nations

Pryor's winners *little rent-seeking*	*intermediate*	*Pryor's losers* *much rent-seeking*
Japan	France	United States
West Germany	Italy	United Kingdom
Belgium	Denmark	Canada
Netherlands	Sweden	Ireland
Norway	Finland	Switzerland
		Australia
		New Zealand
low 20: 7.76	6.16	5.99
low 40: 21.04	18.16	17.79
low 60: 38.96	35.48	34.81
low 80: 62.52	59.18	58.74

Note: See Pryor (1984, p. 160-161) for the classification and the logic behind it.

Table 4.   Average Income Shares for Nations
Grouped by Age of Democracy

democracy [re]established since the end of WW II	*democracy established between 1914 and WW II*	*democracy even before 1914*
Japan (13)	United Kingdom (47)	United States (61)
West Germany (16)	Ireland (42)	Canada (67)
France (20)	Sweden (48)	Switzerland (93)
Italy (20)	Finland (48)	Australia (73)
Belgium (20)		New Zealand (86)
Denmark (20)		
Netherlands (20)		
Norway (20)		
low 20: 6.99	6.98	5.54
low 40: 19.64	19.43	17.74
low 60: 37.26	36.63	34.26
low 80: 60.99	60.38	58.06

Note: The numbers in parentheses provide the age of democracy in 1965. The United Kingdom is regarded as a democracy only since 1818 when universal adult male suffrage was introduced. See Weede (1984, p. 366) for the 'age of democracy' in 1965 and Hewitt (1977, p. 457) for the information which I have used in calculating it.

suffrage are achieved. Non-democratic interruptions lead to mere reductions of the number of years of full democracy rather than to an entirely new beginning in the counting of years. Only the scores of West Germany, France, Italy, Belgium, Netherlands, Denmark and Norway are affected by this issue. Hewitt's alternative indicator increases the age of these democracies and thereby blurs the distinction in age between the democracies in the first and second columns of Table 4. Given Hewitt's indicator, a dichotomization between democracies younger than 50 years old (in 1965) and older ones is more meaningful than the trichotomization in Table 4.

Collapsing the first two columns of Table 4, as is implied by a rejection of the uninterrupted age of democracy indicator, would hardly affect results. The major differences in income shares in Table 4 obtain between the relatively inegalitarian and oldest democracies and the other two groups of younger and more egalitarian democracies. Collapsing the two younger groups by counting the democratic experience of continental Europe before the end of World War II does not affect this contrast.

There is only a single nation in the data set which complicates matters, so that a simple combination of the first two columns of Table 4 does not provide exact results, i.e., Norway. According to Hewitt (1977, p. 457), the Norwegian age of democracy in 1965 is 62 years which puts the nation into the very old democracy column. While a reclassification of Norway would marginally improve the income distributions of the oldest democracies as a group, it would *not* suffice to get rid of the fact, that the income shares of the lowest 20, 40, 60, and 80 percent are lower in older than in younger democracies. So, the focus on *un*interrupted years of democracy is not necessary in order to replicate the main conclusion from Table 4.

An unexpected finding as the one displayed above calls for some deliberations about alternative explanations. Olson's (1982) theory as well as Pryor's (1984) rating scale or my age of democracy indicator give much weight to wars and, in particular, to lost wars. The great wars of the twentieth century have been extremely destructive. By and large, those nations who have for some time suffered from military occupation have also provided the battle-grounds.[16] While Anglo-Saxon nations provided many of the troops to defeat the Axis powers in World War II, their home territories suffered in between no and negligible damage. So, much more property must have been destroyed in the young democracies and in Pryor's 'winner'-category than in the old democracies and in Pryor's loser-category. Loss of property has to be concentrated on the propertied classes rather than on the poor. So, the destructive power of war itself may have equalized income distributions in young democracies.

Although there might be some kernel of truth in the alternative explanation it does not convince me as the main or even a major reason for the pattern of findings in Tables 3 and 4. First, the differential impact of military destruction provides no plausible explanation for the findings themselves. In Table 3, all societies in Pryor's 'winner' and intermediate categories, except for Sweden, did suffer significantly from the war. Nevertheless, we do not find a great contrast between the two columns at the left, where almost all societies suffered from the destruction of property, on the one hand and the column at the right on the other hand, where destruction of property varied between nothing and very little. Instead the greater contrast is between the two categories where almost all nations in both columns suffered significantly from the destruction of property. In Table 4, the most severely war-affected societies constitute the left column. But differences between these nations and either non-affected or little-affected nations in the intermediate category are weak. Instead we find a much more pronounced contrast between the intermediate and the right column where, with the possible exception of Finland, property destruction was rather limited at worst.

Second, one should put the findings in Tables 3 and 4 in a wider perspective. As has been demonstrated elsewhere (Bernholz 1986, Weede 1984, 1986a, 1986b, 1987), both Pryor's rating scale and the age of democracy variable are significantly related to economic growth.[17] Where the comparative youth of the democratic political system has given distributional coalitions less time to overcome the freeriding tendency, less time to establish themselves and to enforce price distortions in favor of their membership or clientele, where (for whatever reason) distributional coalitions are encompassing—and these are the characteristics which Pryor's index and my age of democracy variable try to assess—there we observe faster economic growth and less inequality than elsewhere. A public choice approach in general, and Olson's (1982) theory in particular, can parsimoniously explain both sets of findings within the same framework.

Third, the logic behind the expectation that property-destruction in war equalizes the distribution of income is not convincing. Obviously property destruction can remove some people, even a large number of people, from the propertied class. While former property-owners become more like those who have always been propertyless ('egalitarian' effect), they become less like the lucky property-owners who found their property largely undamaged at the end of the war (inegalitarian effect). Since capital and property are scarce after destructive wars, they should command scarcity premiums on markets. So, it is theoretically dubious that the egalitarian impact of destruction should outweigh the inegalitarian one.

Fourth, the impact of property destruction is not a plausible candidate for explaining differences in low 40 and, even less, in low 20 income shares. These people could not lose significant amounts of income-generating property through war, because they never had it. The war-related destruction approach seems more plausible if we are interested in top 20 or its inverse low 80 income shares. Actually, both Pryor's scale and age of democracy are less strongly related to low 80 (and, implicitly, top 20) than to low 20 or low 40 income shares.

In itself bivariate analysis is not satisfying. Given a small number of cases multivariate analysis is not necessarily an improvement. In my opinion, 16 or 17 cases support nothing more than two independent variables simultaneously. Here combining a union or socialist strength indicator with one for economic development or taxation and government spending produces nothing in addition to Table 1 above and lots of insignificant regression coefficients and even insignificant equations. But the combination of one of the two successful indicators of rent-seeking and either indicators of economic development *or* some of the more successful indicators of union or socialist strength might be more interesting.

I did calculate 56 multiple regressions with income shares as dependent variables and two independent variables, i.e., fourteen regressions for each group of income receivers from the low 20 to the low 80 percent. One independent variable was always *either* the 'age of democracy' *or* Pryor's (1984) index of rent-seeking, while the second independent variable *either* referred to one of the indicators of economic development *or* to Korpi's (1983) 'time with left cabinet representation,' or to Cameron's (1984) 'organizational unity of labour,' or to his 'confederation power in collective bargaining,' or to his 'works councils and codetermination.' Fifty-four out of these 56 regressions either confirmed only the significance of the relationship between the stronger correlate of the respective income share (see Table 1) or produced entirely insignificant equations. The two exceptions explain low 40 and low 60 percent income shares by the negative impact of 'age of democracy' and the positive impact of Korpi's (1983) 'time with left cabinet representation.' As is implicit in Table 1, the effect of 'age of democracy' remains stronger than the effect of 'time with left cabinet representation.' It might be that the aging of democracies leads to a deterioration of income distributions because of more and more rent-seking, but that long-serving socialist cabinet ministers may successfully fight the trend. In my opinion, however, one should not take this token multivariate finding as anything more than a hunch and an incentive for future work.

CONCLUSIONS

Although I have been primarily concerned with the 'democratic class struggle' and 'public choice' approaches to income inequality, one of the most surprising findings of this paper concerns the relationship betwen the level of economic development on the one hand and the size distribution of income on the other hand. On the basis of previous work with global samples of nations rather than samples restricted to industrial democracies (e.g., Ahluwalia 1976; Kuznets 1963; Paukert 1973; Weede 1980, 1982), one should have expected a positive relationship between the level of economic development and low 20 to low 80 percent income shares within the subset of industrial democracies. Instead I find consistently negative relationships here, although only those with low 20 or low 40 income shares are significant.

Often one accepts cross-national patterns as a substitute for longitudinal evidence where the latter is poor or not available. Needless to say that such a procedure is hazardous. Still, this paper calls the comfortable message of earlier studies into question which linked economic development with a trend towards equality at least for industrial democracies. While the data base of this study is narrower than the data base of previous studies, the quality of the most recent data for industrial societies is obviously superior to older data for these societies and less open or less developed countries.

Recently, some longitudinal data on the distribution of income have been collected for West European countries by Kraus and published by Flora (1987, p. 643-674). By and large, these longitudinal data seem to demonstrate a trend towards more equality in a majority of West European countries. So, the available cross-sectional and longitudinal information on the relationship between economic development and income inequality is inconsistent with each other. The reason behind this discrepancy might either be the difference between survey-based and income tax-based inequality data or the difference between cross-sectional and longitudinal analysis. While the issue is certainly too complex to be solved as a by-product of an analysis concerned with the 'democratic class struggle' and 'public choice' approaches to inequality, the cross-sectional evidence supplied here looks good enough to me to undermine the widespread confidence that economic development and time is with the poorer strata of society.

The 'democratic class struggle' line of reasoning received little *robust* support in the computations presented above. Earlier as well as simultaneous unionization is unrelated to low 20, low 40, low 60, or low 80 percent income shares. Left votes as a percentage of the electorate or the left cabinet share in the decades before the measurement of inequality seems to matter as little as simultaneous leftist government control. But longstanding left cabinet representation, the organizational unity of labor, confederation power in collective bargaining, and co-determination are somewhat related to *some* income shares. Yet, the fact that none of the measures of working class mobilization or socialist strength correlates significantly with low 20 percent income shares, unless you eliminate the Japanese case from the analysis, should be deeply disturbing to unqualified adherents of the 'democratic class struggle' approach.

This is not the only paper that calls the democratic class struggle approach into question. Jackman (1980) found some relationship between socialist strength and higher low 80 percent income shares,[18] but none between socialist strength and low 40 percent income shares. If true, this is odd from a democratic class struggle perspective. Weede (1982) found insignificant relationships between socialist strength and income inequality and not even the sign always confirmed to 'democratic class struggle' expectations. Moreover, socialist strength seemed more closely, although still insignificantly related to reduced growth than to better shares for the poor.[19] Finally, Pampel and Williamson (1986) found no robust relationship between their indicators of working class strength and reduced inequality.

Of course, there are studies which do claim some egalitarian impact of socialist strength, like Hewitt's (1977). Significantly his study does not investigate low 20, low 40, or even low 60 income shares at all. Instead it focuses on top 5 or top 20 percent income shares or overall measures of income inequality, such as the Gini index. Similarly, Muller (1988) has recently argued that a country's years of democratic experience reduce income inequality. But his study includes less developed countries and refers to top 20 percent income shares and the Gini index only. Moreover, I (Weede 1989) could not replicate Muller's results with more recent inequality data from the World Bank (1987). Nor did Muller's finding survive a control variable for human capital formation, i.e., operationally: literacy rates.

At most partisans of the 'democratic class struggle' approach may point to some controversial evidence according to which working class or socialist political power reduces the privileges of the top income receivers. But there seems to be no evidence that working class mobilization and socialist political power help those who are most in need of help. The empirical evidence certainly does not support the view that unions and social democratic parties have succeeded in improving the material lot of the poor.

From the 'public choice' perspective the poor performance of 'democratic class struggle' indicators consitutes little surprise. The 'rational ignorance' of most lower class voters and the headstart of privileged interest groups in the rent-seeking game should greatly reduce the egalitarian impact which democracy and working class organizations might otherwise have. In Chan's (1987b) radical interpretation of Olson's (1982) theory, and implicitly of the public choice approach, the headstart of privileged groups in rent-seeking does not only deny the redistributive fruits of democracy to the lower classes and to the absolute majority of voters, but makes democracy compatible with regressive redistribution. Here, it is found that older democracies suffer from smaller shares for the low 20, low 40, low 60, and low 80 percent. Moreover, Pryor's rent-seeking scale by and large reconfirms these findings.

There is one aspect of the 'democratic class struggle' line of reasoning that is compatible with Olson's (1982) theorizing. In Olson's view, encompassing distributional coalitions do much less damage than narrow interest groups. 'Organizational unity of labour' and 'confederation power in collective bargaining' refer to encompassing working class coalitions. So, the positive correlations of these two-indicators with low 40, low 60, and low 80 percent income shares are compatible with the public choice approach. The masses do not lose the redistribution game where they have established truly encompassing organizations. In general, however, democracy permits the proliferation of lots of distributional coalitions, most of which are narrow and hurt the poor as well as the majority of income receivers or voters.

Whereas some writers tend to be critical of all administrative transfers and others make an exception for progressive transfers, nodbody seems to favor regressive redistribution as a matter of principle. Nevertheless, democracies might become more and more afflicted with regressive redistribution over time. To make things even worse, the accumulation of distributional coalitions over time in democracies seems to make the poor lose twice. Here, I have documented that the lower and middle classes receive declining shares in aging democracies. Other research has documented that aging democracies suffer from declining economic growth rates (Bernholz 1986; Weede 1984, 1986a, 1986b, 1987). Put together, the poorest strata suffer from a shrinking piece of the pie and needlessly reduced growth rates at the same time.

According to 'public choice' theorizing, the villains in the story are distributional coalitions and their rent-seeking activities. The problem with democracy is its permissive attitude towards interest groups. If aging democracies suffer from reduced growth and less equality, then democracy might become a self-defeating cause. It is little consolation that Olson's (1982) theory predicts similarly bleak futures for other kinds of stable regimes.

ACKNOWLEDGMENTS

I appreciate the computational assistance of Ulrich Albrecht and Juergen Schwuchow as well as the careful criticism of an earlier draft of this paper by J. David Edelstein. None of them is responsible for any remaining errors.

NOTES

1. Of course, the concept of the median voter is most meaningfull where preferences can be ordered along a single dimension (or approximately so). In a two-party system the necessity to include the median voter among your adherents is stronger and more obvious than it is in a multi-party system. Where multi-party systems approach two-bloc systems, the difference between them and two-party systems loses much of its importance.

2. The publicness of public goods refers to given groups. What is a public *good* for some group, may be a public *bad* for another group, even for a more encompassing group containing the first group.

3. I have chosen this way of analysis and presentation, because it is theoretically difficult to make any predictions about the signs of the relationships between putative explanatory variables and middle quintile income shares. In my way of presenting results an equalizing impact of some variable should always lead to positive correlations.

4. The 'working class mobilization' index itself is derived from unionization and left votes. Korpi (1983, p. 39) describes his index-making in these words: "On the basis of their combined ranks on the level of unionization and share of the electorate voting for left parties, we have divided the countries into three groups having low, medium, and high levels of working-class mobilization." Norway, Sweden, Denmark, Belgium, United Kingdom, Australia, and New Zealand are classified as highly mobilized and scored 2. Finland, Netherlands, West Germany, France, Italy, and Japan are classified as medium and scored 1. The United States, Canada, Ireland, and Switzerland are classified as low and scored 0.

5. The 'weighted cabinet share' is an index "where the proportion of seats in each cabinet held by socialist parties has been weighted by the socialist share of seats in parliament and by the duration of the cabinet. This weighted cabinet share can be interpreted as an indicator of the working class's ability to exercise political influence" (Korpi 1983, p. 41). Only Sweden and Norway are classified as high and scored 2 on this index. Finland, Denmark, Belgium, United Kingdom, Australia, and New Zealand are rated medium and scored 1. The United States, Canada, Ireland, France, Netherlands, West Germany, Switzerland, Italy, and Japan are rated low and scored 0.

6. The scale for 'time with left cabinet representation' is justified by the following argument: "Where the participation of labor parties in government is stable and of long duration, we can expect different types of conflict strategies than in countries where socialist representation in government has been irregular or sporadic" (Korpi 1983, p. 41). Sweden, Norway, and Switzerland are rated high and scored 2. Finland, Denmark, Ireland, United Kingdom, New Zealand, Netherlands, Beligum, West Germany, and Italy are rated medium and scored 1. The United States, Canada, Japan, Australia, and France are rated low and scored 0.

7. The logic of Cameron's product is that control of government by leftist parties should be scored as strong only if the left holds many portfolios *and* if the left also constitutes a major part of the necessary parliamentary majority. The product is high only, where both conditions

are simultaneously met. Neither many portfolios in leftist hands, nor many leftist deputies in parliament suffice.

8.   Obviously, the reference year (1965) for age of democracy is arbitrary. But any other year (after 1955 when the youngest democracy was born) would provide exactly the same coefficients of correlation and significance levels. Table 4 below contains the age of democracy in 1965. Whether the age of democracy should refer to uninterrupted democracy only or might be defined differently shall be discussed together with Table 4 in some more detail.

9.   Elsewhere, (Weede 1987) I have scored 'winners' 2 and 'losers' 0. Here, I have reversed the scale in order to get the same expected sign for all correlations of distributional coalition, price distortion and rent-seeking indicators with income shares. Table 3 contains the ratings of nations on this scale.

10.   While Choi provides two different versions of his index, these are so extremely similar that I have chosen to use only the 'A' version of it.

11.   While age of democracy correlates -0.40 with GDP growth in 1960-82 and -0.60 with GDPC growth, Choi's A index correlates -0.71 and -0.73 with these growth rates. See Weede (1986a, p. 201).

12.   While both Kuznets and Lenski posit a curvilinear relationship between the level of economic development and inequality, they still differ on specific issues. According to Lenski (1966), the transition from agrarian to industrial societies leads to a reduction of income inequality. According to Kuznets, the reduction of income inequalities in most Western industrial societies started only at the beginning of the twentieth century. Moreover, Lenski tends to explain the equalization process largely by ideological and political factors, whereas Kuznets largely explains it by sectoral productivity gaps and the reallocation of labor between sectors in the process of development.

13.   Chan (1987a) calls the curvilinear relationship between the level of economic development and inequality into question without using the best-fitting specification, i.e., regressing Gini or income shares on logged GNP or energy consumption per capita and its square.

14.   Since the measures of inequality and leftist strength are not independent of each other, it is not strictly justified to regard the 44 correlations (4 income shares times 11 indicators of leftist strength) as independent tests of the same basic idea. Obviously, low 20 percent income shares affect low 40, low 60, and low 80 percent income shares. Similarly, Korpi's and Cameron's unionization percentages largely depend on the same facts, because of the overlap in the period of observation. Nevertheles, I feel that summarizing these correlations, *as if* they were independent tests is meaningful and justified under the assumption that measurement errors in different pairs of variables tend to be independent of each other. If you reject this assumption and the corresponding interpretation, you might still notice that indicators of leftist strength tend to correlate lower with income shares of truly poor groups than with more inclusive groups containing the medium income receiver. The fact that some indicators of leftist strength are merely trichotomies might bias some of their correlations with income shares downwards. Since the same holds true for some indicator of rent-seeking, the relative performance of 'democratic class struggle'- and 'public choice'-derived expectations should remain unaffected by this technical issue.

15.   The focus on manhood rather than adult suffrage may irritate some readers. But it is meaningful for the purposes of this paper. The dependent variables concern income inequality between households and social strata. Whether only adult males or all adults vote, should not affect the balance of power and privilege between households and strata. As soon as all men may vote, the poor get a new weapon at their disposal. Of course, my reading of the public choice approach makes it unlikely that the poor successfully wield it.

16. Of course, Eastern Europe suffered even more from World War II than Western Europe. But East European countries are not considered in this study of industrial democracies.

17. Pryor (1984) himself disputes this interpretation. But I believe to have shown that his data, if used properly, support Olson's (1982) theory (Weede 1987).

18. This is an implication of Jackman's (1980) findings concerning top 20 percent income shares.

19. Unfortunately, the printers had badly distorted Table 5 of my paper (Weede 1982) to which this remark refers.

REFERENCES

Ahluwalia, M.S. 1976. "Income Distribution and Development," *American Economic Review* 66: 128-135.

Albert, H. 1978. *Traktat* über Rationale Praxis. Tuebingen: Mohr.

Bernholz, P. 1977. "Dominant Interest Groups and Powerless Parties," *Kyklos* 30: 411-420.

Bernholz, P. 1986. "Growth of Government, Economic Growth and Individual Freedom," *Journal of Institutional and Theoretical Economics* 142: 661-683.

Buchanan, J.M., Tollison, R.D. and Tullock, G. 1980. *Toward a Theory of the Rent-Seeking Society*. College Station: Texas A and M University Press.

Cameron, D.R. 1984. "Social Democracy, Corporatism, Labour Quiescence, and the Representation of Economic Interest in Advanced Capitalist Society," Pp. 143-178 in Goldthorpe, J.H. (ed.), *Order and Conflict in Contemporary Capitalism*. Oxford: Clarendon.

Chan, S. 1987a. "Comparative Performance of East Asian and Latin American NICs," *Pacific Focus* 2: 35-56.

Chan, S. 1987b. "Growth with Equity: A Test of Olson's Theory for the Asian Pacific-Rim Countries," *Journal of Peace Research* 24: 135-149.

Choi, K.A. 1983. "A Statistical Test of Olson's Model," Pp. 57-78 in Mueller, D.C. (ed.), *The Political Economy of Growth*. New Haven: Yale University Press.

Downs, A. 1957. *An Economic Theory of Democracy*. New York: Harper and Row.

Flora, P. 1987. *State, Economy, and Society in Western Europe 1815-1975. Vol. II: The Growth of Industrial Societies and Capitalist Economies*. Frankfurt/Main: Campus.

Hayek, F.A. 1960. *The Constitution of Liberty*. Chicago: University Press.

Hewitt, C. 1977. "The Effect of Political Democracy and Social Democracy on Equality in Industrial Societies," *American Sociological Review* 42: 450-464.

Jackman, R.W. 1980. "Socialist Parties and Income Inequality in Western Industrial Societies," *Journal of Politics* 42: 135-149.

Jackman, R.W. 1986. "Elections and the Democratic Class Struggle," *World Politics* 39: 123-146.

Korpi, W. 1983. *The Democratic Class Struggle*. London: Routledge and Kegan Paul.

Kravis, I.B., Heston, A.W. and Summers, R. 1978. "Real GDP Per Capita for more than One Hundred Countries," *Economic Journal* 88: 215-242.

Kuznets, S. 1963. "Quantitative Aspects of the Economic Growth of Nations. VIII: The Distribution of Income by Size," *Economic Development and Cultural Change* 11: 1-80.

Lenski, G. 1966. *Power and Privilege: A Theory of Social Stratification*. New York: McGraw-Hill.

Lipset, S.M. 1960. *Political Man: The Social Bases of Politics.* New York: Doubleday.

McKenzie, R.B. and Tullock, G. 1978. *Modern Political Economy.* Tokyo: McGraw-Hill Kogakusha.

Muller, E.N. 1988. "Democracy, Economic Development, and Income Inequality," *American Sociological Review* 53: 50-68.

Nie, N.H. and Verba, S. 1975. "Political Participation," Pp. 1-74 in Greenstein, F.I., and Polsby, N.W. (eds.), *Handbook of Political Science, Vol. 4: Nongovernmental Politics.* Reading, MA: Addison-Wesley.

OECD 1984. *Historical Statistics 1960-1982.* Paris: OECD.

Olson, M. 1965. *The Logic of Collective Action.* Cambridge: Harvard University Press.

Olson, M. 1982. *The Rise and Decline of Nations.* New Haven: Yale University Press.

Pampel, F.C. and Williamson, J.B. 1986. *Social Welfare Spending and Social Equality: Explaining Cross-National Patterns and Change.* University of Iowa: Manuscript.

Paukert, F. 1973. "Income Distribution at Different Levels of Development," *International Labour Review* 108: 97-125.

Pryor, F.L. 1984. "Rent-Seeking and the Growth and Fluctuations of Nations," Pp. 155-175 in Colander, D.C. (ed.), *Neoclassical Political Economy: The Analysis of Rent-Seeking and DUP Activities.* Cambridge, MA: Ballinger (Harper and Row).

Taylor, C.L. and Hudson, M.C. 1972. *World Handbook of Political and Social Indicators.* 2nd ed. New Haven: Yale University Press.

Tollison, R.D. 1982. "Rent-Seeking: A Survey," *Kyklos* 35: 575-602.

Tullock, G. 1983. *Economics of Income Redistribution.* Boston-The Hague-London: Kluwer-Nijhoff.

Weede, E. 1980. "Beyond Misspecification in Sociological Analyses of Income Inequality," *American Sociological Review* 45: 497-501.

Weede, E. 1982. "The Effects of Democracy and Socialist Strength on the Size Distrubution of Income," *International Journal of Comparative Sociology* 23: 151-165.

Weede, E. 1984. "Democracy, Creeping Socialism, and Ideological Socialism in Rent-Seeking Societies," *Public Choice* 44: 349-366.

Weede, E. 1986a. "Catch-up, Distributional Coalitions, and Government as Determinants of Economic Growth or Decline in Industrialized Democracies," *British Journal of Sociology* 37: 194-220.

Weede, E. 1986b. "Sectoral Reallocation, Distributional Coalitions and the Welfare State as Determinants of Economic Growth Rates in Industrialized Democracies," *European Journal of Political Research* 14: 501-519.

Weede, E. 1987. "A note on Pryor's criticism of Olson's Rise and Decline of Nations," *Public Choice* 52: 215-222.

Weede, E. 1989. *American Sociological Review* 54:865-868.

Weede, E. and Tiefenbach, H. 1981. "Correlates of the Size Distribution of Income in Cross-National Analyses," *Journal of Politics* 43: 1029-1041.

World Bank. 1987. *World Development Report 1987.* New York: Oxford University Press.

AUTHOR INDEX

Abrams, P., 89, 106
Abzug, B., 274, 296
Accame, F., 116, 137
Adas, M., 184
Adcock, C., 274, 296
Ahluwalia, M. S., 309, 320, 325
Albert, H., 304, 325
Albo, X., 184
Aldrich, J. H., 18, 19, 30
Alencastre, G.,180n.8
Alexander, L., 253, 263
Alier, A., 241n.5
Althusser, L., 67, 87, 180n.2,
      182n2.3, 182n.24, 184
American Civil Liberties Union
      Fund, 99, 106
Amigos de Casa Marianella, 102,
      106
Amnesty International, 103, 106
Andersen, K., 296n.3, 296
Anderson, 67
Anderson, P., 174, 178, 182n.23,
      184
Appaduarai, A., 184
Appleby, G., 150, 184
Aranda, A., 154, 184

Archivo Notarial Alavarez, 180n.6
Arendt, H., 254, 257, 258, 263
Arlen, M. J., 250, 263
Assefa, H., 243
Austin Religious Community for
      Central America, 94, 106
Aveni, A., 30, 43, 65

Back, K., 31
Bainbridge, W. S., 2, 33
Bakan, D., 270-271, 296
Baker, R. K., 278, 296
Bakuniak, G., 68, 87
Balibar, E., 180n.2, 184
Ball, S., 278, 296
Ball-Rokeach, S. J., 36, 38, 60,
      62n.2, 65
Barnett, M. A., 273, 296
Barry, T., 95, 99, 106
Basadre, J., 167, 184
Bassett, C. A., 100, 109
Basta!, 91, 93, 97, 98, 99, 100, 101,
      102, 103, 104, 105, 106-107
Bau, J., 97, 107
Bauer, Y., 262n.4, 263
Bauman, Z., 250, 262n.7, 263

327

SUBJECT INDEX

Abboud, General
  role in Sudan civil war, 205,
    209
Accommodation
  in families, 191-192, 192-196
Agency, human, 182n.23
  mode of production approach
    and, 176
  political economy approach and,
    176;
  see also, Gender: self-concern;
    Masculinity: self-concern
All Africa Conference of Churches
  role in settling Sudan civil
    war, 208, 224-231
Althusser, L., 174
Amin, Idi
  role in Sudan civil war, 219
Amnesty International, 103
Ankrah, Kodwo
  role in All Africa Conference of
    Churches, 224

Bakan, D.
  self-concern and other-concern,
    270-271

unmitigated agency and commu-
    nality, 281
Banzer, Col. Hugo, 96
Barnet, Richard, 277
Berger, Susan, 132

Carr, Canon Burgess
  role in World Council of
    Churches, 224, 229,
    242n.23
Carter, Jimmy, 102
Catholic Church
  Italian peace movement and,
    125-133
Cerro, Sanchez, 166, 167, 181n.18
Chan, Steve
  radical interpretation of Olson,
    304
Churches, U.S.
  response to sanctuary move-
    ment, 102
Cognitive maps
  gender and, 282-283
Collective behavior
  income redistribution and, 304-
    305

Elder, Jack, 94, 101
Espinar, Peru, rebellion
see, Rebellion, Molloccahua,
Peru
Ethnicity
in mode of production approach,
173
*Europe and the People Without
History*, 140, 143, 146,
175, 177
Families
accommodation in, 191-192
accommodation to housework
in, 192-196
conflict processes in, 196-199
division of labor in, 189-191
Femininity
characteristics of, 270
conceptions of security and, 291-
293
conceptions of war and peace
and, 272, 273-274, 284-291
differential value of, 274-276
other-concern and, 270-271
social construction of, 267-269
Feminism
definition of power and, 295-296n.1
household division of labor and,
189-190
perspectives on masculinity, 276
Fife, Rev. John, 102
Foreign Policy, U.S.
Immigration Reform and Control Act of 1986, 99
liberation theology and, 95-96
LIC strategy and, 95-97
mood theory and, 94-95
response to Central American
immigration and, 98-99
response to sanctuary movement
and, 100-101

response to revolution and, 94-
97
Frank, 143
Freedom Summer, 4, 5-7
applicants at Berkeley, 8
history at Berkeley, 7-9
history at University of Wisconsin at Madison, 9
see also, Recruitment, Freedom
Summer
Freire, Paolo, 93

Garang, Col. John
role in Sudan civil war, 238,
241n.7
Gender
attitudes towards violence and, 278
attitudes towards war and peace
and, 278-279
characteristics of, 270
cognitive maps of war, peace,
and security and, 282-283
competitive behavior and, 272-273
conceptions of security and, 267,
271-272, 276-277, 281, 291-
293, 294-295
conceptions of war and peace
and, 267, 269, 272, 273-
274, 277-280, 281, 284-291
conflict and, 270-271
core constructs and, 280-281,
291, 292, 293
differential value of, 274-276
hypotheses about war, peace,
security and, 281-282
self-concern and other-concern
and, 270-271, 279, 288-
289, 294
social construction of, 267-269,
271, 280, 293-294
structures which reinforce, 271

★ ★ ★

Indices prepared by Richard
    Kendrick

Research in Social Movements, Conflicts and Change

Edited by **Louis Kriesberg,** *Department of Sociology, Syracuse University*

REVIEWS: "... recommended for graduate libraries."
— *Choice*

" ... The papers are generally of excellent quality ... a useful series of annual volumes ..."
— *Social Forces*

"... an excellent series of original articles ... the papers are broad in scope and methodologically diverse ... a welcome departure from the traditional 'social roots' approach and offers new insights into 'feedback effects' of social movements ... useful anthologies that are theoretically informed and timely."
— *Political Sociology*

Volume 1, 1978, 350 pp. $63.50
ISBN 0-89232-027-3

James M. Fendrich, Florida State University and Ellis S. Krauss, Western Washington State University. **The Decline of The 1960s Social Movements,** Anthony Oberschall, Vanderbilt University. **Models for the Relationship Between the World of Women and the World of Men,** Jessie Bernard, The Pennsylvania State University. **Author/Subject Index.**

Volume 2, 1979, 293 pp. $63.50
ISBN 0-89232-108-3

Volume 3, 1980, 266 pp. $63.50
ISBN 0-89232-182-2

Syracuse University. **The News and Foreign Policy: An Examination of the Impact of the Newsmedia on the Making of Foreign Policy,** Dina Goren, The Hebrew University. **The Aristocracy of Labor: An Empirical Test,** Peter Dreier, Tufts University and Al Szymanski, University of Oregon. **Multinational Corporate Expansion and Nation-State Development: A Global Perspective,** Richard G. Braungart and Margaret M. Braungart, Syracuse University. **Intervening in School Desegregation Conflicts: The Role of the Monitor,** James H. Laue and Daniel Monti, University of Missouri, St. Louis. **The Slowing of Modernization in Middletown,** Howard M. Bahr, Theodore Caplow and Geoffrey K. Leigh, University of Virginia. **Author Index. Subject Index.**

Volume 4, 1981, 385 pp. $63.50
ISBN 0-89232-201-2

CONTENTS: Introduction, Louis Kriesberg. **Collective Behavior and Resource Mobilization as Approaches to Social Movements: Issues and Continuities,** Ralph Turner, University of California, Los Angeles, **Repression of Religious Cults,** David G. Bromley, University of Hartford, Anson D. Shupe, Jr., University of Texas, Arlington and Bruce C. Bushing, James Madison University. **Defensive Strikes of a Doomed Labor Aristocracy: The Case of the Printers in France,** J.W. Freiberg, Harvard Law School and Centre d'etude des movements sociaux, Paris. **Comparative Perspectives on Industrial Conflict,** Lillian J. Christman, Resources for Evaluation, Analysis and Planning, Washington, D.C. and William R. Kelly and Omer R. Galle, University of Texas, Arlington. **Capitalists vs. the Unions: An Analysis of Antiunion Political Mobilization Among business Leaders,** Richard E. Ratcliff, Syracuse University and David Jaffee, University of Massachusetts, Amherst. **Class Struggle, State Policy and the Rationalization of Production: The Organization of Agriculture in Hawaii,** Rhonda F. Levine, Bowdoin College and James A. Gesscwender, State University of New york, Binghamton. **Expansion of Conflict in Cancer Controversies,** James C. Peterson, Indiana University, Bloomington and Gerald E. Markle, Western Michigan University. **The Miami Riots of 1980: Antecedent Conditions, Community Responses and Participant Characteristics,** Robert A. Ladner, Barry J. Swartz, Sandra Roker and Loretta S. Titterud, Behavioral Sciences Research Institute, Coral Gables, Florida. **Welsh Nationalism in Context,** Charles Ragin, Northwestern University and Ted Davies, Indiana University, Bloomington. **Social Mobility and Modern Art: Abstract Expressionism and Its Generative Audience,** Judith Huggins Balfe, Douglass College, Rutgers University. **Transnational Networks and Related Third Cultures: A Comparison of Two Southeast Asian Scientific Communities,** John Useem, Ruth H. Useem, Michigan University, Abu Hassan, Othman Universiti Kebangsaan,

Movements: A Theoretical Perspective, *Richard G. Braungart, Syracuse University.* **Taylored Work Groups: Managerial Recollectivization and Class Conflict in the Workplace,** *Gerard J. Grzyb, University of Alabama.* **Worker Ownership: Collective Response to an Elite-Generated Crisis,** *Joyce Rothchild-Whitt, University of Louisville.* **Power, Insurgency, and State Intervention: Farm Labor Movements in California,** *Theo J. Majka and Linda C. Majka, University of Dayton.* **Plant Closings and the Conflict Between Capital and Labor,** *John F. Zipp, Washington University, St. Louis.* **Majority and Organized Opposition on Effects of Social Movements,** *Herman Turk, University of Southern California and Lynne G. Zucker, University of California, Los Angeles.* **Center-Periphery Conflict: Elite and Popular Movement in the Boston Antibusing Movement,** *Bert Useem, University of Illinois, Chicago.* **Mobilizing the Tax Revolt: The Emergent Alliance Between Homeowners and Local Elites,** *Clarence Y.H. Lo, University of California, Los Angeles.*

Volume 7, 1984, 299 pp. $63.50
ISBN 0-89232-496-1

Volume 8, 1985, 205 pp. $63.50
ISBN 0-89232-571-2

Volume 9, 1986, 280 pp. $63.50
ISBN 0-89232-594-1

Guest Editors: **Kurt Lang** and **Gladys Engel Lang,** *Department of Sociology, University of Washington*

pendence Movement: A Test of a New Model, *Maurice Pinard and Richard Hamilton, McGill University.*

Supplement 1 - The Alinsky Legacy: Alive and Kicking
1987, 274 pp. $63.50
ISBN 0-89232-722-7

by **Dietrich C. Reitzes,** *Roosevelt University* and **Donald C. Reitzes,** *Georgia State University.*

CONTENTS: Getting Aquainted. Understanding Alinsky: Influences and Underlying Themes. Realigning and Reestablishing the Linkage Between Alinsky and The Social Sciences. Three Alinsky Community Organizations. The Industrial Areas Foundation. The IAF in Texas and California. Heather Booth: The Midwest Academy and Citizen Action. Neighborhood Organizations, Coalitions and Training Centers: The Works of Thomas Gaudette, Gale Cincotta, and John Baumann. Fred Ross and Cesar Chavez: Two Independent Organizers. Wrapping up and Closing the Gaps. Bibliography. Index.

Volume 10, Social Movements as a Factor of Change in the Contemporary World
1988, 286 pp. $63.50
ISBN 0-89232-723-5

Edited by **Louis Kriesberg,** *Deparmtent of Sociology, Syracuse University,* **Bronislaw Misztal,** *School of Humanities, Griffith University,* and **Janusz Mucha,** *Jagiellonian University.*

CONTENTS: Foreword, *Bronislaw Misztal, Griffith University in Brisbane.* **Introduction,** *Bronislaw Misztal, Griffith University at Brisbane and Barbara A. Misztal, University of Queensland.* **Social Movements, Old and New,** *Charles Tilly, New School of Social Research in New York.* **The Trajectory of Social Movement in America,** *Mayer N. Zald, University of Michigan, Ann Arbor, Michiagan.* **The Crisis of Fordism, Transforma-tions of the "Keynesian" Security State, and New Social Movements,** *Joachim Hirsch, J.W. Goethe University in Frankfurt am Main.* **Peace Movements and Government Peace Efforts,** *Louis Kriesberg, Syracuse University.* **Union Action and the Free-Rider Dilemma,** *Bert Klandermans, Free University of Amsterdam.* **Democratization Processes as an Objective of New Social Movements,** *Barbara A. Misztal, University of Queensland and Bronislaw Misztal, Griffith University in Brisbane.* **The Coming Revolution,** *Leszek Nowak, Warsaw University.* **The Solidarity Movement in Relation to Society and the State: Communication as an Issue of Social Movement,** *Pawel Kuczynski and Krzysztof Nowak, Warsaw University.* **Peasant Movements in Poland,**

Disputes, *Martin Patchen, Purdue University.* **A Structural Analysis of International Conflict and Cooperation,** *Thomas F. Mayer and Adele G. Platter, University of Colorado.* **Peace and Deterrence,** *Matthew Melko, Wright State University.*

Volume 12, 1990, 344 pp. $63.50
ISBN 1-55938-065-9

CONTENTS: Microstructural Bases of Recruitment to Social Movements, *Roberto M. Fernandez and Doug McAdam, University of Arizona.* **Ambiguity and Crowds: Results from a Computer Simulation Model,** *Norris R. Johnson and William E. Feinberg, University of Cincinnati.* **Alternative Social Movements in Contemporary Poland,** *Bronislaw Misztal, Indiana University.* **The Historical Structuring of a Dissident Movement: The Sanctuary Case,** *David Kowalewski, Alfred University.* **Strategies in the Italian Peace Movement,** *Carlo E. Ruzza, Harvard University.* **Rebels and Theorists: An Examination of Peasant Uprisings in Southern Peru,** *Benjamin S. Orlove, University of California, Davis.* **Conflict Over Housework: A Problem That (Still) Has No Name,** *Marjorie L. DeVault, Syracuse University.* **The Sudanese Settlement: Reflections on the 1972 Addis Araba Agreement,** *C.R. Mitchell, The City University, London.* **Genocide and Social Conflict: A Partial Theory and a Comparison,** *John L.P. Thompson and Gail A. Quets.* **Personal Security, Political Security: The Relationship Between Concepts of Gender, War, and Peace,** *Terrie Northrup, Syracuse University.* **Redistribution and Income Inequality in Industrial Democracies,** *Erich Weede, Forschungsinstitut fuer Soziologie, West Germany.*

Volume 13, In preparation, Summer 1991
ISBN 1-55938-239-2   Approx. $63.50

JAI PRESS INC.

55 Old Post Road - No. 2
P.O. Box 1678
Greenwich, Connecticut 06836-1678
Tel: 203-661-7602

JAI PRESS

Symbolic Interaction

Editor: **David R. Maines,** *The Pennsylvania State University.* Associate Editors: **Spencer Cahill,** *Skidmore College,* **Patricia Clough,** *Fordham University, Lincoln Center* and **Stanley Saxton,** *University of Dayton*

Symbolic Interaction is a scholarly journal devoted to the empirical study of human behavior and social life. It examines the nature, forms, conditions, and consequences of communicative interaction within, between, and among such social actors as individuals, groups, organizations, institutions, communitites and nations.

Contributions are not only from sociologists and social psychologists, but also anthropologists, philosophers and specialists in speech and communication. Topics covered include: the social construction of reality; the negotiation social orders; the link between power and meaning; socially motivated interpersonal control; the dynamics of situated interaction; the acquisition and transformation of social identities; and socialization through the life cycle. The journal also carries special features such as: Interviews with eminent social scientists; reviews symposia on current books of importance; sets of featured articles on topics of emerging interest, as well as commentaries, reviews, and updates by foriegn-based corresponding editors.

Volume 13 (I990)   Published Semi-Annually
Institutions: $90.00   Individuals: $45.00
Back Volumes 1-12 (1977-1989) $90.00 per volume

Outside the U.S.A. add $10.00 to above rates for surface mail or $20.00 to the above rate for airmail

JAI PRESS INC.
55 Old Post Road - No. 2
P.O. Box 1678
Greenwich, Connecticut 06836-1678
Tel: 203-661-7602